KU-435-974

DAYANANDA SARASVATI
His Life and Ideas

J. T. F. JORDENS

DELHI
OXFORD UNIVERSITY PRESS
CALCUTTA CHENNAI MUMBAI
1997

Oxford University Press, Great Clarendon Street, Oxford OX2 6DP

Oxford   New York
Athens   Auckland   Bangkok   Calcutta
Cape Town   Chennai   Dar es Salaam   Delhi
Florence   Hong Kong   Istanbul   Karachi
Kuala Lumpur   Madrid   Melbourne   Mexico City
Mumbai   Nairobi   Paris   Singapore
Taipei   Tokyo   Toronto

and associates in

Berlin   Ibadan

© Oxford University Press 1978
First published 1978
Oxford India Paperback 1997

ISBN 0 19 564225 2

KING ALFRED'S COLLEGE
WINCHESTER

294.5455
JOR   KA0265 0649

Printed in India at Wadhwa International , New Delhi 110 020
and published by Manzar Khan, Oxford University Press
YMCA Library Building, Jai Singh Road, New Delhi 110 001

DAYANANDA SARASVATI

KA 0265064 9

To Ann–Mari.

Preface

The concept of this book grew slowly out of my teaching and study of nineteenth century India, and it has taken five years in the making. During these years I have become indebted to many people and organizations without whose support this work would have been impossible. My University, the Australian National University at Canberra, helped me by providing study leave to work in India and in London, and the Australian National University Library staff have been most patient and helpful in searching for and acquiring obscure publications. My special thanks go to the Leverhulme Foundation which granted me a Fellowship to spend many months in India collecting material. In the South Asia Seminar, organized by the Department of Asian Civilizations and Professor D.A. Low's Section of Modern South Asian History, I was given useful criticism and encouragement by my A.N.U. colleagues when I presented progress reports on my research. In particular I wish to acknowledge C. Dobbin's helpful criticism of my chapter on Bombay.

My research in India was facilitated by the enthusiastic assistance of many other friends and institutions. The officials and librarians of the Sārvadeshik Ārya Pratinidhi Sabhā of Delhi and of the Gurukul Kangri were most hospitable and unreservedly helpful. At Hoshiarpur I enjoyed the friendly hospitality of the Sadhu Ashram, and I particularly treasure the memory of my daily evening walks with the late Vishvabandhu. At Ajmer I received the full cooperation of the Dayananda Ashram and the Vedic Yantralaya: Shri Karan Sarda and Dr Bhavanilal Bharatiya became close friends overnight. My meeting and subsequent correspondence with the late Shri Ram Sharma of Una also gave me a lot of support.

In the course of my research I became indebted to the officials of many libraries and institutions. These included, in Delhi, the Indian National Archives, the Nehru Memorial Museum & Library, and the libraries of Delhi University, of the Theologate of the Society of Jesus, and of the Anglican Brotherhood; in Bombay, the Bombay Asiatic Society, the Prarthana Samaj archives, the Bombay University Library, and the Bombay Marathi Granthalay; in Calcutta, the Asiatic Society, the National Library, the Sadharan Brahmo Samaj, and the Goethals Library of St. Xavier's College; also the Baroda M.S. University Library; the Gujarat Vidyapith of Ahmedabad; and, in London, the British Museum, the India Office Library, and the S.O.A.S. library.

My very special thanks go to A.L. Basham, who has encouraged and advised me from the first. He took the trouble of going through the whole manuscript, and his knowledge was always a sure guide. I also owe a debt of gratitude to our Research Assistant, Miss Mary Hutchinson for invaluable editorial help. I should not forget the typists, in particular Mrs P. McCusker and Mrs M. Tie, whose patience has been inexhaustible.

The views expressed in this book, however, are entirely my own and full responsibility for any errors or oversights lies with me.

Last, but not least, I should thank my wife, Ann-Mari for her unwavering kindness, encouragement, and assistance. She put up with my absences and with the pressures of my work, was always ready to read or listen to my latest chapter, and gave me her valuable opinion as a historian and a stylist. My children Christopher, Rani, Justin, and Tara, will at last find in this publication the full explanation of the frightful mess I have been making in the study in these last few years.

J. T. F. JORDENS

Australian National University
Canberra, 1978

Contents

Contents

Note on Diacritics and Translations

The transcription of Indian terms and proper nouns is a vexing problem. At the start of my study I was inclined to be a purist and used diacritics for all personal and geographical names. However, this usage enormously complicates the task of typists and printers, and gives the text a forbidding visual heaviness. I decided to compromise. No diacritics have been used for the names of persons or places, so that even Swāmī Dayānanda Sarasvatī has had to do without them. My indological instincts have, however, prevented me from depriving pre-nineteenth century figures, such as Pānini and Rāmānuja, of theirs. I have also decided to use diacritics when referring to Indian languages such as Hindī, Urdū, Bengālī, etc. For nineteenth century names I have chosen the most usual spelling, and I have respected the spelling which writers such as R.C.Dutt and P.C.Mozoomdar have themselves preferred for their names.

For the transliteration of Sanskrit words I have adopted the system used in M. Monier-Williams' *Sanskrit-English Dictionary*, with a couple of simplifications: *sh* is used for both palatal and cerebral sibilants; and the dots under the cerebral consonants ṭa, ṭha, ḍa, dha, ṇa, and under the final letters h and ṃ, have been omitted; similarly I have dispensed with the upper sign of the ña. A similar method is used for the transcription of terms from Hindī and other North-Indian languages.

The translations from Indian and European languages that feature in the work are all my own. I must, however, acknowledge the considerable help given by Dr V.G.Kulkarni with translations from Marāthī.

Abbreviations

AUTO   Autobiography of Dayananda, published in *The Theoso-phist*. Our references are to the original Hindī version published in *Paropkārī* 17, No. 5 (March 1975).

GHI   Ghāsīrām, *Maharshi Dayānanda Saraswatī kā Jīvan-Charit*, vol.I, Ajmer, 1957.

GHII   Ibid., vol.II.

DSS   *Dayānanda-Shāstrārth-Sangraha*, ed. B. Bhāratīya, So-nipat, 1969.

GR   Graham, J. Reid, 'The Arya Samaj as a Reformation in Hinduism with special reference to caste', unpub-lished Ph.D. thesis, Yale Univ., 1942.

L   Lekhrām, *Maharshi Dayānanda Saraswatī kā Jīvan Cha-ritra*, transl. from the original Urdū by Kavirāj Raghu-nandansingh 'Nirmal', ed. Pandit Harischandra Vid-yālankār, Delhi, 1972.

MI   Munshīrām Jijñāsu, ed., *Rishi Dayānanda kā Patravya-vahār*, vol.I., Gurukul Kangri, 1910.

MII   Ibid., vol.II, 1935.

PP   *Pūnā-Pravachana arthāt Upadesh-Manjarī*, ed. Y. Mi māmshak, Sonipat, 1969.

PV   *Rishi Dayānanda Saraswatī ke Patra aur Vijnāpan*, 2nd ed., Y. Mīmāmshak, Amritsar, 1955.

PVP   *Rishi Dayānanda Saraswatī ke Patra aur Vijnāpanon ke Parishisht*, ed. Y. Mīmāmshak, Amritsar, 1958.

S   Sarda, Har Bilas, *Life of Dayananda Saraswati, World Teacher*, 2nd ed., Ajmer, 1968.

SPI   *Satyārth Prakāsh*, 1st ed., Banaras, 1875.

SPII   Ibid., 2nd edition. Our references are to the edition prepared by Y. Mīmāmshak, Sonipat, 1972.

YM   Y. Mīmāmshak, *Rishi Dayānanda ke Granthon kā Itihās*, Ajmer, 1949.

Introduction

Anyone lecturing on nineteenth century India soon becomes aware of how unsatisfactory the available biographies and studies of Swami Dayananda Sarasvati are. Although he was one of the giant figures of his era, none of these works presents a clear picture of the man, of his development, and of his involvement in the contemporary world; and most were really repetitions, rearrangements, and synopses of the early biographies of Lekhram and Devendranath Mukhopadhyay.[1] These two had done valuable pioneering work in tracking down oral and printed sources, and had collected a mass of data that otherwise would have been utterly lost. Every student of the life of Dayananda owes them an enormous debt of gratitude. Lekhram's volume did not really get beyond the collating stage: the documents and testimonies are not even arranged chronologically. However, in many ways his work has the value of a primary source because it contains numerous verbatim reports of eyewitnesses' stories, and also several transcripts of the Swami's discussions. Mukhopadhyay added new first-hand material to this as the result of his tireless travels in search of documents and witnesses; but he too was unable to finish his task.

Ghasiram completed Mukhopadhyay's work, and adding to it the materials collected by Lekhram, he put it all into proper chronological order. Thus originated the voluminous standard Hindī biography of the Swami. But even this work, although it systematically covers the whole of Dayananda's life, really does not present more than the vital raw materials for a historical biography proper, and even these materials themselves are too limited, being restricted only to the actions and sayings of the Swami himself.

Practically all subsequent biographers simply used that work and went very little beyond its narrow confines. Even Har Bilas Sarda's extensive English biography adds little to that of Ghasi-

---

[1] Complete references for all works and authors mentioned in this introduction can be found in the Bibliography.

ram, and consequently suffers from the same basic deficiencies.
Two notable exceptions must be mentioned here. In his unpublished Ph.D. thesis J. Reid Graham made an effort at writing a
more historically-oriented biography of the Swami, and in this
he broke new ground. However, his biographical sketch constituted only the introductory part to his main topic, the attitude
of Dayananda and the early Arya Samaj to caste. Therefore,
although valuable, it is limited in scope. K.W. Jones' unpublished
Ph.D. thesis was the first properly historical study of part of the
Swami's life, his work in the Panjab. It thoroughly explores the
social and political background, and places the Swami and his
Samaj squarely in the Panjab of the eighteen-seventies and -eighties.
It is a masterly study, but it treats only a small period of
Dayananda's life and does not consider his theological develop-
ment.

Like Ghasiram's work the biographers generally fall short in
several ways. First of all, their chronological listing of the Swami's
acts, words, and writings does not transcend a mere chronicle.
They fail to place Dayananda at the different stages of his life into
the proper regional and historical context. The events recounted
seem to exist by themselves in a rarified atmosphere, where the
region and the decade remain immaterial. The writers do not
ask such questions as what it meant to grow up as a brahmin
youth in Kathiawar, or why the city of Mathura had such a decisive influence on the Swami's development. Although they describe the success of Dayananda in the Doab, in Calcutta, in
Bombay, in Panjab., and in U.P.,[2] they do not analyse that success
in social terms. There is little or no indication of the respective
levels of the Swami's success in those various localities, and no
hint as to which social groups became attracted to the Arya Samaj
or what the reasons were for their interest. These writers do not
ask the important question why the Swami spent the last years
of his life in Rajputana, or why he became involved in the movements for the promotion of cow-protection and of Hindī.

Another general flaw in these works is that they do not try to
understand how and why the Swami's ideas, attitudes, and theories

---

[2] U.P.: for the sake of simplicity we use this abbreviation throughout this work
to refer to that area of North India that is now called Uttar Pradesh. It was called
the United Provinces of Agra and Oudh between 1902 and 1947, and before 1902
it went under the name of North-Western Provinces and Oudh.

changed over the years. One basic reason for this is that many of the biographers themselves belonged to the Arya Samaj and tended to look upon their Swami as a *guru*; the changes in his conceptions and approaches were played down, if not gently suppressed. In this context it is remarkable that none of these works includes a study of the first edition of the Swami's most important work, the *Satyārth Prakāsh*. This was written at a pivotal time in Dayananda's development, in 1874, shortly after his visit to Calcutta and just before the establishment of the Arya Samaj in Bombay. It contains the Swami's first full statement of his opinions on a wide range of subjects. Copies of this work are now extremely rare, and practically unavailable outside a few major Arya Samaj institutions. The discovery of a copy provided me with the most essential source for a meaningful study of the development of the Swami's ideology.

As my work progressed I discovered other important sources hitherto neglected, such as the first edition of Dayananda's *Sanskārvidhi*, Damodar Sundarlal's *History of the Bombay Arya Samaj* in Gujarātī, Gopal Rao Hari Deshmukh's biographical sketch of the Swami in Marāthī in his journal, the *Lokahitavādī*, of 1884, and a most rare set of the first sixteen fascicules of Dayananda's *Rigvedādibhāshyabhūmikā*, published in 1877-8, containing complete lists of subscribers from all over India. I was also helped in my work by the recent timely discovery and re-publication of some long-lost works such as Dayananda's first pamphlet, the *Bhāgavata-Khandanam*, the earliest biography of the Swami by Gopal Rao Hari, and the original Hindī version of Dayananda's autobiography published in English in *The Theosophist*. Some recently published works also added new material: Y. Mimamshak's *History of the works of Swami Dayananda*, his *Appendices to Dayananda's Letters*, and B. Bharatiya's *History of the Paropkarinī Sabbā*, all three in Hindī. None of the sources mentioned in this paragraph have hitherto been used in the writing of the Swami's biography.

In the course of my research it became increasingly clear that only a full biography of the Swami would satisfactorily present my findings, because nearly every period of his life had acquired a somewhat new perspective. The study of Kathiawar showed that he owed as much to the land of his birth as did Gandhi, and the study of Mathura clarified the reason for a major turning-

point in his life. Dayananda's long years in the Doab revealed
a clear and gradual development, and his short stay in Calcutta
a critical re-direction of his thought and attitudes. New sources
clarified the reasons for the foundation of the Arya Samaj in
Bombay, and the Swami's final years acquired a significant new
perspective. Moreover, the systematic study of all the works of
Dayananda showed that there had been a constant dynamic
transformation in many important aspects of his ideology, such
as Vedic revelation, the idea of God and the soul, the theory of
creation, the concept of Hindu nationalism,[3] and the role and
function of the Arya Samaj. Only a full biography would do
justice to the many facets of that transformation and would satisfactorily explain the internal and external factors that influenced it.

A biography that took all these new elements into account
would have to employ two different yet related historical approaches. On the one hand it must explore the Swami's ideas and
theories, their gradual growth, and their relationship not only
to the new trends of thought in nineteenth century India but also
to traditional Hinduism. Such a work would have to contain a
close study of all the Swami's writings, and of the ideas that influenced him through his reading or through personal contacts.
Thus it would have to have the perspective of the history of ideas.
On the other hand, the study of the Swami's involvement in social
and religious reform in various parts of India necessitated a social analysis. The society in which Dayananda moved, the classes
and castes he encountered and influenced, needed to be analysed
in their regional and historical setting. Therefore, the work must
also present slices of social history.

These two approaches go hand-in-hand in this study. Occasionally, in whole chapters or substantial parts of them, one or
other perspective dominates, as the activities of the Swami and
his writings are successively analysed. Such alternation seemed
unavoidable in this type of work. However, the final chapter
integrates those two perspectives into an overall view. There an
effort is made to identify the basic trends in the Swami's dynamic

---

[3] 'Hindu nationalism': we use this term in this work in the sense of a nationalism
deeply rooted in Hindu culture and religion, the sense in which it has been used,
for instance, by Von Jürgen Lütt in his work *Hindu-Nationalismus in Uttar Prades*
1867-1900, Stuttgart, 1970. Cf. also C.H. Heimsath, *Indian Nationalism and Hindu*
Social Reform, Princeton U.P., 1964, ch. VI.

growth, to indicate the guiding direction of his thought and action, to trace·his dominant ideas through their manifold transformations. Thus this biography seeks to understand Dayananda in his time, as an integral part of the vigorous atmosphere of nineteenth century India; though he was a stubborn and robust individualist, yet he was a man intensely receptive to the many ideas, old and new, that made up the intellectual ambiance of his period.

CHAPTER I

A Brahmin Youth
from Kathiawar

Our information on the early years of Swami Dayananda Sarasvati derives completely from the two accounts he gave of his own life, the first in a lecture at Poona in 1874,[1] the second in the biographical notes he wrote for, *The Theosophist* five years later.[2] As the Swami persistently refused to divulge the names of his father and of his home town,[3] it is impossible to check his account against other sources. The task of verification is rendered even more difficult by the fact that over fifty years elapsed between the time he left his home and the first search for his birthplace and ancestry, by which time all those who knew him as a youth would most probably have died. Nevertheless, the autobiographical fragments contain much concrete and useful information for an understanding of his background and development. As it is impossible to verify all this information with independent sources, the question whether the autobiographical accounts can be taken as credible documents becomes all the more crucial.

This question has been answered in the negative by opponents of the Arya Samaj, who even ventured to propose an alternative family background for the Swami. However, their story is rather fantastic, and it does not contain even the slightest element susceptible of objective proof: it strikes one as the fabrication of a nasty mind.[4] Dayananda's account, on the other hand, has the convincing ring of truth. Not one single fact or situation he relates contradicts what we know from elsewhere about Morvi, the Kathiawari state he said he was born in, or about the brahmin sub-caste to which he claimed his family belonged. Moreover, the circumstances and events depicted are very straightforward, and do not claim an exalted status for his family or for himself. His parents appear simple people with their qualities and deficiencies. The flow of events too is natural and plausible, and at no stage does it involve the extraordinary or the supernatural. The whole reads as an account, not as a thesis: it does not set out to prove anything, nor does the child and the youth it portrays flaunt marks of greatness, brilliance, or extraordinary sanctity. A few events seem to be slightly embroidered. For instance, the tragic deaths of his young sister and favourite uncle, and the famous episode in the Shiva temple are recalled as having had a deep religious influence on the youth. That in itself is not implausible, and it also seems natural that when a man of over fifty looks back upon his youth, he should attempt to recall in a special way those events which he now sees as having had a particular influence on his later development, so that, when he picks those events out of the many other experiences and shows them up in greater relief than they may have actually had at the time they occurred, he is not really doing any violence to historical truth, but in fact is enhancing it.

But if the Swami's story is indeed a true one, and not a veil to hide some banal or hideous truth, why then did he so obstinately keep his ancestry a secret? He himself has answered this question:

I do not write here the well-known names of my father and of my home town for the following reason: if my parents and my family are still alive, they would come to me, and an obstacle would be put in the way of my task of reform. For I would have to attend to their service and expend my energy and my possessions in keeping them company, which I do not wish to do.[5]

In Poona he said that if he revealed his real name, 'then those kinds of complications, from which I have cut myself off, would pursue me again'.[6] He did not want to become involved in the demands and the aggravations of family affairs lest they take him away from the work he was dedicating his life to. This might seem a weak excuse for an independent man of over fifty, but in the Gujarati context the pressures of family and friends, especially if they are in some trouble, on a powerful and influential relative, can easily become endless and relentless. But that was not the only reason: there was another even more urgent fear that made Dayananda conceal his identity: the fear of being considered a *guru*, a saint, and of being divinized and worshipped after death. Kathiawar was full of monuments to saints of all religions and sects, monuments most often erected on the very spot where the holy man was born, or where he was buried. Dayananda was genuinely horrified at the thought of that possibility. When it was suggested that a memorial in his honour be erected, he retorted, 'Throw the ashes of my body somewhere in a field, thus they will be of some use; but do not make a memorial, lest that be the start of some idolatry'. That fear was a very basic reason why he never revealed his birthplace and stipulated in his will that his body should not be buried in *sannyāsī* fashion, but be cremated like those of all ordinary Hindus.[7]

The Arya Samaj and the biographers of the Swami have come to a now generally accepted conclusion that within the state of Morvi the town of Tankara had the honour of being Dayananda's birthplace. The early biographer Devendranath Mukhopadhyay did the essential painstaking research to establish this by several visits to Kathiawar to investigate places and documents, and to interview possible witnesses.[8] Although details of his argumentation may be challenged, the convergence of a great number of points makes for an acceptable argument. His starting point was the few clear details that are contained in the autobiographical fragments: the Swami's birthplace was a township, and a taluka with dependent villages within the state of Morvi. It was situated near the border of the state, it contained families of Audichya brahmins, and there was a Shiva temple nearby. It may seem an impossible task to select a town with so few definite data. However, Morvi was a very small state, and there were scarcely half a dozen places that could be described as townships. In the circumstances the process of elimination became quite feasible, and Devendranath concluded that only Tankara fulfilled all the requirements.

He then set out to find in Tankara a family that could conform to all the details given by Dayananda. He was looking for a family that had an ancestor who was all the Swami said his father was: a Sāmavedī Audichya brahmin, landholder, tax-collector, and money-lender, a devout Shaivite, whose elder son disappeared at the age of twenty-one. The search was a difficult one because official papers that might confirm oral testimony did not exist for that time. Devendranath claimed he had found such a family, and stated that Dayananda's father was called Karshanji Lalji Tiwari and that the Swami's given name was Dayaram Mulshankar, known as Mulji.

This part of Devendranath's thesis does not have the strength and cohesion of the first part, as it depends largely on questionable oral testimony. However, a reasonable hypothesis has been put forward. One may conclude that Dayananda's birthplace was very probably Tankara, and it seems unlikely that any further evidence could come forward to either strengthen or weaken that probability. As for the particular family, here the probability is only slight. For the Arya Samaj the last is naturally an important point, but for our purpose it does not really matter, because it does not contribute any vital new information. In the reconstruction of Dayananda's background, we therefore accept Tankara to have been the town of his origin, and overlook the doubtful details given by those who claim to belong to his family.

According to Dayananda, the following were the circumstances and events of his early years, as collated from both autobiographical fragments. He was the first-born of a brahmin of the Sāmavedī branch of the Audichya caste in a town of the state of Morvi, and he had two brothers and two sisters. His father was a devout and strict Shaivite: he duly performed the daily *Pārthiva Pūjā*,[9] the worship of the clay *linga* representing Shiva, and his Vedic *Sandhyā*[10] ritual. He conscientiously observed important Shaivite rituals like the *Shivarātri*[11] in the temple, with their obligatory fast, was a regular visitor of temples and religious festivals, and attended the public readings of the *Purānas*.[12] He was an important and wealthy man: not only was he a landowner who possessed tracts of land and some fifteen houses, and an official tax-collector, with a number of sepoys under his command to execute his revenue and police duties, but he also conducted a money-lending business. Thus he combined property and business with an official status.

He saw to it that his eldest son got a proper education. From the age of five Mulji, as we will call him for convenience's sake, was taught the *devanāgarī* script and the customs of his family and caste, and he was made to learn by heart some verses of the *Dharmashāstras*, those ancient works that detail the ritual and social duties of the orthodox Hindu. At the age of eight he was administered the sacrament of initiation, invested with the *Yajnopavīta*, the holy thread of the twice-born, and taught the sacred *Gāyatrī Mantra* and the daily *Sandhyā* ritual.[13] Then his studies started in earnest: he learned to recite verses of the *Yajurveda*,[14] and also a set of prayers to Shiva, called the *Rudrādhyāya*. When he reached the age of ten his father insisted, notwithstanding the protestations of his mother, that Mulji should start the daily practice of worshipping the *linga* of clay. He now acquired a special pandit to teach him Sanskrit grammar, and his study of the *Yajurveda* progressed so that by the age of fourteen he had memorized most of it, and also some texts of the other *Vedas*.

His father used to take Mulji on his visits to temples, religious festivals, and *Purāna* recitations, implanting in his son the conviction that the worship of Shiva was the best of all. He then decided that the time had come for his son to participate in the important *Shivarātri* temple ceremony, which included a fast and an all-night vigil. The mother protested again, but was again overruled. The father prepared his son by telling him the *Shivarātri* myth, the beauty and majesty of which appealed to Mulji. All went well in the temple, but around midnight, as the priests were sleeping in the porch, the devotees found the vigil too much and all, including Mulji's father, slowly subsided into slumber. But Mulji held on to his vow and kept himself awake. Then he saw to his horror some mice running over the emblem of Shiva and eating the offerings. This set him meditating on the relationship between the great god Shiva of the myth and the passive stone idol being polluted in front of him, and he found it impossible to reconcile the two. He awakened his father and expressed his doubt. Though his father's explanations were reasonable, they did not satisfy him. By now he too was overcome by hunger and sleep, and his father, no doubt mellowed a little by having been caught napping, allowed him to go home, provided he did not break his fast. But the mother quickly fed the son some sweets before he went to bed. This led to another confrontation between the parents, but this time Mulji's mother, with the help of an uncle, managed to convince the father that he should not insist on so many religious practices, but let his son get on with his studies, which did not leave him much time for *pūjā*.

So Mulji's studies continued, and he now moved on to works dealing with Vedic terms, their meaning and etymology, the *Nighantu*[15] and the *Nirukta*,[16] and to a further study of the ritual system of the Pūrvamīmāmsā[17] school. Then two successive deaths in the family deeply affected the young boy: the sudden death by cholera of his younger sister at the age of fourteen shocked him into an apparently unfeeling numbness, and that of his favourite uncle, his teacher and friend, caused him to break into tears and hysterical sobbing. These tragic events shook him so much that he meditated on the cruel shortness of life and on that great aim

of liberation from life and death, *moksha*,[18] which could be attained
by asceticism and *yoga*. He talked about these reflections to his
friends, and when his parents came to hear of it, they decided
that his marriage was overdue, and should be arranged as soon
as possible. On Mulji's plea, they agreed to wait till he was twenty.
At that stage his father also insisted that his son should start to
take up some responsibility in the family's zamindari duties, but
the young man refused. Instead, he asked his parents to let him
go to Banaras for further studies in grammar, science, and
Āyurvedic medicine.[19] He met an absolute refusal from both
parents, but still managed to get another year's grace before the
wedding. He spent this time studying under a pandit in a village
neighbouring their zamindari. But his parents knew that he would
not change his mind and therefore speeded up the marriage negotiations. When Mulji completed his twenty-first year, he realized
that all had been finalized, and that within the family circle there
was no avoiding the inevitable: now the only way left to realize
the dream that haunted him was flight. So one evening he quietly
slipped away from home and set out on his journey in search of
moksha.

Besides the information this account gives of Dayananda's
background, it also reveals a good deal about his personality
and character. His father was obviously a strict and determined
man, and his son inherited that strong will and determination.
In a society where the father's word was law, he was able to with-
stand the family pressure to get him married till he was twenty-
one. In fact, by that age his peers would all have been fathers
of a family, as Gandhi was. That same stubborn determination
gave him the strength to run away from a comfortable home
to the insecurity and unfamiliarity of a homeless life. He was
driven by a thirst for learning: in a state where education was
at its lowest ebb, and cursory even in brahmin families,[20] and in a
family where the eldest son was expected to assume the weighty
official and business responsibility considered his right and his
duty, he managed to avoid his initiation into the secular world
and to devote himself wholly to study over a long period. He
was fascinated by religion: his father's deep devotional nature had
found an echo in his son that far exceeded his expectations, as it
had engendered a search for the essence of religion beyond its
outer practices.

One can safely assume that such a determined and individual-istic young man, intellectually curious, obstinate, deeply in-terested in religion, and belonging to a prominent family involved in business and public affairs, must have had his eyes wide open to the world around him. If a Gandhi, who left Kathiawar after only nineteen years, was so deeply influenced by his Kathiawari background, as many recent studies have shown,[21] Dayananda too must in these twenty-one years, unimpeded by family re-sponsibilities or monetary worries as he was, have noticed and absorbed much of that background. It is therefore imperative, in order to fully understand the Swami's later development, to explore the peculiar Kathiawari background of a Shaivite brahmin youth of Mulji's calibre.

Whereas Gandhi the Modh Bania was an integral part of that ambiance of Kathiawar where 'Kshatriya values held sway in the political sphere and Jain-Vaishnava values in the religious sphere',[22] Dayananda's situation within the brahmin community gave him quite a different perspective. The brahmin group was not a dominant one in Kathiawar, and it contributed only about seven per cent of the Hindu population. Yet in some ways the brahmins were very markedly different from the other Hindus through their distinctive religious adherence: practically all of them were Shaivites. In fact, apart from the kshatriya Shaivites, Shaivism in Kathiawar was the preserve of the brahmins, whereas other Hindus belonged to the different Vaishnavite sects.[23] This adherence to Shaivism set the brahmins apart. It connected them more closely with the ancient history of the area: the earliest great dynasties were either Shaivite or Buddhist. The most striking remaining evidence that Kathiawar had indeed been the ancient land of Lord Shiva was no doubt the temple ruins of Somnāth. This temple existed and was famous at least from the second century A.D., and in the following centuries it not only exerted great influence on Saurāshtra, as in ancient times the peninsula was called, but from the tenth century its impact on South India has been described as a 'spiritual conquest'.[24] It was also from Saurāshtra that hailed the saint Lakulīsha, founder of that most influential Shaivite sect, the Pāshupata. The founder himself quickly attained divinization, and his influence spread all over

India. The great philosopher Madhvāchārya recognized his system as one of the major ones, and the Pāshupata movement later became associated with the great resurgence of Shaivism in the seventh century, which spread all over the country.[25]

The great Shaivite past was still very visible in Mulji's youth in the glorious architectural remains of Somnāth and in the innumerable Shiva temples dotted all over the countryside: almost every village and town had its Shiva temple. Many of them were very old, and they easily outnumbered all other Hindu temples.[26] The Maratha domination of Kathiawar in recent years had revived that Shaivite heritage: one of its main influences was greater Shaivite propaganda. One important figure in this respect was Vittalrao Deoji, who built several Shaivite temples. This influence was strongly felt in Tankara, which was ruled in Dayananda's youth by Seth Gopal Medel Narayana of Baroda, who was famous for his vigorous advocacy.of Shaivism.[27]

The brahmins were in yet another and deeper way rooted in antiquity. Only they, through their Sanskritic rites and learning, kept the old Vedic traditions alive, whereas other Hindus practised Purānic rites. Their social and religious customs were still regulated by the most authoritative works of *dharma*, the *Mitākshara*, the *Nirnayasindhu*, and the *Dharmasindhu*. This is no wonder, as the great majority of Kathiawari Shaivites were Smārtas.[28] These did not properly constitute a sect, but they were 'that collection of brahmins who represented orthodoxy *vis-à-vis* the many sects'.[29] They trace their origin to the great philosopher Shankarāchārya and to his master Kumārīla, the theologian of the ritual system of the Pūrvamīmāmsā. They reaffirmed Vedic rites and Vedic *dharma* in reaction to Buddhists and Jains, and created all over India an élite of orthodox brahmins who were the guardians of the old traditions. The loyalty of the Smārtas, therefore, lay with the Vedic rites, and with the old rules of *dharma*. The philosophy they adhered to was the Advaita Vedānta of Shankara, and among the great gods of the Hindu pantheon, all of whom they recognized as proper recipients of worship, they preferred the favourite deity of Shankara himself, Shiva. Although their worship was centred on Shiva, they were not strictly speaking a Shaivite sect, but rather the representatives of orthodoxy with a strong attachment to the worship of Shiva.[30] Not only were they numerically very strong in Kathiawar, but some of them at least had a vital interest in their religion and its reform. This is evident from the fact that when in 1895 a Smārta reform organization was founded in South India, a similar one was organized in Kathiawar.[31] Thus their religious connection as Smārtas and Shaivites linked the Kathiawari brahmins very closely to the traditional ancient Sanskrit roots of Hinduism and to the ancient glory of Kathiawar history.

Naturally not too many Kathiawari brahmins were very conscious of that particular heritage. Like other castes of the peninsula, they were a very splintered caste, divided into over fifty divisions.[32] In fact there were several sections of 'fallen' brahmins, who had mostly been reduced to an inferior status precisely because they cut off their connection with the *Shāstras* and Shaivism. Some brahmins, deprecatingly called Bhojaks, or eaters, had adopted Jainism, others like the Guglis, Abotis, and Kandolias, had become Vaishnavites. The Rajgors, priests of Rajputs and Oswal Jains, had been expelled from their branch, and so had those like the Kanbi-Gors, Darji-Gors, Gandhrap-Gors, Hajam-Gors, Koli-Gors, and Machi-Gors who had become priests to low-caste people.[33] Even apart from these degraded sections, the brahmins on the whole had no claim to learning: recitation of the ritual by rote was the limit of the education of most.[34] In fact, that largest section (63 per cent) of the brahmins, the Audichyas, to which Mulji's family belonged, mostly made their living by alms.[35] However, the degradation of many brahmins and the low educational level of most of the others, may well have increased among the real élite the consciousness of their status as carriers of the most ancient traditions.

From the general description the *Gazetteer* gives of the brahmins, and in particular of the Audichyas, it seems evident that Mulji's father was quite an unusually religious, educated, and enterprising man among his caste-fellows. In fact he conformed more to that small élite (5 per cent) of Nagar brahmins who had achieved a leading position among the brahmins, played an important part in politics, and had a stake in landholding and money-lending.[36] These were the real carriers of the full and rich brahmin tradition of the peninsula. They stood apart not only from all other Hindus, but also from the generally poor quality of Gujarati brahmins. They were the custodians of a heritage deeply rooted in the ancient history of the Shaivite kings, for a time revived by the Marathas, and even more deeply rooted in the Sanskritic tradition of the most ancient *Shāstras*. Very few Gujarati brahmins would have received the education Mulji acquired: an education whose every aspect would have intensified his attachment to Sanskrit learning, the *Shāstras*, and Shaivism.

In this context one may well wonder if Mulji ever heard about the reform movement started in 1824 by Madhavgar of Nadiad, who came to live in Kathiawar. He was a strict Shankarite Vedāntin who condemned all idol worship and did not believe in the incarnations of Vishnu. He deprecated the observance of fasts, and the performance of the *Shrāddh* commemorative rituals for the dead, and he did not give credence to pollution by touch. He taught that the giving of alms should be restricted to the old and the needy. His movement had no actual seat, and no supreme authoritative *guru*. The message was spread by dedicated teachers in yellow robes, living frugally, refusing any kind of honour or presents, except the necessary food and clothing, and carrying Shaivite rosaries of *rudrāksha* seeds.[37] It is remarkable that every single one of these points later became an integral part of Dayananda's own programme. It may well be a coincidence, but it is just possible that young Mulji met one of these teachers in his youth or during his journey through Kathiawar.

In contrast with the ancient heritage of the Shaivites, the traditions of the Vaishnavites must have appeared to Mulji as recent and multiform. Although many sites in the peninsula, like Dwarka, were associated in ancient legend and literature with the Krishna cycle, Vaishnavism as a major religious force was a comparatively recent phenomenon. It was only in the sixteenth century that its upsurge started in Gujarat with the advent of the great *bhakti* poet Narasimha Mehta; and when the Vallabhāchārya sect established a firm hold over the merchant community, its success was assured. One cannot assume that Mulji knew very much about the Vaishnavite sects, but to a religiously inquisitive observer some salient characteristics must have been quite obvious. First of all they covered about half of the total Hindu population, whereas the Shaivites made up only about one tenth. Practically all Vaishnavites were non-brahmins, and those brahmins who had closely identified themselves with them were considered 'fallen' brahmins. Though they were a very large group, they were splintered into some ten main sects, imbued with a sectarian rivalry which had led to many internal subdivisions. Some could claim a few hundred years of existence, but quite a few had been founded relatively recently, from fifty to a hundred years before. Thus they were all comparative newcomers compared with a Shaivism of hoary antiquity.[38]

Their books and rites too set them ages apart from the Shaivites. Their adherence was to the *Purānas*; in fact two of the biggest sects, the Vallabhāchāryas and the Swāmīnārāyanas, considered the *Bhāgavata Purāna* their most authoritative text.[39] This work must have been known to Mulji since the Swāmīnārāyanas were particularly strong in the area from Ahmedabad to Rajkot and had an important seat at Morvi.[40] The Purānic ritual of the Vaishnavites was profuse and full of pomp and ceremony, and constrasted with the simplicity and solemnity of Shaivite worship.[41]

Besides Hinduism, there was also Jainism, about which Gandhi said that 'its influence was felt everywhere and on all occasions'.[42] In a land where for centuries commerce had dominated, the commercial classes were two-thirds Jain and one-third Vaishnavite. In the whole of Kathiawar there was one Jain to every seventeen Hindus, but in the northern quadrangle comprising the area of Navanagar-Morvi-Wardhwan-Rajkot the proportion was more like one to ten.[43] They were not concentrated in a few urban centres, but penetrated every village,[44] and the whole fabric of society 'from the millionaire banker to the village grocer',[45] and their temples were scattered in profusion all over the peninsula.[46] Another indication of the importance and vitality of the Kathiawari Jains lies in the fact that the first modern Jain reformers came from the peninsula. Vijayadharma Suri (1868-1922), an extensive writer in Sanskrit, Gujarātī, and Hindī, was born in Kathiawar, initiated at Bhawnagar, and did his first monsoon season at Limbdi not far from Morvi. The monk Ratnachandra, author of Sanskrit and Gujarātī works and Jain dictionaries, was also a Kathiawari.[47] Morvi state was the birthplace of Rajchandra Rajivbhai, a poet and thinker of considerable influence.[48] Raychand Mehta, another Jain thinker from Kathiawar, had great influence on Gandhi, and so did another reformer, more interested in legal matters, Virchand Gandhi, born of Kathiawari parents. He was a graduate of Elphinstone College, Bombay, became the secretary of the Jain Association of India, and represented Jainism at the famous World's Parliament of Religions in Chicago in 1893.[49]

Thus Jainism was firmly established in the peninsula. Gandhi and his family, sharing a sub-caste with Jains, were closely connected with them, but the brahmin boy Mulji would not have had any such kind of relationship. Presumably his father, prominent in the money business, did have some dealings with the Jains. But the Jain presence was too close and strong to escape Mulji's attention, and he must have become familiar with some of the main characteristics of the community. In contrast with Vaishnavite Hinduism, Jainism was not a recent phenomenon. Kathiawar was claimed to be the land where Arishtanemi, the twenty-second Tīrthānkara, died, and where the first Jain canon was fixed in an important Council.[50] The increasing Jain influence reached its peak in the thirteenth century under the great monarch Kumārapāla, whose fame rivalled that of the Shaivite kings, and was devastated when the Muslims razed their temples, shrines, and libraries. The architectural glory of ancient Jainism, created 'in the sunshine of royal favour',[51] shone as much as that of Shaivism, at its fabulous sites of Girnar and Shatrunjaya, where thousands of temples still draw hosts of pilgrims.[52]

In the field of Sanskrit learning no Gujarati outshone the Jain Hemachandra (1088-1172), politician, grammarian, and literateur of prodigious output, 'the first great literary man who was born in Gujarat, worked for Gujarat and created the group consciousness of Gujaratis'.[53] So the Jains, for all their difference, shared with the Shaivites one peculiar quality, that of having a vital connection with the antiquity of the ancient land of Saurāshtra.

On the level of social life the Jains were barely distinguishable from the Vaishnavites with whom they shared the same caste divisions: socially they were closer to the Vaishnavites of their own subcaste than to the Jains of a different one.[54] They had adopted many Hindu ways and customs. Their temple worship was mostly conducted by brahmins, and was largely identical with its Hindu equivalent, and there were even Hindu idols in some Jain temples.[55] Their four sacraments were the same as those of the Hindus, and were mostly performed by brahmins, and they celebrated the same festivals.[56] Nevertheless, there were some differences in the ritual. 'Jains do not give any meaning to the bathing in holy rivers, they cremate their ascetics, they do not offer gifts to the dead, they do not practise widow-burning.'[57] It is important to note that none of these differences entails any ritual pollution, and thus they did not prevent the closest social and ritual contact with the Vaishnavites. This affinity was so, strong that many Jains had lost the sense of the special identity of their faith,[58] a fact that worried the census officials[59] and made von Glasenapp anticipate a possible complete absorption of Jainism into Hinduism.[60]

One group stood out in bold perspective among the Jains: the Sthānakavāsī or Dhūndhiyā sect. The iconoclastic onslaught of the Muslims, while it drove most Jains into an even closer union with the Hindus, stimulated others to rethink their position, especially about idol worship. In the nineteenth century this sect was mostly found in Kathiawar,[61] and it was particularly strong in Morvi: the raja of Morvi's prime minister was a Sthānakavāsī, and a monk of the sect was his special confidant and counsellor. The strength of the sect in Morvi is also indicated by the fact that its great modern reform leader Rajchandra Rajivbhai was born in that state. Tankara lay on the route between two Sthānakavāsī strongholds, Morvi and Rajkot, and thus witnessed the constant travel of their monks and nuns between the two centres. Mulji could not have missed them.[62]

In 1452 Lonka Sha, a rich merchant of Ahmedabad, founded a sect called after him the Lonkās. While he was engaged in the pious work of having some sacred Jain books copied, he noticed that idol worship was not mentioned anywhere. He therefore tried to restore Jainism to its non-idolatrous original purity. Two centuries later his sect was in need of reform, and a group broke off, who called themselves Sthānakavāsīs, 'dwellers in private houses' as distinct from monasteries, and who were nicknamed the Dhūndhiyās or 'seekers'. They differed from the other Jains in their radical rejection of idol and temple worship and of pilgrimages. They strongly insisted on a strict moral life for all, and severe discipline for their monks. These were probably the very first non-idolatrous sectarians the future iconoclast Dayananda ever saw.[63]

We can safely assume that Mulji was aware of the three salient characteristics of Kathiawar Jainism: its connection with hoary antiquity, its social fusion with the Vaishnavites, and the non-idolatrous sect of the Sthānakavāsīs. He was probably in ignorance of many of the details of their beliefs and customs, but two Jain usages stood out in bold contrast to the Hindu background. The feasts and ceremonies of *Shrāddh*, the periodic commemoration of the dead, foremost in importance among Hindu rites, were particularly elaborate and costly in Gujarat, to the extent that they were one of the main causes of impoverishment and indebtedness.[64] Although the Jains followed the Hindu custom in most sacraments, they did not practise *Shrāddh*, but confined themselves to a simple funeral ritual,[65] a fact that impressed the author of the *Rās Mālā*.[66] The body of the Hindu *sannyāsī* was not cremated like that of other Hindus, but buried or exposed to the elements by being thrown into a river or left in a forest, a ceremony that took place quite frequently in that land of saints *par excellence*.[67] Here again the Jains diverged completely: their monks were cremated exactly like the laymen.[68] On account of the frequency and the public nature of these two important rites, it seems certain that Mulji was aware of them. As Swami Dayananda he would take a stand against old and universal Hindu traditions when he condemned *Shrāddh* and devised a simple funeral rite instead, and when he specified in his will that his own body 'should not be buried, or thrown in the water, or exposed in the jungle', but that it should be cremated with the simple funeral ceremony he prescribed for all Hindus.[69]

One of the major characteristics of the Vaishnava-Jain ethos of Kathiawar was its insistence on *ahimsā*, non-violence, with its resulting aversion to the slaughter of animals and the practice of strict vegetarianism. Both Dayananda and Gandhi became strong protagonists of non-violence and vegetarianism, and both singled out cow-protection as the central aspect of that attitude. The initial impetus for the growth of that ethos came from the ancient doctrine of *ahimsā*, shared by Hindus, Buddhists and Jains, but stressed and promoted most vigorously by the last. The ethos had been strengthened in the Middle Ages by the *bhakti* movement, in particular by the cult of Krishna, the divine cow-herd, so popular among the Vaishnavites. This aspect had given it a strong mythological and emotional aura. The Jains had started in Gujarat that peculiar institution, the 'Pinjarapol', or refuge for animals.[70] Unproductive animals were cared for and the institution also had representatives at cattle-sales and slaughter-houses trying to save animals by buying them up, sometimes even going so far as spiriting away herds. This tenderness for animal life had so influenced some Rajputs and even some Muslim zamindars, that they assisted the Jains in these activities.[71]

Mulji could not but have been influenced by that pervading ethos of non-violence, but his Shaivite background insulated him from its emotional aspect. Shaivites approved of the killing of animals and the consumption of meat at least in a ritual setting: the daily sacrifice and the *Shrāddh* ceremonies included the consumption of *pindas*, balls of meat.[72] In this context it is interesting to note that the Jains of Gujarat suffered persecution from the Shaivite ruler Ajayapāla, the successor of the great Jain patron Kumārapāla. This Shaivite animosity was probably partly caused by Kumārapāla's drastic edict banning all animal killing, even the ritualistic slaughter so important to the Shaivites.[73] Although Dayananda did by the end of his life condemn all animal killing and all consumption of meat, this radical attitude took long to develop. And though for him the protection of the cow became the central act of non-violence, its rationale was purely economic, and it never acquired that emotional and symbolic slant characteristic of the approach of Gandhi, for whom the cow was a 'symbol of the entire sub-human world' and cow-protection as it were the essential ritual of his religion.[74]

The ancient land of Kathiawar distinguished itself in yet another way from most of India in that it was in a special way the land of *sādhus*, *sannyāsīs*, monks, saints, and holy beggars. The census of 1872 shows that although Kathiawar had only about 24 per cent of the total population of Gujarat, it supported 43 per cent of the number of ascetics listed: that means that in Kathiawar the number of ascetics per hundred people was nearly four times the number for the whole of Gujarat.[75] Moreover, there was an additional constant stream of holy men on their way to the many great places of pilgrimage in the peninsula. The countryside was dotted with the innumerable monuments, from simple stones to shrines, erected for the veneration of saints of all sects and religions. Asceticism was a constant and pervading phenomenon, and it also had a special flavour in this area 'infused, as it was, with the unconquerable will-power of the Jain monasticism'.[76] Indeed, it was the most radical and the most ubiquitous Jain monk who set the standard of rigid asceticism, a standard which no Kathiawari with aspirations to be a *sannyāsī* could ignore.

Gandhi came to asceticism proper by a circuitous road, but when he took it up it definitely had Jain overtones.[77] Mulji, on the other hand, adopted the ascetic life in the most direct way by running away from home and becoming a *sannyāsī*. His Shaivite and Smārta background directed him straight to the Shankarāchārya order of the Dandīs.[78] But his initiation into that order still left many options open to him, as he was completely his own master. He could have chosen to live a relatively easy life as a wandering teacher, or even a quiet, orderly, and comfortable life in a monastery, which in fact he was at one stage offered with the promise of a wealthy abbotship in the near future.[79] But he chose differently: he became the rugged, self-disciplined, frugal *sannyāsī*, who braved the harsh cold land of Kumaon, roamed the stark Vindhya ranges, and astounded the people of the Doab by his unflinching endurance of hunger and cold. It was only very much later in life that he moderated this routine for the sake of his work of reform. That 'unconquerable will power of Jain asceticism' had also shaped his early concept of the true seeker of *moksha*, and in that way both the 'naked fakir' and the naked *sannyāsī* betrayed their common Kathiawari background.

Gandhi, born in a family that had provided prime ministers to Rajput rulers, became deeply involved in politics, and his Kathiawari background profoundly influenced his political methodology.[80] Mulji's father, as a tax-collector, was at a low level involved in civil and police administration, but there is no reason to suppose that he was involved in higher politics. Dayananda himself was never interested in the game of politics, but he did present a theory of statecraft and administration. One wonders if the political situation of Kathiawar had any influence on his thought. As a young man he seems to have taken no interest in political matters, but some salient aspects of the Kathiawari condition could not but have impressed themselves upon his mind.

Kathiawar, like Rajputana, was a land of Rajputs, divided into a great number of small states and estates, where two-and-a-half million people were ruled by over two hundred princes of various ranks. The great Rajput tradition of chivalry was constantly sung by the Charans and the Bhats, hereditary bards. Political power was concentrated in the princely courts, where the alliance of Rajput and brahmin was often the tradition, and where access to power and favours depended mostly on personal relationships. The feudal pattern that bound together in mutual dependence the big and small chieftains, the landowners and their tenants, was enormously intricate. Upon the disintegration of Mughal power at the death of Aurangzeb in 1707, Kathiawar had come under the sway of the Marathas for whom the peninsula was primarily a source of income, realized by the regular collection of tribute by the army whose tax-collecting expeditions often brought devastation. The combination of these circumstances made Kathiawar in the early nineteenth century into 'one of the most lawless countries in the world', where chiefs oppressed their underlings and fought one another endlessly, and outlawry and pillage became an accepted pattern of life.[81]

As Maratha power waned, and the British came into the picture in Western India with the collapse of the Maratha Confederacy, the situation improved slowly. Colonel Walker managed to put a stop to the annual incursions of the Maratha armies in 1807, and in 1820 a British political agent took up residence in Kathiawar. Improvement was slow but steady, and disturbances continued in diminishing bursts until 1850.[82]

As Mulji's youth in the peninsula spanned the years 1824-46, he must have been aware of the general and obvious conditions. The rule he saw around him everywhere was a rule of Rajputs and their courts, often influenced by brahmins. But the great fragmentation of that rule made it ineffective and self-destructive; the land was in constant chaos, and the people suffered immensely. That chaos, however, was being steadily and markedly overcome by the overall superintending power of British rule through the political agent and his court. It is no wonder that with that background, Dayananda throughout his life kept a special interest in the Rajput princes, that his first major work contained praise for the pacifying influence of British rule, and that his ideal Indian state was a centralized one under a benevolent and capable king, whose power had to be checked by the concern for the well-being and the will of the people as a whole.

When the autobiographical details are thus integrated with the Kathiawari background, there emerges a reasonably clear picture of the kind of young man Mulji was when in his twenty-second year he set out on that long journey in search of *moksha*, which would eventually transform him into the 'Luther of India'. His character traits were boldly marked: a singular determination, a thirst for knowledge, and a passion for the religious quest combined with the psychic strength to give up everything for the sake of his goal. As a brahmin and a Shaivite he saw himself as heir to the authentic ancient traditions of Hinduism, which were deeply rooted in Vedic and Sanskritic lore, and far superior to all the splintered Purānic sects. His Smārta background attached him closely to the Advaita Vedānta of Shankara, and to the ancient *Dharmashāstras*. With the very air of Kathiawar he had absorbed the ethos of cow-protection and vegetarianism, but as a Shaivite this commitment was not total, neither was it emotional. His ideal of the searcher for *moksha* was to some extent determined by the stern ideal of Jain asceticism. As he stepped into the wider world, these were some of the basic attitudes and leanings he carried with him as part of the make-up of his Kathiawari Shaivite and brahmin background. The unfolding of his adult life would show how strong these leanings were: the Vaishnavite sects and their scriptures would always remain the prime target of his critique of Hinduism, his attachment to Advaita and Shaivism would only slowly recede, whereas his adherence to the *Shāstras* would increase with the years, as would his promotion of cow-protection and vegetarianism. Only very late in life would he moderate his fanatical pursuit of extreme asceticism. Above all, more and more would he insist that the root, the essence, the glory of real Hinduism lay in the most ancient Vedic scriptures and Sanskrit lore.

CHAPTER II

The Search for *Moksha*
Leads to Grammar

Young Mulji, though courageous, was certainly very inexperienced
in dealing with the world outside his home environment. He
soon got 'kindly relieved' of all his money and valuables by a
party of begging brahmins.[1] His speedy initiation at Shaila into
the order of Lala Bhagat, a vaishya saint famous for the temple
to Rāmachandra which he built,[2] sounds perfunctory: his main
aim seems to have been to acquire anonymity with his new outfit,
'a reddish-yellow garment', and with a new name, Shuddha
Chaitanya.[3] He soon left, making his way east now, to Kot
Kangra near Ahmedabad, where he remained for three months.[4]
He stayed among a group of *sannyāsīs*, but the rich young
man was not very convincing yet, and the company was not the
best: he was the butt of the ridicule of the others, and also suffered
the sarcastic attention of a Rānī, a lady of a princely family,
who had been 'caught in the snares of the *sādhus*'.[5] He naively
talked with a passing *sādhu*, who lived near his home town and
knew his family well, and told him he was going to join the religious
festival at Siddhpur, about seventy miles to the north, where
he had heard there were Dandī *sannyāsīs* of Shankarāchārya's
order. That is where Mulji's father, who had been informed by
the *sādhu*, angrily caught up with his runaway son. He publicly
called him a matricide, ripped the robes off his body, and put
him in the close custody of his sepoys to be escorted back home
to family and a waiting bride.[6]

But Mulji's determination equalled that of his father: he escaped
during the night, taking with him that last bitter memory of a
degrading scene, and resolved never again to divulge the name
of his family or of his home town to anyone. He made his way
to Baroda where he found what he was looking for: serious
scholars to study with. At Chetan Math he was initiated into
Vedānta philosophy, a term which to him would always mean
Advaita Vedānta, by Brahmananda and other *sannyāsīs*. 'They

convinced me of the axiom "I am *brahman*", or "*brahman* and the *jīva* are identical"; I had already absorbed a little of that belief from my first reading of Vedānta, but here it became my firmly established conviction that I was identical with *brahman*.' Thus a most important basis for his future development was laid, and its influence would last until the final years of his life. For the whole of 1847 his study of Vedānta continued, first in Baroda, and then near Chanoda-Karnali, twin towns south-east of Baroda on opposite banks of the Narmada river.[7]

This was a particularly holy spot for Hindus, sometimes referred to as the Allahabad or the Banaras of the South.[8] Under the tuition of Paramananda Paramahamsa he now tackled the study of Vedāntic texts. He mentions in particular the *Vedāntasāra* of Saradānanda, an elementary treatise on Shankara's Advaita, and the *Vedānta Paribhāshā*, another elementary treatise on the same text by Dharmarāja. The future Dayananda had already that great ability to concentrate on his work and sweep aside obstructions: 'During this time as a brahmachārin, I sometimes had to prepare my own meals. I felt this constituted an obstacle to my studies. Therefore I felt that it would be a good thing to enter into the order of *sannyāsa*.' As a member of that order he would then be entitled to be fed by the Hindu lay folk. However, perhaps because this motive did not seem good enough, and also because he was still too young, he was at first refused ordination by the two monks he approached. But his insistence soon bore fruit: Purnananda Sarasvati from the Shringeri Math of the South initiated him as a *sannyāsī* in the order of the Dandīs, and gave him the name he would make famous, Dayananda Sarasvati.[9]

This decision of Mulji was a momentous one: at the same time it reinforced the bonds with the Shaivism of his youth, and mapped the broad lines of his future development. The order of the Dandīs is amongst the most highly respected orders of Hinduism. It belongs to the Dashanāmī, the ten orders claiming direct descent from the great Shankarāchārya. Whereas six of these include married men called Gosains, the group of four referred to as Dandīs is restricted to unmarried *sannyāsīs*, and recruited exclusively from the brahmin caste.[10] Philosophically, their special interest is naturally in Advaita, a fact that was to strengthen Dayananda's attachment to this brand of thought. The branch of the Sarasvatī Dandīs into which Dayananda was initiated falls under the jurisdiction of the Shankarāchārya of Shringeri Math, who is also the spiritual head of the Smārta brahmins to which Mulji's family probably belonged. Among the four *Vedas*, the *Yajurveda* is specifically entrusted to the care of this branch. This links up with Mulji's early study of this *Veda*, and the great commentary on the *Yajurveda* which he was to write in the last years of his life. The guiding symbol of the Sarasvatī Dandīs is the great Upanishadic aphorism *Aham Brahmāsmi*, 'I am *brahman*'.[11]

Apart from Advaita philosophy, the Dandīs are known to have a special interest in Patanjali Yoga.[12] Indeed, the traditional interpreters suggest that the Sarasvatīs are so called not only on account of their major concern for knowledge, but also because of their achievements in the practice of Yoga.[13] It is no wonder then that after his study of Advaita Dayananda devoted many years and a lot of energy to the study and practice of Yoga and its secrets.

The initiation ceremony on the banks of the Narmada beautifully symbolized Mulji's entry into a new life. After rites of purification and the 'act of determination', the candidate performed the funeral ceremonies for all his ancestors, symbolically enacted his own funeral and made offerings to himself as a *pitri*, a deceased ancestor. Now that he was free from his obligations to his family, he was shaved clean and gave away all his possessions. Next he performed a series of sacrifices which freed him from all his obligations to the gods. The cutting off of all ties with this world was finally completed by discarding his sacred thread and cutting off the tuft of hair on the crown of his head. He then immersed himself in the womb of the waters, emerged naked, and took seven deliberate steps, as Gautama who later became the Buddha is said to have done at his birth: a new man had been born. The initiating *guru* then prostrated himself before the new *sannyāsī*, and handed him the outward signs of his new status: a water-pot (*kamandalu*) and a staff (*danda*). Dayananda donned a loincloth to cover his nakedness before men, and thus was ready for the search for *moksha*.[14] In the true Dandī tradition, the ceremony had a strong Vedic character: practically all the elements of the initiation, the incantations, the sacrifices, the readings, were taken from Vedic lore, and completely lacked any suggestion of sectarianism. Yet the Dandī also uses two symbols that indicate his special dedication to the great god Shiva: the rosary of dried seeds (*rudrāksha*) worn around the neck, and the three horizontal lines of ashes on the forehead.

The new *sannyāsī* was now a fully-fledged Dandī at the early age of twenty-three, an achievement attributable to his own initiative and persistence. In every way he was now a free agent: he had paid in full his three debts to the sages, the fathers, and the gods,[15] and thus he now transcended the ritual and social duties of the *varnāshrama dharma*; as a consecrated Dandī, he had no further obligations except to his own search for wisdom and *moksha*: the order does not impose any requirements of staying in a monastery or of consulting one's *guru* or superiors.

Dayananda's first action was characteristic of his determination: he surrendered his *danda* to his *guru*, 'because there are many ceremonies connected with the *danda*, which could interfere with my studies'.[16] The *danda* obviously entailed a number of ceremonies, as Oman has noticed, 'the dandis . . . do not worship Shiva, but only their own *danda*'.[17] A similar abdication of the *danda* is described by a modern *sannyāsī*: '[The *guru*] then gave me the *danda*; I bowed to it, and flung it far into the River, saying "Keep this *danda*, Mother Gangā, for I have no more leisure for rules".'[18]

Dayananda continued for some time to live at Chanoda-Karnali, no doubt pressing on with his studies of Advaita. When he heard of a great exponent of Yoga, called Yogananda, living at Vyasashram, he became his student, learning the theory and practice of that science. Thence he proceeded, probably towards the beginning of 1848, to Sinor to study grammar under Krishna Shastri: he obviously felt the necessity for further language training in order to cope with the texts.

From then on, first back at Chanoda, after that near Ahmedabad, and finally at Mount Abu, Dayananda seems to have concentrated on Yoga. Two Dashanāmī monks, Jwalananda Puri and Shivananda Giri were his tutors at the first two centres, and at Mount Abu another called Bhavani Giri. It was from Mount Abu that he made his way to the Kumbh Melā of Hardwar at the end of 1854.[19] About eight years had elapsed since Mulji ran away from home, and he had been a Dandī now for over six years. He had spent these years in the study of the two subjects most dear to the Daṇḍīs: Advaita and Yoga. He obviously had fairly soon made an important option: his study of Vedānta did not last long, and covered only elementary texts. It was Yoga that attracted him, and its pursuit occupied him for some twelve years. In Dayananda, from the early days, action and practice won out over theoretical search.

A *sannyāsī* is naturally attracted to the great places of pilgrimage, and on the occasion of the Kumbh Melā this attraction almost becomes a compulsive duty.[20] It was, one presumes, the call of the Kumbh and also the desire to visit Badrinath and Joshimath, the famous northern monastery founded by Shankarāchārya, that drew Dayananda northwards. One imagines that he reassumed his *danda*, and set forth, now a mature man of over thirty, with a view of life soundly advaitic and a body steeled and a mind whetted on the anvil of Yoga.

When in the year 1855 Jupiter once more entered the sign of Aquarius, the full Kumbh Melā, the most important by far of all Hindu *melās*, was held at Hardwar, where the divine Ganga comes down on earth. Hundreds of thousands of pilgrims assembled from all over India for this holiest and most beneficial of pilgrimages. They went about their devotions individually or in small groups: taking ritual baths, offering gifts, visiting shrines, listening to religious instruction. But at the Kumbh Melā all these usual pilgrim activities were somehow subsumed by and focussed on that central mass-involving event of the procession of the *sannyāsīs* followed by the immersion in the river at the most auspicious moment.[21]

Weeks before the great day, the monastic heads and their followers started to converge on Hardwar. Among them the Dashanāmīs were the most prominent, for it is they who usually lead the great procession. They pitched their camps near the river, the heads of the monasteries flying a simple ochre-coloured banner, whereas the heads of the Ākhādās, or militant Dashanāmī monks, flew their individual standards on lances. In the procession the *nāgas*, the naked militant monks, would lead the procession, with their captain on the back of an elephant, followed by the other Dashanāmīs. But at the precise moment of the entry of Jupiter into the sign of Aquarius, it would normally be the Shankarāchārya of the Shringeri Math who would first enter the water.[22]

Anyone looking for Dayananda on that immensely important occasion at Hardwar would have expected to find him with his co-monks in the camp of the Sarasvatī Dandīs of Shringeri Math. But that was not where he was: for the duration of the *melā* he stayed at the Chandi temple, four miles away on a high wooded and lonesome hill, where he 'kept practising yoga in the solitude of the jungle'.[23] Nothing can better illustrate Dayananda's frame of mind at the time. Although he had come to Hardwar, probably in convoy with other *sannyāsīs* on their way north, the *melā* itself held no interest for him: his mind was completely absorbed in Yoga. It is not as if he had become blasé because he had seen it all before; this was his first Kumbh, his first visit north, his first chance to meet the spiritual head and the colleagues of his order. Every single one of these 'firsts' would constitute a reason to excite any Hindu. But not for Dayananda, who was not even curious: his preoccupation with Yoga was so great that it seems close to obsessional.

He spent the whole of 1855 in the mountain country northeast of Hardwar. In 1816 this area, the Kingdoms of Garhwal and Kumaon, had been ceded to the British after the Gurkha war. The narrow strip frequented by Dayananda lies along the head-waters of the Ganga, the Bhagirathi, and Alaknanda rivers. From Hardwar, the panorama rises to a magnificent string of glacier-garlanded peaks forming the Kedarnath-Badrinath group between twenty-two and twenty-three thousand feet high.[24] The rivers have eroded steep and narrow valleys amid the rocky peaks, with the highest villages and shrines lying between ten and twelve thousand feet: Kedarnath, Badrinath, and Mana. The country, now made accessible by motorable roads, was then extremely rough and was accessible only by mountain tracks. The highest spots were snowbound for at least four months of the year, and the priests·of Kedarnath and Badrinath used to spend the winter in the lower-lying centres of Ukhimath and Joshimath.

Notwithstanding its near inaccessibility, that area, and in particular Kedarnath and Badrinath, has been from the earliest times among the foremost places of pilgrimage for all Hindus.[25] Hindu mythology gave it the name Kūrmāchala, the modern Kumaon, recalling the second incarnation of the god Vishnu when he visited the earth in the form of a tortoise. This was the land where the scriptures pictured the meetings of gods and god-

desses with the sages and ascetics of early times. The hillmen
still sing the praises of the Pāndava brothers, who finished their
earthly wanderings here, their last stop on the way to the heavens
of Indra. The Langur Hills are called after Hanuman who sanctified them by his austerities.[26] It was the highest ambition of
many Hindus to perform that holiest and most effective of all
pilgrimages: some used to commit suicide by flinging themselves
from the Bhairon Jhap after inscribing their names on the temple-
walls.[27]

But Dayananda did not come as a pilgrim of that kind. His
pilgrimage was not the journey to a place, a shrine so sacred
that heaven there touched the very earth, and the air itself breathed
holiness; his pilgrimage was a search for ever better teachers to
open up even deeper secrets of Yoga. 'I felt a strong desire to
visit the surrounding ice-clad mountains to ascertain if there
really lived somewhere a perfect sage and ascetic.'[28] That is the
one purpose and hope that kept him going during that year, as
his itinerary clearly demonstrates.

After his stay in the jungle of Chandi, he proceeded to Rishikesh,
where 'in the company of yogis and *sannyāsīs* I continued my
study and practice of Yoga'.[29] In those days Rishikesh was 'a
mere collection of a few houses and temples and one small line
of shops dotted about the bank of the Ganges amid heavy under-
growth'.[30] From there Dayananda walked east to Tihari, capital
of the state of that name. Here he had his first encounter with
Tantric works: these were brought to him by a pandit who had
invited him to a meal. When the Swami walked in he saw the
bloody spectacle of goat's meat, skins, and heads, was sickened
to the core, and declined to take part.[31] But he immersed himself
in the Tantric works the pandit gave him, and came to the conclusion that they were full of obscenities and of sin, and that
they were mind-destroying.[32] One quite understands that the
erotic practices of Tantra must have repelled him enormously:
yet one cannot but wonder how far he in fact delved into the non-
erotic yoga of Tantra. It took him a whole year before he actually
got rid of the books dealing with the mystical neurology of Hatha
Yoga and Tantra,[33] and he confessed another six months later
how he had got into the habit of taking *bhang*, or Indian hemp.[34]
These are two indications at least that Dayananda at this time
took certain aspects of Tantra seriously, and probably used some

of its methods in the context of Yoga.

Three days' walking brought Dayananda to Shrinagar, a central stop-over town for pilgrims, where Shankarāchārya is said to have attacked the tāntrikas. He read more Tantric literature and discussed it with the local pandits, but spent most of the two months he was there with a *sādhu* called Ganga Giri in his hermitage on a wooded mountain, discussing Yoga. Back on the road, he only mentions in passing Rudraprayag, the holy confluence of the Alaknanda and the Mandakini, where the sage Nārada performed his austerities, and Agastamuni, where the sage Agastya used to do penance. These were but short stops on his way to a mountain peak, called Shivapuri, where he spent four months, no doubt studying and practising the new aspects of Yoga he had discovered.[35]

After leaving this lonely retreat, Dayananda visited Guptakashi, where the gods secretly performed penance to please Lord Shiva,[36] Gaurikund with its hot springs, Bhima Gupha, and Trigunanarayan, where Shiva and Pārvatī were married in the Golden Age.[37] The next stop was Kedarnath,[38] one of the holiest places of Shiva worship. The temple is under the care of the Jangam Gosains, ascetics of the Lingāyat sect about whom Dayananda learnt all he could.[39] He must have been fascinated by these sectarian Shaivites, who had broken with caste, idolatry, and pilgrimages, who rejected the *Vedas* and the brahmins' authority, and whose doctrine in many ways resembled the 'qualified monism' of Rāmānuja.[40]

After this break, Dayananda set forth into the surrounding mountainous country 'in quest of those true ascetics',[41] and roamed around for twenty days in a gruelling and disheartening search. He finally reached and ascended Tunganath peak, some ten miles east of Ukhimath. 'Having seen the disgusting display of idolatry in the temple, I hastened to descend the peak the next day'. He got lost in the fearsome jungle, but 'by dint of tremendous exertion', he managed to reach Ukhimath in full darkness. He slept the night there and the next day he returned to Guptakashi, only a couple of miles to the north, for a well-deserved rest.[42]

Then he went back to Ukhimath with the purpose of 'examining closely its famous monastery'.[43] Ukhimath, 4,300 ft. above sea level, is the winter-resort of the priests of Kedarnath, and a stop on the way for the pilgrim returning from Kedarnath and going on to Badrinath. The head of the Kedarnath temple resided there permanently, and was in charge of the considerable revenues the shrine commanded.[44] Dayananda was not impressed by this famous and wealthy monastery, and its great display of ritual and of rich stores. The abbot, on the other hand, was very impressed with this headstrong *sannyāsī*, and offered to adopt him as his disciple with the tempting prospect of one day succeeding to the headship of the monastery and becoming the master of its wealth. Dayananda refused, saying that he could have had such riches in his father's house, and he explained to the abbot that the real object of his search was 'the knowledge of truth, true Yoga, and through them final liberation, *moksha*'.[45]

Brushing aside an invitation to stay on for a while, Dayananda soon pressed on to Joshimath, where he stayed in the company of *shāstrīs* and *sannyāsīs* of South India, and learned some new aspects of the science of Yoga.[46] Joshimath was the winter-resort of the Badrinath priests, the place sanctified by the *Jyotir-linga*, the *linga* of light of Lord Shiva that appeared to Shankar-ācārya on his memorable visit. Dayananda then pressed on to Badrinath, where he was the guest of the *rawal*, the head of the monastery, traditionally a *nambūdiri* brahmin from Kerala, of Shankarāchārya's own caste.[47] Dayananda does not even mention the famous Vishnu temple, and left after a few days on another search for 'genuine yogis', who, so the *rawal* had heard, occasionally visited the *math*.[48]

He set out one early morning, following the Alaknanda river towards its source. He passed the village of Mana, and, working his way up the mountain, found himself once more completely lost. No wonder, because the terrain was frightful. He was right in the jungle, and even the Mana pass itself, that leads into Tibet, was nearly fifty years later described as follows:

The necessity of travelling for many miles over the vast accumulations of loose rock and debris brought down by ancient glaciers, or which violent atmospheric changes have thrown into the valley from the mountains on both sides, renders the Mana pass one of the most difficult in this part of the Himalayas. Its actual elevation too exceeds that of any other pass in the division which leads into Tibet. The road or rather the track, for there is generally nothing that even deserves the name of a path, ascends constantly the main valley of the Saraswati until it reaches the water-parting which forms the boundary with Tibet.[49]

Exhaustion, hunger, thirst, and countless leg-wounds reduced

him to a state 'more dead than alive'[50]: Dayananda reached
the point of despair. In fact, the *Theosophist* autobiography does
not recount his feelings to the full, but he tells us more in his
Poona lectures: 'the thought came to me that for once and all
I would let my body freeze in this ice and thus free myself from
the troubles of this world'.[51] Although the very physical exhaustion and near-frozen condition of his wounded body were
no doubt partly the cause of this black despair, the feeling of
complete failure in his objective was another major cause. For
nearly a year now he had been roaming this holy land in search
of great yogic masters, and his search had ended in utter frustration. The moment of despair soon passed: 'But it came to
my mind that one should shed one's body only after having
acquired true knowledge.'[52] So he mustered his tremendous will-
power once more and somehow he got his shattered body back
to Kedarnath that very night.[53] This one final day of horror
made up his mind: next day he left for Rampur, down the slopes
towards the valley of the Ganga.

At Rampur he stayed at the house of the famous holy man
Ramgiri, whose strange behaviour intrigued him at first; but
soon he found out that he was not a genuine yogī, and moved
on to Drona Sagar, where he passed the winter months from
December 1855 to March 1856.[54] This was the time for him to
reflect on that year he had passed in the holy land of Kumaon.
He recalled his frustration and despair, 'to shed my body on
these mountains, that had been my wish'.[55] But he shook off
those feelings, and continued his studies of the books he had
acquired. Of these he mentions four explicitly. There were two
treatises on Hatha Yoga, the *Hathayogapradīpikā*, a classical
treatise by Svātmārāma, and the *Gheranda Samhitā*, a later
work. The two other works are difficult to identify.[56] Dayananda
experienced great difficulty in understanding the mystical physi-
ology with its *nārīs* and *chakras*. His mind, as his later works
clearly show, was inclined towards the literal, the pragmatic,
the rational; and he always found it difficult to cope with the
symbolic and the mythological. But he obviously tried hard.
The way in which he finally cut the knot is typical of his literal
and pragmatic rationalism. This happened after the winter at
Drona Sagar, when he reached the Ganga near Garhmukteshwar.
He pulled a corpse out of the river and set to the gruesome task

of cutting it up with a knife. 'I then carefully examined the heart
and compared it with the descriptions in the books. I did the
same with the head and the neck. I came to the firm conclusion
that there was not the slightest similarity between the texts and
the corpse. I then tore the books to pieces and threw them into
the river with the remains of the corpse.'[57]

Thus Dayananda put a dramatic full stop to his experiments
after his pilgrimage to the mountains. Taking stock of that gruelling year, he must have found little positive to put on the credit
side. He had discovered a new dimension of Hinduism and Yoga,
that of Tantra, but only to reject it after having studied and probably sampled some of its non-erotic practices. The real yogīs
he came to search for and learn from could not be found even
in a nearly suicidal hunt. The monasteries and shrines and their
inmates generally disgusted him, and he avoided them as much
as he could: in fact more than half his time in the mountains
was spent in utter solitude, in the study and practice of Yoga,
which he still hoped would transport him into the realm of *moksha*.

Dayananda left the mountains at the beginning of 1856, and
we know he arrived in Mathura to study under Swami Virjananda
at the end of 1860. Little is known about these five years. Coming
down the Ganga from Garhmukteshwar he visited many places
between Farrukhabad, Kanpur, Allahabad, and Mirzapur; and
he arrived for his first visit to Banaras in September 1856. He
did not find what he sought for, and continued his journey after
twelve days.[58] A couple of miles south of Banaras, in Chunargarh,
he stayed at the Durgā temple. It was there, 'where I spent ten
days, that I left off eating rice altogether, and lived only on milk.
I devoted myself, day and night, to the practice of Yoga. Unfortunately, there I did a very wrong thing: I got into the habit
of using *bhāng*. Several times I became completely unconscious
under its influence.'[59] This is a very significant fact which
Dayananda obviously felt to be of great importance, especially
when connected with the dream that followed one of his intoxi-
cated states.

Why did Dayananda start taking *bhāng*? There is one purpose
that may be ruled out right away: as a stimulus to the appetite:
'its appetizing powers are of great value to begging Brahmans,
who under its influence can at a caste feast eat enough to last
for twenty-four hours or more'.[60] That is a kind of pastime

Dayananda never indulged in; he was always a most abstemious man. When one takes into consideration the type of man he was, and particularly his unwavering single-mindedness, one has to presume that his taking of *bhāng* was connected with his obsessive study of Yoga. He had been at this study now for over eight years, and had looked everywhere for a *guru* who would teach him how to break open the doors of perception, the doors of *moksha*. But they had remained closed. He had no doubt by this time mastered a great deal of the art of concentration and meditation, but that final trance, or at least that final certainty in the trance of having entered into a supreme state of freedom, kept eluding him. Is it a wonder then that he turned to the help of drugs? Since ancient times they had been connected with the mystical tradition of India. Particularly in his contact with the tāntrikas, and in the perusal of their literature he must have come across the praises of *vijayā*, the classical term for *bhāng*.[61] Would *vijayā* give him that final victory? Obviously it did not, it only produced an 'unfortunate habit', of which he rid himself as soon as he clearly realized it did not help him in his purpose. This realization seems to have come to him as the sobering result of a dream he dreamt when under the influence of *bhāng*: 'I thought I saw Mahādeva and his wife Pārvatī. They were talking, and I was the subject of their conversation. Pārvatī was saying to Mahādeva, "It would be best if Dayananda got married", but the god did not agree with her, and he pointed to the *bhāng*'.[62]

It would be a rather risky venture to try and give a psychological explanation of this dream. There are, however, some very obvious elements in it that give some clues about Dayananda's state of mind. The two actors in the dream are the tantric couple *par excellence*, Shiva and Pārvatī, his *shakti*. The goddess is saying that Dayananda should get married, or in other words should link his life with a *shakti*. But Shiva disagrees because of the Swami's use of the drug. All the elements of the dream have a direct tantric reference, and in a way indicate that *tantra* did really influence and disturb the *sannyāsī*. But the dream also indicates that Shiva did not agree with Pārvatī. Thus the dream is about an option, a choice that now has to be made by Dayananda: to follow Pārvatī's direction, or to cut himself completely loose from *tantra*, and to heed Shiva's hint. We do not know when exactly Dayananda took his final option, but we know that he took it, never to be revoked, there and then or soon afterwards.

In fact, after this event, a complete curtain comes down over Dayananda's life from mid-1857 till the end of 1860, because his break with the Theosophists prevented the publication of further instalments of the autobiography in their journal. All he tells us is that he travelled south into the fearful jungles of the Vindhya range, towards the hills from where the Narmada takes its rise.[63] Was he still chasing the perfect yogis beyond the rainbow? Possibly, because he was certainly still searching in Banaras towards the end of 1856. Speculation is vain, as not a single, clue is available on the way in which these next three years were spent.[64] All we know is that he went towards the fountain-head of the Narmada, another pilgrimage to the sources. But his great 'pilgrimage to the sources', the one that was to remain linked to his very name, the return to the *Veda*, was still many years away.

Though the groves of Brinda, in which Krishna disported with the Gopis, no longer resound to the echoes of his flute; though the waters of the Jamuna are daily polluted with the blood of sacred kine; still it is the holy land of the pilgrim, the sacred Jordan of his fancy, on whose banks he may sit and weep, as did the banished Israelite of old, for the glories of Mathura, his Jerusalem.[65]

Mathura, once one of the shining centres of flourishing Buddhism, a glory perpetuated in the magnificence of the Buddhist sculpture of the Mathura style, became in the Middle Ages one of the most sacred cities of the Hindus. Its claim to holiness comes from the single fact that it was the birthplace of Krishna. The antics of the child Krishna and the amours of the youth have hallowed not only Mathura but the whole *Braj-mandala*: over five hundred square miles of its environs is holy ground consecrated by one or other of the many legends of the rich and charming Krishna-cycle. The devout pilgrim traverses this land in a two-week trek[66] that brings him to the 'five hills, eleven rocks, four lakes, eighty-four ponds, twelve wells, twelve woods, and twenty-four groves'[67] that constitute the traditional peregrination. 'For nine months in the year festival follows upon festival in rapid succession, and the ghats and temples are daily thronged with new troops of way-worn pilgrims'.[68]

The growth of Mathura into a great centre of the Krishna-cult dates from the early seventeenth century when first Vallabha, founder of the sect of the Vallabhāchāryas, and then his son Vitthalnāth stayed there. The cult was given impetus by the celebrated Bengali Gosains Rūpā and Sanātana,[69] and in the middle of the nineteenth century the Mathura area boasted of no less than fifteen of the seventy Maharajas, religious leaders of the sect.[70] The celebrated Vishrant Ghat, where Krishna rested after slaying the demon Kamsa, is the principal ghat of the city, surrounded along the Yamuna by a dozen more ghats up and a dozen more down the river.[71] Scores of temples crowd the city, thronged by the pilgrims, who are no doubt aware of the popular saying that, 'while Banaras is good for one thing, namely, to die in; Muttra is good for four, namely, to be born in, to live in, to marry in as well as to die in'.[72]

That is where Dayananda arrived in November 1860. He was then a mature man of thirty-six. His whole adult life had been devoted to some study of Vedānta but mainly to that of Yoga. He had combed the holy land of Kumaon and the rugged peaks of the Vindhyas in search of the perfect *guru* who would show him the way to *moksha*. But so far this search had remained fruitless. One would like to know what happened to him in those last three years. What frustrations and new discoveries made him at that stage give up that search for *moksha*, and take the road to Mathura in order to study grammar under the guidance of Swami Virjananda Sarasvati, the famous blind *guru*?

Although the question remains unanswerable in detail, a general answer suggests itself. During these last years Dayananda became convinced that the deepest secret of religion and *moksha* lay hidden in the Hindu scriptures. He probably tried to study them, but soon found how difficult they were, and how inadequate his own knowledge of Sanskrit was. The key to Sanskrit is grammar. So, if he wanted to unravel the teachings of the scriptures, he had to become a master of Sanskrit. No doubt he had heard of the great *guru* of grammar, Virjananda, and with the single-mindedness so characteristic of him, he set out for Mathura to sit with youngsters at the feet of the master.

There is no doubt that the nearly three years during which Dayananda studied under Virjananda radically changed the direction of his life: this pivotal time transformed the individualistic searcher for *moksha* into the man who would become 'the Luther of India'. This transformation cannot have been the result of the content of the *guru*'s formal teaching; grammar is what he taught. As Dayananda himself testifies: 'When I met him, he told me that grammar could be learned in three years. I took the firm decision to study under him'.[73] The biographers tell us that he studied Pānini's great grammar, the *Ashtādhyāyī*, and its chief commentary, the *Mahābhāshya* of Patanjali. The biographers mention no other specific work, except perhaps some works conducive to the understanding of Vedic Sanskrit. They quite definitely agree that no single *Veda* was studied.[74] There are also indications that Virjananda may also have read some Vedāntic texts with his pupil.[75] But, as Dayananda left Mathura before the three years were completed, it seems quite conclusive that the formal curriculum of study itself did not go beyond grammar.[76]

As it certainly was not the content of his study that changed Dayananda's view of life, it must be other factors: the only ones that can be historically ascertained without venturing into the fabrications of the pious imagination, are the total influence of his *guru* combined with Dayananda's own reaction to Hinduism as he saw it around him. In fact the line his development took after leaving Mathura will confirm the strong influence of these two factors.

If Dayananda does not seem to have taken much notice of the Hinduism around him so far, why should he have taken notice now? Simply because its presence constantly assailed all his senses. Dayananda lived in a cell on the ground floor of the Lakshmīnārāyana temple on Vishrant Ghat, the principal ghat of Mathura.[77] The famous Hindu traveller Bholanath Chunder visited Mathura at the time Dayananda studied there, and described this ghat as follows.

The most sacred spot in all Muttra is the Bisramghaut, where Krishna and Buldeo rested from their labours of slaying Kunsa, and dragging his corpse to the riverside. They had also washed their bodies and clothes at this ghaut; in imitation of which the pilgrim also has to perform his ablutions and devotions here. There is no broad flight of steps properly to deserve the name of a ghaut. The top, however, is crowned with many beautiful temples and shrines. It makes a gay scene every evening to perform here the vespers in honour of the Jumna. Large crowds assemble to witness the ceremony. The spot is illuminated. Bells and cymbals ring on every side. The women shower flowers from high balconies, and incense is burned loading the air with a sweet perfume.[78]

The house where Virjananda taught was on the most important road leading from the Holi Gate to Vishrant Ghat. In his cell, at his *guru's* home, and on the way from one to the other, Dayananda lived and moved and worked the whole time in the very heart of Mathura, in the thick of all religious and pilgrim activity. This fact is an important one, because this was really the first time Dayananda had had such a prolonged and intimate contact with the chaotic reality of living Hinduism. No doubt he had been to the Kumbh Melā at Hardwar, but he was never close to it; he had been to Allahabad and Banaras, but only for very short visits when he was preoccupied with anything but popular Hinduism. Here in Mathura he was physically immersed in the thick of it for nearly three years, and the living Hindu devotee was right under his eyes all the time. Later on, in his *Satyārth Prakāsh*, he described Mathura as follows:

It is not true that 'Mathura is exalted above the three worlds' [as the saying goes]. But in it there are three very rapacious species, who make it hard for any one to enjoy any happiness on the ground, in the water, or in the air. First there are the Chaube brahmins who are ready to demand from anyone who goes to take a bath their tax, ever shouting, 'Give, O devotee, so that we may fill up on *bhāng*, pepper and sweetmeats, and bestow blessings on you'. Then there are the tortoises in the river, always ready to bite, so that it is difficult even to take a bath in the ghat. And thirdly, there are the red-faced monkeys off the ground. They snatch turbans, caps, jewels, and even shoes: they bite, attack, would even kill. These three are the objects of worship of the 'popes' and their disciples![79]

The tortoises and monkeys of Mathura are infamous, and the Chaubes are described by Growse as 'a low and ignorant horde of rapacious mendicants ... [who] may always be seen with their portly forms lolling about near the most popular ghats and temples, ready to bear down on the first pilgrim that approaches.'[80]

As a youth in Kathiawar Dayananda had known the strength of Vaishnavism as the majority religion, and the relative weakness of the Shaivite minority. However, Mathura was much worse: here the pervasion of Vaishnavism was overpowering and stifling to a Shaivite. Bholanath Chunder remarked, 'The most favourite local deity now is Krishna, who is adored in nearly all the temples abounding in the town which owns his exclusive jurisdiction. Shiva has no right, title, or interest in this city. He has only one temple dedicated to him, and appears to have been permitted to reside much as a foreigner holding a passport - as an inter-loper.'[81] In Kathiawar the temples of Shiva were the most numerous, and most brahmins were Shaivites, except only for the fallen ones. Mathura did have quite a high proportion of brahmins, nearly twenty per cent of the Hindu population. But of these many brahmins barely one in four was a Shaivite.[82]

It was here in Mathura that Dayananda came to know from close up the sect of the Vallabhāchāryas, who were to remain the special target of his criticism of sectarianism: he wrote a special pamphlet against them, and in his *Satyārth Prakāsh* devoted the longest criticism of any sect to them. In some way one might say that the book *par excellence* of Mathura Hinduism is the *Bhāgavata Purāna*, the most famous of the *Purānas*, the holiest text of the Krishna *bhakti*. Practically every holy spot in the *Braj-mandala* is connected with the myth of Krishna as told in the tenth book of the *Bhāgavata*. No doubt the recitation of the *Bhāgavata* and of the *Prem Sāgar*, its Hindi equivalent, was one of the great devotions of the Mathura Vaishnavites.[83] In fact, one could say that the *Bhāgavata Purāna* was, apart from his grammar books, the one book that would have been forcibly and continuously brought to Dayananda's attention in Mathura.

Thanks to the pioneering work of Devendranath Mukho-padhyay, a fairly complete picture can be gained of Swami Virjananda Sarasvati (1779-1868), and of his life and work. Born in the Panjab, he was blinded by smallpox at five and orphaned at eleven, and he left the harsh home of his uncle at the age of fifteen. After wandering around the Himalayan slopes, he found a *guru* in Swami Purnananda, who initiated him into the order of the Sarasvatī Dandīs, to which Dayananda would also belong. He made grammar his special study at Kankhal near Hardwar, Banaras, and Gaya. He then lived along the banks of the Ganga in the Doab. By far his favourite place was Soron, where he lived for altogether about fifteen years.[84] Later on Dayananda too would gravitate towards that *varāha bhūmī*, the land of the Boar, where Vishnu as the Boar incarnation came to save the world, the greatest pilgrimage place of the Doab. By this time Virjananda had added the teaching of grammar to his study of it.

A new chapter opened in his life when the Maharaja of Alwar asked him to become his teacher. After initial reluctance, Virjananda accepted, and spent about three-and-a-half years tutoring the prince. The biographers recount how one day, because the Maharaja was absent from his lesson, the irascible *guru* packed his bags and left. After a period of illness at Soron, he became the guest of Raja Tikamsingh at Mursan, and of Maharaja Balwantsingh of Bharatpur. Neither of these stays lasted long, and in 1845, now aged over sixty-five and with a reputation firmly established, the blind *sannyāsī* moved to Mathura and opened a regular school of grammar, which was financially supported by the ruling princes of Bharatpur, Jaipur, and Alwar.

Another decisive turning point in his career was a *shāstrārth*, a public dispute conducted formally in Sanskrit. This was a sordid affair, full of intrigue and deception, as distasteful as the one Dayananda would be subjected to later on in Banaras. A pandit named Krishna Shastri, a famous master of grammar and logic, arrived in Mathura, and soon became the favourite protégé of an immensely wealthy Vaishnavite Seth clan. Moves were made to have a public dispute between him and the Shaivite Virjananda. However, when all was arranged, the Pandit avoided appearing, whereupon Virjananda too withdrew. So the dispute was held between their respective disciples. The topic of discussion was an abstruse grammatical point.[85] The Seth, who was Pandit Krishna Shastri's patron, himself presided over the affair, and within a short time summarily declared his pandit's side the winners. Virjananda was very angry, especially when the Seth managed, with the help of money, to acquire a decision in favour of his pandit's side from the pandits of Banaras. He complained to the pandits, he complained to the collector of Mathura, but to no avail. He then closed his school for some time, and when he opened it up again a great change took place. 'After this event, a new era started in the Mathura school. The grammar books that so far had been taught, the *Siddhāntakaumudī*, the *Shekar*, the *Chandrikā*, the *Manorama*, etc, were once and for all thrown out. And their place was taken by the one and only *Ashtādhyāyī* of the sage Pānini.'[86]

This change might not seem very important, for its real significance appears only in the context of a new interpretation of the whole of Hindu literature which Virjananda was evolving, and which he clarified soon afterwards. This is the vital distinction between *ārsha* works written by the real sages of ancient India, the *rishis*, and *anārsha* works composed by others. Devendranath

Mukhopadhyay recounts that the Swami used to apply three criteria by which the wheat could be sifted from the chaff. The books written by the *rishis* always begin with either *OM* or *ATHA*, the others commence with an invocation to a particular deity. Secondly, whereas the *rishis'* compositions exhibit a universal character, the others are full of sectarian bias and hatred. And lastly, the commentaries on the *rishis'* works were all written by recognized teachers like Shankarāchārya and Patanjali; if these teachers have not written a commentary on a particular work, that is a sign that it was not really composed by a *rishi*.[87]

To Virjananda this distinction was not a purely formal or academic one, as his subsequent interventions prove. First he tried to enlist the help of the British commissioner of Mathura in the encouragement of the *rishis'* books. Naturally, he found no help in that quarter; neither would Dayananda when he tried a similar approach many years afterwards. He then turned to the Indian princes, several of whom admired him and supported his work. When he heard of the great 'Durbar' for the ruling princes of Rajputana to be held at Agra by Lord Canning in 1859 after the successful suppression of the Mutiny, he saw his chance to put his case forward. He went to Agra and pleaded with Maharaja Ramsingh of Jaipur, but he only got vague promises of future help. His later letters to the rulers of Kashmir and Gwalior, and even to Queen Victoria herself, also proved fruitless.[88]

Virjananda had indeed a concrete plan to submit to the princes: the convening of a 'Sārvabhauma Sabhā', a universal council of Hinduism, which was explained in a long document under that heading.[89] He tells very little about the composition and function of this council, except that the princes should be involved. The main point he makes is about the degeneration of Hinduism, and the remedy for its renaissance. There are two types of *gurus*, he says: the ancient *guru* whose wisdom became recorded in the books of the *rishis*; and the later *guru* whose teaching should be restricted to the oral interpretation of these works. The curse of Hinduism has been the multiplication of writings by all kinds of teachers. This has led to the multiplication of sects and to the practical oblivion of the *rishis'* works. A proof of the strength of his conviction lies in the fact that Virjananda had two manuscript books on grammar composed by himself thrown into the

river by his disciples.[90] The function of the *Sārvabhauma Sabhā*
would have been to find means to halt the proliferation and propagation of secondary sectarian writings, and to support proper
language study through which to renew the study of the books
of the *rishis*. It is important to note that the one work to be twice
mentioned in this document as an example of these untruthful,
worthless sectarian works, is none other than the *Bhāgavata
Purāna*.

That, then, was the *guru* to whom Dayananda turned for
help in the study of grammar. It is obvious that Virjananda must
often have discussed his favourite ideas with his favourite pupil.
The key idea is the judgement that the degeneration of Hinduism
is fundamentally connected with the proliferation and influence of
'spurious' works of a sectarian nature giving rise to numerous
sects, accompanied by a parallel neglect of the real sources of
Hinduism, the books of the *rishis*. The implication is that the
regeneration of Hinduism can come only through a renewal of
the study and influence of those books and the elimination of
sectarian works and groups. This key idea was also an expression
of a deep concern, a concern new to Dayananda: the concern
for Hinduism and for the Hindus, as distinct from the narrow
individualistic concern for personal *moksha*. This concern which
his *guru* communicated to him was constantly being reinforced
by his close experience of real Hinduism in the heart of Mathura.
For the rest of his life Dayananda was to be preoccupied with
that concern and the search for ways to reform a Hinduism torn
asunder by the sects. He would also remain fascinated by the
idea of the real sources of Hinduism, and he would soon begin
that 'pilgrimage to the sources'. But it would take many years
before this vague idea would find its final formulation.

Apart from a few anecdotes illustrating the irascible nature
of the *guru* and the dogged persistence of his pupil, little concrete
is known about these three years of study. A Gujarati brahmin
provided Dayananda with shelter and food, so that no material
anxieties would impede his studies. At the end of his schooling,
Dayananda, in the true Vedic tradition, took his parting present,
his *dakshinā*, to his *guru*: some of the cloves Virjananda liked
so much. But the blind *guru* is reported to have addressed his
pupil thus: 'I want from you a new kind of *dakshinā*. Promise
me that you will, as long as you live, devote everything, even

give up your life, to the propagation in India of the books of
the *rishis* and the Vedic religion. I will accept from you the fulfilment of that promise as my *dakshinā*.'⁹¹ Dayananda agreed and,
with the blessing of the one and only *guru* .he would ever have,
the great master of grammar, he set out on the first stage of his
new quest.

The four years that elapsed between the time Dayananda left
his *guru*, April 1863, and the time he participated in the Kumbh
Melā at Hardwar in March 1867, are of very great importance
in the development of his thought and his approach. Virjananda
had given him a superior grammatical technique, the idea of
the difference between the books of the *rishis* and others, a concern
for the regeneration of Hinduism, and probably also some rein-
forcement of his Advaitic approach. Mathura had given him
insight into the sorry state of Hinduism, and it should be remembered that the Hinduism he had witnessed was practically one-
hundred per cent Vaishnavite. These were the basic elements of
the new Dayananda, and all of them were still very vague, and
needed to be tested and developed. He moved around within
the triangle Mathura-Gwalior-Ajmer, never further than two
hundred miles from his *guru*. He stayed for long periods at the
different places: one-and-a-half years at Agra, seven months at
Gwalior, six at Karauli and Jaipur, three at Pushkar and Ajmer,
another four at Jaipur and two more at Agra. The period is closed
off by his final visit to Virjananda at the end of 1866.

The sources for our knowledge of this period are the Poona
lectures, Lekhram, and Ghasiram; the other biographies add
nothing new. But there is towards the end of the period a very
important independent testimony of the state of Dayananda's
thinking in the writings of the missionaries who met him in Ajmer,
in particular of Reverend John Robson.⁹² In addition, there is
now available the text of the short pamphlet criticizing the
Bhāgavata Purāna, written by Dayananda towards the end of
this period in Ajmer and published in Agra in 1866.⁹³

The first major impression one gets from the sources is that
this is a very different Dayananda indeed: he has become a public
preacher and teacher. He teaches grammar, Vedānta, Yoga, and
works like the *Bhagavadgītā* and the *Manusmriti*. He advises
people on matters of reading and ritual. He publicly preaches

against idol worship and Vaishnavite sectarianism, and, at least
in the early part, preaches Shaivism and distributes *rudrākshas*.
He has discussions with pandits, Jains, and missionaries, and
starts to participate in public disputes, *shāstrārths*. He even
makes approaches to British officials' about religious matters.
The *sannyāsī* who used to avoid crowds and publicity and seek
the solitude of nature and of his own soul, has become an ardent
preacher and a public figure. Virjananda and Mathura certainly
have transformed the lonely seeker for *moksha* and given him
a completely new kind of impetus.

Yet, to Dayananda this was essentially a time of further study
and reflection. He stayed for long periods at the same place,
was in regular contact with Virjananda,[94] and, when urged to
get on with reform work, he answered, 'This is for me a time
of reflection'.[95] Later on he recalled in more detail: 'From
Mathura I went to Agra where I stayed for two years. There
were available many ancient books of the *rishis* and also many
new books. I reflected on them. Then I stayed at Gwalior. There
too I considered all the books that were available.'[96] This is
the time when he first came into contact with the *Vedas* proper
since his memorization of *Yajurveda mantras* in his childhood.
The information is conflicting. Ghasiram says that he got a copy
of the *Rigveda* from the Raja of Jaipur's library while he was
in Agra for the first time.[97] Lekhram mentions that at that place
he only saw parts of the *Veda*, went in search of it on leaving
Agra, and that he was studying the *Veda* later on during his stay
in Karauli in May-October 1865.[98] On the other hand, Reverend
Robson, recalling conversations with Dayananda in Ajmer in
June 1866, writes that 'he knew only the Yajur Veda', 'he candidly
acknowledged that he had not read the Rig Veda', and 'the first
copy of the Rig Veda he saw was in my possession, that edited
by Max Müller'.[99] One has to take into account here the possibility of misunderstanding, because the conversation would have
been in Sanskrit. However, it is safe to say that during this period
Dayananda had started his study of the *Veda*, but that, difficult
as the task must have been even for one so versed in Sanskrit
grammar, he was only slowly advancing in this task. In fact
it is clear that at this time it was not the *Rigveda* but other works
that influenced him most.

Whereas at Agra he refused to read the *Panchadashī*, an exposition of Shankara Vedānta by Mādhava (14th cent.), because it was 'man-made',[100] at Jaipur he got very involved in the teaching of the *Upanishads*. Ghasiram explicitly mentions the *Nirālamba*, the *Brihadāranyaka*, and the *Chāndogya Upanishads*,[101] and Lekhram speaks of the 'ten *Upanishads*'.[102] Moreover, he is now also studying Shankara's own *Tattvabodha*.[103] This is quite a new departure, and Lekhram comments: 'In those days Swamiji taught Vedānta, and he used to indicate the unmanifest Lord (*nirākāra paramātmā*) by the name of Shiva. He did not mention Shiva the husband of Pārvati; in fact he was against him. He was still wearing the *rudrāksh* beads and applying ashes, and teaching others to do so'.[104] When later in Pushkar he was asked what the name of the Lord was, because some call Him Brahmā and others Vishnu, etc., he answered, '*Saccidānanda* is the name to repeat, no other'. At that time, says Lekhram, he did not venerate Vishnu or Shiva, but only *parameshvar*.[105] In Pushkar too he declared that he only recognized *saccidānanda* or *parameshvar*, and, when asked about the name 'Shiva', he answered, 'We do recognize Shiva, but the name Shiva means "the auspicious one". The other Shiva who is the husband of Pārvati, him we do not recognize'. [106]

It is evident that Dayananda had discovered, or rediscovered, the Vedāntic idea of the absolute. The terms he uses are all Vedāntic, as are the works he was studying. Robson recalled that at that time Dayananda believed in the identity of the divine and human spirits, and added that his argument was chiefly based on the omnipresence of the divine spirit.[107] These Vedāntic concepts forced him to rethink aspects of the Shaivism that had dominated his teaching since he left Virjananda. He now clearly dissociated his god from the Purānic Shiva, and the end-point of this reappraisal is that Shiva is reduced to being just one of the names of God, indicating the auspicious nature of the Lord. To say that Vedāntic ideas re-assert themselves does not necessarily mean that Dayananda now denied the personality of the absolute: it remains for him the *parameshvar*, the Supreme Lord. However, there still remained in his conception the unresolved problem of the relationship of these two aspects. The final verses quoted in his pamphlet against the *Bhāgavata Purāna* also indicate

this strong Upanishadic flavour with a theistic background:
they are the famous verses in the first chapter of the *Kena
Upanishad*:

> That which is unexpressed with speech
> That with which speech is expressed —
> That indeed know as Brahma,
> Not this that people worship as this.
> That which one thinks not with thought
> That with which they say thought is thought —
> That indeed know as Brahma,
> Not this that people worship as this.[108]

This unresolved problem combined with the obvious change
in his interpretation of 'Shiva' explains the ambiguities and even
the contradictions we find in the different sources. Whereas
Dayananda himself in the Poona lectures clearly states that 'on
my arrival at Ajmer I commenced to criticize the Shaivite theology
also',[109] Lekhram says that 'he criticized the idol of Shiva, and
only taught Shiva himself',[110] and Ghasiram declares that in
Pushkar he still converted people to Shaivism and told them
to wear the *rudrāksh*, and that in Ajmer too he was still defending
Shaivism.[111] The changing ideas of Dayananda also explain the
account given by Robson. In fact, somehow the latter put his
finger right on the problem when he said, 'At that time he had
not broken with orthodox Hinduism, nor did he seem to doubt
his pantheistic creed,[112] though theistic instincts seemed to trouble
him and embarrass him in discussion'.[113] Another typically
Advaitic belief is attributed to Dayananda by Robson: 'he could
not accept that he had committed sin'.[114]

A clear development can now be noticed. When Dayananda
left his *guru*, he was, probably partly through his influence and
that of the hostile Vaishnavite atmosphere of Mathura, very
much the protagonist of Shaivism and the antagonist of Vaishnavism and of its main scripture, the *Bhāgavata Purāna*.[115] In
Jaipur he got involved in the great controversy between Shaivites
and Vaishnavites. This controversy led to the conversion of the
king to Shaivism, a mass-conversion of Vaishnavites, and the
flight of some Vaishnavites from the city, a commotion so serious
that it was reported by the British political agent.[116] Perhaps
the distasteful aspects of these events helped Dayananda realize
that the Shaivism he supported was as sectarian as the Vaishnavism

he attacked, and this realization was reinforced by his study of Vedānta, whose lofty idea of the absolute made him see more clearly the absurdity of all Purānic deities. Thus he moved towards a non-Purānic concept of the divinity, and progressively Shiva was reduced to being only a name of the Lord. The final break is not described by the biographers, but is to be found in the last paragraphs of his *Bhāgavata-Khandanam*: 'Abandon the application of ashes, abandon the wearing of the *rudrāksh*, and do not adore me, the Lord of the universe, in the form of a Shivalinga.'[117] A clear sign of his uncertainty in the discrimination of authoritative books is the fact that this final quotation showing a total break with all expressions of sectarian Shaivism is taken from the *Vishnupurāna*.[118]

Dayananda's conception of revelation and scriptural authority, his answer to the question 'which are the books of the *rishis*?', was thus still evolving. Throughout the period the *Bhāgavata Purāna* was the main butt of his criticism, and his pamphlet on this work indicates the criteria he was using to establish its spurious character. Basically he argued that it could not have been written by the *rishi* Vyāsa because it suffered from three fundamental flaws: it contained blatant grammatical errors; it indulged in vilification of the great *rishis* and heroes of ancient times, and of the householders' *āshrama*; and it was full of internal contradictions. These criteria are important and would remain an essential part of his continuing critique of worthless books.[119] Compared with the criteria Virjananda proposed, it is noticeable that whereas the *guru's* criteria concern mostly matters of form, Dayananda's criteria concentrate on the content of the works, their ethical and logical acceptability.

It is noteworthy, however, that while Dayananda was attacking the *Bhāgavata Purāna*, he was also teaching and defending the *Devī Bhāgavata*, a work of the Shākta sect of a later date, for which the Shāktas claimed the place of the *Bhāgavata* in the list of the eighteen great *Purānas*, a claim supported by Dayananda in his *Bhāgavata-Khandanam*.[120] We are also told that during this period, at Gwalior in 1864-5, he recommended for reading both the *Kurma* and the *Linga Purānas*,[121] and in the list of recommended books at the end of his pamphlet, the *Harivamsha Purāna* is included.[122] Dayananda was still very uncertain about the books of the *rishis*, an uncertainty also revealed by Robson's remarks: 'He still believed in caste as laid down in the laws of Manu, and when confronted with some of these laws he maintained they were divine but with the impatience of a man who felt himself in a false position. In the same way he acknowledged some of the legends in the Saiva Puranas to be immoral, and when pressed changed the subject as quickly as possible'.[123]

Besides the *Upanishads*, there is one other work that strongly drew his attention, the *Manusmriti*,[124] an interest that did not wane until the end of his days. The Reverend Robson mentioned how he held to the *varnāshrama dharma* according to Manu. His interest in influencing political authority, which certainly originated with Virjananda, was probably strengthened by his study of Manu's conception of kingship. In Ajmer he had a talk with Major Davidson, the Deputy District Commissioner, about the duty of the Raj to prevent religious malpractice, and he had a conversation with Agent-General Brooks about the prevention of cow-slaughter.[125]

As for religious practice, it is reported that at the beginning of the period the Swami was not completely against all forms of idol worship, at least tolerating the worship of an iconic representation of Shiva, although not that of the *linga*.[126] But at the end of the period he was already the 'uncompromising iconoclast', as Robson called him,[127] for whom all idol worship was anathema, and who even rejected the *rudrāksh*, for so long a cherished symbol of his Shaivite convictions. The practices he advocated were the *Sandhyā* ritual, of which he published one version for the three *varnas* in Agra in 1864,[128] and the recitation of the *Gāyatrī Mantra*.[129] The *Sandhyā* version he published was very probably a rather orthodox one, different from the rite he was to advocate in his later years. Ghasiram indeed makes the observation that it contained the rite of making offerings to the sun, *sūrya ko argh denā*, and insists that Dayananda did not mean that one should adore the sun as God.[130] At this time Dayananda also used to teach some forms of *Hatha Yoga* for health's sake,[131] and seems to have used and distributed certain herbal preparations, an art into which he was no doubt initiated by Virjananda.[132]

The Dayananda who visited his *guru* for the last time in December 1866 had come a long way since he left him four years earlier. Although most of his ideas were still in an uncertain and evolving state, definite directions were discernible. He was working himself progressively free from the Purānic and sectarian aspects of religion. He had found in Vedāntic concepts a firm foothold for his theological thinking, and he was continuously narrowing his study of Hindu lore in a definite direction: the *Vedas*, Vedānta, Manu. The religious practices he advocated too were taking a pronouncedly Vedic turn. At the same time he became increasingly involved in discussion, teaching, and preaching; the target of his propaganda tended to be the religious élite: pandits, *gurus*, *sannyāsīs*, brahmins, people in authority. He had had a first minor taste of publication. Here, however, there still remained the restraining influence of *guru* Virjananda, who could see no good in secondary religious writings. This side of Dayananda's propaganda effort would not become prominent until much later. That was the Dayananda, Swami Dayananda, who received his *guru*'s blessing, and who, at the age of forty-two, a pandit in his own right now, set out for Hardwar, once again answering the call of the Kumbh Melā.

CHAPTER III

The New Reformer
in the Rural Doab

When in early 1867 Jupiter was once more about to enter the sign of Aquarius, Hardwar was again the site of the great Kumbh Melā, and thousands of pilgrims started to move up the narrow mountainous roads weeks before the auspicious day. None would miss out on visiting Rishikesh, that most sacred spot some twenty miles further up from Hardwar. As their climb brought them about six miles above Hardwar, they noticed alongside the road a banner inscribed *Pākhand Khandinī*, 'Heresy refuted', flying over an enclosure containing some ten huts. Curiosity, and the prospect of a welcome rest after a six-mile climb, made them enter the enclosure, and they were handed a small Sanskrit pamphlet entitled *Bhāgavaṭa-Khandanam*. As they moved inside they were drawn to the centre of attraction: a magnificent-looking Dandī *sannyāsī* in conversation with pilgrims and pandits. He completely dominated the group with his splendid physique, his enthusiasm, and the clarity and conviction of his rich voice. It was good to sit down and just look at him, letting his sonorous Sanskrit resound in one's head. Those who tried to understand what he was saying, were surprised that they could follow his simple Sanskrit. They were even more surprised when they realized that this Swami was denouncing as false and worthless all those things that made Hardwar and the Kumbh Melā what they were: idol worship, Purānic legends, incarnation myths, sects, and holy rivers.

This was clearly a major planned enterprise of Dayananda: he set out to propagate his ideas in a place where and at a time when they were bound to reach the greatest possible number of listeners. He had arrived one month before the date of the Kumbh, and set up his headquarters at Saptasarovar, on the road between Hardwar and Rishikesh, a strategic spot past which their very progress would take nearly all pilgrims. He had brought thousands of copies of his pamphlet against the *Bhāgavata* for distribution, and gathered around him a team of two *sannyāsīs* of his own order and some six brahmins. His whole time was taken up by instruction and discussion.[1] This was indeed a systematic onslaught on the evils of Hinduism at a centre where they were magnified to absurdity, and where the audience of the preacher was countless, representing the whole Hindu spectrum. It is easy to imagine that the Swami had high hopes. What impression did he make, however, upon the hundreds of thousands of pilgrims, herded along to Rishikesh and a bit dazed by an overdose of the opium of religion? Even if they were struck by his forceful, sincere, and unselfish preaching, to them he was just another of the hundreds and hundreds of pandits, swamis, and *sannyāsīs* who were marketing their particular brand of Hinduism at the Kumbh fair. They could not buy it all; even the sampling of as much as they managed to taste had already given a lot of them religious indigestion, if not nausea.

These salesmen with their greed and insincerity, and the gullibility of the sheepish pilgrims disheartened Dayananda deeply. Gradually his enthusiasm waned, and he felt that he was like a voice crying in the wilderness, and that in a way he was himself still a part of this *melā*, of this market-place of Hinduism, and needed to completely dissociate himself from it all. He then decided on this complete break. He gave away all he had, though it did not exactly constitute a rich man's possessions: a few books, some woollen and silken garments, some small change, his eating pots. He only kept his loincloth.[2] His disgust was so deep that he even took a vow of silence; but, fiery reformer as he was, that vow did not last long.[3] Dayananda's first major attempt at reform had resulted in heartbreak. For the next two months we find him wandering about, desolate and half-starved, avoiding people and keeping himself to himself, as at Garhmukteshwar where for two weeks he just sat on the sands of the bank of the Ganga.[4]

In this state of mind he descended from Hardwar via Garhmukteshwar to Ramghat. From there he roamed, a lonely, forlorn, and unknown *sannyāsī*, down the Ganga to Farrukhabad, and back to Anupashahar, unwittingly surveying as it were the area where he was to spend the next five years: a narrow strip about a hundred miles long on the banks of the Ganga. During this time he would not, except for his one trip to Kanpur, Banaras, and Allahabad, visit any major city. Not that he was ever far from

the cities; within fifty miles of his field of operation there were
many sizeable cities: Delhi, Mathura, Agra, Kanpur, Aligarh,
Meerut, Mainpuri, Bareilly, and Moradabad.

What, then, was this area like, and why did Dayananda choose
it after his bitter disappointment at Hardwar? The choice was
not a deliberate one like the one he made when going to Hardwar.
After wandering desolately down the Ganga to Farrukhabad and
back, it was in the western part of the area that his new type of
reform work started, in Anupashahar and Karnavas. Ghasiram
noted this first stage quite perceptively: 'At this time he did not
engage in any particular preaching or denunciation. His main
concern was with the uplift of the brahmins: he taught them
to perform *Sandhyā, Gāyatrī*, and *Agnihotra*, and he urged them
to go and learn grammar at Dandīji's school at Mathura.'⁵
Karnavas was a kshatriya village,⁶ and there he concentrated
very much on the same approach. The gradual decision to work
for so many years in this area has to do with this new approach
to the élite of brahmins, kshatriyas, and pandits, and over the
years one can see this approach steadily develop. It should be
remembered that Dayananda's disappointment at Hardwar mainly
stemmed from his observation of the power and influence exercised
on the masses precisely by this élite. Another factor that no doubt
influenced him in his decision was the fact that Virjananda had
spent all in all about fifteen years in this area, especially at Soron.⁷
The *guru* must have told his pupil about these years, and to have
been the prize pupil of Virjananda probably meant a great deal
to the local people. Pandit Angadram, for instance, who threw
away his idols when convinced by Dayananda, and was imitated
by many, was himself a former pupil of Virjananda in Soron.⁸
Moreover, from the Doab, Mathura remained close enough
whenever Dayananda wanted to send somebody for special
language training.

The Doab had been since the very beginning of the nineteenth
century under British administration. This largely eclipsed the
power of the local princes, who, therefore, would not become
a focus of the Swami's efforts, as they were to be later in Rajputana. Power and influence was largely concentrated in the
local religious and social elite. The area Dayananda worked in
covered mainly parts of the districts of Bulandshahr, Etah,
Badaun, and Farrukhabad. The only sizeable town he frequented

was Farrukhabad. This strip along the Ganga constituted 'a level plain, the monotony of which is broken only by the numerous village sites and groves of dark-olive mango-trees which meet the eye in every direction. [It is] highly cultivated, and the fields are never bare except in the hot months'.[9] It is one of the most highly cultivated areas of India and 'in many ways provides a type-section of Indian agrarian life and problems'.[10] It is very fertile, yet population presses hard on its resources. It was then essentially rural, with mostly large, even-spaced villages, with slight urbanism, so that even the middle-size towns were no more than enlarged villages.[11]

There was, however, a way in which the area was a special one: the high incidence of brahmins and pandits made it ideal for the kind of work Dayananda took up. The district of Bulandshahr had a high proportion of brahmins: about one in eight Hindus belonged to that caste.[12] Although the overall proportion in Etah was lower, they were heavily concentrated in the northern area of Kasganj and Soron, where Dayananda used to work: it has one third of the total number of brahmins in the district,[13] so that in Soron pargana the brahmins constituted half of the Hindu population.[14] In fact, Dayananda was once given the advice, 'Go to Soron, there are 10,000 brahmins there'.[15] In Farrukhabad district the brahmins were less than ten per cent of the total Hindu population, but again the heaviest concentration was along the Ganga: in Kampil pargana, for instance, the brahmins constituted the majority Hindu group.[16] Thus, this tract along the Ganga had an abnormally high concentration of brahmins.

The reason for this was obviously the many holy places along the sacred river and the high incidence of religious fairs and festivals.[17] The biographers tell us that several visits of the Swami to particular places were initiated precisely because of local religious fairs,[18] and at many other places his visits coincided with some religious festival. This pattern of coincidence changed considerably after his trip to Banaras: then he tended to go only where he had schools, where he had followers, and where people wanted him for their religious needs.

Going down the Ganga, Ahar comes first, abounding in temples of some antiquity, and the scene of four fairs attracting large crowds. Anupashahar's main claim to fame was its monthly religious fairs,[19] and Karnavas, a very small village, saw up to 100,000 pilgrims at its yearly fair and its old temple of Shītalā Devī.[20] Ramghat, in the near vicinity, drew pilgrims from all over India, for bathing in the Ganga, and its many temples were constantly visited on the occasion of many religious festivals.[21] Soron, the mythical scene of the descent of Vishnu as the Boar incarnation, was the most important place in the area, with its bathing ghat at Garhiyaghat. It was a truly pan-Hindu pilgrimage centre, on the pilgrimage route of many Hindus. Garhiyaghat had fifty to sixty temples, and thirty large *dharmashālās*, rest-homes for the pilgrims, which were kept busy practically throughout the year.[22] Kakora on the northern bank of the Ganga attracted as many as 300,000 pilgrims for its great fair.[23] Kampil, mentioned in the *Mahābhārata* as the capital of southern Panchāla, where king Drupada held his court, had, apart from its ancient ruined temple of Rāmeshwarnāth Mahādeva, rows of temples and bathing ghats thronged by many devotees at its two religious fairs.[24] Farrukhabad itself was not a pilgrimage centre, but it contained numerous Hindu temples, and especially, the spacious and lofty temple of the Sādhs.[25] The banks of the Ganga in the Doab thus constituted a continuous centre of Hindu élite, and a focal religious area for the surrounding districts. Yet it was rural and somehow leisurely, very different from Hardwar or Banaras or Mathura, where the concentration of pandits, *sannyāsīs*, temples and shrines, and the hundreds of thousands of pilgrims were too overpowering and stifling, especially at times of religious fairs, as Dayananda had so bitterly experienced at Hardwar.

It is not intended here to give a detailed chronological report of the work of the Swami: the standard biographies spend hundreds of pages on it. What is attempted is to understand the development of the reformer and thinker and to discover in what way and under what influence he changed in these years, so that it becomes clear how and why the Swami who in early 1872 set out for Calcutta was different from the one who took the direction of Hardwar in 1866 with the blessing of his *guru*.

After his initial forlorn wanderings, Dayananda soon adopted a regular way of life which changed little. He continued his absolute asceticism: he possessed only his loincloth, not even an eating bowl, and his food and shelter depended completely on the charity of the pious. He did not allow any form of soft living to impinge on his life. We are told that if at a certain stage he used to chew tobacco, it was only because of persistent pain in his gums.[26] Several witnesses recall his prolonged daily meditations and the very short periods of sleep, uncovered, with his head on a stone, be it summer or winter. At the start of the period he did not even have one book with him.[27] However, his continuous need for more study made him acquire certain books. The Reverend Scott gave him a copy of the Gospels[28] and we are told that, at the time of the Farrukhabad dispute, 'he had some small and some large Vedic works copied, some ordered, and he also ordered some books from Germany which duly arrived'.[29] He always spoke a very clear and simple Sanskrit. It is difficult to imagine that he would not have picked up at least the simple bazaar Hindī of the North. Yet, it is quite clear that he did not feel confident enough in that language to carry on a discussion: we are told that he did not speak Hindī,[30] and it is several times asserted that he used an interpreter when conversing with people who knew no Sanskrit.[31]

The basic critique of Hinduism which Dayananda presented at Hardwar does not seem to have changed much in these years. He primarily attacked idol worship, sectarianism, and the many superstitious beliefs and practices. But, without ever relaxing this continuous onslaught, which made him many enemies, he devoted more and more time to positive instruction in Vedic practices. He was for ever instructing people in the use of the *Gāyatrī mantra*, and in the proper performance of the *Sandhyā*. The ritual prerequisite for these practices was the *Upanayana*, the ceremony of the investiture with the sacred thread. He found that even in these essential rites a number of abuses had developed, and he gradually clarified his own ideas on the proper Vedic rites and instructed people accordingly.

In Karnavas he noticed the widespread custom among the kshatriyas to have their sacred thread ceremony performed at the time of their wedding instead of in childhood: he rectified the custom wherever he could.[32] In Soron, that great centre of brahmins, he was told that in the 2,500 brahmin homes, only very few knew any Sanskrit, and very few even had the sacred thread ceremony performed upon them. Some gave the excuse that they had no money, to which Dayananda replied, 'If an old man dies you spend thousands of rupees, and you are not able to spend two rupees on the sacred thread'. He instructed as many as he could, and had the *Sandhyā* ceremony written down and distributed amongst them. When a pandit objected that they were not entitled to perform *Sandhyā* since they had not yet received the sacrament, quoting Manu to prove his point, the Swami answered, 'Do not say that, the *dharma* has to be protected in every possible way',[33] thus affirming that to him *dharma* transcended the *Shāstras*.

Brahmins had the tendency to treasure the *Gāyatrī* as their exclusive privilege, but Dayananda asserted that it belonged equally to the three *varnas*.[34] In fact he had copies of it made and distributed among the people.[35] It is also recorded that he was the first to teach a woman the sacred *Gāyatrī*: she was a devout old lady who came to see him at the end of her life.[36] When a pandit criticized him for reciting the *mantra* in a loud voice, because unworthy people might hear it, Dayananda got very angry and said that one should recite it loudly without any hesitation.[37]

The Swami was continuously busy with teaching the proper way to perform the Vedic Five Great Sacrifices. His ideas clarified themselves, and towards the end of the period he declared that the *Sandhyā* should not be performed thrice daily, but only twice, a ruling to which he would adhere to the end.[38] He had the ritual of the Five Sacrifices written down by a pandit for a follower who kept forgetting the details.[39] In fact, the edition of this text was to be one of his very first publications in 1875.

Much has been written, especially by opponents and in answer to them, about the Swami's concept in those days of two controversial issues: his conception of *Shrāddh*, and his attitude to meat-eating. As for the first question, Ghasiram mentions in a vague way, without indicating his source, that 'in those days it is said that the Swami was in favour of *Shrāddh*',[40] implying that here the traditional repeated memorial ceremonies for dead ancestors were referred to. Dayananda was certainly later on a consistent opponent of these ceremonies, for which countless Hindus spent great sums of money and literally ruined themselves. He held that this service for the dead should be replaced by service of the living. In fact, during this period he already advocated that 'service of the living'. However, though the biographers state that the Swami already completely condemned

Shrāddh for the dead,[41] it does not appear that his condemnation was so radical, in view of the ambiguity in this matter that is still to be found in his 1875 *Satyārth Prakāsh*.[42]

The second question about meat-eating is similarly involved. In the same passage quoted Ghasiram says that: ... in those days Swamiji used to say on the subject of meat-eating that the *Shāstras* did not prohibit meat-eating, and that they contain provisions for the two types of food; who wishes to eat it, let him eat it, who does not, let him abstain.'[43] Meat-eating is connected with *Shrāddh*, because the *Laws of Manu* prescribe in the ceremony the offering and consumption of balls of meat. It is also connected with that section of the Five Great Sacrifices called the *Balivaishvadevas*. As Dayananda seems not to have been totally against the consumption of meat even in 1875 when he wrote the first edition of his *Satyārth Prakāsh*, it is safe to assume that his attitude was still a tentative one. Dayananda worked a lot in this period amongst the kshatriyas, many of whom were regular consumers of meat. The fact that no single clear statement against the practice is to be found anywhere supports the assumption that Dayananda did not explicitly preach against it.

At this time the Swami organized the performance of two great public *yajnas* or rites. The first one was held at Karnavas. Its object was to arrange for a big group of kshatriyas to perform *prāyashchitt*, or penance, and to receive the *Yajnopavīta*. About forty learned brahmins from neighbouring towns were invited to come and recite the *Gāyatrī* for a whole week. Then brahmins learned in the *Vedas*, appointed as specialist priests, *brahmā, hotā*, and *ritvij*, performed the rite, and afterwards the *Gāyatrī mantra* was taught. After the ceremony the leavings of the sacrifice were distributed, and the recipients of the sacrament offered their fee to the officiating priests according to their means.[44]

The other great *yajna* was held at Farrukhabad: it was the imposition of the holy thread on Lala Jagannath. Again there was a week-long recitation of the *Gāyatrī* by eleven pandits, for the sake of *prāyashchitt*, and there also was a continuous performance of the *havan*. The sacrament proper and the instruction in the *Gāyatrī* followed a three day fast and finally presents were distributed to the pandits.[45]

These two big rituals had some interesting aspects that reveal Dayananda's attitude to Vedic ritual. He obviously still believed in a vicarious removal of the results of sin by penance, recitation, and fasting. He was careful to make use of the specialist ritualists and to see that their fees were paid. Dayananda made the rites as Vedic as possible, but he was not yet prepared, as he would be later, to boldly do away with the use of specialists, of ritual fees, of fasting and penance.

To assess the development of Dayananda's thought in this period Lekhram's series of interviews with people who had met the Swami proves very useful, suggesting the authenticity of a primary source; and the accounts of missionaries have the advantage of having been written down at the time without the hindsight, so often distorting, of later accounts.

One of the central problems that continued to exercise Dayananda's mind was the question of the respective authority of the many sources of Hinduism. There is a constant clarification of his ideas through discussion, instruction, and study. Nowhere do we yet find a mention that he actually taught any part of the *Vedas* proper, except the few *mantras* that form part of the *Sandhyā*, and except for the fact that the *Vedas* were part of the curriculum of the Sanskrit schools he started, which will be considered later. His teaching was primarily concerned with the *Laws of Manu*.[46] Judging by the use he makes of Manu in his later works, this teaching must have centered on moral instruction. In one place this teaching of Manu is coupled with the *Mahābhārata*,[47] and it is safe to assume that the accent here too was on *dharma*, perhaps on sections of the *Shānti* and *Anushāshana Parvans*. The only other explicit instruction that is mentioned is the teaching of the *Upanishads*[48] and of Vedānta.[49] Dayananda's concentration on Manu and on the *Upanishads* is thus in direct continuity with the preoccupation noticed in the years immediately after his stay at Mathura.

Many more references are made not to actual teaching, but rather to the books considered authoritative by the Swami. As for the *Purānas*, he now finally reached the conclusion that all eighteen had to be considered as non-authoritative. At Karnavas, right at the beginning of the period, he affirmed that 'all *Purānas* are like the *Bhāgavata*',[50] and this is repeatedly asserted,[51] never to be doubted again. He now also discovered that the *Purānas*, even if worthless as religious guides, did have some value of their own as containing precious historical records.[52] As for the *Laws of Manu*, years earlier the Reverend Robson had noted Dayananda's uneasiness when confronted with some verses of Manu.[53] Now he accepted that some parts of Manu could not be considered authoritative.[54] The same is said about the *Rāmāyana* and the *Mahābhārata*; an excellent witness recalls that during his first visit to Karnavas the Swami accepted both as authoritative, but that on his second visit less than a year later, he declared that they contained several errors.[55] Towards the end of the period the *Bhagavadgītā* was put in the same category.[56] Obviously Dayananda made up his mind about the texts as he became more familiar with them: his decisions seem always to have been the result of personal investigation.

A very important declaration on this subject was published by Dayananda in Kanpur on the eve of his visit to Banaras. The accuracy of this signal document is attested by the pandit who published it[57] and by its complete coincidence with the list published by the principal of the Banaras Sanskrit College, Dr Rudolf Hoernle, in the *Christian Intelligencer* of March 1870: Hoernle says that his list was written down for him by the Swami 'with his own hand'.[58] This deliberate and accurate document warrants detailed consideration.

The *Rigveda*, the *Yajurveda*, the *Sāmaveda*, the *Atharvaveda*: in these four *Vedas* we find the definition of the *karma-kānda* (section on duties), the *upāsanākānda* (section on worship), and the *jnānakānda* (section on knowledge). One should understand that the first includes from the *Sandhyā* to the *Ashvamedha*; that the second includes from *Yama* to *Samādhi*; and that the third includes from *nish-karma* to *parabrahma-sākshātkāra*.[59]

This list is a traditional one, but what interests us most is the fact that the *Brāhmanas* are not explicitly mentioned. It seems quite clear that up to now Dayananda considered the four *Vedas* to include their respective *Brāhmanas*. Each *Brāhmana* is in fact closely attached to a particular *Veda*, and Hindu pandits generally considered them as one integral whole. But for Dayananda, who wanted to found Hinduism firmly on Vedic revelation alone, the need to distinguish between them became increasingly pressing. The fact that at the time of the Kanpur declaration he still included the *Brāhmanas* with the *Vedas* can be proved from different sources. Ghasiram, towards the very end of the period, says, 'Formerly he did not accept the separateness of *Vedas* and *Brāhmanas*, but now he started to do this, and he accepted the *Brāhmanas* only in so far as they were in accordance with the *Vedas*.'60 Dr Hoernle notes explicitly, when reproducing the Swami's list, that the four *Vedas* included their respective *Brāhmanas*.61 And thirdly, the Banaras dispute shows the same by implication: Dayananda quoted several *Brāhmana* texts as texts from the *Vedas*, and did not object when the pandits did the same.62 However, at this very time the germs of doubt about the absolute validity of the *Brāhmanas* were already growing in his mind, as a remark of Dr Hoernle suggests: 'he once admitted to me that the *Brāhmanas* did contain modern interpolated portions, and that any passage sanctioning idolatry was to be considered, as such, as a spurious portion.'63 Again we see that it is the analysis of the content of the works that made Dayananda decide about their validity.

Although the Swami did not teach any Vedic texts during this period, his personal study gathered momentum. During his long stay in Farrukhabad in 1868-9, he had Vedic works copied and ordered, some even from Germany.64 The contact and debate with the Banaras pandits must have strongly urged him on in his study. Lekhram tells us that after that experience, the previous hectic pace of his life changed considerably. He continued to preach, and visited his schools, but, 'he stayed for weeks at different places studying Sanskrit works, and devoting more time especially to the parts of the *Veda*.'65 He was for three months in Farrukhabad, but, apart from a single public dispute, 'the rest of his time was taken up by the study of *Vedas* and *Shāstras*'.66 In Mirzapur, on his way back from Banaras, he 'employed a Bengali to teach him English and to read to him Max Müller's translation of the *Veda*'.67 Here he also had several meetings with the Reverend R.C. Mather, an eminent missionary of the London Missionary Society who had been in India since 1834.68 Mather asked him why, if the current commentaries of the *Vedas* were incorrect, he himself did not write one. Dayananda's answer, as reported by the missionary, was that an ordinary mind was not capable of making a commentary on the *Vedas*, because it was difficult to grasp their meaning as long as the intellect was not purified by asceticism.69

Apart from the final clear separation of the *Vedas* from the *Brāhmanas*, there was yet another way in which Dayananda started to differ from the pandits and to clarify his conception of revelation. In those days the pandits generally held that many

Vedic works had been lost over the centuries: these works contained the full proof for all the aspects of contemporary Hinduism. In his later writings Dayananda made his rejection of this theory quite clear. But Dr Hoernle's article says that at Banaras the Swami already 'denied altogether the possibility of the loss of any *Vedas*',[70] an opinion confirmed by the report of the Banaras disputation.[71]

By this time Dayananda had made great strides in his personal study of the *Vedas*. In Ajmer in 1866, the Reverend Robson had judged his knowledge of the *Vedas* to be rudimentary,[72] but since then Dayananda had come a long way. In his own report of the Banaras disputation, he declared that 'he had considered the whole *Veda*, starting from the *Rigveda*',[73] and this is confirmed by a very reliable witness, Dr Hoernle: 'He is well versed in the *Vedas*, excepting the fourth or *Atharva Veda*, which he had read only in fragments, and which he saw for the first time in full when I lent him my own complete MS copy.'[74] Hoernle continues, 'he is more practically conversant with them than most, if not all, of the great pandits of Banaras, who generally know them only at second-hand, or even less.' In fact, the same witness even indicates the general approach to Vedic interpretation that is already taking firm shape in Dayananda's mind: 'At any rate, and this is the most remarkable feature distinguishing him from other pandits, he is an independent student of the *Vedas*, and free from the trammels of traditional interpretation. The standard commentary of the famous, Sayanacharya is held of little account by him.'[75]

One wonders what conception Dayananda had at this stage of the origination of the *Vedas*. His Kanpur declaration lists twenty-one *Shāstras*, which he called *parameshvarārshirachitāni*, 'composed by the Lord and the *rishis*', without any further specification, and without distinguishing the *Vedas* from the other works.[76] Principal Hoernle does give a clue when he says that according to Dayananda, 'God is the creator first of the *Vedas*, then of the world, hence the *Vedas* are eternal as compared with the world; but non-eternal as compared with God'.[77] This again is the germ of an idea, developed later, but still in an uneasy state of vagueness: the *Vedas* here definitely include the *Brāhmanas*: these were supposed to be God's work, yet as we saw, he already had doubts about their full authenticity. The Banaras disputation also touches on this problem. When asked, From whom do the *Vedas* originate?', Dayananda answered, 'From the Lord', and declared that the relationship between God and the *Vedas* was one of cause and effect.[78] Another report makes it even more specific: 'The *Vedas* exist in God. At the beginning of creation the Lord propagated the *Vedas*, and after that the *rishis* did.'[79]

The remainder of the Kanpur declaration lists the other books accepted by Dayananda as 'true *Shāstras*', containing special sciences. The list is a traditional one: the four *Upavedas* on medical, military, musical, and mechanical sciences; the six *Vedāngas* on pronunciation, ceremonial, grammar, etymology, prosody, and astrology; twelve *Upanishads*, expounding the knowledge of *brahman*; four philosophical *Sūtras* with commentary, the *Brahmasūtras*, *Kātyāyanasūtras*, *Yogabhāshya*, and the *Vākovākya*; and finally the *Manusmriti* and the *Mahābhārata*. 'These twenty-four *Shāstras* (including the four *Vedas*) were composed by the Lord and the *rishis*.'[80] When all his statements are taken into account, it seems that Dayananda's conception at the time was that the *Vedas*, including the *Brāhmanas*, were created by God and revealed through the *rishis*, and that the other authentic *Shāstras* were the compositions of the *rishis*. At the end of this period the *Brāhmanas* were classed with the latter group.

After quoting Dayananda's list, Hoernle observed: 'Whatever else is considered as Shastras by the orthodox Hindus, notably the six Darsanas or philosophical systems and the eighteen Puranas he repudiates as false.'[81] Of course, Hoernle was right about the *Purānas*, but his statement on the *darshanas*, or systems of philosophy, seems incorrect. Admittedly, Dayananda had not explicitly included the six *darshanas* in his list, but he did include two *Sūtras* of the *darshanas*, the *Vedāntasūtras* and the *Yogabhāshya* together with an obscure work on logic called *Vākovākya*. In other words, three of the *darshanas* are represented in the list. Moreover, the list of authoritative works cited by Dayananda in his disputation included the 'Sūtras* of Vyāsa, Jaimini, Bodhāyana, Kātyāyana, etc.'[82] Thus all lists did include some, if not all, systems of philosophy. Dayananda at this stage obviously felt the importance and the value of the philosophical works, but the impression is that, apart naturally from Vedānta, his study had not yet advanced very far, and that he was still unsure of, or at least unacquainted with all the basic texts of the *darshanas*. The Kanpur document suggests that up to this time Dayananda did have some faith in astrology. When describing the *Jyotisha Vedānga*, on the science of the stars, he wrote that 'it is the knowledge of past, present and future'. He added that in this science only one work should be considered authoritative, the *Bhrigusamhitā*.[83] Later he made a clear distinction between the science of astronomy and astrology, and, repudiating the latter as a fraud, he specifically condemned the *Bhrigusamhitā*.

Another very important question exercised Dayananda's mind during these years: the problem of the nature of God. In the years after Virjananda he had completely rejected the Purānic and mythological aspects of divinity and had clung to an uneasy and unresolved combination of the Vedāntic absolute and the personal Lord, still holding the identity of the soul and *brahman*. It was a great step forward, but it left many questions unanswered, even unasked. Some of these questions he now investigated and decided, specifically the questions about the identity or distinction between the soul and God, and about the reality or unreality of the world. His answer was now definite and repeatedly asserted: *brahman* and the *jīva* are distinct entities,[84] and the world has a reality of its own.[85] These doctrinal positions are opposed to the Advaita Vedānta of Shankara, at least as it was interpreted at the time by those whom the Swami called the 'Neo-Vedāntins'. It is in fact in the context of his many discussions with them, or in the context of discussions about Shankara, that the question mostly arose. Ghasiram mentions a discussion with a Neo-Vedāntin that lasted no less than a fortnight,[86] and the problem was such an important one that Dayananda wrote a pamphlet against their position,[87] a book unfortunately lost and so far unrecovered. It is significant, that his first writing was against the *Bhāgavata Purāna*, and his second one an attack on Neo-Vedānta: these publications indicate what problems exercised Dayananda's mind at the respective periods.

Little is known about the finer details of Dayananda's position. He did not accept at this time that Shankara himself taught the identity of *brahman* and *jīva* or the unreality of the world. These doctrines, he said, were wrong conclusions by the Dandīs of the Shankarāchārya order.[88] He no doubt recalled his first Dandī teachers who convinced him of these tenets. When he was asked:

There are two commentaries on the *Vedāntasūtras*, the one of Shankara,
called *advaita*, the other of Rāmānuja, called *dvaita*; which one should
we follow?' Dayananda answered, 'Neither by itself is right: but there
is both *bheda* (distinction) and *abheda* (non-distinction). *Brahman* is all-
pervading, and therefore he is *abheda*, and *brahman* is not identical with
the *jīva*, and therefore he is *bheda*.'[89]
These statements have still an air of unsophistication, but one
should remember that these are later reports by people who themselves were not theological specialists, and who intended only
to give a rough statement of Dayananda's conception at the time.
The missionaries were better qualified, and more explicit. The
Reverend Scott wrote: 'He is a Vedāntist. "God", he says, "is
eternal and perfect. By his fiat the universe was developed in
this order: space or ether, air, fire, water, earth, then animal
beings."'[90] Dr Hoernle's statement is so clear that it deserves
to be quoted in full:

There is only one God with all those attributes generally ascribed to Him
by monotheists. He is the creator first of the *Vedas*, then of the world,
hence the *Vedas* are eternal as compared with the world; but non-eternal
as compared with God. The names of God are manifold; he is named
in the *Vedas* Vishnu, Atma, Agni, etc., according as one aspect of the Divine
nature is prominently remembered. Though God is distinct from the world —
for Dayananda rejects the Vedantic and ordinary Hindu pantheism — yet He
is also immanent in the world as the principle of its life and existence. . . .
Incarnations (avataras) for the salvation of mankind never took place,
nor can they ever take place; it is incompatible with the nature of God
to become incarnate.[91]

The supporting pillars of Dayananda's theology had thus by
this time been firmly planted: he believed in a transcendent,
personal God-creator, who is yet immanent by his power. The
perfection of God implies the logical impossibility of incarnations.
The *Vedas*, created by God prior to the world's creation, occupied
a special place between God and the world. Many questions
still remained unanswered, particularly those connected with the
precise modalities of the creation of the *Vedas* and of the world.
The first explicit attempt to answer these questions would be
made in 1875, in the first edition of the *Satyārth Prakāsh*.

Thus the problems of authoritative books and of the nature
of God were foremost in Dayananda's mind, but there is another
concern, both theoretical and practical, that increasingly transpires from the biographies: the concern for morality. As noted
before, his teaching was then primarily a teaching of the moral

precepts contained in the *Manusmriti*, in short of *dharma*. But the Swami was no slavish repeater of rules and prohibitions. Again and again he stressed the importance of inner morality as against the formal implementation of rules, and he judged the value and validity of formal rules with the touchstone of inner righteousness. Thus he set himself in this sphere too quite apart from most other pandits, who considered their function to be the casuistic interpretation of the laws and the play of one authority against another.

When, after having eaten food offered to him by a Sādh, Dayananda was told by a brahmin that he had become polluted as a result, his answer was that food can be polluted only in two ways: if the money used to buy it has been acquired in a manner that caused someone unhappiness, or if the food has been mixed with some impure substances.[92] The basic principles of morality and hygiene applied here invalidated in one stroke the thousands of pages on food-pollution in the *Shāstras*, and the even more numerous food taboos of the Hindu castes. On another occasion he was asked which of two people was a better man, the one who had received the sacrament of initiation but did no good works, or the other who had not received the sacrament, but was devoted to good works. His answer was quite definite: the latter was the better man.[93] While teaching a rich merchant who had spent a fortune building two temples, Dayananda said:

You have spent your money in vain. In twenty to fifty years they will tumble down. It would have been better if you had done a deed that would have benefited some people of this country. You could have arranged the marriage of the daughter of a poor man; you could have arranged the marriage of these many thirty-years old maiden daughters of Kanauj brahmins; you could have built a school for boys and girls, or opened a training centre for arts and crafts, from which the country and the people would have benefited. Instead, you have wasted your hundreds of thousands in vain.[94]

He noticed how people got caught in the web of endless, unnecessary, and ruinous litigation, and criticized the British administration of justice, advocating a system of village *panchāyats* and a local courthouse in the market town.[95]

This serious quest of Dayananda for the morality of social life brought him into confrontation with the contemporary caste system with its strait-jacket of unjust privileges and disabilities contracted simply by birth. But it does not seem to have yet become a major concern of his. At Farrukhabad he gave proof from the *Manusmriti* that he who does not possess any knowledge of the *Vedas* is a shūdra, whosoever's son he may be.[96] Elsewhere he declared that the kayasths were originally vaishyas, but that the consumption of meat and liquor had caused them to drop in status.[97] It is Hoernle again who gives a clear statement of Dayananda's thought on caste. Robson had reported in 1866 in Ajmer that Dayananda 'still believed in caste as laid down in the Laws of Manu', but with a certain uneasiness.[98] In Hardwar his thought had progressed. There he refuted the interpretation by a Banaras pandit of the *Purushasūkta*, the classical proof of the divine institution of caste: 'The Brahmin was his mouth, his arm was made the Kshatriya, his belly became the Vaishya, and from his feet the Shūdra was born.' The pandit took this literally, and as a proof of the fact that caste was a divine creation. Dayananda replied that its meaning was not literal, but that it meant that in society the brahmin, man of knowledge, was similar to the mouth; the kshatriya, the warrior, to the arms; the vaishya, the merchant, to the belly; and the shūdra, the servant, was similar to the feet.[99]

According to Hoernle's report, Dayananda's theory of society had now taken a quite definite form:

This [caste] the reformer considers only as a political institution made by the rulers for the common good of society, and not a natural or religious distinction. It is not a natural distinction, for the four castes were not created by God as distinct species of men; but all men are of equal nature, of the same species, and brothers. It is not a religious institution, for the salvation of men and their fate in the other world does not depend on its observance. The castes are simply different professions or guilds (adhikaras), established by the state to guard against confusion and mutual interference, and for the better accomplishment of the different works. Each class was made up into a guild and furnished with its rights and privileges and made hereditary. But, as the whole classification is a creation of the state, any Sudra, who is deserving of the promotion, can be made by the state a Vaisya or Kshattriya or Brahmana, if he qualifies himself for the work of the respective class. Likewise any Brahmana, who deserves the degradation, can be made by the state a Sudra. In fact, any Brahmana who is disqualified for his work, becomes at once a Sudra *de jure*, and a Sudra, who qualifies for it, becomes at once a Brahmana *de jure*; though neither can become so *de facto* also either by his own will or the will of others, as long as the state does not make him so.[100]

This document reveals some important points. When Dayananda talked about caste, he did not refer to the numerous castes and sub-castes that were the factual divisions of Hindu society, but to the four *varnas* or orders of Hindu society. The first were mostly referred to by the word *jāti*, derived from the root *jan*, 'to be born'. This word *jāti* Dayananda used in the sense of 'species', e.g. the human species; to him the *jātis* in the sense of caste had no validity whatsoever: he completely ignored them. He rejected the justification of caste, or rather class, by birth: it should depend on qualities and qualifications. By denying that class is a religious institution, he asserted that all the *Shāstras* say about it is of a secular nature, and therefore changeable, except where it expresses a moral law. However, he still accepted that the rights and privileges of the classes were hereditary, and that any re-classification could only be done by the state. Since at that time, at least in British India, the state machinery was not concerned with caste, which was considered a Hindu religious matter, Dayananda's statement about re-classification remained a theoretical one. It was not one intended to call for specific action, but rather an attempt to give the social orders a moral basis. 'If someone commits *adharma*, impious acts, then his sacred thread should be taken away', said the Swami.[101] This, nevertheless, was not an invitation to action but rather a statement of principle, as is confirmed by a story of Lekhram: 'There was a story going around that he used to call the Jats kshatriyas. People said that thus he was uttering a wicked thing: the Jats are not kshatriyas. But this was not confirmed from the mouth of any Jat, and I never met a single Jat to whom the Swami would have given the sacred thread.'[102]

The Swami completely rejected the religious validity of the many caste taboos about food that were prevalent among the Hindus. He declared that food could only be polluted by the sin that may be involved in its acquisition or by the admixture of impure substances.[103] When on a particular occasion he decided to take his meal outside the *chaukā*, the ritually prepared place, he said that he was not afraid of caste taboos or being declared outcaste,[104] and when a missionary asked him if he would eat his food, he answered, 'Certainly, I can eat your food; in fact I can eat the food of any man however humble he may be, if it so pleases me.'[105] Many instances are recorded during this period when the Swami deliberately acted against the food taboos by accepting food from persons considered ritually impure;[106] once he even invited a Muslim inside while he was having his meal.[107] Although, as a *sannyāsī*, he was, strictly speaking, above these rules, his radical attitude offended the orthodox. Later in life he would take very great care to avoid giving such offence.

With this increasing concern for morality, Dayananda was probing for the basic moral principles that should direct everyone's life. At Allahabad he had a discussion with a *sādhu* about *pravritti* and *nivritti*, the dedication to action and the abstention from it. The *sādhu* propounded the classical theory that action is inferior to inaction, and that the real seeker for *moksha*, the man who lives at the highest level of religious endeavour, should abstain from all activity in favour of contemplation. Dayananda retorted:

Those who sing the praises of *nivritti*, their life is not better than that of animals. It makes people lazy. They teach others the way of *pravritti*, but they themselves roam about, begging to fill their bellies. A life full of action, that is real life. To perform the good works ordered by the *Veda*, that is the real way of renunciation. Those people are entitled to be called alive, who spend their life in works for the good of mankind.[108]

Dayananda here affirmed the principles that action is the very core of life, and that action should be directed towards the welfare of man. He was not promoting a secular, humanistic type of activism, as another aphoristic saying makes quite clear. In a discussion about the Ganga, he declared, 'That is only water. *Moksha* does not come from water, it comes from works'.[109] Action, therefore, was the basic duty of man as somebody reaching out for *moksha*, as *homo religiosus*. Dayananda's thought had reached here one of its most basic and commanding principles, one that would never cease to dominate his thinking and direct his discrimination when judging the acceptability or non-acceptability of religious ideas and practices.

The Kanpur declaration confirms this concern for morality in the way it incorporates basic ethics into its scheme of the eight *gappas*, things to be avoided, and the eight *satyas*, or truths. Of the eight *gappas* four refer to religious superstitions, the other four condemn the use of intoxicants, adultery, theft, fraud, conceit, and lying. The eight *satyas* include, apart from the religious duties of study of the *Shāstras* and performance of the Vedic rites, a list of moral duties that have relation to the stages of the householder and of the *sannyāsī*. It concludes with a general call 'to eliminate by wisdom and by science all the evils that spring from birth and death, joy and sorrow, lust and anger, greed, error, and bad company', and to strive to obtain '*moksha* by transcending the five elements, and by the elimination of all the evils of ignorance, egoism, attachment, hate, and the fear of death'.[110]

Connected with this concern for morality is another doctrine that now emerged and that also would remain part of his teaching: sins cannot be forgiven,[111] they must be paid for by suffering. The Reverend Scott admirably summarized the doctrine as follows: 'Depravity is the result of ignorance. Restoration to purity is to be effected by the acquirement of knowledge and the infliction of punishment.'[112] The law of karmic retribution is an inexorable one, and later on Dayananda progressively eliminated all the exceptions to this rule that centuries of Hinduism had invented.

During this period Dayananda adopted a new means of propagating his ideas by the foundation of Sanskrit schools. The influence of his guru Virjananda was obviously still at work. He founded four schools between early 1869 and the end of 1870, at Farrukhabad, Kasganj, Mirzapur, and Chalesar. The reason for this venture is obvious: the proper knowledge of Sankskrit was essential for the reform he envisaged. He himself acquired this knowledge through Virjananda, and he occasionally sent promising aspirants to his *guru* for training. However, Virjananda died on 14 September 1868. Dayananda never aspired to a role similar to his *guru*'s, but he knew from personal experience how necessary a proper language training was for the task of reformation. The traditional Sanskrit schools produced the traditional pandits, whose knowledge was inadequate and who wasted their time on valueless, unauthoritative works. There was a need, and the only way to provide for it was for Dayananda to start his own schools.

The first opportunity presented itself at Farrukhabad, where Dayananda's success had been the greatest.[113] Among his disciples was a prominent banker, Lala Pannilal Seth Vaishya, who was planning to build a Shiva temple. Under the influence of Dayananda's teaching he changed his mind and offered the money to him for the foundation of a Sanskrit school.[114] All the schools were similarly funded through the generosity of followers of the Swami, mostly through the combined contributions of a group of donors.

Student numbers were reasonably high in Farrukhabad, where they rose from fifty to a hundred, whereas in the three other schools they remained constant at around twenty. Food and clothes, and, if necessary, accommodation were provided by the schools. The curriculum included the study of the *Ashtādhyāyī*, the *Manusmriti*, and the *Vedas*. Students were expected to perform the *Sandhyā* rites twice daily, and if they failed to get up before sunrise for the rite, they had to fast till evening. They were supposed to spend all their time at the school, and only occasional visits to village or town were allowed. Regular tests were held, and the diligent students were rewarded with special food.[115] The first two teachers were both recruited from Mathura, probably students of Virjananda. But very soon, within less than two years of the opening of the first school, at least four graduates of the Far-rukhabad school were appointed. It was obviously a problem to get the right teachers: both the Farrukhabad and the Mirzapur schools, the only ones of which we have the complete list, went through five successive teachers in their short existence.

The experiment was a failure: the schools at Farrukhabad and Chalesar lasted for about seven years, the others less than four. They were all closed down by the Swami himself, and where he could he diverted the funds that remained to the publication costs of his *Vedabhāshya*. He realized that the schools did not achieve their objective, to become centres of training in and the dissemination of his Vedic religion. Some of the pandits reverted to the defence of sectarian Shaivism in his absence,[116] others mismanaged the institution.[117] Students too were a problem: sometimes they enrolled first to get the clothes and books provided, and then stayed away. But, worst of all, they tended to go back to their old sectarian Hinduism after the completion of their studies.[118] Soon after his return from Calcutta, Dayananda closed two schools, and let those of Farrukhabad and Chalesar run on for another three or four years. These were more successful, and especially the Farrukhabad school did produce a number of pupils who later on made their mark in life, probably because that town had the greatest number of Dayananda's followers. In fact the three main pandits who later assisted him in his writings and publications, Dineshram, Bhimasena, and Jvaladatta, were all students of that school.[119] But even there he had eventually to admit to the general failure of his experiment, and, except for a short-lived trial later on in Banaras, which did not last even two years, he would not again venture personally into that aspect of reform.

Looking back over that lustrum on the banks of the Ganga, a clear development can be seen in Dayananda's life, thought, and action. After his disappointment at Hardwar and a time of retreat and reflection, he initiated a new kind of reform work concentrating on the leading castes and the pandits in a basically rural area where they were present in great numbers. His negative denunciation of contemporary Hinduism was to a greater and greater degree counterbalanced by a positive instruction in Vedic ritual and moral life. At the same time his fame as a challenging and successful debater spread further and the local pandits, defeated by the Swami, imported more eminent pandits from bigger centres. The key issue in all these debates was idol worship, and more specifically: was idol worship sanctioned by the scriptures? This process of challenge, success, and fame, finally brought the Swami to Banaras.

Banaras was the great citadel of idol worship, where temples were 'as plenty as blackberries', and where idols were 'more numerous than the swarming population'. There the many sects of Hinduism thrived, but they were all 'only varieties of idolatry under different guises'. Banaras was also 'the capital of the India of the Hindoo', 'the head-quarters of Hindoo orthodoxy, enjoying and exercising the metropolitan authority throughout Brahmindom, that Rome once did throughout Christendom'. When Dayananda arrived in that city thus described by the contemporary traveller Bholanath Chunder,[120] to challenge the Banaras pandits, that very challenge propelled him from the rural obscurity of the Doab into the national limelight of pan-Hinduism. The fact that the Banaras pandits took this challenge seriously made the Swami into an important public figure. Hoernle, certainly a neutral observer, remarked that the Swami caused great commotion and excitement in the town.[121] The press now considered Dayananda newsworthy, and wrote about his activities and ideas. Some papers even became very enthusiastic, like the *Hindu Patriot*, which commented that on hearing the Swami, 'we have come to believe that the golden age of India has not completely come to an end'.[122]

From all accounts the debate was a grand occasion. It was arranged by the Raja and held in Anandbagh in the presence of many notables of the town. The Swami was surrounded on the podium by no less than twenty-seven prominent pandits, although only six of these actually participated in the discussion. Thousands of people attended and the police was present to keep order. The available reports of the proceedings, one by the Swami himself and the other by a Bengali pandit, show that Dayananda kept the attacks of his opponents at bay with great self-assurance and competence. He had a constant struggle to bring the pandits back to the precise topic, 'that idol worship is or is not taught in the scriptures', and no pandit managed to produce conclusive proof for their side. Then the end came quite suddenly. One pandit read a text to the Swami, who did not recognize the passage and asked to inspect the manuscript. He was handed the leaflet and started to examine it in silence. As he was doing so, the pandits rose in unison and declared Dayananda defeated. The crowd then started to pelt the Swami, and the police had to intervene to protect him.[123] There is no doubt that this sudden closure of the debate and the proclamation of Dayananda as the loser was a mischievous act on the part of the pandits, who could not afford to come out the losers in that citadel of orthodoxy. No doubt the Swami recalled how his *guru* Virjananda had suffered a similar unjust humiliation in Mathura.[124] The injustice committed emphasized in fact the importance the pandits attached to the Swami's challenge. Hoernle's comment is extremely revealing:

But, whether gotten ill or well, their [the pandits'] victory had certainly the result they desired. The change was very remarkable in the state of things before and after the disputation. As quickly as the excitement had arisen before, so quickly it subsided afterwards. Whereas, before, multitudes flocked to see him, those who came afterwards might be easily counted. The reformer himself was practically excommunicated, and any one who would visit him after his refutation was threatened with the same measure.[125]

But how did all this affect Dayananda himself? On the one hand the dispute had confirmed his faith in his own method and scholarship, and his low opinion of the competence of the pandits had been vindicated. Yet two other aspects of the situation could not have escaped his sharp and clear mind. First, he did need yet more study of *Vedas* and *Shāstras* so as not to be outwitted again by a pandit's surprise question. And, secondly, he must have wondered, seeing the complete collapse of his impact and influence after the dispute, in how far these public debates really were of any great importance in his work of reform.

It is evident that after Banaras his lifestyle changed. Ghasiram, who wrote seventy pages about the first period along the Ganga before Banaras, has only ten pages on the second period. And he repeats[126] Lekhram's observation that during the latter period Dayananda spent little time on debates, but looked after his schools, and stayed for weeks and months at once place, mostly occupied in the study of the *Shāstras*, and more especially the *Vedas*.[127] For Dayananda it was once more a time for consideration and evaluation, looking back on his reform efforts and the very meagre results of his work in the rural Doab. He certainly did exert great influence on a number of people, who tried to live a new life. But the trouble was that they often had to face strong opposition from their caste: they sometimes were declared outcaste or at least were threatened with this.[128] As a result many did not dare to openly follow the Swami's teaching, and some who had that courage quickly slipped back into their old ways.[129] They were only individuals, and as such extremely vulnerable; they needed the protection of an organization, of a community, to shield them against these pressures, and so far Dayananda had not provided such support. Even his schools easily lost their converts.[130] The reaction of the people of Banaras to the demands of orthodoxy[131] also demonstrated the strength of the system and the weakness of the individual iconoclast. The Swami needed to seriously reconsider his practical approach.

This reconsideration must also have been influenced by his discussions in Banaras with reformers from the great cities. Before coming to Banaras he already had talked in Kanpur with the Brahmo Kshetranath Ghosh,[132] but in Banaras he had his first prolonged contact with representatives of modern Hindu reform movements. Two prominent members of the Bombay commercial classes, Jaikishendas Jivanram and Dharmsi, the brother of the famous Shet Lakhmidas Khimji, had talks with the Swami.[133] They no doubt informed him about Karsondas Mulji's fight against the Vallabhāchāryas, and his search for the true pre-sectarian Vedic religion. They would also have spoken about the efforts and organization of the Prarthana Samaj in their city. They urged the Swami to pay a visit to Bombay in the near future.

Dayananda also met two Calcutta people, barrister Chandrashekar
Sen, a leading figure of the Brahmo Samaj, and pandit Satyavrat
Samashrami of the Bengal Asiatic Society, who published a detailed
account of the Banaras *shāstrārth*.[134] They described the activities
and organization of the Brahmo Samaj, and invited him to their
city, an invitation reiterated by Debendranath Tagore, the great
leader of the Adi Brahmo Samaj, when he met the Swami a few
weeks later at the Kumbh Melā in Allahabad.[135] To Dayananda,
the frustrated rural reformer, these discussions must have opened
the window to a totally new world.

But these years in the Doab brought a great development in
the Swami's thought. When he came down from Hardwar there
had been much dead wood and uncertainty left in his thought,
but by now much had been cleared up. The four *Vedas* now
stood prominently apart as the only revelation, created by God
and promulgated by the *rishis*. They contained the blueprint of
the ideal religion and the ideal social system. All other books
were considered secondary, man-made, and therefore liable to
contain errors. His personal study of the *Vedas* had progressed
very considerably indeed. His idea of God had now become
more precise, and the main tenets of his theology had been firmly
established, a strong and logical framework for future refinement.
There had been a great step forward in his thinking on ethics: moral
action lies at the very basis of religious life, and the law of Karmic
retribution holds sway over it. His ideas on ritual too had taken
clear shape. He now had a firm grasp of what he felt the religious
life was all about. Hoernle put it succinctly and pointedly: 'The
worship or service of God consists chiefly in the following three
acts: first and foremost the study of the *Vedas* with a view to
the knowledge of God; then the observance of the moral laws
as the will of God; thirdly, the worship of God by fire or the homa
sacrifice. The observance of these is the means of salvation.'[136]

Dayananda's reflection and study during those final two years
along the banks of the Ganga must have concentrated on the
clarification of these ideas in the *Vedas*, and on the method he
should employ to bring to the people that authentic worship
and service of God. Except for Farrukhabad, significantly the
biggest urban centre frequented in these years, there was little
to show for his work in the rural Doab, and as an effort at con-

verting people Banaras had been a failure. What new road should
he take now?

A last question should be asked: what and who influenced
Dayananda during this period? The nature of the sources makes
this a difficult question to answer. The overriding impression is
that Dayananda's thinking and course of action was primarily
influenced by the challenge of contemporary Hinduism around
him, its superstitions, its institutions, its leaders. He fought the
abuses wherever he met them. He was constantly buffeted by a
fierce opposition, which occasionally did not shirk from using
vicious and violent methods, abuse, slander, and physical threats
to his life. It is in the heat of that confrontation that he evolved
his ideas and methods. And at the same time he kept looking
into the *Vedas* for answers. But, as he felt in the latter part of this
lustrum, he was too closely and constantly involved in struggle
and controversy, so that he was not getting very far in his study
and his thinking. What he needed were distance and peace to
work things out in his mind, hence the quiet two years after Banaras.
Dayananda was then, and would remain a man who had to solve
his problems for himself, by study and more study, by trial and
error, never accepting things from hearsay or second-hand.

Yet, there must have been other influences at work. Three
groups of people re-appear frequently enough in the biographies
to make one wonder how far they influenced the Swami: the
Neo-Vedāntins, the missionaries, and the Sādhs. Dayananda had
frequent discussions with those followers of Shankara whom he
called Neo-Vedāntins. These were quite an active and influential
group among the nineteenth century Indian intelligentsia. The
biographers mention a number of discussions between the Swami
and the Neo-Vedāntins,[137] and one in particular with Pandit
Jotisswarup, which lasted no less than fourteen days.[138] When
Dayananda planned to open a Vedic school in Banaras, one of
his primary aims was to counteract the errors of the Neo-
Vedāntins,[139] and the only book he wrote during the period was
one against Vedānta.[140] It was a Vedāntin who accused him
of being an atheist and a Christian in disguise.[141] It is also significant that the *Vedāntasūtras* were specifically included in the
twenty-one *shāstras* of the Kanpur declaration. All this indicates
that Dayananda was in fairly constant contact with the Vedāntins,
and that Vedānta was foremost in his mind. The main influence

on Dayananda from this contact and study was the growing clarification of his ideas on God and his relation to the soul and the world. This influence remained with the Swami nearly up to the end of his life.

Did the missionaries have any noticeable influence on him? Only four meetings with missionaries are recorded in the sources. At Farrukhabad, a Padre Anlan, two English Padres, and some Indian Christians came to arrange a discussion, but they called it off because they knew no Sanskrit. To them Dayananda asserted that sins cannot be forgiven.[142] At Mirzapur the Reverend Mather came to see him from time to time, but all we know about it is that he suggested to Dayananda that he should himself write a commentary on the *Vedas*.[143]

The two other meetings are much better documented, because the missionaries themselves wrote a record of them. At the great annual fair of Kakora, the Reverend T.J. Scott had several interviews with the Swami, which he described in his *Missionary Life in the Villages of India*. The Reverend Scott obviously had a great admiration for the Swami, and they talked about God and the forgiveness of sins. He told Dayananda the Christian position on each subject they discussed, and he presented him with a copy of the New Testament.[144] The most extensive record is that of Dr Hoernle. He too had several meetings with the Swami, and gave repeated expression to his admiration of him. Dayananda gave him some autobiographical details, and obviously conversed long about his own ideas on many subjects, which are very clearly and objectively presented by Hoernle, who wrote that, 'He has read the Gospels, though I do not think very carefully'.[145]

Dayananda had read the Gospels, no doubt the copy he received from the Reverend Scott, and the exchange of ideas with these intelligent men conversant with theological thought may have helped him to clarify his own. One feels that Hoernle grasped the essence of Dayananda's thought much better than the other witnesses whose comments are reproduced by the biographers. But apart from that, especially since missionary work was not very important in that area at that time, it seems quite clear that any influence on Dayananda on the part of the missionaries was minimal.

Dayananda spent a lot of time at Farrukhabad, and it was there that his preaching was most successful. This city was the main centre of a very special sect, that of the Sādhs. They were an extraordinary community. According to the 1891 census Farrukhabad district had 1,866 Sādhs,[146] and it was by far their biggest centre: their total number did not exceed six thousand.[147] They formed a closed community, living together in their own quarter of the city, providing generously for the needy among them.[148] They did not observe caste and rejected the authority of the brahmins.[149] They believed in one God, whom they called *Satya Guru* or *Satya Nāma*, who was considered the creator of the universe. They believed in the doctrine of reincarnation[150] and for them the means of final liberation from the round of rebirths lay in a devout life consisting of the veneration of God and the observance of strict morality.[151] They rejected all idol worship, pilgrimages, observance of auspicious days, the ritual of *Shrāddh*, and most Hindu usages and ceremonials. Their own religious meetings, conducted weekly, consisted mainly in readings from their holy book. This work, called *Pothī*, is in Hindī, and it is a collection of sermons and songs in the manner of the medieval *bhakti* saints: in fact it contains a number of Kabīr's songs and also extract from the *Ādi Granth* of the Sikhs, itself a compilation of medieval *bhakti* poetry.[152] They had no regular priesthood. 'That man who in each particular division, happens to be the most respectable, who can read, repeat their hymns and relate their traditions is their chief, though always with limited authority.'[153]

The doctrine of the *Sādhs* put great stress on moral living, as is evident from their thirty-two laws, which were condensed into 'Twelve Commandments'.[154] Major injunctions were vegetarianism and non-violence, and the continuous pursuit of truth in word and action. They prohibited all forms of intoxicants and insisted that man should avoid all luxurious living. Their marriages were monogamous, and every Sādh was required to work for his living and to avoid all mendicancy. Crook comments that, 'they are hardworking and industrious; it is considered disgraceful to be dependent for support on another; beggary is unknown among them.'[155]

Dayananda had an especially close relationship with the Sādhs, who came to consider themselves as his helpers, providers and protectors, keeping guard over him as he slept, and even beating up those who threatened their Swami.[156] Two incidents give a flavour of this close relationship. When he was criticized by Hindus for accepting food from a Sādh, whom they considered low in ritual status, Dayananda retorted that food can only be spoilt by dirt or by the tainted money that procures it.[157] Another time a Sādh asked him, 'What is man's duty', and received the answer, 'To be merciful and truthful like God'.[158]

It is immediately obvious that practically everything about the belief and the life of these people would have appealed very greatly to Dayananda. His close contact with them must have strengthened his conviction that authentic moral and religious living was possible even in the midst of the excesses of Hinduism. He must have learnt also from observing the Sādhs that for such a life to be viable and lasting depended on the strong support of a group of people all dedicated to the same ideal; that it needed some kind of association, organization, of the community to remain alive and unaffected by outside influences. He may well have noticed the other side of the medal. No doubt the Sādhs formed a hospitable community: they took him to their hearts, as they did around the same time Mrs Kellogg, the wife of a missionary, who commented on their open and gracious hospitality.[159] But, on the other hand, they were still a closed community, isolated within caste barriers, averse to propaganda, an esoteric community[160] which as such did not hold out hope for that regeneration of Hinduism Dayananda aspired to.

When the Swami went up to Hardwar he had sought a pan-Hindu audience, but had experienced only disappointment. His work among the élite of the rural Doab was crowned with some success, but it remained an influence on isolated individuals, and because its roots in society were not deep enough, the tender growth often withered soon. The visit to Banaras was an important turning point, even if Dayananda himself did not fully realize it at the time: he had suddenly become a figure of all-Hindu importance. Moreover, he had talked with modern reformers from Bombay and Calcutta. They had been impressed by his personality and his ideas, had urged him to visit their cities, and given him a first glimpse of a different field of work and of a different approach. But before the Swami acted on these invitations, he once again immersed himself for two years in more study and in a review of his methods.

CHAPTER IV

Calcutta: A Cauldron of New Ideas

On reading the biographies of Swami Dayananda one gets the impression that his stay in Calcutta was not a very crucial one: the Swami is said to have astounded the sophisticated Bengalis by his lectures, and to have picked up some useful hints from his talks with Keshub Chandra Sen, but there is no suggestion that Calcutta influenced him profoundly. Yet, if one compares the ideas and approaches of the peripatetic preacher of the Doab with those of the Swami in 1874 as they are described in the biographies and in the first great work the Swami wrote that year, the *Satyārth Prakāsh*, the difference is very great indeed, and it appears that the key to the understanding of this transformation is to be found in Calcutta.

In April 1872 Dayananda left Banaras and started his unhurried journey eastwards: it took him eight months with only six stops on the way to reach Calcutta. Obviously he continued the pattern of study and reflection that had regulated his life after the Banaras disputation, staying for long periods in the same place. He only spent a fortnight in Mughal Sarai and Monghyr, but one month each in Arrah and Patna, two months in Bhagalpur, and nearly four in Dumraon. The biographers mention very few public performances by the Swami in those eight months. He held a *shāstrārth* on idol worship at Arrah, and another at Patna, which soon broke up when the pandits started to quarrel among themselves. At Arrah he gave two lectures on Vedic *dharma*, and at Bhagalpur one on the duties of man.[1] Apart from this there is mention of a few discussions with various individuals. At Mughal Sarai he had an exchange of views on sin and its forgiveness with the Reverend Lalbihari De, and at Dumraon a discussion on Vedānta with the famous Shaivite pandit Durgadatta. A conversation with the District Magistrate, H. W. Alexander, mainly about caste, took place at Arrah. On his last stop before Calcutta, at Bhagalpur, Dayananda debated the nature of God with European

and Indian clergymen, and caste and interdining with the local
Brahmos.[2]

That is the total extent of his public appearances during these
eight months according to his biographers. It is clear that the
Swami was not seeking the limelight, nor was he in heavy demand
in this area previously unvisited by him. Study and reflection
took most of his time: he was still clarifying his thoughts, preparing himself for the big test in Calcutta, and taking all his time
to journey there. He had already met some westernized Indians,
and some Brahmos, and he was no doubt keen to find out more
about the Brahmo Samaj and its leaders, and about the religious
and cultural vitality of Calcutta which he only knew from hearsay.
His contacts so far had been primarily with the traditional leadership of Hinduism, and he must have realized that he needed to
be much clearer in his own mind about the reform he was striving
for, in order to be able to present it convincingly to the western-
educated élite of the great metropolis.

The information on these eight months is so scanty that it is
impossible to discern new developments in his thought. An
interesting episode occurred at Arrah. Here the Swami founded
a Sabhā, a society for the promotion of the Vedic *dharma*. Nothing
more is known about this abortive venture, except that after a
couple of meetings the Sabhā ceased to exist altogether.[3] It indicates, however, that the idea of an organization was already
stirring in Dayananda's mind even before he visited Calcutta.

When the Swami arrived in Calcutta on 16 December 1872,
his first overriding concern was not to teach, but to learn. This
is quite evident from the record of his activities. He was for three
weeks in Calcutta before he ventured to present some of his views,
and that was not to a large public audience, but to a select group
at Keshub Chandra Sen's Lily Cottage. His big public lectures
did not start until the beginning of March, that is two-and-a-half
months after his arrival. In the first seven weeks he met a number
of people in private discussions, and visited institutions. In early
February he left Calcutta and spent three weeks in isolation,
digesting all the new ideas that were crowding his mind. It is
only after that period of seclusion that he ventured on to the
public platform. The man who stood up before the critical audience
of the metropolis was already very different from the rural reformer of the Doab: he had given himself time to meditate on

what he had learnt and to work out his own considered conclusions.

These first seven weeks the Swami spent in Calcutta were obviously very crucial for this development, and to understand what new ideas he absorbed, it is necessary to know whom he met and what he saw in Calcutta. The information of the biographers is rather scrappy, and one gets the impression that the only really influential contact the Swami had was with Keshub. But even the little information the biographers possess has never been thoroughly considered. A recently discovered document throws considerable additional light upon the Swami's contacts in Calcutta. Hemchandra Chakravarti, a preacher of the Adi Brahmo Samaj, became the Swami's personal pupil in Calcutta, and was in constant contact with him. He kept a diary, and the section that deals with the Swami's stay in Calcutta has recently been published.[4] This daily record, succinct as it is, has considerably enlarged our knowledge of the Swami's range of visitors, and of the topics of their talks. Thanks to it we now have a list of some thirty people who had discussions with Dayananda. An analysis of that list makes it now possible to assess more accurately the currents of thought the Swami encountered.

The invitation to come to Calcutta had been extended to Dayananda by the leaders of the Adi Brahmo Samaj; he was looked after by them and put up in a house belonging to the Tagore family, and he was the main guest at the annual festival of the Samaj held at the Tagores';[5] his closest associate was Hemchandra, and he had several meetings with Rajnarayan Bose, the current President of the Samaj.[6] An important qualification shared by these people, and one that would have pleased the Swami greatly, was that they were all well conversant with Sanskrit. But the most striking characteristic of the Adi Brahmos in the early seventies was that they formed the spearhead of a newly-emerging movement of proud Hindu nationalism against the inroads of westernization in Bengali society.

The acknowledged inspirer of this movement was Rajnarayan Bose, with the strong support of the Tagore family. In the mid-sixties he had founded the 'Society for the Promotion of National Feeling', the prospectus of which envisaged a Model School for Indian Music, a School of Hindu Medicine, publication of works on Indian history and culture, promotion of the study of Sanskrit, and protection of the vernaculars against the influence of English. His initiative directly led to the establishment of the 'Hindu Mela' in 1867 by the Brahmo Nabagopal Mitra, and the subsequent formation of the 'National Society'. The aim of all these organs was to counteract western influence by the promotion of knowledge and awareness of the greatness of Indian culture.[7] This national feeling was closely linked to the Hindu religion and the Hindu heritage according to Nabagopal's dictum, 'The Hindus are destined to be a religious nation'.[8] That same connection was eloquently proclaimed by Rajnarayan in his famous lecture of 1872 entitled 'The Superiority of Hinduism'. He read this text to Dayananda and presented him with a copy.[9]

In this lecture twelve reasons were listed why Hinduism was in every way superior to all other religions. Although some of these reasons would not have met with Dayananda's approval, others had a great impact on his thought, as we see them developed and increasingly accentuated in his later works. Rajnarayan argued that Hinduism contained within its scope the fullness of human knowledge, including the political and economic sciences: Hinduism was 'like an ocean containing gems without number'. Whereas other religions, like Christianity, Islam, and Buddhism derived from a historical figure, Hinduism predated history in its hoary antiquity. Admittedly, Rajnarayan's concept of the scope of Hinduism was much wider than Dayananda could accept; it included the Puranic and Tantric developments. However, the two basic ideas of the all-comprehensiveness and the non-human pre-historical origin of Hinduism were adopted by the Swami. But he transferred these qualities to the *Vedas* and they became for him the cardinal proof of the superiority of the Vedic religion over all others.[10]

The eloquent affirmation by Rajnarayan and the Tagores of the greatness of Hindu culture in comparison with other cultures was reinforced by other personalities the Swami met: the political thinker Akshaychandra Sarkar, the historian Rajnikanta Gupta, and the educator and journalist Bhudev Mukhopadhyay were all imbued with this spirit of Hindu revival in the face of the inroads made by westernization.[11] Dayananda's key concept of the superiority of Hindu religion and culture is one that is linked with his very name, and it has been taken for granted that it was the outcome of his Vedic studies. However, in the biographical works one cannot find for the period before Calcutta a single reference that indicates that the Swami had at that time even thought about Hinduism in 'national' terms, or in terms of comparison with other religions. He certainly had loudly proclaimed the excellence of the Vedic faith, but he had done this completely within the context of Hinduism itself. This attitude is clearly confirmed by what Hoernle wrote at the time of the Banaras disputation: 'The reformer is not unacquainted with Christianity. He has read the Gospels, though I don't think very carefully. I had some conversation with him about it. But at present his mind is too much occupied with his own plans of reformation to give any serious thought to the investigation of the claims of another religion.'[12] It was in Calcutta that this context suddenly widened, because the people the Swami met had to think of Hinduism in relation to other religions, especially Christianity and Islam. One must conclude that the Adi Brahmo Samaj group were the people who set the Swami's mind firmly in the direction of thinking of Hinduism in national terms, and in comparative terms, although Dayananda did not agree with them as to what constituted authentic Hinduism and what its sources were.

There was another way in which the Adi Brahmos deeply influenced the Swami. We have seen how Dayananda during his stay in the Doab became increasingly interested in the problem of the nature of God and in questions of morality. During his stay in Calcutta Debendranath Tagore's *Brahmo Dharma* was read to the Swami, and the biographers report that Dayananda's reaction was that the book should rather have been called 'Discourses upon the *Upanishads*'.[13] But no biographer has hitherto compared the *Brahmo Dharma* with the Swami's writings, possibly thinking that the Swami had dismissed it flippantly. But that he certainly did not: a close comparison of Debendranath's work with Dayananda's first *Satyārth Prakāsh*, written a year after he left Calcutta reveals some remarkable similarities.

Debendranath's work is in the form of reflections on nearly three hundred texts, the great majority of which are taken from the *Upanishads* and from the *Manusmriti*, with some from the *Mahābhārata*, the *Vedas*, and the *Mahānirvāna Tantra*.[14] In the *Satyārth Prakāsh* Dayananda gave over forty quotations from the *Upanishads*, nearly half of which are to be found in the *Brahmo Dharma*. As for Manu, Dayananda used forty-two per cent of

the verses used by Debendranath. These correlations are far too
great to be accidental: the Swami definitely drew on the *Brahmo
Dharma* for his own work.

But the similarities go beyond the mere use of texts. The *Brahmo
Dharma* set out to give a complete picture of the beliefs and of
the life of a Brahmo. The first part of the book, in sixteen chapters,
concentrates on doctrinal matters: the nature and attributes of
God, creation, the relation of man to God, and the means and
quality of man's knowledge of God are treated in special chapters.
Dayananda had special chapters on precisely these same topics.
Two ideas are constantly stressed by Debendranath: God's im-
manence, particularly in the soul; and God's role as judge of
the actions of man in dispensing rewards and punishments. These
two ideas are also clearly dominant in Dayananda's work. There
are even some quite specific doctrines on which Debendranath
insisted and which recur in identical form in the *Satyārth Prakāsh*:
there was an original creation of the world, before which nothing
existed besides God;[15] in the act of creation God himself was
not transformed into matter and the world;[16] the monistic concept
nirguna is given a very special interpretation, 'being above all
qualities found in created beings'.[17]

The remainder of the *Brahmo Dharma*, the last two chapters
of part one and the fifteen chapters of part two, deals with general
and special ethics. In these matters one can naturally expect a
fair amount of similarity without having to postulate direct
influence. About marriage, Debendranath wrote that the bride
should be chosen for her qualities, and should not marry too
young, and that the partners should marry only after having met
and ascertained each other's character, all conditions Dayananda
too was to stress. Two themes run through Debendranath's work
as constituting the basic conditions of a moral life: the necessity
for truth in thought, speech, and deed, and the obligation to lead
a life of activity. These certainly are also the basic conditions
proclaimed by Dayananda for a moral life. There are also some
points of special ethics mentioned by Debendranath that very
often recur in the Swami's *Satyārth Prakāsh*: man should shun
evil company and seek the company of the wise and virtuous;[18]
gifts should be given only to worthy persons, and specifically
to those in real need;[19] fasting does not constitute austerity.[20]
It is also remarkable that Debendranath devoted three pages to

the moral obligation of the witness in court to do his utmost to speak the truth;[21] Dayananda too was to treat this extensively in his own work.

These correlations and similarities both in broad themes and in details of doctrine are too great to be accidental. They prove conclusively that Dayananda studied the *Brahmo Dharma* very carefully indeed, and that the ideas of the Maharshi had a definite influence on his own evolving conceptions in the areas of both theology and ethics.

Another very influential personality who met Dayananda, and must have discussed with him questions of morality, was Akshaykumar Datta, hailed as the 'first moral teacher' of Bengal.[22] His *Dharmanīti* was a remarkable treatise of ethics, dealing extensively with the family, education, and the state, in a stringently logical fashion. The book vehemently attacked the current social evils of early marriage, polygamy, oppression of widows, etc. and set out the arguments against early marriage, and for pre-marriage courtship. Akshaykumar's ideas on education were very advanced for his age, as was his conception of the duties of the government.[23] The Swami must have felt a great affinity with him on many matters, especially as he was also an accomplished sanskritist, and had published an important study on Hindu sects.[24] On the other hand, Akshaykumar Datta, the Brahmo who had been primarily responsible for 'freeing the Brahmo Samaj from the thraldom of the *Vedas*', had become a rationalistic agnostic.[25] The Swami probably saw this development in a most brilliant man as the very consequence of his repudiation of the *Vedas*.

The ebullient Keshub Chandra Sen liked the Swami from their first meeting, and they saw a lot of each other. At that time Keshub was at the apogee of his career and influence. He had visited Britain in 1870, in 1871 he had founded his Indian Reform Association, and in 1872 his efforts at marriage reform had been crowned by the passage of the 1872 Marriage Act, which legalized Brahmo marriages. In those days, says Heimsath, Keshub was universally recognized as 'the most vigorous religious and social reformer in the land', and his writings and speeches, and 'the fearless espousal of the causes he undertook' were an inspiration to all reformers.[26]

The Swami cannot but have been highly impressed as the organizational achievements of Keshub unfolded before his eyes. The

Brahmo Samaj itself was a very important institution with a membership of about six thousand. The Indian Reform Association, open to non-Brahmos, with its five sections of Cheap Literature, Charity, Female Improvement, Education, and Temperance, penetrated the whole society. Keshub took Dayananda on a tour of his institutions.[27] At the Bharat Ashram, a group of families lived a communal life, and the building also housed the Female Normal School and a girls' school, with the Brahma Niketan, a boarding school for boys, nearby. There were also the Working Men's Institution and the Industrial School, established at the end of 1870, and Keshub's own press, so vital for his work of propaganda. Dayananda was probably less impressed by the Brahma Mandir, the architectural symbol of Keshub's syncretism, a grotesque amalgamation of Hindu, Buddhist, Islamic, and Christian styles.

In their private discussions the two reformers touched on some basic differences in their beliefs. The Swami defended his own faith in the doctrine of the transmigration of souls, and tried to prove to Keshub, who believed in the multiplicity of revelation, that only the *Vedas* constituted the true revelation.[28] When Keshub expressed his regret that Dayananda did not know English, since if he had done so he could have become his companion on his next visit to Britain, Dayananda retorted that it was a greater pity that the leader of the Brahmo Samaj knew no Sanskrit and spoke in a language most Indians could not understand.[29] Keshub did in fact give the Swami two useful concrete pieces of advice, which he readily accepted. The first was the suggestion that he cover his nakedness, as it would be shocking to the audiences and the gatherings he would attend.[30] Dayananda adopted this suggestion immediately. Later on, in Kanpur, he himself gave as the reason for covering his body that his contact with all kinds of people, and especially the presence of ladies at meetings and lectures and during visits to homes, necessitated it to avoid giving offence.[31]

Keshub's second suggestion was more important and far-reaching: that the Swami should lecture not in Sanskrit, but in Hindī, so as to reach a greater number of people.[32] An incident in Calcutta provided another strong argument for changing to Hindī. The *Indian Mirror* of 22 February 1873 reported that: 'After the lecture Pandit Maheshchandra Nyayaratna translated into Bengālī, but he did not translate correctly, because he said things which the Swami had not said. The students of Sanskrit objected to the Pandit's translation.'[33] It took some time before Dayananda could put this suggestion into practice, as his Hindī was practically non-existent. At Kanpur, in November 1873, the Swami 'had started to speak some *bhāshā*', says Lekhram,[34] but it was not until May-June 1874, at Banaras, that Dayananda gave his first lecture in Hindī. Even then, according to Lekhram, it did not go very well as yet: 'hundreds of words, and even sentences still came out in Sanskrit'. At that time the Swami gave as reasons for his use of Hindī that with Sanskrit he did not reach the common people and that the pandits often mistranslated his words.[35] Ghasiram notes that, as a result of the use of Hindī, more common people and fewer pandits tended to be present at his lectures from then on.[36]

In the sphere of language the Bengalis were in those days discussing questions such as the respective importance of English and the vernaculars, and if there should be a national language in India. So far these problems had not exercised the Swami's mind; he had been content to use Sanskrit, the *lingua franca* of all pandits. The Bengalis introduced Dayananda to the current discussions on language. He met ardent promoters of the vernaculars versus English in Rajnikanta Gupta, Jayakrishna Mukhopadhyay, Rajnarayan Bose, Bhudev Mukhopadhyay, and Rajendralal Mitra.[37] In fact, the latter two became leaders of the nineteenth-century movement for the adoption of Hindī as a national language.[38] They were probably the first people to suggest to the Swami this cause which he was to espouse so enthusiastically in later years.

Dayananda must have become deeply aware of the great influence of Christianity on Keshub's syncretic religion, especially as this would have been pointed out to him by his friends of the Adi Brahmo Samaj. It was a trait he thoroughly disapproved of. In his meetings with the followers of Keshub, the Swami also became acquainted with the dissension that was about to split Keshub's Brahmo Samaj of India. In P.C.Mozoomdar he met an ardent admirer of Keshub,[39] a promoter of the 'Keshub-cult', who was to become his master's right hand in his New Dispensation.[40] But the Swami also met Dwarkanath Gangoli, the radical reformer, who was to become a leader of the break-away Sadharan

Brahmo Samaj.[41] This group was dissatisfied with Keshub's increasingly autocratic regime and with his doctrine of 'Great Men' and 'Inspiration'. According to this doctrine, with the progress of history God specially inspires great men, who become the mouthpieces of new revelations. Increasingly Keshub saw himself as a man thus inspired. In fact, during Dayananda's stay, on 25 January 1873, he delivered his famous Town Hall lecture on Inspiration.[42] This concept of revelation was completely contrary to Dayananda's own belief, and he must have realized that Keshub's assumption of the role of an infallible *guru* was one of the main reasons for the internal division in the Samaj. It was a lesson he was never to forget.

Dayananda's many meetings with Pandit Ishvarchandra Vidyasagar must have been among the high points of his visit.[43] Whereas the Swami stood at the beginning of his public career, the Pandit, only four years older, had finished the most productive part of his life; his strength had been sapped by illness and a great load of debts and frustrations.[44] But his achievements had been remarkable. At the age of twenty-one he had been appointed Head Pandit of the Bengālī Department of Fort William College, and ten years later he had become Principal of Sanskrit College. He had established a string of twenty model schools, and no less than thirty-five girls' schools, and had just succeeded in having the Hindu Metropolitan Institution which he directed affiliated to Calcutta University. Against the fierce opposition of the great majority of Hindus, he had successfully carried out a campaign in the fifties to have the Widow Remarriage Bill passed, and was currently fighting his frustrating battle against the polygamy of *kulinism*. As early as 1847 he had established his own Sanskrit Press; by now he had published no less than twenty books, mostly educational textbooks, and edited ten Sanskrit texts.[45] His conversations with Dayananda focused on the problems of women and of education. Dayananda found in Vidyasagar a man after his own heart, steeped in the tradition, and basing all his projects for reform soundly on the teachings of the *Shāstras*. It was with Vidyasagar that for the first time he talked about his own concept of *niyoga*, which was to become his own ideal solution to the problem of widows.[46]

Vidyasagar's arguments for widow-remarriage were strengthened by those of his supporters whom Dayananda met. In 1865 the lawyer Umeshchandra Mitra had written a Bengālī drama in support of widow-remarriage; [47] and Ramtanu Lahiri had been a constant supporter of the Pandit,[48] as was A.K.Datta.[49] Dr Mahendralal Sarkar, an eminent scientist who was soon to found the Scientific Society, wrote impressive articles proving the necessity of later marriage, using arguments from both the *Shāstras* and from medical science.[50] One of Vidyasagar's most eminent supporters was Raja Jayakrishna Mukhopadhyay, who also sought the Swami out in Calcutta.[51] His achievements in Uttarpara in the field of social services had become legendary: he had founded a High School, a Charitable Dispensary, a Popular Library, and no less than thirty schools. He had provided in his area a superb network of educational establishments and of services to the needy, thus showing what the dedication and generosity of one man could achieve for the people.[52]

The Swami's interest in scholarly matters led him to visit the Asiatic Society, accompanied by Pandit Rajkumar Vidyaratna, later famous under the name of Ramananda Bharati.[53] He bought some Vedic and Upanishadic texts and had a talk with Pratapchandra Ghosh, the assistant librarian, a pioneer in historical-novel writing and a scholarly historian of renown.[54] He also discussed ancient history with R.C.Dutt, the civil servant who was to make a name for himself as a sanskritist and historian.[55] His conversations with Rajendralal Mitra about ancient Indian history must have been most instructive.[56] This pioneer historian, 'the finest fruit of the growth of Indology', was at the time the Vice-President of the Asiatic Society. He had edited numerous works for the *Bibliotheca Indica* series, had translated the *Chāndogya Upanishad* into English, and was deeply committed to the support and development of the vernacular through his editorship of two journals of the Vernacular Literature Society.[57] Conversations with these historians, and others like Rajnikanta Gupta[58] and A.K.Datta, opened Dayananda's eyes to a world of historical scholarship of which he had been hitherto little aware.

One of the Swami's prime motives for his visit to Calcutta was to investigate the possibility of founding a Vedic school. He had talked about it with Debendranath in Kanpur,[59] and in Calcutta a special discussion session was held about the matter;[60] there it was decided that if Sanskrit College did not start to teach the *Vedas* a special school should be established. In fact at that

time a rumour was going around that the Lieutenant-General of
Bengal proposed to close Sanskrit College. Dayananda's reaction
was typical: 'there is no use for such a college in which the *Vedas*
are not taught'.[61] He also complained to his Bengali friends
that in that great centre of Hindu reform, 'the rich people's sons
learn Persian and English, and only the sons of the poor are left
for the study of Sanskrit'.[62] But Dayananda's plan for a Vedic
school did not really arouse the Calcuttans; whatever enthusiasm
some may have had, it seems to have quickly evaporated when
the Swami left.

Up to this time Dayananda's concern with education had been
a limited one: he had thought of Sanskrit schools only as a necessary medium for the training of pandits who would be dedicated
to the propagation and study of the ancient religion. In his first
Satyārth Prakāsh he was to tackle the problem of education in
its widest context. This is no wonder, because during his stay
in Calcutta he met some of the foremost educational thinkers
and practitioners of the time. We have already mentioned his
tour of Keshub's schools; he also visited Raja Prasanna Kumar
Tagore's Sanskrit school.[63] In Bhudev Mukhopadhyay he met
one of the greatest educationists of Calcutta. Bhudev was a staunch
promoter of Hindu culture against anglicization, a cause he had
defended in his young days among the Young Bengal group of
Hindu College. He was deeply orthodox, and one of the first
to promote Hindī as an all-India link language. In his long career
as a headmaster and as Inspector of Schools he had become a
pioneer in teachers' training, and from 1868 he had been the
editor of the *Education Gazette*.[64] Vidyasagar and Jayakrishna
Mukhopadhyay were both deeply involved in educational work,
and so was Rajendralal Mitra.[65] We have already mentioned the
advanced educational theories of A.K.Datta's *Dharmanīti*. In
Ramtanu Lahiri, the disciple of Derozio, Dayananda met one
of the greatest and most beloved teachers of the time.[66] It was
contact with these men that opened Dayananda's eyes to the
basic importance of a broad educational programme for the
uplift of the whole society.

So far Dayananda's work of propaganda had been carried out
by the living word, and only twice had he cautiously ventured
into print during the ten years since he left his *guru* Virjananda.
During the next ten years he was to pen manuscript after manu-

script, and his press could scarcely keep up with his writings. Again it was his experience in Calcutta that revealed to the Swami the value of the written word. Keshub and Vidyasagar both made their influence felt primarily through the written word, and they both established their own presses to facilitate distribution. Many of the personalities the Swami met were constantly involved in propagating their ideas through publication. Bhudev Mukhopadhyay and Kristodas Pal were editors of the *Education Gazette* and the *Hindu Patriot* respectively. A.K.Datta and A.C.Sarkar exerted profound influence through their writings, and the scholar Rajendralal Mitra was an editor for the Vernacular Literary Society. Rajnikanta Gupta lived by his writing,[67] and Dwarkanath Gangoli was a journalist and prolific author.[68] In fact, publication was the most powerful organ of propaganda of the Bengali reformers, and one Dayananda had scarcely touched.

Although Dayananda had studied Manu and some of the didactic treatises of the *Mahābhārata*, statecraft in itself had not been a concern of his; he had only touched on it in relation to specific problems he encountered within the world of Hinduism: the propagation of the true *Shāstras*, the curtailing of cow-slaughter, the restructuring of society according to the four *varnas*. In his *Satyārth Prakāsh* he was to propose an overall theory of the state and government. Some very important questions were currently being discussed by the Calcutta intelligentsia: what was the nature and function of the state, and how should one view the British Government in India? A.K.Datta's *Dharmanīti* attempted to answer some of these questions,[69] and A.C.Sarkar too was an advanced political thinker, especially on the question of 'nationhood'; to him the four bonds of nationality were territory, language, religion, and dress.[70] In 1873 he started to edit the *Sādhāranee*, 'the most powerful organ of educated public opinion in Bengal' at the time. Rajnikanta Gupta was another nationalist whose writings concentrated on political matters.[71] The Swami also met several people who were actually involved in the processes of administration. Kristodas Pal and Yatindramohan Tagore were at the time members of the Bengal Legislative Council,[72] and Bhudev Mukhopadhyay and the great barrister W.C.Bonnerjee played an important role that would lead to the last-named becoming President of the first session of the Indian National Congress in Bombay in 1885.[73] Three of the Swami's contacts,

Dwarkanath Gangoli, Rajnarayan Bose, and A.C.Sarkar were to be on the first executive of the Indian Association in 1876. Through his contact with these people Dayananda was stimulated to think out his own concept of statecraft, and also to make some evaluation of the British Government of India.

The Swami must have been overwhelmed by the striking variety of beliefs he found among the Calcutta intelligentsia, who represented a fascinating spectrum of different mixtures in their conceptions of Hinduism, of religious reform, and of social reform, ranging from the conservative orthodox to the agnostic rationalists. Among those on the orthodox side the attitudes towards social reform were as different as they were among those who stood for religious reform. Some reformers were very westernized, others were ardent promoters of a Hindu cultural revival. Dayananda cannot but have been struck by the extreme individualism of the Calcutta intelligentsia. Among those he met very few would have found themselves in full agreement on the basic question of religious reform in its relation to social reform, on the issue of westernization versus cultural revival, and on matters of statecraft and politics. Their conceptions of the essence of Hinduism, the sources of true religion, and the implementation of religious reform, were amazingly divergent. Perhaps there was only one conviction they all shared: denial that the *Vedas* presented the unique and definitive revelation. And Dayananda may well have diagnosed that refusal as the root cause of their disagreements.

Nevertheless, all these people had a great deal in common, not so much beliefs as attitudes. They were all deeply concerned about the state of Hindu society, its educational backwardness, its injustice and cruelty, its cultural degradation, its religious enslavement, and its political insensitivity. Moreover, they went beyond mere concern: they were deeply involved in the task of regeneration of that society by devoting their energies to journalistic and other writing, politics, educational work, social reform causes, religious innovation, cultural revival. In this they were the leading representatives of a whole new urban class, aware of and receptive to new ideas, and ready to participate in reform. This must have been a rather overwhelming revelation to the roving reformer of the Doab, a sleepy rural tract dominated by the inflexible orthodoxy of pandits and brahmins.

No wonder that the Swami felt the need to retire after seven weeks, and quietly consider his experiences. He left Calcutta for three weeks,[74] and when he came back he felt ready to stand up in public with confidence. His public lectures started on 2 March 1873. One would wish to have a more extensive report of these lectures, but what is available gives some idea of the new trends in his thought. However, the total impact of his experiences in Calcutta was not to show itself fully until a year later when he wrote his *Satyārth Prakāsh*.

The Swami's careful preparation bore fruit: his lectures, no more than ten in all, were a great success, although they were delivered in his usual simple Sanskrit and lasted for up to three hours. The *Amrita Bazar Patrika* and the *Indian Mirror* reported them with both admiration and astonishment.[75] The best sources for the content of his lectures are the articles published in the *Dharmatattva*,[76] which voiced the general astonishment of the Calcuttans thus, 'Though he is a complete stranger to western science, his discourses on all subjects are so excellent that people are struck dumb'. The Swami's lectures concentrated on the positive exposition of his central ideas: the nature of God and of revelation, the worship of God, and the duties of man.

Dayananda's theory of monotheism was not one that was new to his audience, but his conception of the *Vedas* certainly was: he said that they were the literal publication of the very wisdom of God, and that they contained a pure monotheism, even if they used many names for the one God. In these doctrinal matters the Swami's contact with the Bengali intelligentsia had not changed his convictions, but rather strengthened them. However, it was the social message of the Swami that interested his audience most; and his ideas on social issues had certainly developed considerably. His denunciation of caste and his advocacy of the four · *varnas* according to quality was not new, but his vehement denunciation of child-marriage certainly was, as was his strong support for widow-remarriage. The Swami also had a lot to say about the education of the young, and the education of girls in particular. The commentators were quite surprised about what Dayananda said about the state of *sannyāsa*: that there is no basic difference between *sannyāsa* and the state of the householder, except that the *sannyāsī* should devote his life completely to the propagation of knowledge and *dharma*, because 'one does not become a religious man just by sitting in meditation in one spot'.[77] The Swami explained what *dharma* meant to him: the combination of the worship of one God with the observance of Vedic rites and a responsible moral life. And in Calcutta where he had heard so much about the stigma attached to the very term 'Hindu', he told his audience that they should discard that derogatory name imposed by foreigners, and call themselves Aryans. The depth and clarity of the Swami's lectures astonished his audience so much that the *Dharmatattva* commented 'that the appearance of such a man is a wonder'.[78]

Although most of the Swami's time was spent with the new intelligentsia, he did have some contact with orthodox pandits too. He had discussions with Satyavrat Samashrami, the pandit who was present at the Banaras disputation,[79] with the renowned Āyurvedic physician Gangdhar Kaviraj, a strong opponent of Vidyasagar,[80] and with Maheshchandra Nyayaratna, the principal of Sanskrit College.[81] Only twice did Dayananda venture into debates with Hindu pandits along traditional lines. He went to Navadvip to meet its famous Navya Nyāya pandits. Keshub, who had brought him there, soon left, before the discussion was over. He was probably bored to distraction. The editor of *Bhāratjīvan* wrote that the pandits caught Dayananda in the net of *nyāya* and managed to bewilder him somewhat. That sounds quite probable, as the extreme subtleties of Navya Nyāya tend to confuse even the sharpest minds. Moreover, the Swami was never enamoured of, or skilled in, the formal play of logic: he used to refer to the language of the logicians as a *kāk-bhāshā*, a language of crows![82]

At Hugli the Swami held his famous *shāstrārth* with the eminent Pandit Taracharan Tarkaratna, the rajpandit of the Raja of Banaras, who had been on the panel of pandits who had 'defeated' Dayananda in Banaras two years earlier.[83] The subject of the disputation was once more 'idol worship in the *Vedas*'. It was again an interchange in the traditional style: quotations were refuted by counter-quotations, and both attack and defence were conducted with subtle arms from the arsenal of grammar. It seems that on this occasion Dayananda came out the clear winner. The account of the dispute, published later in the year,[84] is a rather strange one: short reports of what Tarkaratna said are followed by long refutations on the Swami's part. In fact, the document reads rather like a justification by Dayananda of his own position, frequently interspersed with harsh exposures of Tarkaratna as a fool and a deceiver. Obviously Dayananda was getting his own back for the unjust humiliation he had previously suffered at Banaras. The pamphlet contains a second part, an account of Dayananda's interpretation of the meaning of the terms *pratimā, purāna, devālaya*, etc., entitled *Pratimādi-Shabda-Vichār*, 'thoughts on the words *pratimā* etc.' It is written in that special style of the *shāstrārth*, quoting texts and applying grammatical and logical principles to them, a rather boring and barren form. One cannot but reflect on the tremendous difference between this exercise and the splendid lectures the Swami gave in the metropolis.

What, then, did Dayananda learn in Calcutta? How was he different from when he stepped off the train only four months previously? The two useful suggestions of Keshub, to wear clothes and to speak Hindī, soon transformed his public appearances, and made him more acceptable and more understandable to a wider public. But these were not the most significant results. More important was the tremendous self-confidence he had gained. The Banaras disputation had already convinced the Swami that he could stand up against the strongest attack of orthodoxy, and now his discussions with the western-educated urban intelligentsia had strengthened that self-confidence. He had defended his ideas against some of the best minds of Calcutta, and they had not managed to shake any of his basic convictions. Even if he had not convinced his hearers, he had gained their respect. He had been struck by the great individualism and utter divisiveness of the Calcutta intelligentsia, and by their unanimous refusal to accept the *Vedas* as a unique revelation, which he saw as the basic reason for their divisions; and it is here in Calcutta that he made up his mind that he himself would write a commentary on the *Vedas*.[85]
But if Calcutta did not weaken Dayananda's basic convictions, it opened up wide new horizons for him. For the first time he learned to see Hinduism in the context of other religions, especially Christianity and Islam, and to affirm its radical superiority. Previously he had thought about Hinduism purely within a Hindu context, and in his contact with representatives of other religions the wider comparative question had not come up: only particular

items of belief or practice had been discussed. There is no doubt that this idea of the superiority of Hinduism originated with the Adi Brahmos and particularly with Rajnarayan Bose. Calcutta also opened the Swami's eyes to the various crucial problems of women: widowhood, early marriage, and lack of education, which were all foremost in the minds of Calcutta reformers. There is no evidence that these problems had exercised Dayananda's mind in the previous period.[86] Moreover, his many meetings with educationists broadened his perception of the education problem; whereas before his interest in education had been limited to the teaching of Sanskrit, now universal education as a powerful agency for the reform of the whole society became an integral part of his programme. In the same way, his hitherto limited concern with the functions and responsibilities of the state widened out into a comprehensive view of statecraft.

Even before he came to Calcutta, Dayananda had initiated a small abortive experiment in establishing a Sabhā at Arrah. The idea of an organization may have originated partly from his observation of the organizing skill of the Christian missionaries. But it was his close experience of the life of the community of the Sādhs in Farrukhabad that planted the idea firmly in his mind. In Calcutta he saw from close up the impressive organization of Keshub's Samaj, its wide appeal across caste barriers, and its penetration of society through its reforming agencies. But he also noticed the negative side: the friction between Keshub's Samaj and the Adi Brahmos, and the growing dissension within Keshub's own organization. In his *Satyārth Prakāsh*, written a year later, the Swami commented that in the span of a few years the Brahmo Samaj had been split into three opposing sections, and that the Samaj was following the old path of the other Hindu sects leading to error and mutual antagonism.[87] This danger of sectarianism was one that the Swami would constantly fear for his own Samaj, and he would take great care to counter it. Another risk involved in Keshub's radical approach came to Dayananda's notice, especially in his conversations with the Adi Brahmos: the fact that the rapid implementation of radical reform tended to isolate people from orthodoxy, and thus diminish the influence of the reformers on the bulk of Hindus. Dayananda himself had previously exposed some of his followers to such danger and in the coming years he became much more cautious in this matter.

One of the greatest lessons the Swami learnt in Calcutta was no doubt the discovery of two most powerful organs of propaganda: the public lecture and publication. His lectures were advertised in the press, drew large audiences and proved a resounding success. Dayananda must have noticed how Keshub's influence was firmly based on his lectures, and on his publications, many of which grew out of these lectures. In fact there was a proposal that his own lectures be published, but unfortunately this did not happen. In the Doab, the Swami had exposed himself too much to the pull and push of the pandits, and his continuous subjection to the demands of controversy had hampered his thinking. That was partly why, after Banaras, he had given himself more time for study and reflection. The first organized result of these meditations was his lectures in Calcutta, which anticipated some chapters in his first great work. The importance of this discovery to the Swami is evidenced by the dramatic change in his pattern of life in the eighteen months between his departure from Calcutta and his arrival at Bombay, as will be described at the end of this chapter.

The discovery of the lecture-method and of publication also involved another discovery, that of a new type of audience. In the Doab the Swami had concentrated on the traditional Hindu élite of brahmins, kshatriyas, and pandits, in a rural setting. The results had been disappointing, except perhaps in the only sizeable city he frequented, Farrukhabad. Calcutta gave him a different audience: the educated, and mostly western-influenced urban middle class. Among them there was a receptiveness to ideas of social and religious reform that was largely absent from his previous public, which was strongly dominated by the many traditional bonds and taboos of caste and religion. In the eighteen months following his visit to Calcutta, only two of the places he visited were small, Kasganj and Chalesar, little towns of about 15,000 inha)itants. In both cases, Dayananda had a special reason for his visit: to inspect the schools he had founded there. All the other places visited were large towns; whereas previously he had deliberately stayed away from them, they now became the prime focus of his attention.

When Dayananda left Calcutta, never to return, the metropolis soon forgot that extraordinary Swami; he was a passing pheno-menon, and had no lasting impact on the local scene. But Dayananda himself was a profoundly changed man. Once again he had faced a completely new situation, one that would have overpowered many a lesser man. He had coped with it, thought about it, and gone away, still very much the same stubbornly individual thinker. He had been strengthened in conviction in his basic ideas, but enormously enriched by new ideas and approaches. Now he had a much more comprehensive view of man and society, of the meaning of religion, of the aims of reform, and of the historical perspective of the contemporary situation. In the next few years he would incorporate these newly discovered perspectives into his basic vision.

On leaving Calcutta Dayananda made his way back westwards, taking about a year for a journey that would bring him through Bhagalpur, Patna, Chapra, Arrah, Dumraon, Mirzapur, Allahabad, Kanpur, Lucknow, Farrukhabad, Kasganj, Chalesar, Aligarh, and Hathras, and finally back to Mathura where he had sat at the blind *guru*'s feet. He totally ignored those rural places in the Doab where he had first preached. He only visited Farrukhabad, Kasganj and Chalesar because his schools needed inspecting. He stayed only two weeks at Farrukhabad and one week each at the other two places, whereas his stay at each of the other cities varied between one and three months. This was quite a radical break with his former pattern of travel.

His whole style of life had also undergone significant changes. From the Calcutta journey onwards he always had a servant with him, and now he travelled with some three pieces of luggage containing books and clothes.[88] When people who remembered him as the naked *sannyāsī* without any possessions remarked on this, he explained that what he kept with him was needed for his work of reading, studying, preaching, and writing, and that 'these things are not against *dharma*'.[89] In the towns where he had schools he used to stay in the schools, but elsewhere he depended on the hospitality of his admirers. It is striking that, in seven out of the remaining ten cities, he was the guest of the local raja. He had become a very important public figure, and the nobles considered it an honour to be his hosts. He entered Aligarh seated on an elephant, escorted by some twenty kshatriyas on horseback.[90] The princes often provided his transport to the next town, and arranged his accommodation there in advance. During this period he started to write many letters, and his correspondence steadily grew in volume from then on. At Aligarh he is said to have had two people writing letters for him in Hindī and in Urdū.[91] Practically none of these early letters have been preserved, but those from 1875 onwards have been collected and published in great numbers. Dayananda no longer drifted from one place to another as he used to do. His movements were deliberate and planned, his accommodation arranged for, his arrival announced. More often than not the time and place of lectures and discussions were made public by notices in the local newspapers. These notices included an open invitation to anybody to come and discuss religious matters with the Swami at his place of residence, and sometimes, if the local conditions called for it, they also contained an open challenge to hold a *shāstrārth*. This challenge, however, was only rarely taken up, and the two public debates recorded, one at Chapra and one at Lucknow, both ended in uproar and confusion among the opponents.[92]

The public lecture had now become his major means of propaganda. At most places he gave several; the number mentioned for Kanpur is fifteen, and for Vrindavan ten.[93] The discourses were mostly held in the most important hall in the locality, and were often attended not only by Hindus, but also by Muslims and Christians, and by the local British officials. The topics of the lectures are not often stated, but it is striking that among those mentioned only a couple were concerned with the denunciation of Hindu practices. Most of them dealt with subjects like creation, the nature of God, *Veda* and revelation, Āryāvarta in Vedic times, the past and present conditions of Āryāvarta. It was in Aligarh in the beginning of 1874 that Raja Jaikishendas, who faithfully attended all the Swami's lectures, pressed Dayananda to have them published in book form, and he promised that he himself would bear all the costs of publication.[94]

A few occurrences during this year are noteworthy, as they illustrate the widening of Dayananda's contacts. At Arrah he had several discussions with a Jain monk, probably in an effort to elicit more information about that religion, which remained so secretive about its holy books. During his stay at Farrukhabad he had a meeting with Mr Kempson, the Director of Public Instruction, and with Mr Muir, the Lieutenant-General of the North-Western Provinces. He asked the latter if he would use his influence to promote the ban on cow-slaughter when he became a member of the India Council in London. He also had conversations with the Muslim reform leader Syed Ahmad Khan. In Aligarh he tried to explain to the Syed his theories on the usefulness of the *havan* sacrifice, and later at Banaras he gave a lecture at his bungalow.[95] Dayananda continued to attract the hostility of the pandits. Both at Kanpur and at Farrukhabad he was again accused of being in the pay of the Christians.[96] His two *shāstrārths* were deliberately disrupted by the pandits, and at Vrindavan, where he had specifically challenged the famous Rangacharya to a public disputation, which the pandit avoided by being conveniently unwell, verses in Sanskrit and Hindī mocking Dayananda were posted.[97] These acts of hostility were of minor importance, however, compared with the general acceptance and admiration the Swami experienced on his travels.

In May 1874 Dayananda returned east to Banaras and Allahabad, where he spent the following five months. Two important issues drew him back to Banaras. First, he had to take care of his Vedic school. He found the arrangements unsatisfactory, shifted the school to new premises, and appointed new pandits. He published an announcement in the press, including the full curriculum, which is not without interest. The first stage of study covers the six schools of philosophy, ten *Upanishads*, the *Manu-Smriti*, and the *Grihyasūtras*. The next stage comprehends the four *Vedas*, the four *Vedāngas*, the four *Upavedas*, and books on astronomy. There was also to be instruction in grammar, and in all the adjunct linguistic and literary sciences. Students were invited from the four *varnas* or classes, but it was explicitly stated that shūdras would be excluded from the study of the *Vedas* proper. Moreover, an Āryasabhā was founded to run the school, and it was planned to publish a monthly magazine called *Ārya-Prakāsh*. Obviously Dayananda had given careful thought to this project, and tried to organize it well so as to avoid the failure which befell his other schools. However, like all his other school ventures, this failed, even more rapidly: by February 1875 the school was dissolved.[98]

It must have been a great disappointment to the Swami to fail once again in this citadel of orthodoxy, where he had previously been so unjustly humiliated at the time of the great public debate. However, the complete success in the second purpose of his visit to Banaras was a great consolation. Only three months earlier, at Aligarh, he had had long conversation with Raja Jaikishendas about the publication of his lectures in book form. The idea had immediately appealed to the Swami. The great impact of the publications of Keshub, Devendranath, Vidyasagar, and others on the urban intelligentsia had completely convinced him that his own message had to get into print if it was to exert any significant influence. So, when the Swami and the Raja met again in Banaras, it did not take them long to reach complete agreement, and immediate arrangements were made for the writing, printing, and speedy publication of the Swami's lectures.

A Maharashtrian pandit, Chandrashekar, was appointed as translator, and the work started on 12 June 1874.[99] It was a major task: the volume published runs into as many as 407 closely printed pages, which did not even include the final two long chapters. Lekhram notes that during his stay of over three months at Allahabad the Swami continued writing his book.[100] It is notable that the biographers mention no public disputes or lectures for this period; writing took practically all the Swami's time. The task was a difficult one because of linguistic problems. Dayananda had ventured on his first lecture in Hindī only one month earlier at Banaras, and at that time Sanskrit still played havoc with his Hindī. He probably dictated his material in Sanskrit to the pandits who then translated it into Hindī. It also seems clear that the Swami did not correct the proofs, as indeed Raja Jaikishendas himself attested.[101] This made it possible for the pandits to slip into the book certain statements Dayananda would not have approved of.

The volume was published in 1875 at the Star Press in Banaras. Not the whole manuscript was printed, however. There were only twelve chapters in the book; chapters thirteen, on the Muslim faith, and fourteen, on Christianity, were not included. It has now been firmly established that Dayananda did in fact write these chapters; they are included in the original manuscript which is held by the descendants of Raja Jaikishendas, and of which the Paropkarinī Sabhā of Ajmer has a photocopy.[102] It appears that they were excluded not for any sinister reason, but simply because their inclusion would have caused a considerable delay in publication. This transpires from a letter sent by Dayananda from Ahmedabad to the Star Press on 23 January 1875. In this letter he urged the Press to get hold of the chapter on Islam which had gone to Moradabad for checking, and to finish printing the whole work within two months, as many people were clamouring for the book.[103]

Thus Dayananda finished writing his *magnum opus* in a relatively short time. But although the actual period of composition was small, one should remember that the book was essentially a reproduction of the Swami's lectures. He had been giving scores of these since leaving Calcutta, and it is in those lectures that his ideas took shape and gradually clarified themselves. It was those lectures Dayananda wrote down for the pundits to translate. He was indeed a novice in the field of publication, and this method was the cause of many imperfections in the book, as the next chapter will show. However, the Swami was now on his way as a publicist of the pen, and he would never look back, constantly improving his methods of composition and publication.

CHAPTER V
The First *Satyārth Prakāsh*

The *Satyārth Prakāsh* of 1875 was the first complete statement by Dayananda of his opinions on a wide range of subjects, and as such it requires extensive treatment. It is especially important because the comparison between this work and its revised edition of 1883 is the one major means of establishing the development of Dayananda's ideas during the last eight years of his life.[1] Moreover, when compared with the ideas of the Swami before his visit to Calcutta, it puts in clear evidence the great impact that city had on his development.

Certain controversies arose about the original *Satyārth Prakāsh,* after the publication of the second edition. Some adversaries of the Arya Samaj contended that the first edition contained the real teachings of the Swami whereas the second edition was written by his followers after his death.[2] This accusation is completely unfounded. Many letters show that Dayananda received proofs from the press, corrected them and sent them back, and that the proofs of the whole book were read by him before his death.[3] Others have tried to discredit the works and the Swami by showing contradictions between the two editions. No doubt there are differences, but they can be explained. First of all, Dayananda may have genuinely changed his mind on particular issues, and it will be shown that in fact he did so. Secondly, since he did not read the proofs of the first edition, some changes or interpolations may have been made by the pandits who prepared the work for publication. This latter argument is adopted by some Arya Samaj writers who are loath to accept a radical change of mind of their Swami, particularly in sensitive matters like meat-eating.

Two criteria prove conclusively that the first edition as a whole is to be accepted as the genuine expression of Dayananda's mind. The first criterion is the expressed judgment of the Swami himself. He did acknowledge that there had been some misrepresentation. When his attention was drawn to the fact that there was a discrepancy between the *Shrāddh* for the living he was preaching and the *Shrāddh* for the dead described in his work, he published in 1878 a notice in the first and second fascicules of his *Vedabhāshya*. First he stated the general principle that the verses quoted were not in themselves authoritative, but only in so far as they conformed with the *Vedas*. Specifically about the service for dead ancestors, he added that 'what has been printed in this matter has been printed by a mistake of the writers or the correctors.'4 Apart from this mistake, there is only one other minor point he ever withdrew, again in a notice in his *Vedabhāshya*: 'Let it be known that on page 107 of the *Satyārth Prakāsh*, line 14, instead of Rohinī was the wife of Baladeva, one should read that Rohinī was the mother of Baladeva and the wife of Vasudeva.'5 Dayananda thus had an easy method of correcting statements of his first edition, and yet these are the only two corrections he ever made. Moreover, it is quite clear from his letters that throughout these years he kept selling his first edition: he was still doing so in 1882, one year before his death when he was writing the second edition.6 No clearer proof can be given of the fact that the Swami himself accepted the work as his own and that the reservations he had were minor ones. When he changed his mind on certain matters he did so openly, though he did not necessarily repudiate his former position. The whole development of Dayananda shows he was not afraid of changing his ideas and of acknowledging this change when confronted with it: he never considered himself at any stage infallible.

When the two editions are juxtaposed it becomes clear that Dayananda wrote his second edition with the first one in front of him. Whole chapters run practically parallel, with minor additions or deletions. Other chapters have been drastically rearranged, but even there the change is more one of sequence than of substance. The use of quotations has changed considerably. In general, the second edition has many more quotations from the *Vedas* and from the philosophical treatises, and the awkward Hindī of the first edition has been polished up. One can say that as far as the substance of the original is concerned, ninety per cent of it is closely, if not textually, reproduced in the revised edition. The Swami himself wrote in his preface to the second edition as follows:

When I wrote this book I did not have a good knowledge of Hindī, because at that time and before, all my lectures, reading, and teaching were in

Sanskrit, and Gujarātī was my mother-tongue. As a consequence the language was impure. I have now gained practice in speaking and writing Hindī. That is why I edit it a second time after correcting the book according to Hindī grammar. Here and there occurs a difference in words, sentences and arrangement, as it seemed proper, for it was difficult to improve the flow of the language without these alterations. But there has been no change in the meaning. However, some special topics have been added. The errors that had remained in the first edition have been set right by removing or correcting them.[7]

Thus it is conclusively proved that Dayananda always acknowledged the first *Satyārth Prakāsh* as his very own.

A second criterion for its authenticity is the internal evidence. Two considerations count here. Firstly, the work has considerable internal consistency, a quality Dayananda always strove for. This is particularly evident in the related tenets of his doctrines about God in relation with the cosmos and the souls, and about the *Veda*. References to these recur constantly throughout the work, and they remain mutually consistent, as will become clear later. Secondly, the ideas expressed are in harmony with those expressed at the same period in independent sources. In the year 1875 Dayananda also published two pamphlets, one against the Neo-Vedāntins, the other against the Vallabhāchāryas.[8] He deals with both these adversaries repeatedly in his *Satyārth Prakāsh*, touching on a wide variety of doctrinal matters, but no contradiction can be found between the two sources.[9] Therefore, both the statements of the Swami and the internal evidence confirm that the first *Satyārth Prakāsh*, except for a couple of minor passages, was indeed his own work, accepted by him and faithfully expressing his ideas at that time.

As for its presentation, this work is of very poor quality and difficult to read. There is no paragraphing: the only division of the text are the chapters. In fact, after about 150 pages, because of the tremendous pressure put upon the press to expedite the work, it gets worse: even the words run together, so that often three or four words and whole lines are printed without any hiatus at all. The only breaks in the text are the strokes indicating quotations, and the pages present themselves as an unbroken succession of tightly printed characters. The style is very oral and didactic, with the unfinished and unpolished character of a narrative or exposé given by someone who is wholly concerned with content and totally oblivious of 'flow, balance, or elegance of expression. The Hindī is rather peculiar: it is very Sanskritic, using only rarely Urdū or Persian words, and often using the gender of the orginal Sanskrit word and not the gender established in Hindī. It also indulges in quite a number of quaint archaisms. Dayananda's difficulties were enormous: he was a born Gujarati whose knowledge of Hindī was still very shaky, trying to write with the help of a Maratha pandit a large volume in a language the prose style of which was still in the stage of formation. Considering these difficulties, the work, with all its imperfections, was a remarkable achievement.

The volume gives a clear idea of the state of Dayananda's knowledge and use of the sources of Hinduism at this time. Although his study of the *Vedas* proper had advanced considerably, the whole book contains only about twenty Vedic references, a small number indeed for one who based his whole system on them. The second edition, composed after long and arduous work at his *Vedabhāshya*, would contain as many Vedic quotations in one single chapter.[10] The first edition contains many more texts from the *Upanishads*, more than forty: this is one indication of the persistent advaitic influence on his thought. The great bulk of quotations, concentrated in chapters three to six dealing with society and the state, come from the *Manusmriti*, —nearly four hundred. The Swami had become quite a master of this favourite text, and he justified his nearly exclusive reliance on Manu.[11] His knowledge of the philosophical schools had increased: in the list of acceptable books he mentions not only the *Sūtras* of the six schools but also the acceptable commentaries.[12] But whereas his quotations from the *Nyāyasūtras* number about forty,[13] those of the other *sūtras* do not even reach twenty altogether.

The list of acceptable and unacceptable books, the first since the Kanpur declaration, remains very much the same.[14] But the criteria for recognizing the authentic books are more clearly developed. Dayananda still accepted the external criteria of the first words: what begins with *Atha* is secondary, what begins with *OM*, is authentic, a criterion he had learned from Swami Virjananda. But he stressed the internal criteria that infallibly indicate that a particular work is not authentic: physical impossibility which discredits all miracles, internal contradictions that offend logic, and infringement of moral principles.[15] Dayananda also gave some historical perspective to the emergence of the

false books. The social and political disruption brought on by
the *Mahābhārata* war caused the corruption of the brahmins,
who started to claim divinity and various privileges, fabricated
many superstitions, and 'started to write books under the names
of the great *rishis*'.[16] King Bhoja, propagator of the study of
Sanskrit, testified that the brahmins interpolated thousands of
verses in the *Mahābhārata* and wrote under false names.[17] In
the section on statecraft, the king is urged to punish those who
read, teach, or write false books, even with the death penalty,
and he is told that the propagation of the good books is a function
of the state.[18] Here we can again detect the persistent influence
of Swami Virjananda.

In Dayananda's discussion of the *Vedas*, occupying half of
his seventh chapter, many issues have become clearer. Three
arguments are used to prove the Vedic revelation. First it is stated
that revelation is logically necessary because of God's infinite
mercy: how could God, like a jealous pandit, have denied knowledge, the most precious treasure, to man, unable to discover it
by himself![19] The very content of the *Vedas* also proves their
divine origin: they possess four qualities totally beyond the powers
of any human author. They are absolutely free from any bias,
they treat adequately *all* branches of knowledge, they are devoid
of anything that may offend morality, and their arrangement of
words, meanings, and construction is so tight and perfect that
they can yield the totality of knowledge. The third proof is a
purely logical one: if there were no single book that has its full
logical justification within itself (*svatah-pramāna*), then it would
be impossible to decide the truth or untruth of all other books,
because they disprove one another, and doubt could not be overcome. The *Veda*, being the wisdom of God, is *svatah-pramāna*,
and therefore the touchstone of all truth.[20]

The method of revelation was by direct communication from
God to the *rishis* Agni, Vāyu, and Āditya who were created at
the beginning of the world. God, present in their mind, taught
them the *mantras* and their meaning, and they heard them 'like
a voice from the sky': that is why the *Vedas* are called *shruti*, 'what
was heard'. These three *rishis* passed it on to others, and through
them it came to the people. Dayananda then introduced a distinction in the use of the word *Veda*, which would prove very
handy in disputations. The *Veda*, as the wisdom of God, is eternal

just as he is. But the *Vedas* as the books or as the recitation of
the *mantras*, are created and not eternal: their existence is co-
extensive with the cosmos, and comes to an end with it.[21]

In justifying the fact that the *Vedas* were revealed in Sanskrit,
Dayananda was concerned to safeguard their universality. If they
had been couched in the language of a particular country, they
would not have been universal; and if they had been revealed in
all languages, the number would have been unlimited. Sanskrit,
therefore, was not the language of a particular country, it was
nobody's mother tongue, and all had to learn it. Dayananda
then went on, without perhaps noticing an inherent inconsistency,
to affirm that Sanskrit was the mother of all languages. It has
certain unique peculiarities: many words express one meaning,
many meanings are attached to one word, creating endless possibilities of derivation. That quality combined with the gradual
diversification of pronunciation gave rise to the birth of the
vernaculars.[22]

Whereas the Bible or the Koran are exclusive scriptures, the
Vedas, said Dayananda, are universal and meant for all mankind.
This does not mean that everyone can study the *Vedas*: the shūdras
who in a properly structured society are those lacking the necessary
intelligence, are excluded.[23] To the objection that God would
have shown his abundance of mercy if he had given the knowledge
of the *Vedas* to all without the need of laborious study, Dayananda
characteristically answered as follows: such a course would have
taken away from man his freedom and also the great contentment
that comes from effort.[24] This answer illustrates two basic
principles of morality that were becoming more and more the
pillars of his ethics: knowledge is the key to right action, and
action constitutes the very nobility of free man.

Thus Dayananda's doctrine of revelation had now reached its
full maturity, although his study of the *Vedas* had still a long
way to go. This study would not substantially change any tenet
of the theory: in fact his *Bhāshya* would be completely based on
that theory from which he never wavered an inch.

Right at the beginning of the work Dayananda gave a description
of the hundred names of God. On account of the inexhaustible
richness of his nature, God is called by a multitude of names.
This is an important assumption that would constantly guide
his interpretation of the *Vedas*. In his mind it was the logical

consequence of his fundamental assumption that the *Vedas* are monotheistic: all *mantras* that somehow refer to the divine speak of necessity of that one true God. This principle invalidates any accusation of polytheism in the *Vedas* and makes all its *mantras* susceptible to a monotheistic interpretation. The list comprises most of the Vedic deities from Agni to Kubera, from Hiranyagarbha to˙ *brahman*, about thirty proper names. Other terms indicate faculties and qualities like intelligence or power, and some indicate elements or even the senses. It is a strange conglomeration, which the Swami tried to rationalize a little in his second edition.

The seventh chapter starts with a discussion of the proof of the existence of God. The objector asserts that the world is self-subsistent, the result of the spontaneous admixture of elements,[25] that God's existence cannot be proved by either inference or intuition and that therefore the proof from testimony (*shabda*, scripture) is also impossible. Dayananda then proceeds to give three proofs. His inferential proof is the classic one of the order of the cosmos that postulates a maker; the intuitive proof lies in the fact that we can perceive God's power, mercy, and justice in this world, and that those who have deep knowledge can achieve the direct vision of God; as scriptural proof there are fifteen texts, of which fourteen are from the *Upanishads*, and only one from the *Yajurveda*.[26] The problem of the existence of God was taken up again in detail• in the final chapter on Jainism.[27] There Dayananda used the *Nyāyasūtras* to refute eight different types of atheism. In fact this section is a paraphrase of select stanzas of Gautama's *sūtras* couched in the specialized abstruse language of the logician.[28]

The nature of God-in-himself, making abstraction from his relationship to man and cosmos, was never of great interest to Dayananda and that aspect of his theology was never much emphasized. He had dispensed with the whole mythological superstructure of Hinduism, and what remained was simple and basic. The fundamental idea was still that of the Upanishadic *sac-cid-ānanda*: God is *sat-swarūp*, *jñāna-swarūp*, and *ānanda-swarūp*, meaning that it is his very nature to be the fullness of being, intelligence, and bliss.[29] God is formless, *nirākār*, which means that he has no body nor could ever be embodied, because this would invalidate his qualities of omnipotence, omniscience, and eternality.[30] For dealing with the awkward concepts *saguna* and *nirguna* Dayananda now used a simple, if not simplistic formula, probably inspired by Debendranath's *Brahmo Dharma*. Both terms apply to the Lord, but with a different connotation: the Lord is *nirguna* because he has none of those imperfect qualities of creatures like destructibility, grossness, etc.; but he is *saguna* because he possesses all those divine qualities like omniscience, etc.[31] Apart from being infinite in wisdom, power, and duration,[32] God is also the holy one, free from all corruption.[33] It is important to note that to Dayananda the activist, activity is an essential quality of God, whose nature contains all powers in potentially unlimited measure.[34]

The theory of God's relation to the cosmos had now taken a firm shape, but a shape soon to be drastically changed: in fact many of these tenets were later to be rejected as errors of the Neo-Vedāntins, which shows the persistent influence of *advaita* on his thought. The central conception around which most of his speculation revolved, and on which it often depended, was that of cosmic cycles. Dayananda accepted the classical Hindu concept of the periodic re-creation and re-absorption of the universe: these he called *anādi srishti*, non-original creation, and *mahāpraloya*, the great absorption. They occur rhythmically when the universe relapses into and re-emerges from the subtle state of matter called *prakriti*. However, and here we have a remarkable doctrine without parallel in the history of Hinduism, this ryhthm is not an eternal one: there was at the beginning of the series an *ādisrishti*, an original creation, and there will come an end to the series in the final re-absorption, *atyant pralaya*.[35] There is no doubt that this was the firm conviction of the Swami: the same idea was repeated in different ways at different times: 'there was a time when the cosmos did not exist at all'; 'even *prakriti*, the subtlest form of the cosmos will be dissolved, and only the Lord will remain'; 'the world, in effect, will be destroyed in its cause, God'.[36] But an even stronger argument for the definiteness of this doctrine is its logical connection with many other tenets, as will become clear.

Since God created the universe 'in the beginning', when nothing existed but he, the material cause of the universe was no other than God's natural potentiality (*sāmarthya*),[37] and that is the cause into which, at the end of time, all that exists will relapse.[38]

Thus God is a real maker, a creator of new beings: 'Brahmā and the *devas* and men are mere *shilpīs* (artisans working on independent pre-existing materials). It is not in the power of anybody to make a new thing. Except for the Lord, there is no real "maker" in this world.'[39] Every one of these propositions was later rejected by Dayananda. Making God into the material cause of the universe obviously had its logical difficulties, and Dayananda tried hard to justify his position.

We must think hard so that no imperfection would be attributed to God. God is omnipotent. He who is omnipotent possesses infinite potential and material. This material is natural to him, just like a natural quality has connection with its possessor; it is not a different thing yet it is not the same. . . .

That potential is extremely subtle and because it is natural, it is not opposed to the Lord, but it exists within him. From it the Lord created the whole cosmos. It follows that the Lord, because he used no distinct thing, has become, by making the world, the material cause of that world, because there exists no other material distinct from him which he could have used to make the world. So he created the world from his natural potential which has the form of a quality. Therefore the Lord himself is the material cause of the universe, but he did not himself take the form of the world.[40]

This last sentence echoes statements of Debendranath's *Brahmo Dharma*.[41] Dayananda's argument is basically the old argument of *bheda-abheda*, the simultaneous distinction and non-distinction of the quality *vis-à-vis* its possessor; the quality here being the Lord's *sāmarthya*. The quality is in a way identical with its possessor, therefore the Lord is the material cause of the universe; but the quality is also distinct from its possessor, and therefore it cannot be said that the Lord changed into the universe.

The process of evolution starts from the subtlest *prakriti*. Its first evolute is *ākāsha*, from which by progressive admixture all the elements and atoms emerge, and thus the whole complex cosmos. The process of dissolution follows the reverse order from the gross through *ākāsha* to the subtle *prakriti*. In this description Dayananda made use of the Vaisheshika atomic theory within his own context of the creation process. He tried to use this atomic theory to explain certain natural phenomena like lightness, heaviness, porousness, etc.: these, he said, depend on the different density of the 'packing' of the atoms. Storm, rain, and lightning are explained rather naively, and the Swami remarks how this kind of scientific knowledge led to the discovery of railways, electricity, telegraphy, etc.[42]

In answer to the question whether our world is unique,

Dayananda affirmed that God has made innumerable worlds, all inhabited by human and other beings, because God does not create anything useless. Among these worlds some abound in happiness and have but little sorrow: they are called the heavens. Those abounding in sorrow are called hells, and those where happiness and sorrow are approximately balanced, are human worlds. But all these worlds are equally governed by the law of *karma*: beings move about in these worlds from life to life, and their peregrinations are determined by the balance sheet of their deeds.[43]

Dayananda refuted the materialists, who held that the spirit emerges from the admixture of the elements, by pointing to those special qualities, desire and will, happiness and sorrow, and particularly knowledge, that differentiate the soul from material things.[44] The *jīva*, in short, is *cetan-svarūp*, and consciousness is its natural form.[45] It is connected with the gross body through the subtle body, the *linga-sharīr*, which consists of the senses and the inner organ that is the seat of intelligence and will. In this inner organ it is the *jīva* who presides, acts, and enjoys.[46] And the Lord, subtler than even the subtlest matter, pervades all these.[47] The sun of his knowledge shines on that pure surface of the subtle body, which reflects what happens in the body and outside: it is in this mirror that the *jīva* sees and knows.[48]

Dayananda insisted that the *jīva* is an active entity and a free agent, fully responsible for his deeds.[49] If God caused man's action, or if he gave him perfect knowledge, that would entail compulsion and would take away man's precious freedom, and destroy that blessed effort without which happiness is impossible. Man's freedom is the greatest gift of God's mercy.[50] When asked, 'why does the *jīva* not perform these deeds that lead to happiness?', the Swami replied, 'Nothing is known properly without the virtue of wisdom, and wisdom is impossible without effort'.[51]

Nyāya is used to proffer proofs of rebirth: the instinctive behaviour of new-born babies presupposes former experience, and the unequal distribution of happiness and sorrow requires a moral ground. Dayananda spurned the objection that sorrow and pleasure are relative and shared differently but comparably by the pauper and the king by graphically describing the luxurious life of the king, contrasting it with the hell of frustration and hunger that awaits the child born of the poor.[52] The mechanism of rebirth consists in the conjunction of the subtle body with a particular embryonic new gross body in the womb.[53] The particular embryo is determined by the *karma* of the previous life that adheres to the subtle body: according to that *karma*, the soul will enter an animal, a human, or a divine body in the appropriate world.[54] The difference between these bodies is due to a different combination of the three basic constituents of nature, the *gunas sattva, rajas*, and *tamas*: in a way they represent the ontological counterparts of *karma*.[55]

The internal logic of his theory of cosmic cycles with their absolute beginning and end forced Dayananda to accept also an absolute beginning and end of the *jīva*. This was an extraordinary doctrine in the Hindu context and he shrank from stating it too bluntly, but it is obvious from various statements that it was his firm conviction. 'The *jīvas* were *created* by the Lord',[56] and at the time of the first creation there existed not one single man.[57] The very process of rebirth had a beginning,[58] 'the very first creation of men happened in the Himalayas'[59], and 'the creation of *jīvas* by the Lord was of all simultaneous'.[60] In fact, to avoid any injustice in God, Dayananda claims that these first beings, not born from the womb, were all created completely equal: they were all in the bloom of youth, innocent of good and evil, and there was no distinction between man and animal. It was only afterwards that *maithunasrishti*, origination by sexual reproduction, started to occur.[61] No specific statement says from what the *jīva* was created. The body and the inner organ derive from *prakriti*, but for the *jīva* itself the question remains unanswered: the presumption is that the *jīva* too in some way originated from the Lord's potential.

The *jīva* that had a beginning must similarly have an end: in the final dissolution when even *prakriti* disappears, the *jīva* too will find his end: 'when *atyant pralaya* occurs, nobody will remain'.[62] Dayananda seemed reluctant and unhappy about this conclusion, and added a word of consolation, 'it will only happen when all *jīvas* have been liberated, and therefore it is a very long time ahead'.[63]

Apart from that limit in time, the *moksha* described by Dayananda is complete and irreversible: 'It is the complete cessation of all sorrow', '*avidyā*, the root of death, is destroyed', and '*karma* is shed with its very root'.[64] Thus the very root the

very possibility of sorrow and rebirth, is irreversibly destroyed.
Moksha is naturally not complete absorption into God, a theory
Dayananda had long since rejected,[65] but rather a union with
God that produces full bliss.[66] Since there can be no enjoyment
without body,[67] the *jīva* keeps its subtle body in *moksha*. In fact,
'without the body the *jīva* itself does not last'.[68] All this fits in
perfectly with the internal logic of the theory of *atyant pralaya*:
there *prakriti* itself is dissolved, and its dissolution must necessarily entail the dissolution of all subtle bodies, and therefore
the end of *moksha* itself.

Thus Dayananda's theory of the soul had at this time strong
characteristics. He stressed to the utmost the freedom and activity
of man, a conviction that would gather even greater strength.
On the other hand, his whole concept of *moksha* would undergo
a profound transformation as he revised his theory of cosmic
cycles in the coming years.

The Swami devoted about one fourth of his work to a critique
of Hinduism, dealing with idol worship, miracles, pilgrimages and
holy men, sects, *Purānas*, modern reform movements, etc. This
savage indictment is full of concrete details of persons, places,
and practices, drawing on a wide variety of sources from *Shāstras*
to folklore. His knowledge of Hinduism had widened enormously
since the *guru* of Mathura diverted his attention from his own
inner development to the sorry state of his fellow-men around
him.

The historical survey that opens the treatment shows that his
knowledge had also gained in depth: he looked for an overall
historical explanation of contemporary conditions, and their
relationship with the Golden Age. It starts out with a panegyric
of that Golden Age in Āryāvarta, the ancient land overflowing
with milk and honey, where the seasons were sweetest, where
gold and gems lay for the picking, where even the poor grew rich,
the land of the *Āryas*, the best of people. There the first men
were born, Sanskrit the mother of all tongues was spoken, and
not only theoretical wisdom flourished but also the practical,
industrial sciences: vehicles were propelled mechanically by the
combination of fire, water, wind, etc. From there wisdom and
science spread over the earth, first to East Asia, then to Greece
and Rome, and thence to England.[69]

When the great war of the sons of Bharat wiped out all good

kings and brahmins, the disintegration started from the very core of society, the brahmins. By neglect of the *Vedas* they lost that key to everything, knowledge. They divinized themselves and ensnared the people in their new-woven nets of superstition. The Jains, who at that time inhabited China and its borderlands,[70] saw their opportunity, entered under the pretext of trade, and established their reign that from Bodh Gaya spread all over the country. By reviling Sanskrit wisdom and propagating their own books they made many converts, and built temples wherein they erected statues of their saints: thus it was that idol worship had its origin in India.[71]

The great teacher Shankarāchārya tried to counteract the disintegration of Hinduism. He studied Sanskrit and the *Vedas* and toured the country defeating the Jains in public disputations and re-converting kings. Thus he effectively started a renaissance, but his premature death at the age of thirty-two brought the collapse of the movement. King Vikramāditya of Ujjain, a couple of centuries later, and King Bhoja of Kanauj half a millennium later, also made serious attempts at reform, but with little success. The brahmins, out of greed, started to build temples, filling them with idols to compete with the Jains. Then the plundering devastation of the Muslim raids brought the country to the nadir of poverty, shame, and social disruption. Finally the Muslims came to stay and established their reign over India. In Akbar they produced one reasonably good emperor, but Aurangzeb undid his achievements by persecuting the Hindus, destroying their temples, and replacing them with mosques. Then the British Raj appeared on the scene. It created the possibility for India to reform itself: there is peace in the land, books are no more destroyed but preserved, and 'it becomes possible to publish books and sell them for five rupees, where previously they could only be had for a hundred'.[72]

Dayananda criticizes at length the corrupt teachings of the *Purānas*, reserving his longest blast for the *Bhāgavata*. He recalled their stories abounding in internal contradictions, logical and physical impossibilities, moral degradation.[73] The section on the sects gives the lion's share to the Vallabhāchāryas, whose leaders are steeped in pleasure, sex, and untold luxury. The many other Vaishnavite and Shaivite sects are also treated, the mediaeval *gurus* like Nānak, Kabīr, and Dādū are accused of bibliolatry, and the sexual perversions of the Tāntrikas are exposed in detail. Among so many false prophets, who claimed to be divine, fabricated new *mantras*, and fought each other with the weapons of spurious texts, Shankara stood out as a non-sectarian reformer. Dayananda accused his own order of the Dashanāmīs of having splintered and wasted his efforts at reform.[74]

Idol worship naturally gets a substantial treatment.[75] It is again proved to be absent in the *Vedas*,[76] and the contention that it was contained in the lost books of the *Vedas* is untrue because they never existed.[77] It is also against reason: the idea that the rite of *prānpratishthā* gives life to inert matter is pure absurdity.[78] To prove idol worship from tradition (*paramparā*) is also worthless, because traditions are being established all the time: true tradition is determined by logic and by conformity with the *Vedas*.[79]

The section on miracles and pilgrimages[80] reads like a pamphlet exploding the myth of the wonders of India. We hear of meat-eating idols, a *linga* that grows when sprinkled with Ganga water, monkeys of enormous size, an idol that smokes the hookah, another that drinks wine, a pond that spouts fire, a temple without flies, etc. etc. Simple logic dissolves all miracles: some are just tricks manufactured by priests, others are simply physically impossible, some are mere physical phenomena. Dayananda denounced repeatedly the deceit of astrology, another trap set to extort money,[81] but he recommended the study of astronomy, and he still prescribed the *Bhrigusamhitā* which he was to denounce later.[82]

This lengthy criticism of Hinduism is summarized in a couple of bitter pages: 'Āryāvarta is full of darkness.' They are full of a harsh condemnation of the gross greed and luxury of the exploiting priests, but also replete with pity for the poor people who cannot afford to fill their bellies, and yet give their last penny to those unscrupulous shopkeepers, who sell wares worth nothing for profits of a thousand per cent.[83] They are 'secret thieves' who should be punished by the king.[84] All in all, Dayananda's exposure of Hinduism is a savage one, and throughout he used two basic criteria for rejection: one is the sword of logic, the other is the touchstone of morality.

Dayananda devoted the last pages of this chapter to the Brahmo Samaj. Apart from the single last line, 'other things of theirs like adoring the one Lord, are good', it is a list of criticisms. Their

belief in a continuous new creation of *jīvas*, their rejection of
rebirth, and their tenet that repentance deletes sin, are denounced
as errors. They reject the *varna*-system because they confuse *varna*
with caste, and they go wrong in denying the symbolic value of
the sacred thread. Dayananda remarked that the Brahmo Samaj
was breaking up into separate sections, and concluded that they
were going the way of the sects, leading to error and hostility.
Finally he made two interesting criticisms. The Brahmos have
an excessive love of English: they only read English books and
neglect their own, especially the *Vedas*. They also declare their
great admiration for Jesus, Moses, Muhammad, Nānak, Chaitanya,
etc., as holy men, but they forget the ancient *rishis* of India. This
is a very interesting criticism, most applicable to the followers
of Keshub. But the nationalist feeling it expresses is one that
was most strongly advocated to the Swami by his friends of the
Adi Brahmo Samaj.[85]

The last chapter about Jainism, of only about eleven pages,
shows clearly that Dayananda's knowledge of it was limited.[86]
He accused the Jains of hiding their books and their beliefs. He
knew of their extensive literature in Sanskrit and Prākrit, but he
did not quote a single Jain text, probably because he had not yet
seen any.[87] Most of his information seems to be second-hand,
some of it probably acquired in discussions with Jains themselves.
He refers to the Jain cosmology, to their list of twenty-four
tīrthānkaras, to their atheism, and to their belief in the divinization of the *jīva*. Their doctrine of mechanical *karma* is denounced
because without the Lord as the just dispenser of the fruits of
karma, the law cannot function. It is most interesting that the
main attack is on the *ahimsā* doctrine of the Jains. The basic
criticism is that their non-violence is literal and mechanical, and
does not take account of wider standards of morality. They
insist on non-killing, but forget that the hatred and enmity they
exhibit to non-Jains is also a form of violence. They forbid the
digging of tanks lest innumerable small insects be killed but overlook the great benefit a tank will confer on many animals and
men. They vilify sacrifice, but do not realize that 'the benefit
of sacrifice is that in the killing of animals there is a little sorrow,
but in it there is also enormous benefit for all beings'.[88]

We have seen how Dayananda condemned by his savage criticism innumerable ritual and social practices of Hinduism. The vast

complex of temple and idol worship, pilgrimages, festivals, sectarian rites, and the many superstitious practices attached to these
were declared worthless, if not harmful and sinful. The caste
system with its innumerable taboos and privileges and its mal-
practices in domestic and public life was denounced. This clean
sweep would have left most nineteenth century Hindus practically
without religious observances and bereft of social and marital
regulations. In Dayananda's mind they had to be replaced on
the religious side by the authentic Vedic rites, domestic, public,
and sacramental, and by the authentic *varna-dharma* in the social
sphere, and these should be combined with the 'good life' directed
by moral principles.

The domestic rites are the Five Great Sacrifices, which include
the recitation of the *Gāyatrī* and the *Sandhyā* prayers in which
man adores God, and venerates the fathers, his fellow-men
and all creatures. These rites are close to the Vedic model,
with a new explanation of meanings: the *devas*, for example, do
not refer to gods but are names of the one Lord.[89] It has already
been shown that by this time Dayananda certainly recommended
veneration and service of the living in preference to that of the
dead 'fathers'. But it appears that even this work cannot be said
to condemn the latter completely, even if the text was tampered
with.[90] Dayananda committed to paper for the first time his
theory of *agnihotra*, the offering in the fire. He described the
rite in great detail and it is noteworthy that meat is one of the
listed ingredients of the sacrifice. The purpose of this rite is firstly
the adoration of God by the accompanying recitation of *mantras*,
and secondly the well-being of the people, which results from the
purification of the air. The wind carries aloft the sweet-smelling
and purifying particles, thus destroying disease-carrying vapours;
in the upper atmosphere they mix with the clouds and purify the
water that comes down as rain. Here Dayananda's inability to
grasp the symbolical and mythical dimension of religion shows
itself again by reducing a rich rite simply to an occasion of praising
God by *mantras* and purifying the air by burnt oblations.[91]

At this time the Swami did not yet consider domestic sacrifices
an absolutely universal duty. In his fourth chapter on the householder he clearly stated that 'all these rites are for people without
knowledge', 'whose heart and soul are not pure', whereas those
who have acquired wisdom,' need not perform them outwardly'

but inwardly, 'by knowledge only'.[92] This exception is *a fortiori* applicable to the true *sannyāsī*, who also offers the *agnihotra* only inwardly.[93]

As for that other great section of Vedic ritual, the public sacrifices, the king should have them all performed 'from the *Agnistoma* to the *Ashvamedha*', with 'full ceremonial and distribution of *dakshinā*'.[94] When on the subject of the air-purifying qualities of *homa*, Dayananda remarked that if the public sacrifices were arranged by the princes and the wealthy, 'there would be immeasurable benefit to all living beings'.[95] That is all that is said about these public sacrifices: the Swami obviously accepted them as a proper part of Vedic religion, but somehow he did not quite know where to fit them in.

Education received special treatment in chapters two and three. The mother plays the most important role in the first five years, and one of her main tasks is to teach the child to speak properly. From the age of five or eight the boys and girls should be taught by a teacher, and learn not only the *devanāgarī* script, but also that of languages of other countries.[96] Both boys and girls should be taught the *Gāyatrī*, but only the boys should receive the sacrament of initiation, and only the sons of the twice-born, not the shūdras.[97] The children should then be sent to school, the boys to schools manned only by men, the girls to schools staffed exclusively by women. The shūdra children are also expected to go to school, but they should be excluded from the study of the *Veda*.[98] The minimum age for finishing schooling is sixteen for girls and twenty-five for boys, but a much longer period is recommended. That is about all Dayananda had to say about school organization: he had suffered serious setbacks with his own schools and probably was not very clear in his mind what the best system would be. In his second edition he had much more to say in this matter.

Dayananda repeatedly stressed the moral side of education, recommending some basic virtues essential to its success. Foremost were two virtues that strongly characterized the Swami himself: truthfulness in every respect, and effort and application. The life of study should have an ascetic slant, free from all type of luxury. The student is given four criteria by which to learn to distinguish true from false, virtue from vice: the *Vedas*, the *Shāstras*, the conduct of virtuous people, and the satisfaction one

experiences in one's own conscience.[99] The curriculum proposed
is the one he detailed for his Banaras school: grammar, philosophy,
the *Vedas*, and the sciences. But now he specifically stated that
the girls should learn 'at least' five subjects: grammar, philosophy,
medicine, music, and art. The happiness of married life, he said,
would greatly depend on having both husband and wife well-
educated.[100]

In a plea for the education of all four classes, of men and women,
Dayananda predicted that until all were educated, there was
no hope for the prosperity of Āryāvarta: education had to be
the key to its renaissance. Then the brahmins would abandon
sectarianism and greed, and properly perform their duty of intellectual and moral leadership, the other classes would forego
deceit and reach happiness and prosperity, and the princes and
the wealthy would take their duty seriously. Thus prosperity
and happiness would return to Āryāvarta and benefit the whole
world.[101]

Dayananda reiterated his theory of the perfect society. The
varna-classification by qualities and merit would replace the
division into caste by birth. The allocation of a *varna* should
be made by the state, after due examination of the graduates from
the schools. The brahmins should be entrusted with ritual and
the pursuit of knowledge, the kshatriyas with government, the
vaishyas with the running of the economy, and the shūdras with
service.[102]

The form of monogamy proposed by Dayananda was quite
new to Hinduism: 'Among the twice born it is not proper that
there should be a second marriage, either of the man or of the
woman.'[103] Contemporary Hinduism allowed polygamy for the
man, and remarriage of the widower; its only restriction was on
the remarriage of high caste widows. Dayananda's general principle extended that restriction drastically: after one marriage
neither the widow nor the widower may contract another one.
That seems an oddly reactionary step for a reformer who was
recorded to be in favour of widow-remarriage: in fact Dayananda
was more liberalizing than any nineteenth century reformer ever
dared to be by proposing a different type of temporary marital
contract between widows and widowers called *niyoga* which will
be treated later.

In the ideal society marriage should be between people of the class, that is assigned to them at graduation: they are probably more compatible.[104] The girls should be at least sixteen, and three years should have elapsed since their first menses. Dayananda ridiculed the old notion that a father's *dharma* is destroyed if his daughter has her menses in his house: 'how can the natural function of a woman be conceived as a sin of the father!' Indeed, said the Swami, it is better for a girl to remain in her father's house than to marry a worthless man. Wedding arrangements should be preceded by inquiries about the candidates, not by means of worthless and fraudulent horoscopes but by proper investigation,[105] and arrangements should not be finalized without the assent of both partners.[106] Dayananda recommended for two reasons marriage between parties who live a great distance apart: the mixture of blood promotes breeding, and the interaction between distant regions fosters peace and harmony among different peoples.[107]

The firm foundation of a happy home is mutual affection, and the constant effort to please each other.[108] It is the woman's duty to be the manager of the household by running its economy. She should also keep up her study of the *Vedas* and assist her husband in the twice daily ritual of the Five Great Sacrifices. She should attend to guests, and she should not feed all the lazy and degenerate *sādhus* that roam about, but only the real *sannyāsīs* and the needy poor, the blind, the lame, and the orphaned. The morning and evening meals are accompanied by the ritual, but the middle part of the day is reserved for work. One feels that it was mainly the work motive that drove the Swami to eliminate the midday ritual, just as he discouraged the siesta, except in the two hottest months.[109] It was Muslim influence that taught the Hindus to imprison their women in the house. The Aryans should remember the Vedic age, when women fully participated in all areas of public life.[110]

The radical institution of *niyoga*, the temporary union of widows and widowers, is here presented for the first time, and Dayananda was to advocate it till the end of his life. Yet it is the one institution which his followers never put into practice: there is not one single report of a *niyoga* being contracted during or after the Swami's life. In his mind the theory had two basic starting points: his deep concern for the sorry state of widows, and the fact that the *Vedas* allowed in certain cases a widow to contract a temporary union with the brother of her deceased husband. The plight of the upper class widow was one of the major social curses of contemporary Hindu society, and one of the very first concerns of Hindu social reform. Dayananda had now become acutely aware of the complications of the situation. The problem was confounded by the prevailing custom of child marriage: many girls were widowed even before the end of infancy. Some sections of the Hindu community like the Kanauj brahmins had created a host of unmarried girls by exacting enormous dowries. The dowry system of some martial classes had caused the widespread custom of female infanticide, and the polygamy associated with *kulinism* in Bengal had multiplied unsupported wives and unsupported widows.[111]

The eradication of those practices would drastically reduce the number of widows, but even then there still remained, according to the Swami, the basic problem of the widow: unloved and unsupported she was often driven to vice, abortion, and infanticide. He saw the solution in allowing the widow to contract a temporary legal union with a widower: however, that decision should be wholly in her hands.[112]

Apart from this moral argument, Dayananda also uses the argument that *niyoga* had a basis in the scriptures. What, then, are the facts in this matter? Some of the most ancient lawbooks permitted the practice of *niyoga* in certain very specific circumstances. The husband, living or dead, should have no son; the elders should approve the union; the partner should be either the husband's brother or a close relation of his; the relationship could last till one or two sons were born, after which it had to be drastically broken off. This usage was very old, alluded to even in the *Rigveda* (x, 40, 2), and was motivated by the great ritual and social need for a Hindu to have a son. It gradually became rarer, and was totally prohibited in the first centuries of the Christian era. Manu first describes the custom and then proceeds to condemn it with great vehemence.[113]

Dayananda radically changed and extended this ancient institution. For him the *niyoga* contract is between a widow and a widower, and must be broken off after the birth of two sons. It is not clearly stated if another *niyoga* contract may be entered into afterwards, but that was probably his idea, since he later affirmed it clearly. He completely omitted the basic condition of the ancient law: that the first union failed to produce male offspring. And then *niyoga* was extended even further: it is possible for a wife to enter into it while her husband is still alive, for the following reasons: if he is absent for a long time, if he becomes impotent or sterile, or if he becomes vile and violent.[114] Similarly not only may the widower contract *niyoga*, but also the husband may have strong reasons to temporarily supersede his living wife; these are lóng absence, hateful behaviour, drunkenness, disease, barrenness, inability to produce a son, and acute quarrelsomeness.[115]

Dayananda thus not only resuscitated an institution that had been shunned by Hinduism for nearly two millennia but greatly extended its application.[116] It was an immensely courageous proposal to deal with a dreadful problem, and although it testifies to the deep concern of the Swami, it also shows that the *sannyāsī* had little understanding of the complexity of marital and sexual problems. For him sex was intimately bound up with reproduction, and he found it impossible to dissociate the two. Although the many sufficient reasons for *niyoga* are often different from the urgent need of offspring, yet whenever he mentions *niyoga* he adds the phrase *putrotpatti*, 'for the sake of begetting a son', and he insists that the contract must be broken off after the birth of two sons. The reasons for *niyoga*, apart from the specific desire for offspring, are that the widow is left without support, financial and emotional, and consequently engages in vice, abortion, and infanticide; the need of the widow is, therefore, most often not offspring, but support, companionship, and sex.[117] The basic weakness of the whole structure is that Dayananda has taken an old tradition, specifically designed for the narrow purpose of providing a son to a deceased husband, and extrapolated it to solve the much wider problem of widowhood, which touches on sexual, temperamental, social, and economic matters.

Dayananda's concept of sexual morality was also dominated by the idea, very prevalent in the Hindu tradition, that man's manhood or seed is an exhaustible treasure of overall vitality that needs to be guarded and carefully husbanded. Parents are warned not to let their children touch their genitals, because loss of seed will cause untold illness and degeneracy.[118] His main argument against polygamy is that it saps man's strength, and womanizing is slated because of that waste of precious vitality leading to disease and premature death. Long *brahmacharya,* meaning protracted storage of vitality, brings to those married at a mature age, a pleasure in coitus which others cannot even imagine, and it also guarantees offspring of superior qualities.[119] The last two stages of life, *vānaprastha* and *sannyāsa* are treated in chapter five. This is a commentary on selected verses from the sixth chapter of the *Manusmriti,* and Dayananda remains too closely entangled with this text and seems not yet to have thought the subject over thoroughly. Little is said about *vānaprastha,*[120] but *sannyāsa* receives extensive treatment. The necessity of this stage of life is justified as follows. The most basic condition for all progress and prosperity is knowledge. Since householders do not have enough leisure to devote to it, specialists are needed to increase and propagate knowledge and to fight ignorance. The *sannyāsī* is best equipped for that task: not being tied down by home and work he is free to move around the country, and being economically independent, he is able to speak his mind to all, even to kings.[121]

Sannyāsa is open to the members of the three superior classes, who have paid their three debts: to the *rishis* by the study of the *Vedas,* to the fathers by begetting a son, and to the *devas* by sacrifices.[122] However, the state can also be taken up in youth without passing through the stage of householder.[123] The main qualifications should be superior qualities: total unselfishness, dedication to knowledge, and freedom from all bias, so that the real *sannyāsī* would be totally different from the contemporary *sādhus,* thieves of others' wealth, seducers of others' wives, confounders of truth, and destroyers of *dharma.*[124] The *sannyāsī's* life should be one of complete asceticism, detached, possessionless, sustained only by alms. He should strive for knowledge with all his power and try to reach *samādhi* through the constant practice of Rāja Yoga.[125] Dayananda still insisted on the special privileges and powers the real *sannyāsī* may acquire. He is free from the performance of all external rites.[126] Once he has achieved knowledge he is no longer bound by *karma,* and he can dispose of his accumulated *karma* by transferring his merits to his friends and his demerits to his enemies. When in the state of *samādhi,* he can shed his body and thus obtain *moksha.*[127] Every one of these special powers will be carefully weeded out in the second edition.

Dayananda devoted the whole tenth chapter to some taboos

of conduct and diet prevalent in Hinduism. He rejected the idea that foreign travel constitutes a sin: the *Mahābhārata* is full of stories about international travels of the great kings and princes. But reason too shows that foreign travel is intrinsically good: it fosters trade and prosperity, opens the mind to other cultures, and gives self-confidence. Some who say that contact with foreigners pollutes, themselves keep white courtesans; it is absurd to accept that contact with a good Englishman would be defiling, whereas that with a prostitute would not! The taboo was invented by brahmins and sectarians, who were afraid that travel would broaden the minds of the people and liberate them from the net of superstitions. 'Evil springs from the heart, not from the location.'[128]

Concerning food taboos too Dayananda put his basic axiom quite clearly: 'there is no direct connection between eating and drinking and *dharma*. *Dharma*, the criteria of which are non-violence etc., is based in the mind; whereas eating and drinking are external actions.' Yet there are two kinds of food, proper and improper, and the norms for their distinction are the medical sciences and the *Dharmashāstras*. From the medical point of view, all foods that promote health and strength are good, and only contaminated foods or drugs that destroy health are bad. The norm of *dharma* excludes food that is acquired by theft or deceit: it is not the food itself that is bad, but the manner of its acquisition.[129]

In this context Dayananda treated the question of meat-eating and the problem of non-violence in connection with the killing of animals. These pages[130] demonstrate conclusively that the Swami's attitude at that time was a qualified one: he did not totally condemn all consumption of meat. Three types of meat are forbidden. Firstly that which is obtained from impure animals, like village pigs and chickens: since they feed on offal, their flesh is contaminated and it would injure health. The second type of forbidden meat is that of those animals that are useful to man, like cows, buffaloes, sheep, goats, camels, etc. The reason here is an economic one: the killing of those beasts would produce very little food in comparison with the food and services to be expected if the animals continued to live. Thirdly, flesh should be eaten only when it has been processed through the *homa* sacrifice: 'because at the time of the slaughter pain has been inflicted, and therefore there is some sin. But when *homa* is performed in the sacrificial fire, then the atomic dispersion of the vapours will bring benefit to all living beings. If from the pain inflicted on one living being some sin has resulted, it will be counted for very little (in comparison).'[131] Therefore the first two reasons given for forbidden meats are hygienic and economic, and have nothing to do with *ahimsā*. The third is connected with it: the *homa* sacrifice tends to nullify the sinfulness of the killing.

Dayananda then elaborated on his conception of non-violence, and he seems to have had a rather biased version of Jain *ahimsā* in mind as his Aunt Sally. Absolute non-violence, he said, is impossible, because all our actions, even the blinking of an eyelid, will cause some pain to some living being. Therefore, one has to judge and weigh the harm done by a particular act against its beneficial results. He applied this principle in his reflections on the *homa* sacrifice, and he applied it again in the case of the killing of wild animals: they would increase unchecked and destroy the very livelihood of mankind if they were not kept down to reasonable numbers. Dayananda therefore still accepted the killing of animals as legitimate in a sacrificial context or as an economic necessity, and approved in certain cases the consumption of their meat.[132]

Hindu food taboos are not only concerned with the food itself, but also with the questions of who touches and cooks the food, and who may share in its consumption. As for the first, cooking is the function of the servant class, the shūdras: it takes too much time and would disrupt the important tasks the other classes have to perform. Dayananda approved of interdining between the twice-born, giving examples from the *Mahābhārata* to prove his point, and adding that interdining is a good way to foster friendliness and unity, whereas the food taboos introduced by the sectarians have created enmities and have made the people of India into weaklings.[133]

Political science was probably Dayananda's very weakest field of knowledge. In his chapter on the state he completely depended on Manu and only occasionally does what he wrote touch on the political realities and possibilities of nineteenth century India. He was a political innocent, but with a deep concern for justice and for the welfare of the people.

The king should naturally be the ideal kshatriya, whose duty it is 'to protect the whole world and to check *adharma*'. The institution of kingship is divine in the sense only that it was created by God, who also created the kingly power, *danda*, for the establishment of truth, justice, and *dharma*. Nevertheless, the king can be removed from office either by his cabinet or by the Sabhā if he neglects his duties. His cabinet of eight should include the prime minister (*divān*), the chief justice, and the commander-in-chief. The centre of the administration is the palace and the fort, and there should also be a Sabhā, a council of wise men, the composition and function of which are not detailed. The cabinet should appoint a number of officials to assist them in the different departments of the administration.[134]

The work of administration essentially covers three fields: the treasury, justice, and social welfare. Taxes should be moderate and the royal treasury should be well administered and used primarily for education and social welfare. The state's social responsibilities are wide. It has to see to it that marriages are not performed before the proper ages, that all children receive a good education (a very advanced notion in nineteenth century India), and that at the end of their schooling they are allotted to a particular class and to a particular family.[135] The state also should support and send out men of wisdom and holiness as teachers of *dharma*, and catch and punish the false preachers: these should be put 'to useful work like pushing a plough'.[136]

Considerable attention is given to the administration of justice, which Dayananda felt left much to be desired: he devoted nearly twenty pages to the subject. Justice should not be a respecter of persons, be they relatives, friends, brahmins, or *sannyāsīs*: no one should be above the law. In fact Dayananda accepted Manu's principle that in certain cases punishment should increase according to the higher status in the class hierarchy. The courtroom, where justice should be administered, is often the place where it is most prostituted: injustice in the courtroom throws guilt not only on the criminal and the false witnesses, but also on the judges and the king.[137] The witnesses are key actors, and are often corrupt. But the Swami offered no original solution to this problem, he only repeated many verses of Manu that disqualify witnesses, sometimes for rather strange reasons. He also unhesitatingly repeated a number of savage punishments prescribed by Manu: branding, amputation, death by burning and by being devoured by dogs, the last two reserved for people convicted of adultery. He insisted that even those *sannyāsīs* and priests who rob the people, but who are not strictly speaking thieves because the misguided people give willingly, should be prosecuted: they are 'secret thieves', and their victims are like innocent children.[138]

There are also some guidelines for foreign relations, diplomacy, and war. Here again, Dayananda flounders in the mass of Manu's material, and picks those elements that seem important to him, although it is hard to see how they are related to reality.[139] One should remember that many of Dayananda's reform proposals only make sense in the context of the perfect Vedic society which did not yet exist. No wonder that he finished the chapter on the state by recalling the lost greatness of Āryāvarta. Then the kings were wise, and knew the secrets of missiles and fire-arms. They had a superior knowledge of medical science, and travelled across the continents by mechanically propelled airships and boats. Their reign stretched over the whole earth, they taught geography to the rest of the world, and even the women of their kingdom were filled with knowledge. Compared with that glorious condition of yore, India today is in a pitious state, worse in fact than any other country.[140]

Some of Dayananda's best observations on government occur in the eleventh chapter, where he devotes six pages to an assessment of the contemporary British Raj. He first acknowledged that the Raj had brought many benefits to India. It had put an end to destructive wars and established universal peace. It had taken measures that promoted economic prosperity by building a good network of roads and increasing arable land. The Raj had also brought personal freedom in religious and other matters: state-compulsion was no more. In the field of education, it had established a school system through which many got an education that ensured employment, and books ran from the presses in great numbers. The courts were accessible to the rich and the poor alike. All in all, the Raj had provided good government.[141]

However, said the Swami, in some areas the Raj had not done the right thing. He criticized the tax on salt and sugar: these were two basic necessities for all, and the tax fell most heavily on the poor. The state should rather increase fourfold the tax on intoxicants, which are harmful to the people. The courts were too lenient on thieves, gamblers, and adulterers. If Manu's punishments by branding, amputation, and death, were re-introduced, they would create a most effective deterrent. The many stamp duties levied by the courts were a crippling burden on the poor. The total and constant involvement of money in court proceedings caused a lot of false witnessing, and tended to protract the court-cases with appeals and counter-appeals. The lawyers and judges should be only concerned with justice and all their mistakes should be made liable to punishment. Justice should be assisted by a good police force composed of honourable men: the police station was too often the place from where endless litigation started.[142] Dayananda also insisted that it is the duty of the state to protect useful animals, like cows, oxen, sheep, which were being indiscriminately killed to the great detriment of society. He proposed the economic argument which he would later develop in detail in his *Gokarunānidhi* pamphlet: 'One cow can feed 100,000 people, but its meat can feed scarcely eighty.'[143]

The regeneration of man and society thus depended, according to Dayananda, on the reforms he proposed for ritual and sacramental life, for the home, for society, and for the state. But it equally depended on the effort of every man to lead the good life, the moral life. Repeatedly Dayananda stated that necessity of practicing the virtues, the most central and important one of which is knowledge, the key to all morality: knowledge makes *dharma* possible because, 'he who has knowledge will never again commit sin', and 'lack of knowledge is the root of all evil'.[144] From knowledge and truth spring a number of virtues that are the essential regulators of social life. Truthfulness in words and action eliminates all treachery, gossip, calumny, hypocrisy. Truth is also the root of justice, and of tolerance and peace. Among the virtues that should shape man's character, Dayananda always gives the central place to self-control, self-reliance and application.[145]

Dayananda's moral man is, therefore, consumed with the thirst for knowledge and truth, he tries to control himself and remains ever active, and guides his relations with others by truth, justice, and tolerance. One cannot but admire how Dayananda has succeeded in stressing essentials and avoiding the trivial in his definition of moral man.

The first *Satyārth Prakāsh* displays a deep concern with a wide range of problems and questions that were outside the ambit of the Swami's preaching in the Doab. Some issues of a social nature now appear in bold relief: poverty and exploitation, the condition of women, the question of universal education, the functions and responsibilities of the state. The utter superiority of the Vedic religion and of the Vedic Golden Age over all other religions and civilizations has now become the central idea of his total concept of reform and revival. This interest in the Vedic age has led Dayananda to a study of the historical processes that brought about the contemporary degeneration of Hindu society. His reflection on moral problems has also widened and deepened, searching for the general principles that must direct the discrimination of good and evil in all concrete circumstances. This striking widening of the Swami's horizons was greatly influenced by his experiences in Calcutta. But it is even more striking that he in no way underwent or absorbed that influence passively. In every instance the new ideas were remoulded and recreated by the Swami in such a dynamic and individual manner that they became his very own, and an integral part of a completely new overall view.

CHAPTER VI

Bombay: The Foundation of the Arya Samaj

His most important and far-reaching decision was taken by Dayananda during his stay in Western India: the decision to found the Arya Samaj, the organization that planted his message and his reform firmly in the soil of North India and that had enormous influence on the later development of Hinduism and of Hindu nationalism. The Swami arrived in Bombay on 20 October 1874 and spent the next eighteen months in the area. During this period he stayed in the city of Bombay on four occasions for periods, varying in length from about six weeks to five months, and totalling about ten months altogether. In between his periods in the metropolis he made three tours of towns of Western India: he continued his policy of concentrating on important urban centres by singling out Ahmedabad, Baroda, and Poona for special attention.[1] This chapter will deal first with the foundation of the Samaj and afterwards with the other activities the Swami engaged in during this period.

The idea of an organization had been in the Swami's mind for some time: he had tried twice to form a society, in Arrah in 1872, and at Banaras in 1874, but both attempts had been short-lived. He had witnessed in Calcutta the extension and influence of the Brahmo Samaj and the effectiveness of its various reform bodies. But he had also noticed the sectarian and schismatic tendencies of the Brahmos. Now in Bombay a combination of factors created the right climate for a renewed attempt. For one, the Swami must have felt better prepared than he had ever been. His ideas on reform had now fully matured: there was his *Satyārth Prakāsh* to prove it. Soon it would roll off the presses and a comprehensive textbook would be available to his followers. This would be supplemented by the two books of ritual and the prayer book he composed in Bombay. Moreover, he was starting to plan the great Vedic commentary that he was to publish in monthly fascicules. His followers would, therefore, be provided with all the necessary materials for effective reform.

His close observation of the Prarthana Samaj in Bombay no doubt helped the Swami to clarify his ideas: he always took time to arrive at important decisions, for impulsiveness was not a characteristic of his nature. This does not mean that he went to Bombay with the express intention of founding the Samaj: there is not a single indication that he had such a plan in mind. After his tour of the Gangetic plains it was only natural for him to look westward again to the land of his origin. The decision to establish the Samaj was taken in Bombay, but, apart from his own greater readiness, the really decisive factor was the demand: there was in this city a group of people who had the right attitude, and who wanted to explore the possibility of collaborating with the Swami. These people came from two different sections of society: some were members of the Gujarati trading castes disenchanted with their own sect, others belonged to the Prarthana Samaj circle which was dominated by Maratha brahmins.

Swami Dayananda had a long-standing invitation to come to Bombay. It had been extended to him at the time of his famous Banaras disputation of 1869 by two prominent members of the Bombay commercial classes, Jaikishendas Jivanram and Dharmsi, the brother of the famous Shet Lakhmidas Khimji. They were present at the famous disputation and were highly impressed by the forceful argumentation of the Gujarati Swami, especially by his attack on idol worship on the basis of ancient Vedic teaching. They felt he might well be the man to give new impetus to their fight against the abuses of Vaishnavism and to strengthen their efforts at reform. That is why they had invited Dayananda to Bombay, and when five years later the Swami decided to visit Western India, he remembered them and informed them of his plan.[2]

The invitation came from people who were the successors to Karsondas Mulji in his fight against the abuses of the Maharajas of the Vallabhāchārya sect. Karsondas himself was a member of the sect, but his long years at the Elphinstone institution and his contact with other reformers had led him to an intensive questioning of the sect's doctrines and practices. This study convinced him that the sect was of very recent date, and that many of its tenets were but perversions of 'real Hinduism'. The publication of his arguments in his paper, the *Satya Prakāsh*, founded in 1855, led eventually in 1860 to a famous court-case, when one of the Maharajas sued Karsondas for libel on account of the allegations he had made in his article entitled, 'The Primitive Religion of the Hindus and the Present Heterodox Opinions'. The libel case exploded like a bomb over Bombay society and brought some of the most prominent Gujarati bankers as witnesses before the bench. The trial ended in an almost complete victory for Karsondas.[3]

One of the central recurring themes of the trial was the question of what constituted authentic, traditional Hindu doctrine as against the later innovations and perversions brought about by the sects. Repeatedly the defence argued along the following lines: 'The religion of this sect is a new system set up at a modern date; and it is a distinctly established fact that, in the proportion that these new and monstrous doctrines have gone forward, the ancient doctrines of morality have gone back and have been superseded.'[4] It is noteworthy that the main burden of proof for that contention was assumed by Dr John Wilson, the Orientalist, as the Indian witnesses were practically all innocent of Sanskrit. The search for that 'authentic Hinduism' as contained in the older scriptures, was continued by Karsondas after the trial. Shortly before his death in 1873, two years before Dayananda's visit, he published a pamphlet in Gujarātī entitled *Ved Dharma*, the 'Vedic religion'. Its contents are most interesting: Karsondas
was in favour of calling the Hindu religion by the title of 'Arya Dharma' and said that the genuine kernel of the Arya Dharma was to be found in the Vedas. In this book he dealt with the language of the Vedas, and the reasons why people were left in ignorance of the Vedas, and said that whatever was written in the Puranas was not written in the Vedas . . . Karsondas in this brochure says that in the Vedas was to be found the nucleus of a pure religion.[5]

This quest for the religion of the *Vedas* was continued by those who carried on his work after his death, foremost among whom were Lakhmidas Khimji and Mulji Thakarshi. A Veda Sabhā had been established in Bombay for that purpose.[6] In the context of that concern and that search it is no wonder that Lakhmidas Khimji's brother was impressed in Banaras by Dayananda, the great protagonist of the *Vedas* and critic of sectarianism. That same context explains why Sevaklal Karsondas, another leading figure of the same group, translated a synopsis of the Banaras dispute into Gujarātī and published it in the *Ārya Mitra* one month before the Swami's arrival.[7] This group of reformers obviously had followed the Swami's career with interest, and the latest reports of his visit to Calcutta showed them how he had now elaborated a plan for the regeneration of Āryāvarta through the revival of Vedic religion: what the Swami was preaching was exactly what they themselves had been searching for.

The other group of people who showed considerable interest in Dayananda were the members of the Prarthana Samaj. The Samaj had been founded in 1867 mainly through the influence of Keshub Chandra Sen who visited Bombay in 1864 and 1867. Its doctrines were largely similar to those of the Sadharan Brahmo Samaj: non-idolatrous theism, rejection of both transmigration and infallible revelation, and eclecticism in the use of religious texts from both Hindu and non-Hindu traditions. In the field of social reform it advocated widow-remarriage and female education, and called for the abolition of child-marriage and of caste. However, whereas the Brahmos tended to expect all their members to try to implement without delay their reform platform, the members of the Prarthana Samaj were more patient. They were in favour of gradualism and opposed to radical innovations and to breaks with traditional society.[8] The great majority of the members were English-educated Maratha brahmins, representing a section quite different from the former group of Gujarati merchants.[9]

There was at the time among the Bombay reformers in general a greater interest in religious matters and in early Hinduism than there was in earlier or later years. In previous decades the Bombay elite had been very involved in various attempts at social reform, but by the beginning of the seventies the social reform movement had abated and had become dormant in most communities. Among other reasons, the increasingly national outlook of the intelligentsia was a major one. They had learnt by experience that social reform action often had a divisive effect: it pitted community against community, and region against region. Across communities and regions it was much easier to agree on political issues than on social matters. Still, the social questions could not be neglected, and people felt that an approach through religious reform might be more unifying, particularly if this study of religion turned away from sectarian multiplicity towards those strong symbols of overall unity, the earliest sources. It was Behramji Malabari's *Notes on Infant Marriage and Enforced Widowhood*, that launched social reform action again in 1884 by hitting upon a social issue that could effectively unite the social reformers of all regions, namely the need for legislative control of the age of marriage of Hindu girls. But in that interim of fifteen years from 1870 onwards, the Bombay reformers showed a much keener interest in religious reform and in the study of the sources of Hinduism.[10]

That was the atmosphere, those were the people, among whom Dayananda arrived when he stepped off the train in Bombay on 20 October 1874, an atmosphere very different from the one he had experienced in Calcutta four years earlier. His reception in Calcutta had certainly been a very warm one, and he had earned the admiration of the Brahmos. But at no stage had there been the feeling that a group of people were actually interested in his idea of return to the *Vedas*, or needed the Swami and looked for leadership on his part. Many Bengalis had admired his radical social platform, not because it was better than theirs, but rather because they were astounded that a Sanskrit-speaking Swami without English had managed to construct such a radical programme. His doctrinal position, particularly on the *Vedas*, they never could take too seriously: it was too offensive to their agnostic rationalism. One can detect their sense of superiority even in the concluding lines of a long and quite sympathetic article on the Swami in the *Dharmatattva*:

The infallibility of the *Vedas*, rebirth, etc., and some sacraments according to Hindu *dharma* are still firmly embedded in his heart. His way is the way of *dharma*, not [yet] the way of love and devotion. If the Swami will manage to climb the next steps of the ladder of *dharma* as successfully as he has mastered that first step, then his influence will soon spread widely.[11]

The Brahmos had very little interest in the *Vedas*, and the study of Sanskrit was not very important to most of them, as Dayananda had noticed. Their social radicalism, especially as expressed in the Brahmo Marriage Act, tended to isolate them into a distinct caste. That was all very strange to the Swami, and in a way Calcutta must have felt to him like a foreign land, and the Bengalis like strangers. Arriving in Bombay, on the other hand, Dayananda, hearing his mother-tongue all around him, must have felt he had come home again, and the active interest in his Vedic programme encouraged him enormously.

The establishment of the Arya Samaj raises a number of important questions. How did Dayananda conceive the role of the

Samaj in society, and how did he see his own function in the Samaj? Who were the people that joined the new organization, and why did they do so? What kind of institution emerged and what were its models? Before attempting to answer these questions it is necessary to look closely at the chronological sequence of events that led to the act of foundation.

The first mention of an organization was made less than a month after the Swami's arrival in Bombay. On 16 November Swami Purnananda, on Dayananda's behalf, published in the papers answers to twenty-four questions that had been anonymously sent to the Swami, probably by the Vallabhācāryas. The last answer contains the following sentences:

If we, the Aryans, discuss with love and without prejudice the Vedic *dharma*, then all kinds of benefits will arise; that is what I wish. For that purpose there should exist a perpetual Sabhā. It would be a wonderful thing if that could come about. That means, by which the manyfold sects may be destroyed, that is the means all should adopt.[12]

This Sabhā, however, was not the Arya Samaj, but rather a supersectarian Hindu Council, an idea conceived by his *guru* Virjananda, to which Dayananda periodically came back.

The idea of founding an Arya Samaj did not originate from above, but rather by pressure and demand from below. This pressure is not surprising because the leading castes of Bombay had over the last decades become very organization-conscious and tended to form all kinds of associations for different purposes. About one month after the Swami's arrival some people already started to suggest the establishment of a Samaj. They were quite serious: between 24 and 30 November some sixty people held several meetings and signed a petition to form a Samaj. The Swami agreed to frame a set of rules and promised that he would support the society by occasional lectures. However, by this time the opposition to Dayananda in Bombay had crystallized, and caste-pressure was exerted on the aspirants with the result that the plan was dropped for the time being.[13]

The next mention of a Samaj occurred at Ahmedabad in December. Dayananda had favourably impressed many people by his lectures, and the leaders of the local Prarthana Samaj invited him to be the special speaker at their annual festival. The *Hitecchu* of 6 January 1875 wrote that Dayananda had suggested at this time that contemporary Hinduism in its sorry state might well be significantly helped by an Arya Samaj and a Vedic school. But the editor commented that he felt that the people of Ahmedabad were still too steeped in their old caste customs and not ready to join such a venture, however much benefit might be expected from it. All Dayananda did at this time was to plant the seed in the hope that it might germinate.[14]

The one occasion when Dayananda ever returned to his native Kathiawar was during his visit to Rajkot in January 1875. And it was there, in the land of his birth, that the very first Arya Samaj was established: apparently it was a wholesale takeover of the local Prarthana Samaj. This had been founded only two years previously, and the branch, being quite young and far removed from its Maharashtrian base, probably did not have the strong theological convictions Dayananda was to encounter elsewhere when he suggested a similar transformation. Thirty people joined the new Samaj, and Dayananda formulated a set of rules which were printed for distribution at Rajkot and elsewhere. The secretary of the new Samaj wrote to Gopalrao Hari Deshmukh that the new Rajkot Aryas had been unable to agree with the Swami's ideas on the marriage age and on *niyoga*, but that their rejection of these points had been quite acceptable to the Swami. This report, confirmed by a note in the *Hitecchu* of 12 January 1875, indicates that from the very start Dayananda was flexible in his expectations. This first Arya Samaj of Rajkot was short-lived: within six months it was disbanded on account of political troubles connected with the very burning issue of the dethronement of the Gaekwad of Baroda by the British.[15]

The Rajkot success must have encouraged Dayananda to find out in Ahmedabad on his way back if the seed he had sown there had germinated. He distributed his Rajkot rules to people interested, and on 27 January a meeting was held to consider the Swami's teachings. There he discussed with various pandits his interpretation of some Vedic *mantras*, and the questions of idol worship and *varnāshrama* in the *Vedas*. The two leading members of the local Prarthana Samaj, Bholanath Sarabhai and Ambalal Sagarlal, who were appointed judges of the contest, declared Dayananda to have won on every topic. Nevertheless, no Arya Samaj was established at that time: it was only the following March that it came about; and of the thirty people who joined it only one came from the ranks of the Prarthana Samaj.[16] The basic reason for Dayananda's failure to convince the members of that Samaj to become Aryas is quite clear: they found it impossible to accept his claim of infallibility for the *Vedas*, however much they sympathized with most of his other ideas. Dayananda tried his utmost to convince them by personal discussion, by spurring Gopalrao on to try to win them over, by sending his *Satyārth Prakāsh* and other publications for study; but he remained unsuccessful: the Prarthana Samajists stood firm on their principle, and so did the Swami.[17]

On the Swami's return to Bombay the movement to found a Samaj had again gathered strength and on 17 February some hundred people held an open meeting in Girgaon, and formed a committee under the chairmanship of Raobahadur Dadu Ba Pandurang to consider rules and regulations. However, there was still considerable apprehension of orthodox retaliation, and this venture too came to nothing.[18] One of the obstacles may have been the crafty proposal of Rajakrishna Maharaj to Dayananda 'to write the identity of the soul and *brahman*-into the rules, a doctrine that could be abandoned later on. That way a lot of people would be attracted to the Samaj.' Dayananda's categorical refusal made him another enemy.[19]

These setbacks, however, did not stop the sizeable number of enthusiasts from forging ahead. Panachand Anandji Parekh was entrusted with the task of rewriting the rules, which were then given a last polish in consultation with Dayananda. Finally, on 10 April 1875, the Arya Samaj of Bombay was formally inaugurated. Twenty-eight rules were adopted, and a committee was elected from amongst the one hundred founding members. There was also a proposal to make Dayananda the leader or the president of the Samaj. He firmly refused this honour, but he accepted enrolment as an ordinary member of the Samaj, and his name duly appears in its place in the alphabetically ordered list.[20] No other Samajes were founded by the Swami himself during his stay in Western India. As a result of his visit, Samaj branches were established at Poona, Broach, and some other towns, but they were all short-lived like the one in Rajkot.[21] When Dayananda moved on after one and a half years, he left behind him only the one substantial and strong branch: the Bombay Arya Samaj.

The leading Hindu castes of Bombay society were all rather small: the Gujarati Vanias, Bhatias, and Lohanas, the Maratha and Gujarati brahmins, the Saraswat brahmins, and the Pathare Prabhus constituted altogether only 15 per cent of the total Hindu population, and the Gujarati Vanias were the largest group with 3.5 per cent. The overall leadership of society was in the hands of two sets of people: the shetias, or Gujarati business magnates on the one hand, and the intelligentsia dominated by Maratha brahmins on the other. This intellectual dominance of the Maratha brahmins was evident in their striking pre-eminence in education, the professions, and the public service.[22] However, during the seventies there began a clear and constant rise of the trading castes, particularly of the Vanias, in the field of education.[23] In this bustling city of personal endeavour and untold opportunities, politics was at a low ebb,[24] and also that former enthusiastic commitment to social reform had become dormant. However, there was a new interest in religious reform: it was felt that this may have a wider national appeal because it was free from the many divisive stresses inherent in social reform.[25]

Who, then, were those people who finally succeeded in founding the Bombay Arya Samaj? Only a few were really prominent citizens. Mulji Thakarshi, a wealthy mill-owner born in Kathiawar, had visited England in the sixties and had played a prominent part in municipal politics, the widow-remarriage movement, and the crusade against the Vallabhāchārya Maharajas. He strongly supported Dayananda right from the start.[26] Lakhmidas Khimji, eminent leader of the Bhatias, was also involved in the fight against the Maharajas and the promotion of widow-remarriage. He was a member of the Bombay Association, and active in municipal politics; on account of his reform activities he had been deposed as the manager of the Hallai Bhatia caste.[27] It was his brother Dharmsi who attended Dayananda's Banaras disputation. Two other prominent figures also assisted Dayananda and the Samaj without actually becoming directly involved in the organization. Mathuradas Lowji, a rich Bhatia philanthropist, was among the early supporters and gave big donations for the *Vedabhāshya*. He was the patron of the young student Shyamji Krishnavarma, an active member of the Samaj. He also tried to promote a public dispute during the second visit of the Swami in 1882, by putting up a prize of Rs 500 for any challenger who could beat the Swami.[28] The Bhanshali shet Chhabildas Lallubhai, very active in municipal affairs and an opponent of the Vallabhāchāryas, similarly supported the Swami. He too was a patron of Shyamji, to whom he gave his daughter in marriage, and his son was a member of the first Committee of the Bombay Arya Samaj.[29] During his visit to Poona, Dayananda also got strong support from the great leader Mahadev Govind Ranade, who was instrumental in having fifteen of the Swami's lectures published. Dayananda corresponded with him, and Ranade sometimes addressed the Arya Samaj of Bombay.[30] Ranade's support was no doubt important in influencing people with reformist leanings, especially young intellectuals, to sympathize with the Swami. Yet, his support always remained general, not implying agreement with Dayananda's Vedic theology: it was the support of one reformer for another. Chandavarkar aptly expressed Ranade's attitude in the following quotation: 'What does it matter if Dayananda says the Vedas and the Vedas alone are the revelation of God? Be that his faith. But let us go deeper and see if, apart from that principle, there is anything which is in accord with our principles'.[31] Ranade found much to support in Dayananda's programme, and the Swami showed his admiration for and trust in Ranade by later including his name among the trustees of his will.[32]

Mahatma Jotirao Phule too showed his appreciation for Dayananda as a reformer by walking alongside Ranade in the procession in honour of the Swami in Poona. This procession was threatened and in fact disrupted by a rival procession organized by opponents, causing some injuries to participants. 'Jotirao's men had joined the procession in large numbers to give protection to the social reformers.'[33]

Whereas the support of these two eminent Maharashtrians remained general, that of Gopalrao Hari Deshmukh, the Lokahitavādī, was constant and concrete. By the time he met Dayananda he was fifty-two, a year older than the Swami, and a reformer and writer of fame. Born of a Deshasth Poona Brahmin family associated with the last Peshwa, he had received an English education and had risen quickly in government service so that by 1875 he was a sessions judge in Ahmedabad. From the forties, when Dayananda was just starting on his long frustrating search for *moksha*, he had been engaged in journalistic writing, containing bitter attacks mainly on the brahmins and their arrogant stranglehold on Hindu society. The *Prabhākar* published his famous *Shatapatra*, 'hundred letters', between 1848 and 1850: their main target was the brahmins who boosted and perpetuated their intellectual pride and supremacy through the 'mysteries' of Sanskrit. He was also deeply involved in the widow-remarriage movement, and became in 1862 with Vishnu Shastri Pandit the co-founder of its mouthpiece, the weekly *Indu Prakāsh*. However, the fiery reformer was ,in his own private life quite orthodox, and at one time he submitted to penance for having attended a widow-remarriage.[34]

He invited Dayananda to Ahmedabad, became a foundation member of the Ahmedabad Arya Samaj, and was later elected president of the Bombay Arya Samaj. He carried on an extensive correspondence with the Swami on a wide range of matters touching on the Samaj, the publication of the Swami's works, the Vedic press, the cow-protection movement, etc. He was also one of the trustees of Dayananda's will, and published in his journal *Lokahitavādī* a lengthy biographical sketch of the Swami immediately after his tragic death. This document proclaims his immense admiration for Dayananda, and the latter's letters prove his admiration and affection for the Lokahitavādī.[35]

Among the supporters of the Swami, therefore, we find only very few individuals from those two leading élite groups, the shetias and the Maratha intelligentsia. The Arya Samaj could not boast great support from those ranks of society. Its main success was among the lower orders. Fortunately a complete list has been preserved of the one hundred founding members of the Bombay Samaj, which indicates the caste, the education level, and the occupation of each member; an analysis of that document gives an accurate social profile of the Bombay Aryas.[36]

The trading castes easily dominated in numbers, with at least fifty-five per cent of the total, but the brahmin proportion was quite considerable with forty per cent.[37] Half of the members were actually engaged in business, twenty per cent in the professions, thirteen per cent in the lower clerical services, and seventeen per cent were students. The overall education level was not very high: half of the membership admits to little formal schooling,[38] only twenty-four per cent had at least matriculation standard,[39] another sixteen per cent mention only their knowledge of English, five note their knowledge of Sanskrit and one of Hindī.[40] So only one in five of the members had reached or passed matriculation standard.

The sizeable brahmin group was forty per cent Maratha and sixty per cent Gujarati. Their formal education level as a group was only a little higher than that of the overall membership,[41] and even they included a significant proportion of people without much schooling, who were all but one Gujarati.[42] Nineteen per cent of the brahmins were in business, all except one Gujaratis; about half were in the professions or clerical services, and a large group were still students.[43]

The two main trading castes represented offer quite different social profiles. Most of the Bhatias, eighty-six per cent, were engaged in business, seventy per cent admitted to little schooling, and only one of their twenty-two members had matriculated. The Vanias, on the other hand, although forty-seven per cent had only a minimum of formal education, had a very large proportion of people with matriculation and above: their forty per cent easily exceeded the twenty-eight per cent of the brahmin group. As for occupation, only just over half of the Vanias were engaged in business, one third in the professions and services, and two of the fifteen were students. These different profiles correspond with the different social situation of the two groups at that time. Whereas the Bhatias were still in the ascending process of their business success, the Vanias had reached their ceiling and were being hard pushed by other rising mercantile groups: they were compelled to move out into education and the professions.[44]

Of the sizeable group of students, seventeen per cent of the total membership, two-thirds studied at Elphinstone High School (3) and College (7), one at Fort High School, one at Grant Medical College, and three at unnamed High Schools. Two-thirds of the group were brahmins, equally divided between Marathas and Gujaratis, and the other third came from the trading castes: two Vanias, two Bhanshalis, and one Soni. The student at Fort High School was Shyamji Krishnavarma, who was singled out by Dayananda for special attention because of his brilliance in Sanskrit. He was later to become a revolutionary.[45]

The first committee of sixteen elected by the hundred founding members had some interesting features. Members of the trading castes had about the same majority in the committee as they had in the total membership but, whereas only half of all members were engaged in business, businessmen overwhelmingly dominated

KING ALFRED'S COLLEGE
LIBRARY

the committee with seventy per cent. Although one-third of the members were engaged in the professions and the services, they had only a quarter of the committee. Even more striking was the position of the brahmins: whereas they had forty per cent of the total membership, they only had twenty-five per cent of the committee, two Maratha and two Gujarati brahmins. As for education, forty-four per cent of the committee were people with little schooling, and only one quarter had matriculation or higher qualifications, which is the same proportion as in the total member-ship. The committee also included one student, the Bhanshali Ramdas Chhabildas Lallubhai, son of the prominent Shet. It is remarkable that of the four members of the writers castes in the membership, two were on the committee, and two of the small number of six Bhanshalis were also included. The single 'Udasi' was also made a committee member, probably on account of his special knowledge of Hindī.

The office-holders were the Vania pleader Girdharlal Dayaldas Kothari, president; the Bhatia broker Thakarshi Narayanji, vice-president; the Vania merchant Panachand Anandji, secretary; the Maratha brahmin Anna Martand Joshi, assistant secretary; the Bhanshali Shet Sevaklal Karsondas, treasurer; and the Gujarati brahmin broker Shamji Vishram, assistant treasurer. Even among the office-bearers the businessmen had a higher percentage than they had in the total membership,[46] and the brahmins' percentage was less than in the total membership.[47]

These figures show clearly that the dominating and leading force in the Samaj were businessmen, mostly Bhatias, Vanias, and Bhanshalis. These were castes that had risen in recent decades, thanks to the growth of the cotton trade and the mill industry. They were searching for a new status to match their new prosperity, especially after the image of their brotherhood had been so severely damaged by the Maharaja Libel Case. Most of the Aryas did not belong to the top layer of their caste: in fact most of the names remain just names, for they are not mentioned anywhere else in the annals of Bombay. However, the few names about which some information is forthcoming, present a remarkably uniform pattern.

In one way or the other they were all connected with the aftermath of religious search produced by the Maharaja Libel Case. Karsondas Mulji had himself initiated that quest in his

Ved Dharma. Lakhmidas Khimji, a major witness in the Maharaja Libel Case, his brother Dharmsi, and Mulji Thakarshi, established the Veda Sabhā to continue the good work. Thakarshi Narayanji, the vice-president of the Samaj, was also a witness for the defence in that case, and continued to play a leading part in the Samaj, being a committee member at least till 1884.[48] Pranjivandas Vadhaji had been from the early days one of the rare open and strong supporters of Karsondas Mulji in his fight against the Hindu establishment.[49] Mathuradas Lowji and Chhabildas Lallubhai had both been on Karsondas' side in his fight against the Maharajas.[50]

The two Bhatia friends Sundardas Dharmsi and Liladhar Hari were also moved towards reform by their disenchantment with the Vallabhāchārya sect. They started their own organization to study earlier Hinduism, the Vedokt Shravan Sabhā, and issued a monthly first called *Hridaychakshu,* but later renamed *Āryadharm Prakāsh* on Dayananda's advice. Their search too was for the original purity of Hinduism free from sectarian corruption. They became friends of Sevaklal Karsondas in 1870, and became founding members of the Samaj.[51] The names of these three appear with regularity in the committee lists for the next twenty years, testifying to the vital role they played. Rajakrishna Maharaj was also involved with this group, but he turned hostile when he realized that the Swami could not be moved from his stand against the Neo-Vedāntins.[52]

The common bond of all these people whose past does not remain completely unknown, is that they were all involved in the reform move set afoot by Karsondas Mulji. Most of them became prominent members of the Samaj, and remained so for a long time. This common background suggests that a great number of the Bhatias and Vanias who joined the Samaj were probably in some way connected with those people, motivated by the same desire for a religious entity of their own, that would be independent of the established oppressive structures. Their eyes were already turned towards the genuine sources of Hinduism, their aspiration was for a purified religion, for a faith that freed them from brahmin and sectarian dictatorship and gave them self-sufficiency and self-respect. It is no wonder that they felt that Dayananda could help them find that ideal, and that is why they decided to found the Arya Samaj.

It seems strange that there were so few brahmins on the council, considering that they did have forty per cent of the total membership. With those numbers, one would rather expect that they would command a majority on the committee: after all, they were by far the most numerous single caste, and the highest in status. But when one looks more closely at the names of those thirty-seven brahmins, it soon becomes clear that there was among them only one prominent figure, the Chitpavan Dr Anna Moreshwar Kunte, whose brother Mahadev was professor of Sanskrit at Elphinstone College, and who was himself once excommunicated for participating in a widow-remarriage.[53] The others belonged mostly to the middle and lower ranks of the professions, and were certainly not a group of outstanding intellectuals.[54] It should also be remembered that twenty-eight per cent of their group were still students. The brahmins of the Bombay Arya Samaj were in no way representative of the intellectual élite; they were a moderately educated group belonging not to the intelligentsia, but rather to the lower middle class strata of schoolmasters and clerks. They were also a group divided in several ways, e.g. between Gujaratis and Marathas, and they lacked that commonly rooted desire for religious regeneration that we detected among the Aryas of the trading castes. In fact the number of brahmins in the Samaj would decline over the years, and their influence within the Samaj would never really increase.[55] Dayananda's general repudiation of brahmin leadership, an aspect of his approach that appealed to many Bengalis and was to be enthusiastically approved by the Panjabis, was probably one of the reasons why he failed to attract the Maharashtrian social reformers, who mostly considered brahmin leadership essential in the reform movement.

In this context there is the question of what happened to that sizeable group of students, particularly of Elphinstonians, who became founding members of the Arya Samaj. This group seemed to augur a good start for the Samaj among the young intelligentsia, and it included two young men who were to leave their mark in history, Shyamji Krishnavarma and Ganesh Shrikrishna Khaparde. On the inspection of the available committee lists of the Bombay Arya Samaj's first twenty years, it appears that only four of these students persisted in their association with the Samaj: Shyamji Krishnavarma, the Gujarati Vania Tulcharam Chunilal, the Soni

Khanji Bhagavan, and only one Maratha brahmin, Moreshwar
Gopal Deshmukh.[56] It seems, therefore, that the initial interest
of the young intellectuals was very soon dissipated.

The Bombay Arya Samaj, therefore, had as its most numerous
and dynamic core a group of businessmen of the rising trading
castes. With only a few exceptions they belonged to the middle
ranks of society; they were neither the very wealthy nor the leading
intellectuals. Over decades they had grown used to all kinds
of cross-caste organizations in social and municipal affairs, and
they knew therefore enough about the way to set up a modern
association. They were motivated by a genuine religious aspiration, mostly having its source in the anti-Vallabhāchārya movement
started by Karsondas Mulji with its inclination towards a purer
and older non-sectarian form of Hinduism. Initially these people
were supported by a miscellaneous but sizeable group of Maratha
and Gujarati brahmins, a group however of no great eminence
or dynamism, and also by a significant group of students. This
support, however, soon dwindled away, and the membership
and leadership of the Bombay Arya Samaj remained in the hands
of those middle class businessmen and professionals from the
trading classes who took the initiative in founding it.

The twenty-eight rules adopted by the Bombay Arya Samaj[57]
constituted a very clumsy mixture of statements of belief, organizational by-laws, and moral precepts. The credal content was
minimal. When one considers in how much detail Dayananda
had worked out his own theological system by this time, this is
a clear indication of deliberate restraint: the Swami had no wish
to impose all his own views on the Aryas. Only two areas of belief
were insisted upon: God and the *Vedas*. The *Vedas* should be
accepted as the principal self-evident authority, and interpreted
with the help of the books composed by the *rishis*. The *dharma*
described in the *Vedas* should be followed by an Arya 'as much
as it was in his power'.[58] The Lord is described by no less than
twenty-five adjectives: he is infinite and perfect in every way,
free from all bodily characteristics and from any birth as *avatār*,
and he should not be represented by an idol.[59]

Although the rules included moral principles and directives,[60]
they mostly dealt with membership and organization. Each province should have a 'Principal Samaj', of which the others would be
branches and on which they should model themselves. The Prin-

cipal Samaj had three special functions: the running of a central Vedic library, the publication of a weekly, and the general supervision of the Samaj schools.[61] The requirements for membership were minimal: one had to be of good character, principled, and concerned with the welfare of the people. The leadership should be reserved for those who lived up to the rules, and only those who were wicked in an excessive and public manner should be expelled, but only after impartial deliberations of the committee.[62]

Each Samaj should be run by a committee, which was open to males and females, and should include a president and a secretary. The committee members were responsible for the general running of the Samaj and they also had two special duties. They should conduct two schools, one for boys and one for girls, staffed exclusively by males and females respectively, in which the ancient scriptures should be studied. No further details are given about these schools, and it seems that Bombay never even started them. The other responsibility of the committee was to send preachers around 'to preach the truth everywhere', an idea no doubt inspired by the use of such propagandists by both the Brahmos and the Christian missionaries. Any alteration of the rules of the Samaj had to be made by the committee after proper deliberation, which had to be preceded by due notification of the proposed change to all members.[63]

The duties of the ordinary members were, in general, to work for the advancement of the Samaj in so far as their family duties gave them the opportunity, and, specifically, to attend the weekly meeting. This meeting should be the occasion for exchanging ideas and discussing practical matters, but it was primarily meant to be a religious function, involving two alternating items: chanting of *Sāmaveda* hymns and lectures on Vedic *dharma*. There was also a rather vague injunction that the Samaj should see to it that the sacraments were duly performed. The members had a financial obligation: they should contribute a regular one per cent of their income to the Samaj and, if on a special occasion they felt like giving a donation, this should be directed to the Samaj. The funds thus collected were to be used exclusively in the running of the Samaj, the periodical, and the schools.[64]

The most striking characteristics of this constitution are two: the paucity of its requirements in matters of faith and religious and social duties, and the insistence on decentralized autonomy.

Dayananda had elaborated a complicated theological system, yet only Vedic infallibility and spiritual monotheism were prescribed doctrinal tenets. His current publications provided a complete guide to ritual, yet no direction was given to follow those rites: in fact the Aryas were left free to continue the ceremonial customs of their caste, as long as they shunned idolatry. There was not a single rule that would prevent a member from continuing to observe all his caste rules: he was not asked to be a social reformer, except in a most general fashion. In fact only gross public misbehaviour could lead to a member's expulsion. Autonomy for each Samaj was the key-word of the organization: it adopted and revised its rules as it pleased. There was no provision for a provincial or national authority: the 'Principal' regional Samaj was not invested with powers, but only with special responsibilities. The Swami's ideas were not held up as in any way binding, and the person of Dayananda was not given any place at all in the constitution, not even as patron. The only guiding principle was the very vague Vedic authority. The aim of the Samaj, as expressed in rules 1 and 17, was kept very broad: the uplift of the whole society in both its spiritual and material aspects.

One could say that the structure of the Arya Samaj was the very opposite of that of Keshub Chandra Sen's Brahmo Samaj of India. Keshub's organization had no formal constitution: he exercised practically dictatorial powers, the members having no formal access to decision making. Dayananda had noticed the disruptive influence of that situation which was to split Keshub's Samaj into two. That is why he gave his own organization a proper constitution, vested all power in the members, and refused to accept any title to authority for himself.

What then did Dayananda have in mind when he encouraged and assisted the establishment of the Arya Samaj? He wanted to bring together all Hindus who agreed on a couple of very broad issues: a dedication to religious and social reform, and a conviction that this reformation had to come through a revival of Vedic religion. Being organized in a body, these people would be more effective in helping one another and in influencing the whole of society. The Swami had no intention of creating a body of 'followers' to propagate his ideas. Reform had to come from the people themselves, who had to take their personal improvement and the uplift of society into their own hands. Dayananda himself would always be available to them for advice, either in person or through his publications, but he would not be their leader. He had a horror of *guru*dom and sectarianism. He recognized the limitations of his own knowledge, and refused to become the *guru* of a group of devotees, and even of one single individual. When Thakur Umrao Singh implored the Swami to be his *guru* and give him a *mantra*, Dayananda replied, 'I do not make anyone my pupil. Those are my pupils who believe in my ideas, and those who help me in my work are my brothers.'[65] His one great fear for the Samaj was that it might evolve into a sect, a process he had already detected in the Brahmo Samaj: that is why he saw to it that the constitution of the Arya Samaj avoided those dangers. Overall authority would reside with no man, but only with the *Vedas*, and direct authority would be democratically shared by the people involved. Just as Dayananda's own goal lay far beyond the establishment of the Samaj, similarly the ultimate goal of the Aryas should lie far beyond their own group, beyond narrow credal inhibitions: they should aim at the final establishment of the unity of *dharma* by striving to persuade all groups and sects to accept the *Vedas*. Indeed, the overall reform of the whole society, which was the Swami's own aspiration, could not be realized by the Samaj, but only by the collaboration of everyone.

All this was made very clear by the Swami in an important speech to those admirers in Bombay who had pressed him for the establishment of the Arya Samaj:

If you are able to achieve something for the good of mankind by a Samaj, then establish a Samaj; I will not stand in your way. But if you do not organize it properly, there will be a lot of trouble in the future. As for me, I will only instruct you in the same way as I teach others, and this much you should keep clearly in mind: my beliefs are not unique, and I am not omniscient. Therefore, if in the future any error of mine should be discovered after rational examination, then set it right. If you do not act that way, then this Samaj too will later on become just a sect. That is the way by which so many sectarian divisions have become prevalent in India: by making the *guru*'s word the touchstone of truth and thus fostering deep-seated prejudices which make people religion-blind, cause quarrels and destroy all right knowledge. That is the way India arrived at her sorry contemporary state, and that is the way this Samaj too would grow to be just another sect. This is my firm opinion: even if there be many different sectarian beliefs prevalent in India, if only they all acknowledge the *Vedas*, then all those small rivers will re-unite in the ocean of Vedic wisdom, and the unity of *dharma* will come about. From that unity of *dharma* there will result social and economic reform, arts and crafts and other human endeavours will improve as desired, and man's life will find fulfilment: because, by the power of that *dharma* all values will become accessible to him, economic values as well as psychological ones, and also the supreme value of *moksha*.[66]

This statement clearly demonstrates that from the very start the Swami conceived his own role in the Samaj as anything but a dominant one. It was not his idea that the Samaj should become the esoteric haven of a select few, but rather that it should be a broadly based and open association that could unite all Hindus of goodwill around the unifying centre of their religion, namely the *Vedas*. These fundamental attitudes of the Swami towards the Samaj would become even stronger as the organization itself grew in later years.

The meetings and discussions that led to the establishment of the Samaj did not take much of the Swami's time, which was mostly devoted to his usual work. The public lecture had become the main instrument of his propaganda, and he now definitely concentrated on the positive side of his message: the history of the Aryan people, Vedic revelation, the doctrines of God and soul, ethics, the uplift of the nation. He had always been reluctant to let the flow of his lectures be interrupted, or to have his long lectures followed by long question sessions. He now solved this problem by a new device: he gave his lectures on alternate days, with a day in between exclusively devoted to discussions.[67]

The best reported lectures are those the Swami gave at Poona. He delivered about fifty lectures in all, some in town, others in the cantonment. The fifteen lectures delivered in town were extensively reported in the papers, and eventually Marāthī and Gujarātī translations, and a re-translation into Hindī were separately published.[68] They covered his favourite topics, plus some especially chosen for the sake of the Prarthana Samaj audience: the proof of rebirth, remarriage, and *niyoga*.

In no other statement did Dayananda express his attitude to *niyoga* and widow-remarriage more clearly and forcefully:

It is not my wish to criticize widow-remarriage in order to give support to those who oppose widow-remarriage . . . what I am saying is that for the twice-born *niyoga* is better . . . In the olden days *niyoga* was practised extensively, and there was little need for remarriage. But in this age both *niyoga* and remarriage have been stopped, and the resulting miserable wickedness is indescribable . . . All these sins are on our heads. Looking at today's blind adherence to false tradition one has to admit that widow-remarriage is altogether better than that.[69]

These words make Dayananda's stand quite clear: in principle, only *niyoga* should be practised by the twice-born; but, if *niyoga* is not acceptable, then let there be widow-remarriage, because it is infinitely better than the contemporary situation. Although he remained inflexible on the principle, Dayananda was quite amenable to practical compromises. This explains his continuing good relationship with reformers and even Aryas who persisted in promoting widow-remarriage.

Six of his lectures dealt with history from the Vedic age to that of the *Purānas* and the sects: Dayananda had been widening his knowledge of history even since the composition of the *Satyārth Prakāsh*.[70] The final Poona lecture was autobiographical, and it has remained one of the most important sources for the knowledge of the Swami's early life. In general, these lectures displayed greater clarity in the development of themes and in the order of their presentation than is to be found in the treatment of similar subjects in the *Satyārth Prakāsh*.

As soon as the Swami arrived in Bombay, his presence and his readiness to discuss religious topics were proclaimed in an announcement in four languages. The Vallabhāchāryas immediately interpreted this as a direct challenge to them: the Swami's hosts were their antagonists, the members of the Veda Sabhā who had invited the Swami especially to fight them.[71] They sent the Swami anonymously twenty-four questions in order to ascertain his doctrinal position. The answers were written and published on Dayananda's behalf by his collaborator Swami Purnananda.[72] Such were the first moves in a confrontation that lasted during the whole stay of the Swami in Bombay. The most crucial question was again about idol worship in the *Vedas*, and it is no wonder that the idea of a public dispute was very much in the air: the Swami's arrival had been heralded a month before by the republication of his Banaras disputation. The Swami's first lecture in the Framji Cowasji Hall on the topic of idol worship was disrupted by his opponents at question time.[73] Next they tried to make the Swami face their own famous Pandit Gattulal in a meeting they planned to stack in their favour. By now Dayananda knew the dangers too well, and he stated his conditions for a fair disputation: equal representation of supporters, equal rights of question and reply, daily continuation until the question was decided, and a complete written report which should be published.

That was too much for the opponents: they arranged a lecture by Pandit Gattulal on the very day that a lecture of the Swami had long been scheduled, thus making sure that Dayananda would be unable to accept their weak demand for a confrontation.[74] The Vallabhāchāryas thought that the Swami's Achilles heel might be grammar, and in February 1875 they arranged a debate of Dayananda with one of their pandits on grammatical points. This disputation took place and the Swami came out the winner.[75] In June they tried again, choosing this time a very reluctant Pandit Kamalanayanacharya, an acknowledged pillar of their sect. In fact, when they issued the challenge Dayananda had left for Ahmedabad, and they thought he had left for good: they claimed that he had fled to avoid the confrontation. The Aryas, however, sent a telegram to Ahmedabad, and the Swami promptly arrived back on the next train. The pandits then had to go through with their boast.[76] We have a detailed description of this dispute from the *Bombay Samāchār*.[77]

It was a grand occasion in the Framji Cowasji Hall, with a capacity audience, among whom there were many shets and pandits. On the centre of the stage a large table was placed covered with over 150 books, the *Vedas*, *Brāhmanas*, *Upanishads*, *Sūtras*, and various *Shāstras*. On the chairman's left there was a chair for Dayananda, and on his right one for the Pandit and, a little below that, eight chairs for *shāstrīs* who were to take notes. The session was started with the reading of a strange document: it was a contract between a devotee of Dayananda and a follower of the Pandit, in which they pledged that, according to the outcome of the debate, the signatory on the losing side would become a follower of his opponent's *guru*! When Pandit Kamalanayana-charya was asked to commence his argument, he started instead to question the other pandits about their sectarian adherence and their qualifications. Dayananda and the chairman Shet Mathuradas Lowji tried to reason with the Pandit and make him get on with the debate, but he just sat there sullenly. Dayananda then proposed that he would first state his case and that the Pandit could criticize it afterwards. But the Pandit was not to be persuaded: he simply left the hall, thus bringing a rather flat finale to what was expected to be a grand occasion.

The opponents nevertheless did not lose hope, and during Dayananda's last weeks in Bombay they produced their final antagonist: Pandit Ramlal, famous primarily as an astrologer, and as such employed by many businessmen. The Pandit was reluctantly propelled by his own fame and by the fear of losing face, into an affair he dreaded, though Gattulal and other pandits coached him all they could. At the debate the poor Pandit kept producing proofs of idol worship alternatively from the *Purānas* and the *Smritis*. Finally the chairman urged him to come to the point and submit a proof from the *Vedas*. Ramlal, put on the spot, admitted that he was unable to do so, and the debate collapsed.[78] This involvement of Dayananda in public debates was not of his choice; by now he knew too well how little they achieved, and how often they ended in uproar or frustration. But he could not ignore the challenge, and his performance certainly put him in the limelight on the Bombay scene.

The Swami also considered private discussions with eminent people as part of his work. In Bombay he had long exchanges of view with the great sanskritists of the Prarthana Samaj, R.G. Bhandarkar and Vishnuparashuram Shastri.[79] He is also reported to have had meetings with the important western scholars Von Bühler, J. Wilson, and Monier-Williams, to whom he no doubt explained his plan for a Vedic commentary.[80] But writing occupied a growing period of his working day. He had now reached the point where he was completely convinced of the power of publication in the work of reform. He had at last completely overcome that reluctance towards secondary writing that Virjananda had instilled in him. During his stay in Western India he wrote six works, five of which were published within that period.

Not surprisingly his first work was the *Vedaviruddhamatkhandana*, a 16,000 word pamphlet against the Vallabhāchāryas.[81] It had a didactic, question-and-answer form, which covered all the important aspects of the sect in sixty-two items. It was a thorough and biting criticism. It concentrated less than the *Satyārth Prakāsh* had done on the history and immoral practices of the sect, though they were mentioned: its stress was rather on doctrinal issues. The Swami took great pains in preparing this pamphlet, as is demonstrated by the many references it contains to Vallabhāchārya works. He quoted the *Anubhāshya*, Vallabha's famous commentary on the *Brahmasūtras*, and also a minor work of his, the *Siddhāntarahasya*. He also referred to the

Vidvanmandana, an important treatise by Vitthala, the son of Vallabha. Moreover, he had consulted contemporary works, the *Shuddhādvaita Mārtanda* of Giridhara, great-grandson of Vitthala, born in 1845, and the *Satsiddhāntamārtanda*, a work of Pandit Gattulal, whom the Vallabhāchāryas unsuccessfully tried to pit against him in debate. Finally, he even mentioned one of the many vernacular works available at the time, the *Rasabhāvanā*. Dayananda took his polemics seriously and prepared for his publications in the best way possible.[82]

Jaikishendas Jivanram, one of the two Bombay reformers who had met Dayananda in Banaras, was a convinced Vedāntist, and he was shocked when the Swami started to denounce Advaita in his lectures. He turned against the Swami and started to attack him in the papers.[83] Another Vedāntist of the same circle, Rajakrishna Maharaj, also switched from admiration of Dayananda to enmity.[84] The Swami then put his criticism of Advaita into print in his *Vedāntidhvāntanivārana*, a pamphlet in Hindī only about a quarter of the length of the previous one.[85] Its construction and argument are clear and simple. Four basic tenets of the Neo-Vedāntins are refuted: that *brahman* and the *jīva* are identical, that man's deepest self is not active, that the world is illusory, and that in *moksha* the *jīva* is utterly absorbed into *brahman*. Both argumentation and doctrine presented in this work are identical with those offered in the *Satyārth Prakāsh*.

In the beginning of the nineteenth century Swami Sahajananda had instituted a reform of Vallabhāchārī Vaishnavism by founding the new sect of the Swāmīnārāyanas. His sect was open to followers of any other sect, who could even continue to wear the symbols of that sect. Sahajananda was an excellent organizer and he had institutionalized in three different orders the administration, the leadership, and the cultural responsibilities of his sect. His success was very great in Kathiawar and Gujarat, and by the seventies the sect was in a powerful position in Western India.[86] Dayananda gave several lectures about the sect, and then devoted a pamphlet to it, the *Shikshāpatrīdhvāntanivārana*, about the same size as the previous one.[87] The method used in this work is the favourite one of the Swami when dealing with any religion: it consists in writing a scathing commentary on its principal sacred text. The most important text of the Swāmīnārāyanas was the *Shikshāpatrī*, a collection of 212 verses. Dayananda quoted a quarter of these verses in his pamphlet and showed in his usual fashion their rational and moral flaws and their deviation from Vedic religion.

These were the three polemical pamphlets Dayananda wrote in Western India. But in his writing as well as in his preaching his involvement in controversy was overshadowed by his efforts at positive instruction. During this time he wrote three more substantial works, of which two dealt with ritual, and the third was a prayer book. The decision of Dayananda to write these works was part of the new approach to the establishment of the Vedic religion he was evolving. His long and mostly fruitless efforts in the rural Doab had convinced him that the regeneration of Hinduism would not be effected through the pandits and the brahmins: they had too big a stake in the *status quo*. His preaching in Calcutta and his contacts with the Brahmos had revealed to him that there existed a group of people who had both the desire and the ability to launch that regeneration: the educated urban middle class. Therefore, he had ever since concentrated his preaching on them. But it was obviously not sufficient to convince them of the abuses of contemporary Hinduism, and of the truth and glory of the Vedic religion: they needed mutual support, hence the foundation of the Samaj. They also needed concrete directions to guide them in their new life and to show them how to worship and how to pray: those three books were written in answer to that need.

In his *Satyārth Prakāsh* Dayananda had already described the historical, doctrinal, and ethical aspects of Vedic life; in Bombay he decided to complement that text with handbooks for ritual and prayer, and thus to provide his followers with a complete guide to leading a truly religious life. He would soon add to that the continuous publication of his commentaries on the *Vedas*, which would give everyone access to the very sources of revelation. His programme of publication was thus a systematic and carefully considered one. These books could effectively take the direction of religious life out of the hands of pandits and brahmins, and put it back into the hands of the people themselves. At the same time they would guarantee that all rituals and prayers remained thoroughly Vedic. In other words, these books created the possibility of taking religious authority away from the incumbents who had abused it with disastrous results, and restoring it to its rightful seats: the infallible *Veda*, and the conscience of the individual.

The *Sanskārvidhi* written with 'the aim of making the sacraments easy to perform for all people, learned and uneducated'[88] was finished in Baroda in early 1876 and published in Bombay in 1877.[89] In about two hundred pages it contains the description of sixteen major sacraments from among those described in the *Grihyasūtras*.[90] Dayananda closely followed the most usual list by including three pre-natal rites, six rites pertaining to childhood and three to studentship, and ending with marriage and the funeral ceremonies.[91] Three chapters were devoted to topics which cannot be properly called sacramental: they described the qualifications and duties of the three stages of life, those of the householder, the hermit, and the *sannyāsī*.

The handbook certainly succeeded in providing a manual for Vedic rites: it abounded with Vedic texts, the Hindī commentary retained the full richness of Vedic terminology, and all sectarian and Purānic elements had been excluded. It also brought a new meaningfulness to the ritual, as all actions and formulas were carefully explained in Hindī. However, the manual did not make for easy use. There were too many long quotations from the *Vedas* and other works, and these were separated too far from their vernacular translations. Moreover, the rubrics were so completely interwoven with the commentary that they were difficult to follow. These defects were corrected by Dayananda in his second edition.

In general there was no change in the *Sanskārvidhi* from the doctrinal positions of the *Satyārth Prakāsh*. On two particular topics, however, the Swami's thought had clarified itself. He had removed the ambiguities from his former treatment of *niyoga*. He made it quite clear now that among the twice-born marriage could only be contracted between a man and a woman who had not been previously married: therefore, the widower as well as the widow had to have recourse to *niyoga* for any further union. It was explicitly stated that *niyoga* might be contracted by someone who already had children, that from any one *niyoga* only two children may be begotten and that up to ten successive *niyogas* might be contracted by any widow or widower. *Niyoga* was not contracted by a sacramental rite proper, but in a ceremony where the partners holding hands made a solemn promise in the presence of the responsible leaders of the community.[92]

Whereas Dayananda's chapter on the hermit and the *sannyāsī* in the *Satyārth Prakāsh* was rather muddled, consisting of a medley of verses from Manu, and drawing a picture of withdrawal from the world and privilege, his treatment of the topic in the *Sanskārvidhi* was much clearer. The main theme was that the state of *sannyāsa* entailed enormous responsibilities of spiritual direction and religious instruction. All references to special social or spiritual privileges had been dropped, and so had the minute external regulations proposed by Manu.[93]

The daily Five Great Sacrifices constituted the backbone of Vedic religion, and Dayananda's preoccupation with them dated back a long time: the first booklet he ever published was on the *Sandhyā* rite, in Agra just after leaving Virjananda.[94] The Bombay edition of the *Panchamahāyajnavidhi* came out in 1875, and a revised but practically unchanged edition in 1878.[95] This handbook of the daily Vedic rites was a much better production than the previous one on the sacraments. Its conciseness and clarity, the proper arrangement of the ritual instructions and the Hindī commentary, made it into a very easily useable manual.

The *Aryābhivinaya* was published in Bombay in 1876. It contains a Hindī commentary on fifty-three select verses of the *Rigveda* and fifty-four texts of the *Yajurveda*.[96] Dayananda wrote that the work was taken up 'on the loving request of many learned and pious persons concerned with the welfare of the people', and that its aim was 'to help the people to have the proper knowledge of and loving devotion to the Lord, so that they may know how to praise the Lord, how to pray and to worship'. He remarked that this commentary gave only one side of the *mantra*-interpretation: it explained the religious truths and values, but omitted the scientific truths often inherent in the same texts. The latter would be fully investigated in his *Vedabhāshya*.

This remarkable work shows a side of the personality of Dayananda that but seldom surfaces in his other works: the man of deep devotional prayer. The book is a collection of meditations on Vedic texts, devotional literature of great directness and fervour. Yet, on close scrutiny, these prayers never waver an inch from the doctrinal convictions of the Dayananda of that period. Every reference to creation, for instance, remains in strict conformity with the theological structure elaborated in the *Satyārth Prakāsh*, which was to be changed so fundamentally later on. The book demonstrates how much Dayananda was a man of one piece:

even in his most meditative and emotional outpourings he neve strayed from his doctrinal structure. The work was also quite an innovation in contemporary Hindu devotional literature. Collections of texts with commentaries, or collections of devotional hymns with commentaries were available, but this combination of Vedic *mantras* with a meditative, prayerful commentary was a new initiative. Dayananda may well have come across some Christian collections of a similar nature. However, the main influence probably came from the prayer literature published by the Brahmo and Prarthana Samajes, since we know definitely that the Swami acquired some of them.[97] Yet these prayers were very different from Dayananda's in that they were carefully purged of all concrete references to both Vedic and Purānic mythology. They had in fact such an air of generality and indefiniteness that many could as well have been part of a Christian or even a Muslim prayerbook. Dayananda's work, on the other hand, was steeped in the rich peculiarity of Vedic lore and terminology, and every sentence had some Vedic reference that would strike a chord in the Hindu mind.

With these three works Dayananda provided for those who wanted to follow the Vedic *dharma* manuals of ritual and prayer readily understandable in the Hindī language, thoroughly Vedic, and free from all the excrescences of corrupt Hinduism. But by this time the Swami had been thinking a lot about another major project: the publication of a full translation and commentary of the *Vedas* in Hindī, which he increasingly considered was to be his major life's work. It was a revolutionary and ambitious project to make available to all the people of India the sacred *Vedas*, which at the time the brahmins and pandits still considered their private domain. To Dayananda the key to India's full regeneration lay in the *Vedas*, and he was deeply convinced that knowledge of the *Vedas* would inevitably lead the Aryans back to their ancient glory. It was in Bombay that he wrote and published the first sample of his Vedic commentary. It was a commentary in Sanskrit on the first *Sūkta* of the *Rigveda*, accompanied by Hindī, Gujarātī, and Marāthī translations. He wrote in the introduction that 'this is the manner in which I will make a commentary of all the *Vedas*. If anybody has any objections to it, let him please inform me, so that I can write my commentary after taking critical notice of them.' The sample was sent to pandits in Banaras, Calcutta and elsewhere, and also to Growse and Griffith, but there is no evidence of reactions on their part.[98]

On leaving Western India Dayananda went back for the third time to the U.P., where he remained about a year.[99] He first spent a fortnight at Farrukhabad, the centre of his first success during his period in the Doab. He gave four public lectures, and the Rev. J.J Lucas expressed his surprise at the enthusiastic welcome for the Swami and at the clarity and forcefulness of his speeches. Dayananda disestablished his local Vedic school when he learnt that the head pandit was teaching Shaivism and that the pupils were not changing their old ways, and he diverted the funds of the foundation to the financing of his *Vedabhāshya*. At the time of his departure he told his many friends that he would only come back to them on condition that they established an Arya Samaj.[100]

The next five months, three of which were spent in Banaras, thence going on to Jaunpur, Ayodhya, Lucknow, and Shahjahanpur, the Swami lived practically in complete retirement, gave no lectures and did not participate in any debates. He was fully occupied with arrangements for the printing and publication of the first fascicules of his *Vedabhāshya*, and with the writing of his important work, the *Rigvedādibhāshyabhūmikā*, 'Introduction to the Commentary of the *Rig*-and other *Vedas*'. By November 1876 his public activity increased again; he gave a series of lectures at Bareilly and at Moradabad, where he also had a lengthy public debate with the Rev. E.W. Parker. He then headed for Delhi, passing through two of the scenes of his earliest preaching, Karnavas and Chalesar. This was the Swami's very first visit to Delhi, and he had very special reasons to visit it now.[101]

Lord Lytton had organized a magnificent durbar in Delhi on the first of January 1877 to celebrate the assumption by Queen Victoria of the title of 'Empress of India'. The rulers of the native states, big and small, would be present, and this seemed to Dayananda a unique opportunity for contacting them and presenting his ideas of reform to these princes who wielded such enormous power over a great part of India. No doubt it was the example and influence of his *guru* Virjananda that inspired the Swami. When after the Sepoy Mutiny Lord Canning had organized a durbar at Agra for the ruling princes of Rajputana,

Virjananda had gone there: he wanted Maharaja Ram Singh to convene a 'Sārvabhauma Sabhā', a universal council of Hinduism to promote the writings of the *rishis*. But nothing had resulted.[102] The pupil was as unsuccessful as the master: apart from a few minor talukdars, only one ruling prince took the trouble to contact Dayananda: Maharaja Tukojirao Holkar of Indore. This idea of a universal council of Hinduism exercised Dayananda's mind considerably: it had been mentioned in the answers to anonymous questions in Bombay, and his Poona lectures had also referred to it.[103]

Another attempt at high level cooperation similarly failed to produce any results. Several eminent reformers were at the time present in Delhi, and Dayananda arranged a meeting to discuss how they could cooperate in their reform work to maximize the results. Those present were Munshi Kanahiyalal Alakhdhari from the Panjab, Babu Navinchandra Ray of the Lahore Brahmo Samaj, Keshub Chandra Sen, Munshi Indramani of Moradabad, Syed Ahmed Khan, and Babu Harischandra Chintamani of the Bombay Arya Samaj. Any attempt at collaboration between these reformers was bound to founder on the rock of enormous doctrinal differences, especially in the matter of Dayananda's unbargainable belief in Vedic revelation. And so it did.[104] But these two events in Delhi show how the hope for a supra-sectarian form of collaboration and organization retained a hold on Dayananda's mind, an idea that strengthened rather than weakened in the coming years.

In March 1877 the famous three-cornered disputation of the Chandapur Melā took place, where Christians, Muslims, and Aryas discussed central religious issues.[105] This time the participants were all prominent figures. On the Muslim side there was Maulana Muhammad Qasim Nanawtawi, the founder of the famous Deoband School for the protection and revival of Islam. He was then forty-five years old and at the height of his power and influence.[106] He was assisted by Maulvi Sayyid Abdul Mansur of Delhi. The spokesmen for Christianity were equally distinguished. They were the Rev. T.J. Scott, missionary of the American Methodist Episcopal Church, then Presiding Elder of Bareilly District, assisted by the Rev. E.W. Parker of the same church. The following year Scott was to become Principal of Bareilly Theological Seminary, and he was the author of several important works, Parker was ordained Bishop in 1900.[107]

The disputation, as reported by the Arya faction, was mainly concerned with problems of creation and salvation. It is· in the record of this debate that we find the first major change in Dayananda's idea of creation. Up to then all his publications had affirmed that the world and the souls were originally created by the Lord out of his own potentiality, *sāmarthya*, and that they therefore had an absolute beginning. Now he stated clearly and repeatedly that both *prakriti* and *jīva* were beginningless. *Prakriti* was eternal dormant matter, the *upādāna kārana*, material cause, and the Lord was the efficient cause, *nimitta kārana*, which fashioned the actual cosmos out of that dormant matter. The *jīva* was eternal, had no beginning and no end, and *moksha* too was endless. Pressing questions from the Rev. Scott could not make Dayananda elucidate any more clearly the exact relationship between *prakriti* and the Lord.[108]

It was during this period that Dayananda finished writing his very important *Bhūmikā*, which was sent to the press at the beginning of 1877. The Swami wrote only the Sanskrit version and left the Hindī translation to his pandits. He must have considered it a very important task, for he wrote no less than seven successive versions of it, so that the pandits could not keep up with his changes: even in the last editions one still finds some discrepancies between the Sanskrit version and the Hindī translation.[109] In fact, Dayananda started to learn English from a Bengali, so that he would be able to read Max Muller's translation of the *Vedas*. But he soon realized that he did not have sufficient time for that study, and had to be content with having someone translate to him from Max Müller's work.[110]

The *Bhūmikā* is a large volume of over four hundred tightly printed pages, divided into thirty-three chapters of very uneven length: they vary from just one page to forty. It is written mainly as a commentary on Vedic texts arranged around a number of topics. About half the volume deals specifically with the *Vedas*, their origin, their nature, and the rules of Vedic interpretation. The rest of the work is devoted to matters of theology, *dharma*, and worship. Some thirty pages deal specifically with Vedic science and technology: astronomy, mathematics, geometry, and the arts of telegraphy, ship-building, and medicine.

This work does not present any major changes in doctrine in comparison with the *Satyārth Prakāsh*, except for the creation theory. This particular case is worth closer investigation, because the *Bhūmikā* presents a transitional stage between the Swami's theory proposed in the *Satyārth Prakāsh* and the one presented at the Chandapur Melā; thus we have before us three phases of the change. Whereas the *Satyārth Prakāsh* ascribed an absolute beginning to the cosmos, an *ādisrishti* when God fashioned the universe out of his own potentiality, the Chandapur discussion rejected both these propositions and affirmed that *prakriti*, the material cause of the universe was without beginning. In the debate Dayananda carefully avoided using the word *sāmarthya*, potentiality, although the Rev. Scott tried to force it on him. The Swami kept insisting on the eternal character of the material cause, 'which is called *prakriti*, *paramānu* (ultimate atom), and other names'.[111]

The *Bhūmikā*'s position lies between those two. Dayananda had already rejected the *ādisrishti*, and he believed the material cause of the universe to be beginningless. But he still referred to that material cause as 'the potentiality of the Lord', and considered the *prakriti* as its first evolute.[112] This continuing identification of the material cause of the universe with the potentiality of the Lord had often led the Swami into logical difficulties, especially in discussions with missionaries who saw it as a weak point. From the Chandapur Melā on Dayananda freed himself from this difficulty by simply dropping completely the concept of *sāmarthya*, and holding on to the statement that *prakriti* is the material cause of the universe: since it is beginningless like the Lord, the question of its origin is a useless one. The third eternal substance is the *jīva*: here we have for the first time Dayananda's doctrine of *traitavāda*, 'the theory of the three ultimate substances'.

Looking back over this year in the United Provinces one gets the feeling that something important is missing — and so it is: Dayananda had come from Bombay after the successful launching of his Samaj, and during this year in the U.P. the subject does not seem to have been raised. No samaj was founded, nor was there even the suggestion that one should be founded, except at Farrukhabad. Admittedly the Swami was fully occupied in the first six months with his *Bhūmikā*, but work or overwork could never stop him doing what he wanted to do. Moreover, in the second half of that year he came out of seclusion and did a lot of public work in different cities where samajes were started a couple of years later. Then why did not Dayananda try at this time to foster the founding of samajes, as he soon would do in the Panjab? The answer is simply that there was as yet not enough demand from the people concerned, no groundswell from below. The Swami never considered the establishment of a local samaj through his initiative or ·pressure: the initial moves and the organizing drive had to come from the people themselves. This attitude of his must have been reinforced by the fate of the Rajkot Samaj. There the branch had been established rather rashly, probably because the Swami had been somewhat carried away by being back in his homeland, Kathiawar. But, if he was rather impulsive there, he had learnt his lesson when he saw how quickly that branch collapsed. The Swami must have felt that in the U.P. it was too early in 1877 simply because the people were not quite ready for a serious and lasting commitment.

CHAPTER VII

Success in the Panjab

When Dayananda left Western India in 1876, his activities had caused quite a stir in certain circles, but the scene there had not basically changed at all. The hundred or so enthusiasts of the Bombay Samaj kept their spirit, but never managed to transform their small branch into an intellectually or socially important group. The Swami spent only sixteen months in the Panjab, two months less than in Western India, and he never was able to pay a return visit. Yet, when he left the land of the five rivers, a new force had clearly been set in motion in Panjab society, a force that had a decisive influence on the history of the province for many years to come. The main reasons for the great success of the Arya Samaj in that area are the peculiar social structure of the Panjab and the special needs and aspirations of an important section of the Panjabi Hindus in the seventies. Since Dayananda did not venture into the native states and limited his activities to the submontane and central districts, the heartland of the Panjab which was under direct British administration, it is these latter districts that need to be looked at more closely.

The Panjab has always been an area of great social and racial diversity, lying at the land gate of India through which over the millennia numerous invaders descended into the land of promise. In the nineteenth century this diversity was greater in the central districts visited by Dayananda: there the population was approximately half Muslim, three-eighths Hindu, and one-eighth Sikh.[1] The Hindus, therefore, constituted a minority community; the Sikhs were more powerful than their number indicates, as they had long been the rulers; and the Muslims dominated in numbers. These three communal groups constituted the most important units of society in the Panjab: in most matters of consequence the deciding factor was which of these groups one belonged to. Even the newly educated Panjabis remained subject to that communal gravitation pull; they tended 'to identify with a religious community rather than with the Western-educated

class as a whole'.[2] There was also a caste system: a broadly parallel
caste hierarchy cut horizontally through the three communities
with aristocratic and religious elites at the top of the ladder and
outcaste groups at the bottom.[3]

Because of its strategic position on the map of the subcontinent,
the Panjab had been the scene of many battles. For longer than
nearly anywhere else in India it had been in the grip of the Muslim
armies, and had recently experienced two centuries of Sikh martial
rule. It is no wonder that here it was the kshatriya caste that
wielded the greatest power and claimed the highest status. In a
land where the Hindus were a minority group and where prince
and soldier were the natural leaders, the brahmins did not have
that dominant status they prided themselves on in most other
parts of India. Prakash Tandon, a very keen observer of his own
society, remarked about the brahmins, . . . 'that they could be
leaders of society, in a position of privilege, I only discovered
when I went to live outside the Panjab. With us the Brahmins
were an underprivileged class and exercised little or no influence
on the community'.[4] In this area of decisive Muslim majority,
the Hindu community was too small to support the brahmins
in their traditional roles of priest and pandit, and they were forced
to spread out into the world of business and government service
to secure a livelihood. This dispersion of the brahmins impeded
even further their cohesion and influence.[5]

In the hierarchy of castes there were, between the ruling castes
(among whom the Rajputs were the dominant group) and the large
body of peasant Jats, several major castes comprising merchants,
professionals, and government servants, — the Khatris, Aroras,
Vanias, and Suds, who were all either Hindu or Sikh. The Khatris
were the most outstanding group, claiming the Rajput descent
suggested by their very name. They held a powerful grip on trade,
were generally literate and prosperous, and also had a long tradition of government service under both the Mughals and the Sikhs.[6]
Sir George Campbell remarked, perhaps with some exaggeration,
that they were, in the Panjab, 'all that the Mahratta Brahmins
are in the Mahratta country, besides engrossing the trade which
the Mahratta Brahmins have not'.[7] Within the Panjab they were
largely concentrated in the areas visited by Dayananda,[8] and
their bases were the cities and the towns. They were a vital community, always attempting to improve their social and religious

status in accordance with the improvement in their economic power and influence.[9]

The introduction of British administration into the Panjab at the time of annexation in 1849 brought profound changes. A multitude of new jobs were created both inside and outside the government services. At first they were filled by imported Western-educated Indians, mostly from Bengal, because no Panjabis had yet received an English education.[10] But educational opportunities soon grew, particularly after the establishment of the Panjab Education Department in 1856,[11] and they were eagerly seized upon as providing the passport to the new employment opportunities. British rule also created a host of economic openings in the grain trade, and in the money-lending business as a result of agrarian indebtedness.[12] These new opportunities were naturally not the kind to have any attraction for the old aristocratic élites, who, deprived by the British of their traditional arena of political rivalry, tended to limit themselves to an empty tussle for honours and protocol precedence.[13] It was the merchant classes, primarily the Khatris, who eagerly grasped the new opportunities.

Education and opportunities were new and they fell on virgin soil, which blossomed soon into a meadow of a very industrious, able and conscientious professional class. The Punjab Khatris had for generations been deprived of their right to administration, and now suddenly opportunities were thrown before them, anyone's to pick up. The Khatris, and soon the other castes, ran forward to grasp them . . . soon they spread all over the Punjab government civil list, the medical service of the army, and the professions of lawyers, barristers, doctors, scientists and professors.[14]

This process by which the Khatris nearly monopolized educational and career opportunities, was assisted by the Panjab Government's policy of religious impartiality which lasted till the late 1880s. Such a policy precluded the British from making special educational and occupational provisions for lagging sections of the community, in particular the Muslims who, as a result, were left further and further behind in the race. Thus the rapidly-rising English-educated élite was dominated by the ambitious Hindu Khatris.[15]

British administration had brought another important new element into the Panjab: the Christian missionaries. The American Presbyterian Mission was first in the field in 1834, and had a vigorous start; within a year they had a High School in Ludhiana, and their own printing press, and their progress across the province was rapid. The Church Missionary Society followed in 1854, and in 1855 the Church of Scotland. Missionary propaganda spread quickly in the areas of education and publication, and new institutions sprang up in many places: orphanages, Zenana Missions for the evangelization of women, and even mission colonies.[16] Two factors tended to reinforce the impact. When the missionaries saw the many new employment opportunities in the Panjab, they invited Indian Christians, particularly Bengalis, to come and take up positions in the new province. Thus they quickly laid a firm foundation consisting of a compact community of educated Indian Christians.[17] Moreover, more than two-thirds of the Britishers of the first Panjab Commission were Evangelicals who strongly believed in the mission of Christianity and tended to support the churches' efforts.[18] Considering that missionary activity was a new experience for the Panjabis, it is no wonder that the fear of a 'Christian threat' was engendered in their minds when they observed the quick and efficient ramification of the various missionary institutions across their province, and the close affiliation between the government and the missionaries.

Although conversions of upper caste people were few, the Christian missionaries made the most of them, and gave them strong publicity whenever the occasion arose. The Reverend Robert Clark arranged for the cream of Christian converts to be presented to Edward, Prince of Wales, on his visit to Amritsar, in 1876, and proudly described the gathering:

There, in one corner of the room, is seated the brother of the reigning Rajah of Kapurthala, who was only baptized a few months ago. . . . There is Imad-ud-din, the learned Maulvie, who is now engaged in writing a commentary on the Bible. There is Rajab Ali, the editor of a native newspaper. . . . There is Imam Shah, the native pastor of Peshawar. . . : At the opposite side of the room conspicuously appear five Rajputs. One of them is a Zaildar, or chief, of twenty-two villages. After tea has been served, Professor Ram Chander (Director of Public Instruction in Patalia State) is called upon to give an address. : . . But the address of the evening is that of Mr Abdullah Athim, an Extra Assistant Commissioner. . . .[19]

Another such public occasion was the inauguration of the Native Church Council at Lahore, where papers in Urdū were read by eight leading intellectuals, converts from all three communities.[20] This happened on Easter 1877, the very date on which the Swami entered the Panjab.

The introduction by the missionaries of aggressive religious

proselytization and controversy was bound to elicit reactions
from the three communities, and especially from those groups
benefiting from the new educational and occupational opportunities. The Muslim community, although in the majority numerically, was the least represented among the social groups that
mattered, and its response was correspondingly weak. The Sikhs
were more active and aggressive. The Nirankári movement
founded in 1851 was mostly concerned with internal religious
matters, but the Nāmdhāri movement was much more widely
influential. Apart from their religious and social aspirations, the
'Kūkās', as they were called, had also political ambitions. However,
the murder of Muslim butchers at Amritsar and Raikot, and the
attempted coup in the state of Malerkotla in 1872, provoked
strong British reprisals which for the time being quietened the
movement. The Singh Sabhā founded in Amritsar in 1873 was
much more a reform organization along modern lines, concerned
with the protection and promotion of the religious and social
values of the community.[21]

But the new rising élite was strongly dominated by the Hindu
Khatris. The Hindu community had had for centuries to cope
with the two proselytizing religions of Islam and Sikhism, and
now, when a new future was opening up for them, they faced the
apparently more serious threat of Christian missionary propaganda.
As the Panjabis were new to this type of threat and its organizational methods, it is no wonder that the leadership of the first
Hindu reaction was undertaken by the Bengali Brahmos who
formed 'the largest, most influential and publicly active section
of the Bengali community' in the Panjab.[22] In 1863 the Brahmo
Samaj was founded in Lahore, with six Bengalis and four Panjabi
Khatris as its members, and by 1877 branches of the Samaj had
been established at Rawalpindi, Amritsar, and Multan. They
opened schools, set up a publication society, established their
own press, and published a monthly in Hindī and Urdū.[23]

Another Hindu organization, the Sat Sabhā, was founded in
1866 by the ex-Brahmo Lala Behari Lal. It was subject to strong
Bengali influence and was in doctrine and organization closely
patterned on the Adi Brahmo Samaj of Bengal.[24] Both these
reform organizations thus had an important built-in weakness:
their inspiration and leadership were Bengali. As the Panjabi
Hindus rose in the administration and the professions, they would

start resenting the 'imported' Bengalis safe in the higher echelons, and this resentment was bound to rub off on the organizations themselves.[25] At both Firozpur and Gujarat the Hindus had found it necessary to form an association to counteract missionary influence. Both these societies were called Hindu Sabhā, but they seem to have been purely local and unconnected phenomena and little is known about them.[26]

Such, then, was the Panjab Dayananda entered at the end of March 1877. He had come on the invitation of some eminent personalities: the famous author and reformist Kanahiyalal Alakhdhari, Sardar Vikramsingh Ahluwalia, an important leader of the Sikh community, Pandit Manphul, and Munshi Har Sukhraj, proprietor of the Kohinoor Press.[27] His activities continued to follow the pattern so firmly established in the previous few years: the Swami went to a town on invitation only, and he expected those who invited him to arrange his travel and accommodation, and the venue, time, and advertisement of his lectures. In the Panjab the initial invitation often came from members of the existing Hindu reform bodies, the Brahmo Samaj, the Sat Sabhā, or the Hindu Sabhā. The itinerary of the Swami shows his awareness of the relative importance of the centres he visited. Half his time was spent in Lahore and Amritsar. All the towns he stayed in were district headquarters, except Wazirabad, where he spent the shortest time. His visit to other towns were as follows: over a month at Rawalpindi, Jullundur, and Multan; and from one to three weeks at Gujaranwala, Gujarat, Ludhiana, Jhelum, Gurudaspur, and Firozpur. Practically all these towns lay in the belt of strong Hindu and Khatri concentration.

Dayananda's programme was such that it must have amazed even the industrious Panjabis: he lectured constantly, often on practically every day spent in a town, and his lectures were never short.[28] Bhagat Lakshman Singh expressed the amazement of the Panjabis thus:

There was, of course, nothing in him of the dreamy mysticism I had learnt to associate with the name of *Sadhu*, a sort of sanctimoniousness which suggested consciousness of a superiority or a desire to appear as a person not easy of access. On the contrary we saw before us a wide-awake man full of life and anxious to impart it to those who came across him.[29]

The topics of the lectures showed no signs of innovation, and the full list of the Multan lectures[30] indicates that the Swami tried to cover all the main aspects of his teaching in his lecture series: all the theological, ritual, and ethical topics were there, and those criticizing contemporary Hinduism and exalting the Vedic age. He did give special lectures on Islam and Christianity, and some on the Brahmo Samaj and Sikhism. A lecture on cow-protection at Gurudaspur suggests that this question, and the allied problem of meat-eating, were gaining importance in his mind.[31]

Very soon the conservative Hindus of Lahore realized that Dayananda was a formidable foe. They disseminated the slander that he was an atheist and a spy paid by the Christians, and they exerted pressure on his host to have Dayananda leave his house. They even established a Sanātanadharmarakshinī Sabhā and organized counter-lectures in the Dharmshālā. They managed to put enough pressure on Pandit Bhanudatta, the Sat Sabhā preacher and an avowed admirer of Dayananda, to induce him to join their own Sabhā.[32] However, their influence does not seem to have been great, and during the subsequent visits of the Swami to Lahore it drops out of the picture altogether. The opposition was also at work in other towns, and their activities sometimes led to disorderly scenes. Lectures were disrupted at Gurudaspur, Rawalpindi, and Multan; and in Gujarat, Wazirabad, and Amritsar it even came to bombardments with stones and bricks.[33]

Whereas in Bombay the question of a public disputation was always in the air, on account of the local republication of the text of the Banaras dispute, and because there was a strong body of learned brahmins and pandits keen on publicly defending orthodoxy, this was not so in the Panjab. Only three public debates were arranged, only one of which was with a Hindu pandit. The latter was held at Gujarat, where the missionaries had been very active and where the Hindus had founded a Hindu Sabhā to counteract their influence. The pandit from Jammu who was to be the Swami's antagonist had been asked to bring his authoritative books to the debate. He arrived with a little booklet containing just a few *mantras*. Thereupon Dayananda exclaimed, 'The whole town of Gujarat cannot produce a single copy of the *Vedas*. Look at the Christians! They are translating the Bible into all languages and they are available for two annas each!' This outburst must have taken the wind out of the pandit's sails, and he just sat there in sullen silence.[34]

Although in general the orthodox opposition was weak, and
no pandit could be produced to effectively oppose the Swami,
they did have some effect here and there. In Rawalpindi their
efforts kept many people away from the lectures;[35] in Gujarat
they prevented the Swami from founding a local Samaj; and in
Multan the newly founded Samäj mustered only a paltry seven
members.[36] Nevertheless, the overall impact of the opposition
was not very great. Dayananda's vehement denunciation of
Christianity deprived them of their main weapon, and the pathetic
intellectual weakness of their pandits made them lose face with
the intellectual élite.

There seems not to have been strong Muslim antagonism
towards the Swami at that time, and although he did give some
lectures about Islam, they were few; whereas the orthodox Hindus
were his constant target, the Muslims were not. In fact some
Muslims were quite friendly. When the Brahmos of Lahore
withdrew their support, the Swami was given a house by the eminent Muslim doctor Khanbahadur Rahim Khan,[37] and the
Amritsar Arya Samaj was established within the residence of
Miyan Jan Muhammad.[38] When the Jhelum Samaj was thinking
of converting a Muslim, Dayananda advised against it as inop-
portune in the circumstances.[39] At Amritsar a public debate
between a Maulvi and the Swami was mooted, but it did not occur
on account of the difficulty of finding a proper interpreter.[40]

In Jullundur a public debate was held, and it was a properly
organized affair: the topics were clearly defined (transmigration
and miracles) and an account was duly published over the signatures of Lala Amichand and Muhammad Husain Mahmud.[41]
It was also agreed beforehand that neither disputant would afterwards claim victory, but that they would let the public record
of the debate speak for itself. Although that particular agreement
was broken by a section of the Muslim community, the disputation
itself was conducted in a civilized and dispassionate manner.
In fact, the record shows that Dayananda met an intellectual
equal, as versed as he was in scholastic debate and in the niceties
of logic. This is not surprising as the Muslims had a long tradition
of experience in that exercise. The argumentation proceeded at
high level, and the competence and composure of Maulvi Ahmad
Hasan did not give Dayananda the chance of scoring with éclat,
which his Hindu opponents often gave him by their very incom-

petence. The Maulvi's self-confident and direct rational arguments stayed closely to the topic, and he certainly came out of the confrontation unscathed. The Swami too argued well, and it was only in his very last submission that he could not resist the temptation of sprinkling a little dash of that pepper which spices most of his debates: 'If the Maulvi Sahib thinks that way, then he should never let himself be overtaken by sleep, because in that state he will forget all he learned while awake.'[42]

In Gujaranwala, a third debate was launched with some Christian missionaries. All the notables of the town were present in the packed church where it was held, but the building could not hold the more than two thousand who spilled out into the courtyard. For two successive nights the dispute ran from eight in the evening, the topic being the identity and difference between God and the soul. Dayananda then requested a change of venue: it should be an open space where all the people could listen. The missionaries went ahead on their own and arranged for the next meeting to be held at midday in the church, which they stacked with their followers beforehand. Such, at least, is the way the Aryas report it. Dayananda refused to go to that session, and arranged for a meeting at four o'clock in an open space not far from the church. He invited the missionaries to come, but, understandably, they declined, probably a little afraid of the combination of a huge crowd and the fiery Swami. Dayananda therefore took the floor himself and gave one of his caustic criticisms of the Bible.[43]

The missionaries were acutely aware of his presence and of the aggressive challenge he represented. Several of the leading Panjabi missionaries of the day had meetings with the Swami. The Reverend E.M.Wherry, who met Dayananda at Ludhiana, belonged to the American Presbyterian Mission and had started an Urdū weekly at the Ludhiana Mission Press which he owned.[44] Dr W. Hooper was a distinguished scholar, who had obtained first-class greats at Oxford and had been a Boden Sanskrit Scholar. At the time he was Principal of Lahore Divinity College, and would later establish the Allahabad Divinity School and become one of the main workers in the revision of the Hindī Bible. He had a discussion in Sanskrit with Dayananda about the *Vedas* and about caste.[45] At Amritsar the Swami met the Reverend C.W.Forman of the American Presbyterian Mission, one of the most influential pioneer missionaries of the Panjab, who had arrived as early as 1849.[46] During their conversation Kanahiyalal entered the room and put some two hundred rupees in front of the Swami to cover his expenses. Someone peeped in afterwards, and seeing the Swami and the missionary with a stack of money on the table between them, spread the rumour that Dayananda had been bought by the missionaries.[47] That accusation had been levelled before at Lahore,[48] but Dayananda's vehement denunciation of Christianity in his lectures soon dispelled the slightest suspicion on that score. Another time a bishop, whose name is not reported, challenged the Swami's translation of a hymn to Prajāpati, and then boasted that the power of the Bible was clearly demonstrated by the fact that the sun never set on the area of its influence. Dayananda retorted that that power did not come from the Bible itself, but rather from the fact the Christians practised the virtues preached in the *Vedas*.[49] The Swami is also reported to have met Father Robert Clark, the eminent leader of the Church Missionary Society in the Panjab since the early fifties.[50]

Such prominent missionaries, by making a point of meeting the Swami, showed their awareness of the importance of his presence and his impact. But it was the emergence of a new idea of Dayananda's, the concept of *shuddhi*, that made them realize how real a threat he was. This was an ancient Hindu concept, referring to the quality of purity necessary for the proper performance of *dharma*, which includes ritual and social duties. By extension the term also indicated the rite by which pollution is removed, and access to *dharma* is restored: it gives back the right to perform the rituals and to participate in the social life of the caste.[51] In the nineteenth century the term first appeared among the reformers in the context of crossing the *kāla pāni*, the black waters. Those who had journeyed outside India would necessarily have had many contacts with polluting materials and persons. They were, therefore, on their return required by orthodoxy to submit to a rite of purification. Many reformers repudiated this rule, and so did Dayananda.[52] The second use of the term was for the reinstatement of a 'lapsed' Hindu, perhaps somebody who had been converted to another religion. Orthodoxy was very reluctant to accept such reinstatement.[53] The pandits forgot that it was an ancient custom: the *Atharvaveda* and the *Brāhmaṇas* prescribe the rite of *vrātyastoma* for readmittance of those fallen beyond the pale of Aryan society, and the later law-books like the *Devalasmriti*, probably written after the early Arab raids, prescribe lengthy provisions for the re-admission into Hinduism of people forcibly converted.[54]

It is significant that it was in the Panjab that Dayananda first mooted the question of *shuddhi*. It was first raised at Ludhiana, the Swami's very first stop in his Panjab tour. The brahmin Ramsharan, who was a teacher at a mission school, was on the point of being baptized. When Dayananda arrived some Hindus asked him to try to prevent it. The Swami gave some instruction to Ramsharan who decided not to go through with the baptism.[55] The problem was brought to Dayananda's attention for the first time here in the Panjab where the Hindus felt the missionary propaganda as a real threat. Six months later Dayananda had obviously thought and talked about the problem a lot, and at Jullundur he gave a lecture on *shuddhi*, and himself performed the reconversion of a Christian.[56] There were other cases. Kharak Singh, once a *yogī*, had been converted by the Reverend Clark of Amritsar, but still had doubts: 'It was at this time that I met again Swami Dayananda . . . I had met him before, when he and I were both *fakirs*. He told me that I had mistaken the meaning of the Vedas, and bade me practice Yoga in order to gain salvation. For a time I followed him and became an Arya, and the Christians left me.'[57]

By the time of the Swami's final stay at Amritsar the threat he represented had become quite clear to the missionaries. About forty students of the mission school were very attracted by Christianity. They called themselves 'Unbaptized Christians', and even formed a society, the 'Prayer Meeting'. The preaching of Dayananda redirected those potential converts, and disturbed the Reverend Waring. He decided to arrange a debate between an eminent convert of his, Pandit Khansingh, who had been a Christian for twelve years, and the Swami. However, on meeting Dayananda, the Pandit was so impressed that he became his follower. The Reverend Waring could not let the Swami get away with such a victory, and invited the Reverend K.N.Banerjee of Calcutta to come and face the Swami. However, the latter clergyman was prevented at the last minute from leaving Calcutta by the illness of his daughter. This episode led to the re-conversion of some Christians.[58] This was the only area where Dayananda showed an active interest in *shuddhi*, although he occasionally reiterated his stand that *shuddhi* was a proper and necessary procedure. But he gave the Panjabi Aryas an idea that would be followed later on in the province, grow into a considerable movement, and spread over the Gangetic plains. The missionaries early realized the potential threat of Dayananda's message, although they would not feel its full impact till the eighties. This powerful Hindu counter-challenge to the missionaries was eagerly welcomed by the Panjabi Hindus, and it certainly constituted an important factor in the Swami's growing popularity. Its impact was reinforced by the first letter from the American Theosophists, which reached Dayananda during his stay in the Panjab: this letter claimed that many Christians of the West were dissatisfied with Christianity and were looking to Indian religions for an answer in their religious quest.[59]

Relations between Hindus and Sikhs had always been close, joined as they were by ties of common traditions, of kinship, and of shared oppression under Mughal rule. Dayananda probably knew little about Sikhism when he came to the Panjab. In his first *Satyārth Prakāsh* he had given the Sikhs only a couple of lines, which they shared with other sects: 'It is noteworthy that in the sects of Nānak, Kabīr, and Dādū, there is no idol worship. But they have too great a veneration of their holy books: that too is a kind of idol worship.'[60] He saw Sikhism as just another unimportant sect of Hinduism, and did not make it a target for attack; he only gave two lectures on Sikhism, in Multan and in Amritsar. The Amritsar reaction was strong: the militant Nihāngas threatened to assassinate him.[61] But this was an isolated incident. There was no real antagonism between the Samaj and the Sikhs. In fact, some individual Sikhs supported Dayananda: Bhai Jawahar Singh assisted him and became secretary of the Lahore Samaj in 1878. This friendly relationship between Aryas and Sikhs did not last however: friction started in the eighties, soon leading to serious Arya-Sikh confrontation.[62]

Like their brothers of the Prarthana Samaj, the Panjabi Brahmos were very interested in the Swami's visit. They received him in Lahore, and for the first couple of weeks he was their guest. However, when Dayananda concentrated his two lectures in the Brahmo Samaj Hall on the *Vedas* and transmigration, thus directly confronting the Brahmos on the key doctrinal differences, they felt slighted and withdrew their support.[63] Dayananda's casual and condescending treatment of their Pandit Agnihotra did not help, and the Swami made himself another bitter enemy.[64] Yet, he wanted good relations, and when the Brahmo Samaj celebrated its fourteenth birthday he came at the end of the prayer meeting with nearly two hundred of his followers to congratulate the Brahmos.[65]

The cooling of relations in Lahore did not mean that other places immediately followed the lead: each group made up its own mind. Both in Rawalpindi and Multan the invitation to the Swami came from the Brahmos, but their final reaction seems to have been similar to the one in Lahore. Some Multan Brahmos seriously considered joining the Arya Samaj; but they were dissuaded by their friends. In Jhelum the Arya Samaj chose an ex-Brahmo as its president, but he soon returned to his former group.[66] Although a few individuals did leave the Brahmos for the Arya Samaj, and even a few Bengalis made that move, lasting in only two cases, the loss to the Brahmos was only a small one.[67] But even if the Arya Samaj did not present an immediate danger to the Brahmos, it took the wind out of their sails by presenting the Panjabis with an alternative reform body: one they could lead themselves, which was free from Bengali dominance, and free also from that taint of excessive westernization that affected Brahmoism.

The Sat Sabhā was only a small organization, very closely patterned on the Brahmo Samaj. The first two meetings of the Lahore Arya Samaj were held in its hall. But the Sat Sabhā members were displeased by the Swami's severe attack on the *Shāshtras* and the *Purānas*, and asked the Aryas to find another venue.[68] In Firozpur a Hindu Sabhā had been established before Dayananda's visit, and this organization invited him. As a result the Hindu Sabhā was changed into an Arya Samaj.[69] The Hindu Sabhā of the town of Gujarat, similarly antedating the Swami's visit, reacted differently. Their leader, Pandit Nandalal, was a strong opponent of Dayananda, and his opposition was probably the reason why no Arya Samaj was established at the time.[70]

Whereas in Bombay it took six months of tentative moves to establish the Samaj, the Lahore Samaj was founded two months after the Swami's arrival, on 24 June 1877. Its initial membersnip was about a hundred, as in Bombay, a number far exceeding the tally of the Brahmo Samaj founded fourteen years earlier.[71] A month later the membership had trebled and a bookshop-library had been opened; and soon afterwards a Sanskrit school was inaugurated, attended by a hundred people.[72] It was a remarkable and rapid achievement illustrating both the impact of the Swami and the way in which he fulfilled a pressing need of the Panjabi Hindus.

A committee of twenty-two was elected and the list is a very impressive one.[73] Half the members had a University degree: five M.A.'s, three doctors, one lawyer, and two B.A.'s. These figures speak all the more eloquently when seen in the context of contemporary higher education in the Panjab. By 1884 the total number of Panjabis who had passed either the M.A. of Calcutta University or the equivalent Honours in Arts of the Panjab University College was only twenty-six. By 1877 not more than a dozen Panjabis could have gained that degree, which means that nearly half that number were on the Samaj committee.[74] If half the committee could boast of a University degree, the presumption is that many other Aryas had matriculation and higher degrees. The Lahore Arya Samaj committee was indeed representative of the cream of educated Panjabis.

Of the twenty-two committee members, only one was a brahmin, whereas probably over eighty per cent were Khatris.[75] They dominated the Samaj as completely as they dominated higher education and the professions. The recorded professions of committee members were as follows: one district judge, one lawyer, three doctors, one headmaster, three government translators, and five clerks in various government offices. If we add to these thirteen the four members who had a B.A. or an M.A. and presume that they too were in the professions or government service, we end up with the probability that at least eighty per cent of the committee were thus employed, and the percentage may well have been higher. The Lahore Arya Samaj committee, therefore, contained some of the best-educated Panjabis, mostly from the trading castes, primarily Khatri, and the number of professionals and government servants was very high.

The information available on the committee members of the other Samajes established in the Panjab confirms the same pattern.[76] Over seventy per cent appear to be Khatris, and the professions are well represented at about sixty per cent, including five lawyers, three magistrates, two doctors, two head clerks and three teachers. Considering the small number of Panjabis with University degrees at that time, the tally is impressive.

Another source gives invaluable information about the composition of the Panjab Arya Samaj, confirming the picture already sketched. About the time of Dayananda's arrival in the Panjab the fascicules of his *Vedabhāshya* started being published, and they contained, usually on the inside of the cover, a list of subscribers. This list, for the period Dayananda was in the Panjab, runs to around 570 names, 170 of which are names of Panjabis, thirty per cent of the total. Apart from the full name and title of the subscriber, the list also gives an address, in most cases the place of employment, and thus it provides information on both the caste and occupation of the subscribers. Naturally not all these people were Aryas, or even followers of the Swami. Nevertheless, the latter would have constituted the overwhelming majority of the subscribers, so that the list tells us something about the Panjabi Aryas. Of the 170 Panjabi subscribers some ninety lived in Lahore. At least seventy per cent of them were Khatris and only eight per cent were brahmins. No less than eighty per cent worked in government offices, a third of these in fairly responsible positions.[77] The Panjabi subscribers outside Lahore present very much the same profile: eighty-five per cent were in government service, half of these in senior positions. It is also noteworthy that the subscribers did not come only from the towns visited by the Swami: an additional twelve towns are mentioned. This document, therefore, confirms that the Panjab Arya Samaj was completely dominated by Khatris, and by people primarily employed in government service.

At Lahore the Bombay rules of the Samaj were studied, and it was decided to rewrite them thoroughly and put them in some logical order. There would be ten basic principles, and all practical and organizational matters would be arranged in a separate section of *upaniyams*, or by-laws. The ten principles have remained unaltered to this day, but the by-laws were later changed.

The ten principles[78] give broad directions concerning creed, objectives, and attitudes. The first two deal with God, 'source of all knowledge', who is described by his attributes, very much as in the Bombay rules. The addition of the attribute of 'holiness', *pavitra*, is probably a result of Dayananda's frequent discussions with missionaries. The third principle refers to the *Vedas*: 'The *Veda* is the book of the sciences of truth. It is the duty of all Aryas to read it and to propagate its study.'[79] Althoug':. the Bombay rules had only a minimal credal content, the Lahore rules cut down even on that. They left out the term *svatah-pramāna*, 'self-evident', 'finding its justification within itself', and did not mention the subordinate relationship of post-Vedic *rishi*-composed works *vis-à-vis* the *Vedas*. Thus they lacked any statement establishing the unique position of the *Vedas* as the norm of all truth. This uniqueness was, however, indicated in the first *upaniyam* by the vague formula that the *Vedas* constituted 'an extraordinary authority'.[80]

These principles were approved by Dayananda, and never changed. He was acutely aware of the implications of formulas dealing with the *Vedas*, and must have been conscious of the omission and approved of it. This does not suggest in any way that his own belief in the *Vedas* had been eroded, but it does clearly indicate that he did not expect the Aryas to accept his belief as a condition of membership. This decision was the outcome of discussions by the Swami with his Panjabi followers, who urged him to allow broader and less precise doctrinal requirements for membership of the Samaj. Mulraj was eminently qualified to speak on this matter: he was closely associated with the Swami and helped formulate the Lahore rules; he was the first President of the Lahore branch and the Swami later appointed him Vice-President of his Trust. Mulraj interpreted the wording of the vital third rule as follows:

Swami Dayananda purposely abstained from entering in the *Niyams* any doctrinal points and philosophical questions. He believed in all he wrote, but he had toleration for the views of others. If a man believed in the ten *Niyams*, the Swamijee thought that he could become a member of the Arya Samaj; whatever his opinions on other subjects might be. He did not make it an essential condition for membership of the Samaj that a man should believe his translation of the Vedas to be correct, or the opinions expressed by him in his works to be sound. . . . He was never required to sacrifice his freedom of thought and speech.[81]

This is clearly confirmed by the second *upaniyam*, which only requires for membership 'belief in the fundamental principles', and no more.[82]

Rule 6 states the objective of the Samaj: 'The principal aim of this Samaj is to promote the well-being of the whole world, physical, spiritual, and social.' The other rules dictate the attitudes of mind that should pervade the members: they should be concerned for truthfulness in all, and should actively dispel ignorance by wisdom; their activity should be guided by *dharma* and their social relations by affection; Aryas should not be content with their personal well-being, but they should have the good of society in mind: they should obey the laws that govern the well-being of all, but where their individual good is concerned, all should be self-governed.

Mulraj understood very well that combination in the rules of a very broad doctrinal basis with the more important stress on those virtues which go to make moral man.

We must be thankful that the Arya Samaj has been placed upon a very broad and catholic basis: the basis of belief in one Eternal God and in the Vedas. . . . On the broad platform of this religion, which is simple and free from philosophical theories, men, whose minds are in different stages of development and who have different modes of thinking, can come together to revive the study of the Vedas and to worship and glorify the Omnipotent Being who was adored by our ancestors.[83]

But, says Mulraj, philosophical niceties do not make one into a saint, it is only virtues that build up moral man, and that is why 'Swami Dayananda took care to include in the articles of faith of the Arya Samaj all that is necessary for the making of a noble, virtuous, and religious man'.[84] The subsequent history of the Panjab Arya Samaj confirms Mulraj's judgment. Dayananda never objected to some Aryas actively promoting widow-remarriage or continuing to be meat-eaters. In his mind there was a clear distinction between the basic principles all Aryas should accept, and the theological system and the body of Vedic interpretation that were his very own. The latter he propagated forcefully with all the power of his speech and his pen, but he never imposed their acceptance as a condition for membership of the Arya Samaj.

The Lahore Aryas also re-wrote all the rules to do with the organization of the Samaj and arranged them into a properly ordered set of *upaniyams* or by-laws. Two omissions from the Bombay rules are noteworthy. The loose hierarchical structure was completely dropped,[85] as was Bombay rule 15, requiring 'that all sacraments including the funeral rites shall be performed according to the *Vedas*'.[86] Here again, the changes are in the same direction: lessening of the requirements and opening up the Samaj for a wider membership. One interesting innovation was the introduction of the annual meeting, which would also be the anniversary celebration of a particular Samaj. This custom was to become an important aspect of Samaj life in the coming years.

Dayananda now effectively started on his major work of publishing a commentary on the *Vedas*. He had already sent samples of his work to pandits and orientalists, from Bombay in early 1875 and from Banaras in 1877, but there had been little reaction.[87] And now Dayananda made a much bolder move. He arranged a meeting with J. Griffith, secretary to the Lieutenant-Governor of the Panjab and Director of Public Instruction, and asked him if the Government would subsidize the publication of his Vedic commentary and would put it on the syllabus of the Panjab Colleges. He also presented him with a sample of his work. The Government passed the document on to the Panjab University, who circulated it for comment to R. Griffith, principal of Banaras Sanskrit College, C.H.Tawney, principal of Calcutta Presidency College, and three Sanskrit pandits of Lahore. Their adverse comments were referred by Dr Leitner, the University Registrar, to the Government. Somehow the Arya Samaj got hold of these documents and on 25 August two submissions were forwarded to the Registrar: one was Dayananda's answer to the objections, the other was a plea for reconsideration by the Lahore Arya Samaj. On 14 November 1877 the negative answer of the Government was communicated to Dayananda and the Samaj. This was one more of the Swami's many attempts to get for his Vedic movement a more general base, beyond all Hindu sectarian and caste configurations, from which it could have an impact on the totality of Hinduism.[88]

Dayananda did not base his request on the claim that his commentary was the only true one, or infallible. He claimed that his own interpretation was primarily based on the pre-*Mahābhārata* commentators, whereas other Hindu and European scholars relied on the later commentaries. His commentary, therefore, had a scholarly advantage in that it tried to approximate more closely to the most ancient sources. Moreover, it would stimulate research: 'My Veda Bhashya by frequently referring to the old pre-Mahabharata commentaries, and taking an adverse view to those of European scholars, will engender a strong spirit of enquiry which will bring truth to light, and improve the moral tone of our schools. As such it is deserving of the patronage of Government.'[89] Two things are noteworthy in these documents. First of all, there are a wealth of references to the Vedic works of European scholars. Dayananda did his best to keep abreast of what European scholars were publishing; every important contemporary Vedic scholar is mentioned.[90] The second striking aspect is the writing and composition of the first document, which was signed by Jivandas, secretary to the Samaj, who probably composed it in collaboration with other committee members. The document is very well composed in fluent and clear English, and is an indication of the quality and competence of the leaders of the Lahore Samaj, and of their thorough understanding of the ideas and aspirations of their Swami. The final paragraph of their submission makes this abundantly clear.

In conclusion the Samaj may be permitted to recapitulate the principal grounds on which it seeks the patronage of the Government of the Punjab for the Veda Bhashya of Swami Daya Nand Saraswati, and to express a hope that the Government may induce all the other Local Governments in the country to combine with it in encouraging this noble and disinterested project of a great reformer and scholar.

1. That Indian philology, if it is to follow a natural course, must begin with a study of the Vedas. Hence a diffusion of their knowledge is highly desirable.

2. That the publication of the present Veda Bhashya has engendered a spirit of enquiry, which it is well to encourage.

3. That a spread of the true knowledge of Vedas is calculated to emancipate the Hindu mind from the trammels of superstition and deep-rooted prejudices.

4. That Swami Daya Nand's commentary is founded on most reliable authorities, acknowledged as such even by European scholars, but which they have not hitherto fully utilized.

5. That unbiased opinions under the present state of circumstances cannot be expected from interested Brahmans or misinformed Europeans. Hence a fair trial should be given.[91]

It was in Lahore also that Dayananda wrote his answer to the criticisms of his *Bhāshya* by Pandit Maheshchandra Nyayaratna of Calcutta. This was later published as a pamphlet under the title *Bhrāntinivārana*.[92] It contains a detailed analysis of all the Pandit's objections in sixty-five pages. The principal accusation

was that the Pandit was running after the European scholars,
'they are not God that we should accept without examination
what they have written . . . Are they greater than our Aryan
rishis that we should follow them above all and dismiss our ancient
true books?'[93] Here too we find another aspect of Dayananda's
'nationalism'.

While in the Panjab the Swami wrote another work, the
Āryoddheshya Ratnamālā, which was published by a litho-
graphical process in Amritsar at the end of 1877.[94] It is a slim
volume containing a hundred definitions and descriptions of key
terms of Hindu religion and philosophy. It was meant as a small
glossary for the people who studied Dayananda's works and
attests to the Swami's sense of pedagogy. There were no new
doctrinal developments, but one definition is of interest: '*Mukti*
is the state of the attainment of God, who is all bliss, after having
been liberated from all evil works and from the unhappy ocean
of birth and death.'[95] The interesting thing is that this definition
avoids the use of any term indicating eternity. In fact, this omission
was deliberate. It was during this period that Dayananda for
the first time stated publicly his new doctrine of *moksha*: 'We
have thought about this question for a long time, and now after
three years of consideration we have become completely convinced
that the fruit of man's limited works is also limited, and that
man's spirit comes back into this world after having enjoyed the
fruits of his good deeds.'[96]

Thus Dayananda had now completed the radical revision of
the ontological scheme presented in his first *Satyārth Prakāsh*.
There he had stated that the *jīva* was non-eternal, and that therefore *moksha* too, although irreversible, would come to an end
in the final dissolution of the world.[97] We saw how he later changed
this doctrine: the *jīva* was an eternal entity; the clear implication
was that the irreversible *moksha* too was without end.[98] But
now he explicitly modified the latter: *moksha* is not an eternal
state, but at the end of the great cosmic cycle it terminates, and
the *jīva* re-enters the world of transmigration. This was a most
extraordinary doctrine, unprecedented in the two millennia of
Hinduism. The only precedent, and one of which Dayananda
could not have been aware, was the *mandala-moksha* of the
Ājīvikas, buried for ten centuries in the tomb of the past.[99]
Dayananda struggled with this problem for years, and he must

have been aware of the extraordinary nature of his solution. Therefore he must have had most compelling reasons for finally proposing it and persisting in his conviction to the end. He concisely indicated his basic argument in the definition itself, 'the fruit of man's limited work is also limited'. He was to elaborate the arguments in his second *Satyārth Prakāsh*, in our study of which they will be fully discussed. It will suffice here to say that the Swami's argument was based on his growing conviction that man's deeds alone earn *moksha*, and that the reward, therefore, must be commensurate with these deeds: since the deeds are by nature finite, the reward too must be so.

Dayananda's correspondence greatly increased during these months. In fact, in March 1878 he wrote a letter from Multan to the Lahore Arya Samaj, asking that they should engage for him another secretary, 'versed in English, Urdū, and Hindī', in order to help him with his correspondence.[100] Only a few letters have been preserved. He wrote frequently to his Bombay collaborators, Harishchandra Chintamani, Gopalrao Hari Deshmukh, and Shyamji Krishnavarma, mostly about the Vedic commentary and about Shyamji's planned trip to England. He also kept in touch with the Samajes of the Panjab. But his letters ranged widely, e.g. they went to a follower in Darjeeling,[101] and to Ramadhar Vajpeyi who had founded a Satya-Nirūpa-Sabhā in Lucknow.[102] His letters to Babu Madholal of Danapur in Bengal were most efficacious. Madholal had founded a Hindu Satsabhā and, thanks to the correspondence, it was transformed into an Arya Samaj in April 1878, a branch that was still flourishing when the Swami visited it for the first time in November 1879.[103]

By the time the Swami left the Panjab, which he would never visit again, an enormous amount had been achieved. His *Vedabhāshya* was being sold all over North India. Bombay itself was taking some 120 subscriptions, with many more in a dozen other towns in Western India, even in Kathiawar. Some ten towns of the Central Provinces figure on the list: in Bengal, apart from several subscriptions in Calcutta, another ten towns are mentioned; and from both Bihar and Rajputana there is also mention of ten towns. But the most striking success was no doubt in the area of the U.P.: no less than thirty towns appear on the list, most with multiple subscriptions. This was a clear sign that the Swami was succeeding in putting the *Vedas* back on the map of North India, and it augured well for his next tour in the U.P.[104] In the Panjab the Swami left behind ten Arya Samaj branches: all the towns he visited had their Samaj, except Ludhiana, which was his first stop, and Gujarat, where the local Hindu Sabhā refused to be converted. Some branches had a strong start, Amritsar with fifty members and Rawalpindi with thirty, whereas others started more modestly, Jhelum with twelve and Multan with only seven members.[105] But the number of branches and of members would soon multiply and go from strength to strength. The Lahore centre was extremely strong, with at least three hundred members at the time of the Swami's departure.

What were the reasons for this resounding success, far greater than any other modern Hindu reformer ever achieved even after many years of preaching? It was the result of a combination of two elements, the particular and pressing needs of a strong, compact section of Panjabi Hindus at that time, and the message of Dayananda. There was the general communal situation of the Panjab, where Islam and Sikhism had for centuries brought about among the Hindus a greater empathy with reform and monotheism; where orthodoxy was never as strong as elsewhere in India; and where the Hindus constituted a minority community, within which brahmin influence was not very great. The merchant classes, particularly the Khatris, were in a crucial stage of development. The changes brought about by the British administration in education, the economy and occupations, influenced them more than any other group, and the rapidly changing group accordingly experienced new needs. The religious and cultural challenge of the British, expressed most strongly in missionary activity, had greatly discredited the weak and stagnant Hindu orthodoxy, so that many educated Panjabis had remained Hindu only on the surface.[106]

To that challenge Dayananda offered a response that was not just defensive, but aggressive: he affirmed the superiority of the monotheistic and non-idolatrous Vedic *dharma* over all other religions, and the cultural and technological superiority of the Vedic Age. The Panjabis warmed to this approach whereas they had remained lukewarm and unresponsive to the endeavours of the Brahmo Samaj. The eclectic syncretism of the Brahmos, and their constant praise of foreign religions and scriptures, did not constitute a solid enough basis of proud self-respect, and their whole approach reminded one too much of the West. Moreover, the Brahmo leaders were mostly Bengalis imported by the British, and the Brahmo Samaj 'always remained a creature of the Bengali community'.[107] To the Panjabi the modern Bengali was somehow a product of the British Raj. This distrust of the Bengali and his pro-British views is also demonstrated by the fact that in the early years the Panjabi Aryas remained aloof from and hostile to the Congress, whose support 'was generally confined to the handful of Bengali and Panjabi Brahmo Samajists who controlled the Lahore Indian Association and published the Lahore Tribune'.[108]

Other aspects of Dayananda's message also found ready acceptance. To a rising élite the doctrine that caste should be attributed not by birth, but only according to quality and merit, was a welcome one. The Khatris were at the time well on the way towards a secure position of educational, professional, financial, and political superiority in society, yet their status, in the traditional sense, remained lower than that of both the religious and aristocratic élites. In previous centuries one particular group of Khatris, the ten *gurus* of Sikhism, had managed to become the leading group in the Panjab, both in religion and in politics.[109] To the nineteenth century Khatris it may have seemed that Dayananda's message offered them a similar opportunity.

To an élite that was ashamed of the exterior apparatus of contemporary Hinduism, and of the poor quality of its traditional leaders, the brahmins, it must have been most acceptable to find that Dayananda was striving to put the religious leadership squarely into the hands of those who were best qualified to undertake it. He bypassed the brahmins and pandits, and gave back to the people the pure Vedic rites and their own great scripture. They could be proud of both, and such a religion was free from all those aspects that figured most in the missionary satirization of Hinduism. Moreover, this religion was purely Indian in every aspect, and thus it freed the Panjabis from any feeling of being denationalized by the process of reform.

When Dayananda left the Panjab his ideas had clarified themselves in several areas, but most importantly, his conception of the aims and function of the Arya Samaj had developed, accentuating even further the trend his thought had taken in

Bombay. The minimal requirements in the Bombay rules regarding doctrinal matters had been lessened, thus opening the doors to a greater range of applicants. The increase in autonomy for the local branches also allowed for greater variety and flexibility. Both these innovations clearly indicate the Swami's concern to stop the Arya Samaj from becoming a sectarian body. He completely rejected being the *Guru*, and, though he continued to expound and propagate his own ideas as forcefully as ever, he accepted dissent and even tolerated it among the leading personalities. He wanted to prevent the Arya Samaj from cutting itself off from the body of Hinduism by the sort of rash social protest the Brahmos indulged in. Although he did not believe in pollution by inter-dining, he personally always avoided any action that might give the orthodox an excuse for claiming he was 'polluted' by eating with non-Hindus.

He firmly believed that the first task of the reformer was to get his ideas accepted: knowledge would gradually lead on to reform action, whereas premature implementation of minor points would only provoke the antagonism of Hindus, and thus endanger the very dissemination of the ideas. That was the type of approach he hoped the Aryas would follow, and one that also appealed to the Panjabis: the Swami gave them autonomy in the direction of their organization, and offered them a programme of radical yet gradual reform that would in no way upset the structure of their society or isolate them from non-Arya Hindus. A great cause of satisfaction to the Swami was seeing that his great project of Vedic commentaries was now at last properly launched all over North India. He never imposed the acquisition or study of them on the Aryas; his main concern was that they spread out over Āryāvarta so that they might influence Hindus as a whole.

CHAPTER VIII

The Final Years: The Founder and the Samaj

When Dayananda left the Panjab there only remained just over five years of his life. Although the pace of his activities had already become hectic, in these last years the intensity and range of his commitments became greater, to the extent that one wonders how one man could cram so much into a day. Because of this great variety, for clarity's sake, it is more convenient to devote different chapters to the various aspects of his work in these final years. This chapter analyses the Swami's role as founder and leader of the Arya Samaj, and the next discusses his various attempts to reach the wider world of Hinduism. Dayananda's work in the native states is studied in the following chapter, and his last publications and the further development of his thought are considered in a fourth chapter.

The chronology of Dayananda's travels in these last years was as follows: a tour of three months in the U.P. was followed by two months in Rajputana and another two years and three months in the U.P. After that he spent a total of two years and one month in Rajputana, interrupted by a six months' stay in Bombay. All in all, of the five years and three months left, two-and-a-half were spent in the U.P., two-and-a-quarter in Rajputana, and six months in Bombay.[1] The Swami now strictly limited his travels: he visited only important centres, on specific invitation, advertising his arrival beforehand; and all the towns visited had received him before, except for Roorkee and Danapur. He now travelled with a considerable quantity of books and quite a retinue of servants, helpers, pupils, and scribes.

The visit to the U.P. was very different from the one before he went into the Panjab. At that time the question of founding branches of the Samaj had not been raised, because it was obvious that the people were not ready and forthcoming. But now the atmosphere had completely changed: the great success of the Samaj in the Panjab and the regular publication of the fascicules of the *Vedabhāshya* heralded the Swami as he came down into the Gangetic plains. No less than sixteen branches were established, some even before his arrival. The Swami's pace of living is all the more remarkable because of a prolonged illness he suffered. He was already unwell at Aligarh, one month after leaving the Panjab,[2] but during his visit to the Hardwar Kumbh Melā in February-April 1879 he was struck down with acute dysentery.[3] This severe attack, however, did not slow him down much. Although the condition eased a little at Dehra Dun,[4] he was still very weak,[5] and got worse again at Aligarh at the end of April. His condition must have been severe indeed to induce him to take a five weeks' rest at Chalesar.[6] But when in early July he reached Moradabad for a week's stay, he was found to have contracted severe sprue, a chronic infection of the bowels, and he could manage only three lectures.[7] The sprue, with dysentery and inflammation of the gums and throat, aggravated by three attacks of high fever, kept bothering him from July 1879 to May 1880.[8] In Badaun, the Swami sadly remarked that poison had been administered to him several times, and that some poison must have remained in his blood. 'Hence', he said, 'my health has been ruined, otherwise I would have lived over a hundred years; but now there is no hope of this body surviving that long'.[9] This feeling seems to have spurred him on to work even harder, and it also made him draw up his first will in August 1880 at Meerut. This protracted and acute illness also helps one understand how a sudden and savage disease would later fatally strike down a man of the physical strength and endurance of the Swami: a chronic illness was brooding under the surface. Notwithstanding his affliction, Dayananda kept up his hectic pace till the end of November 1879, when he settled in Banaras for nearly six months. This prolonged stay seemed to have restored him to health.

During these tours he continued his usual routine of lectures and discussions, but more and more time was devoted to writing and to his growing correspondence. Wherever he was, whatever his state of health, there was always a series of public lectures. At key places they increased in frequency. During his three weeks at the Kumbh Melā he set himself a very demanding timetable: from nine to eleven he was available for consultation, from one to five he gave his daily lecture followed by discussion, and from seven to nine he gave special instruction to select people.[10] When he paid a three-and-a-half months' visit from November 1880 to Agra, a town he had not been near since 1866, he gave thirty-two lectures, the subject-list of which has been preserved. They covered the whole field of his thought and endeavours: God, the *Vedas*, prayer, ritual, diet, moral and political duties; there also were lectures on scientific knowledge in the *Vedas* and on cow-slaughter.[11] As a result, an Arya Samaj was established in the town. A similar intensive series of twenty-six lectures at Ajmer in May-June 1881 resulted in the founding of a branch there that would continue to flourish.[12]

Public debates had long been one of the Swami's propaganda tools, but in the Panjab they were not the fashion; of the three debates conducted there, two quickly collapsed, but the third was formal and properly recorded. In the U.P. and Rajputana, debates were more in demand, and Dayananda often showed his readiness to participate by throwing down the gauntlet on his arrival in a town. However, his attitude had hardened; he was never prepared to take part unless formal rules were drawn up and agreed to down to the last detail. There had to be an important patron and a neutral, trustworthy chairman; the topics had to be clearly defined; the time available to the speakers had to be decided; impartial scribes had to take down every word and the full report had to be published over the signatures of chairman and participants.

The negotiations, oral and written, were sometimes very protracted, and the net effect was that as many as ten proposed debates fell through. This was the case with the famous Muhammad Qasim Deoband whom Dayananda had already faced in the three-cornered dispute at the Chandapur Melā of 1877. Two further attempts to arrange a debate with him at Roorkee and at Meerut, proved unsuccessful.[13] The same thing happened to the negotiations with the Sanātana Dharma Rakshinī Sabhā of Meerut,[14] the Sanātanīs at Hardwar,[15] the Muslims of Dehra Dun,[16] and Pandit Angadram at Shahjahanpur.[17] On a later occasion at Dehra Dun, both the Hindus and the Christian missionaries were instantly put off by the Swami's conditions,[18] as were the pandits of Ajmer.[19] Only in three instances could the parties arrive at an agreement, and a dispute took place.

During his visit to Ajmer in November-December 1878,

Dayananda had a formal debate with the Reverend Grey and Dr Husband of the Scottish Presbyterian Mission, about some points in Genesis. One Muslim and two Hindu scribes took everything down in writing. The Swami opened with his usual type of attack, based on a naive and literal interpretation of the text, and the missionaries gave their considered answer. The pace of the debate was excruciatingly slow, being little more than boring dictation from both sides. The first day's session produced only a few paltry pages of text, and the missionaries were completely exasperated, as was the chairman, Judge Amichand, who re-marked, 'We will be here for six months!' The clergymen declined to continue the debate in the same way, and suggested that written communications and answers should replace the painful dictation sessions. However, Dayananda refused to alter the agreed method, and the debate was discontinued in such a manner that the Aryas interpreted it as another victory for their Swami.[20]

Another debate took place at Bareilly. The antagonist was the Reverend T.J.Scott, and the exchange lasted for three days, from 25 to 27 August 1879. The successful conclusion of this occasion no doubt had much to do with the genuine friendship that had sprung up between the two disputants. They had first met over ten years previously, when the Swami was preaching along the banks of the Ganga. For four days then they had discussed God and salvation, and the foundations of mutual respect had been laid.[21] They had faced one another again in the Chandapur Melā disputation of 1877.[22] At Bareilly the debate focussed on three questions: rebirth, divine incarnation, and forgiveness of sins, all three central and weighty theological issues in the systems of both participants. It was a good exchange and both put their case clearly and forcefully. Scott showed himself the intellectual equal of the Swami and was able to make his points in a leisurely and assured manner. Not once did the Swami resort to his heavy sarcasm or his sledge-hammer type of denunciation. The debate came off very well, without claim or pretence of cheap victory by either side, and it brought the two even closer together.[23] In fact, shortly afterwards, the Swami visited the Reverend Scott's church and gave a small address, and Scott never missed the opportunity of hearing the Swami lecture.[24]

This type of public debate, intelligent, dispassionate, but slow-moving, must have had but little popular appeal, and could not have made a great impact on the few people present: its propaganda value was minimal. No wonder that the Swami, who strove to a greater and greater degree to maximize the thrust of his influence, set such strict conditions that most potential challengers withdrew.. In some instances he replaced the oral confrontation by written controversy; this was more economical of time, and, through publication, it could easily reach a larger number of people. When the pandits of Farrukhabad tried to embarrass him by sending a list of twenty-five questions, he published a careful answer in the local Arya Samaj journal, the *Bhāratsudashāpravartak*. The topics raised ranged widely: the duty of *sannyāsīs*, the forgiveness of sins, the eternity of atoms, God and free will, creation, freedom, *moksha*, diet, marriage, astrology, *Shrāddh*, suicide, etc.[25]

Raja Shivaprasad similarly tried to put the Swami in an awkward position by sending him a list of questions just before the latter's departure from Banaras. These were all carefully answered by Dayananda in a pamphlet entitled *Bhramocchedan*, 'The destruction of error'. When the Raja published an answer to this, a rebuttal came forth from the Swami's pen, entitled *Anubhramocchedan*. The issue raised in this controversy was the well-worn problem of the difference between the four *Vedas* and the *Brāhmanas*: the Raja objected that Dayananda had not conclusively proved that the former were self-evident revelation whereas the latter were not. At the start the exchanges were polite, but as the controversy grew the sarcasm and even abuse on both sides became harsh.[26] Dayananda simply could not ignore the challenge of a man of the standing of the Raja. He had served with distinction in the native states, and had a great number of writings to his credit: as a result he had been granted the C.S.I. and the title of Raja. At the time of the debate he was Inspector of Schools in Banaras, and well known for his pioneering work in the Hindī language: he was in fact the *guru* of Bharatendu Babu Harischandra.[27]

The intellectual climate in those native states Dayananda visited was quite different from that prevailing in British India. The power and influence of orthodoxy was greater and often it was in close alliance with the princely families. Education, the press, and an English-educated bureaucracy, those three activators of modernization, had been slow in emerging and in developing a platform and a receptive audience for the reformer. In these areas the public disputation was still a potentially powerful means of getting a hearing and making an impression on both the population and the Rajas. In fact, the initiative for the debate sometimes originated with the princes themselves.

In Masuda the Rao Bahadur tried to organize two debates. He invited Dr Schoolbred from Mewar for that purpose, but the clergyman was satisfied just to listen to Dayananda's lecture and declined to debate. Then the Rao instigated the local Jain community to put forward a Jain scholar. Sādhu Siddhakaran of the sect of the Dhūndhiyās was duly called. By chance he met Dayananda on the road during a morning walk. They made each other's acquaintance, and that was the first and last time they met face to face: the actual debate took the form of written communications. The Swami first sent a long list of questions to the Jain monk, and they were duly answered; but the second, even longer, communication of Dayananda remained unanswered. The *sādhu* simply declined to continue, 'After all, I am a *sādhu*', he said, and went on his way. The discussion centered around the Jain monks' custom of wearing a piece of cloth over their mouths to avoid swallowing any insects, an aspect of their rigorous practice of *ahimsā*. The debate never reached any depth and except for the one short answer of Siddhakaran's, remained largely an indictment of 'Jain absurdities' by Dayananda.[28] However, the encounter had a considerable effect on the local community, as will be related later.[29]

The last formal debate was held in Udaipur between Dayananda and Maulvi Abdul Rahman, a local judge, on 11, 13, and 17 September 1882. The discussion was mostly about the *Vedas*, with the Maulvi attacking and the Swami defending their position as unique revelation. The Maulvi was a sharp logician, but he soon found that it was quite impossible to lure Dayananda into a logical impasse. His doctrine of Vedic revelation had become neatly articulated, and consisted of a number of closely related tenets. Strictly speaking, none of these could by themselves survive the acid test of logic, but in the arena of a public debate Dayananda was very nimble in moving from one tenet to the other and thus forestalling the complete logical demonstration of any one of them. The Maulvi tried hard to pin him down, but after three days he must have been quite happy to terminate the show: at no time was he able to force the Swami into a logical quandary.[30]

During this period the Swami was drawn into another type
of controversy with some Jains that lasted two years. The first
shot was fired by Seth Thakurdas of Gujaranwala in the Panjab
in his letter of 13 July 1880 to Dayananda. It started as a slow
correspondence, grew into a press campaign, and ended two
years later in Bombay with the exchange of legal notices by the
parties' solicitors. About thirty letters, notices, and documents
went to and fro, and the controversy became public property
through the involvement of the press on both sides.[31]

His letters show that Thakurdas was not a very well-educated
man, but he was doggedly persistent. His contention was that
Dayananda had misrepresented the Jain faith and slandered the
Jains by lumping together into one religion Buddhism, Jainism,
and the atheistic Chārvāka. The offending passage was on page
402 of the first edition of the *Satyārth Prakāsh*, where a number
of verses were reproduced as representing the Jain view.
Thakurdas affirmed that they were not part of the Jain scriptures,
and simply asked Dayananda to declare where they came from,
adding that if the Swami could not prove that they came from
Jain sources, he should say so, and withdraw them with an apology.
This seems to be a straightforward matter that could have been
cleared up in no time. However, Dayananda made a tactical
error in underestimating the inquirer and delegating his Aryas
to deal with the matter. The result was that Thakurdas was treated
rather rudely. When after two letters he received an answer,
it came not from the Swami but from the secretary of the Meerut
Arya Samaj. His next two letters were similarly answered by
Samaj secretaries. These answers were offensive in that they
kept harping upon the ignorance of the writer, and urging him
to arrange a *shāstrārth* between the Swami and 'a worthy Jain
scholar'. In fact the Aryas on their own initiative started cor-
responding with the Jain scholar Atmaram, whom they thought
to be the man behind the scenes. Moreover, their answers to
Thakurdas were consistently evasive in that they did not even
attempt to answer his one question.

At last, after six letters and four months, Dayananda himself
entered the controversy with two letters of 6 and 14 November.
These letters were much more reasonable and courteous than

those of the Aryas, and they attempted to answer both Thakurdas' query and additional questions sent by Atmaram. About the offending verses referred to by Thakurdas, the Swami said that 'all those verses are from the works of a follower of the system of Brihaspati, named Chārvāka, whose system has another name, Lokāyata, and who was a follower of the Jain sect.'[32] At last we have a straight answer. The verses do indeed come from the famous *Sarvadarshanasamgraha*, where they are ascribed to Brihaspati and Chārvāka, whose school is said to be also called Lokāyata.[33] However, this much is only half an answer, because Dayananda had also to prove that this Chārvāka system was in fact a sect attached to Jainism.

By this time the controversy had become quite public and was being aired in the newspapers. In October 1880 Dayananda had written to Karsondas Sevaklal, the Bombay Arya Samaj secretary, asking him to collect all books on Jainism that he could lay his hands on.[34] Dayananda's most complete answer to the question about the inclusion of Chārvāka in Jainism is contained in the letter dated 14 November 1880. In this letter he quotes five books in support of his argument. These five books are not listed among those collected by Krishnadas Sevaklal in Bombay,[35] but they do feature in the list of books found in the possession of Dayananda at the time of his death.[36] This means that at the time of the controversy, even as he wrote to Bombay for more books on Jainism, he already possessed quite a few which he used in the correspondence.

What, then, are Dayananda's arguments for lumping the Chārvākas and Jains together? He shows how the names of the saints of Buddhism and Jainism are completely interchangeable, and that this interchange in fact occurs in the books of the Jains themselves. This leads him to the conclusion that they are one and the same sect. He goes on to argue that the Chārvākas are a sub-sect of Buddhism, quoting the *Ratnāvalī*. Therefore, he says, 'I have proved what I set out to prove, namely the connection between the two sects'. In his argumentation he also refers to the fact that the three sects have much in common doctrinally, the basic common doctrine being their atheism.[37]

Although today Dayananda's contention may seem unjust and unjustifiable, the matter looks different when we put it in the context of the state of Jain studies in the nineteenth century: for

Jainism was a neglected branch of Indology. One of the main reasons for this was that the Jains were very secretive about their scriptures, which they started publishing only at the very end of the nineteenth century. Dayananda's repeated accusations in this respect were completely justified. The result of this absence of texts and the ensuing lag in the study of Jainism was that among orientalists the exact relationship between the Jains and the Buddhists remained a disputed question.[38] 'At first the similarities between Buddhism and Jainism induced scholars to think that they were branches of the same tree. Some held that Jainism was anterior (H.T.Colebrooke, J. Stevenson) whereas others considered the Jainas to be a Buddhist Sect. (H.H.Wilson, E. Burnouf, Th. Benfey, Ch.Lassen, A. Weber).'[39] It was only at the end of the century that the Germans Bühler and Jacobi settled the matter, and not even then was their theory universally accepted. It is, therefore, not surprising that Dayananda too was confused, especially since he was aware of the theories of the European scholars.[40]

While the correspondence with Atmaram was going back and forth, Thakurdas became increasingly frustrated and hostile, as he felt that he was being rudely ignored. He sent a notice to all samajes daring them to declare openly their support for the Swami's position, and threatening that if they did so they would become equally challengeable in court. Their answers did not satisfy him. He then enlisted the support of the Jain Raja Shivaprasad, whose book entitled *Itihāsatimiranāshaka* had been quoted by Dayananda in support of his assertions. The Raja backed up Thakurdas. He wrote that the distinction between Jainism and Buddhism had now been conclusively proved by a German scholar, and that the preface of his book clearly said that not all its statements were to be taken as his own opinion, but rather as a basis for criticism and discussion. Thakurdas kept up his barrage, and in early 1882 he published several notices challenging the Swami to a *shāstrārth*. He even came to Bombay and met the Swami, but he was not to be appeased. In June he sent a notice through his lawyers, and Dayananda sent an answer through his own. This answer was couched in such terms that it took all the wind out of Thakurdas' sails. No offence was intended, it stated; if anyone convinced Dayananda that the verses were opposed to the principles of Jainism he would delete them from the second edition;

and any objection to the sale of the book should be referred to the publisher. No doubt Thakurdas' lawyers convinced him that the law could do no more for him, and the matter rested there. The controversy with Jainism throws considerable light on Dayananda's efforts at scholarship. He had with him in his travelling library at least ten books on Jainism, two of which were manuscripts, plus an anthology of Jain texts selected and copied by himself.[41] For this anthology he may have used the books collected for him in Bombay by Karsondas Sevaklal. This was an impressive collection: it comprised no less than sixty-one manuscripts, varying from 250 to 18,000 verses in length, many of which were said to be three to four hundred years old; there were also twelve printed books. Sevaklal not only collected the books, but he also wrote a short description and prepared a table of contents of each.[42] From the quotations contained in the second edition of the *Satyārth Prakāsh* one gathers that Dayananda did in fact consult these Jain books, held for him in Bombay, for the composition of the section on Jainism. We also know that he did make an effort to gain awareness of the state of scholarship reached by Western orientalists.

On the whole there was during this period little change in the Swami's propaganda activities, but there was a definite shift in emphasis. He continued his practice of preferring important centres and in general tried to build on the support he already had: he did not seek out new places to pioneer in, except for the native states which will be treated later. The public lecture remained a very important instrument of influence. But increasingly he devoted more time to writing and correspondence. He now avoided public disputations with their narrow ambit and impact: he preferred the written word that reached a wider public, and even the few debates he held were duly recorded and published.

Since his success in the Panjab, a new and important sphere of activity had been added to his endeavours: the establishment and direction of local branches of the Arya Samaj. The success story of the Panjab had preceded him. We get some idea of this from an analysis of the list of subscribers published in the *Vedabhāshya* instalments between early 1877 and the middle of 1878, when he came down into the Gangetic plains. By that time he had at least one hundred subscribers in the U.P., spread over about thirty different townships. There was a great difference in the type of person subscribing compared with the Panjab. There both the members of the Samaj and the subscribers were overwhelmingly from the trading castes, with only a very small sprinkling of brahmins and kayasths; this distribution faithfully reflected the composition of the rising Panjabi élite. In the U.P. the pattern was quite different: about twenty-two per cent of the subscribers were from the trading castes, about twenty-three per cent were brahmins, about forty-five per cent belonged to writers' castes, and the kshatriyas represented some ten per cent.[43] These proportions closely conform with the way in which the advance in education and employment was more evenly spread among those castes in the U.P.

These figures, naturally, are only of subscribers to the *Vedabhāshya*, even before the samajes were founded, and not of actual members, and thus indicate only the potential Aryas. But there is one document that sheds some light on the composition of the samajes in this area: a complete list of the initial 83 members of the Meerut Arya Samaj.[44] The caste composition of this membership was as follows. Forty-one per cent belonged to the trading castes, thirty-four per cent to the writers' castes, and twenty-two per cent were brahmins, with about three per cent kshatriyas. Although the trading castes were the largest group, they were counterbalanced by a good proportion of brahmins and writers, whereas in the Panjab the first were utterly dominant. In fact, this is even more apparent in the composition of the committee: five of the eleven members were brahmins, four were writers and only two came from the trading castes, thus putting the balance of leadership clearly on the side of brahmins and writers.

The distribution of occupations was also somewhat different from the one prevailing in the Panjab, where the overwhelming majority were Government employees and professionals. In the Meerut list, which gives the occupations of forty-five people, we notice that half of these were employed in Government offices, some thirty-five per cent were professionals, and fifteen per cent claimed the more traditional status of zamindar, tahsildar, and quanungo. As sixty per cent of the 38 names that bear no indication of profession were vaishyas, one may presume that many of these were in fact engaged in trade. The overall impression is that the Aryas of the U.P. were spread over a wider area of both caste and occupation than they were in the Panjab: this reflects the fact that the modernizing and opportunity-creating influence of the Raj had affected a more diversified section of society, and that the brahmins and kayasths played a leading role in this group.

During Dayananda's tours of the U.P. seventeen new samajes were established, five of which were founded even before his arrival.[45] a fact which indicates the keenness of his local followers. The great majority of these branches were concentrated in the north-west, the area of Rohilkand and the Doab, between the Yamuna and a line going through Kanpur and Sitapur, the area contiguous to the Panjab. East of that line there were only four scattered samajes. This concentration of branches in the Panjab and Western U.P. added strength to the new organization. In only five of the centres visited by the Swami was no branch established at that time, but specific reasons account for most of these cases. Although he visited Aligarh twice, once for four days and later for a week, he was quite ill on both these occasions,[46] and his week's visit to Allahabad was similarly spoiled by illness.[47] His five weeks at Chalesar were purely a period of rest and recuperation.[48] Saharanpur was also visited twice, but on both occasions it was a brief stop-over on the way to Hardwar and Meerut.[49] The Swami spent three weeks at Bareilly, where he held his famous debate with the Reverend Scott, yet no samaj was founded at the time: however, one came into being some time after he left.[50] The two weeks spent at Muzaffarnagar, where he gave ten lectures, did not produce a branch of the Samaj.[51] On the whole, the founding of samajes was a success story, and only Muzaffarnagar looks like a failure.

But the growth of the Samaj continued unabated in the following years: by the time of the Swami's death the total number of samajes had risen to seventy-nine.[52] That means that in the last three years of the Swami's life, when he was absent from the northern area, the number of branches more than doubled. The greatest increase took place in the Panjab and Western U.P., where the growth was well over one hundred per cent.[53] The fact that this rapid development occurred in the absence of the Swami demonstrates that the Arya Samaj had by 1880 definitely acquired a momentum of its own.

Now that so many branches of the Arya Samaj had come into being, one has to ask what kind of guidance and direction Dayananda gave them, and what authority he exercised. There is no ready answer to this question. It has been shown that the Swami wanted the branches to be autonomous, that he did not set up a central authority, and that he refused to occupy an official post such as president or act as a *guru*.[54] But perhaps his assertive nature got the better of him. The answers to these questions lie scattered in the 'occasional reports of the early biographers and in the volumes of the Swami's incoming and outgoing letters. In these last years his correspondence was very extensive, and only part of it has been preserved. The great majority of letters do not deal directly with Samaj affairs, but with his multifarious other involvements: the Press and his publications, his travels and controversies, the cow-protection movement, the Theosophical Society, and advice to the native princes. Nevertheless, there are a sufficient number of letters extant dealing directly with the Samaj to give an idea of how the Swami saw and fulfilled his role, and how the Aryas regarded his leadership.

At Roorkee Dayananda was asked if he would give his permission for a meeting of the committee. He replied that his permission was unnecessary as he was not himself a member. He was immediately made a member and he proceeded to tell the Aryas that they should always act in accordance with a majority decision.[55] He seems to have adhered strictly to his explicit policy of non-intervention: not a single letter can be found that actually gives orders to a branch of the Samaj. He certainly offered his advice when he was asked, or when he thought it necessary. When a young man, who had been expelled from the Amritsar Samaj for stealing books, met him at Hardwar, confessed his theft, and promised to reform, the Swami asked the Amritsar Aryas if they would take him back.[56] In Agra he advised an Arya to accept appointment as trustee of a Hindu temple, because in that position he might be able to exert worthwhile influence on the expenditure of the temple's riches.[57] When the Ajmer Samaj re-converted to Hinduism a Christian convert, a young widow with two children, the Samaj leaders reported the incident to the Swami and sought his advice on what should be done.[58]

When the Swami judged it necessary, he voiced his dissent in no uncertain terms. On hearing that the Lahore Samaj was collaborating with the Brahmos in promoting the cause of widow-remarriage, he wrote to Lala Jivandas as follows·

These Brahmos are different inside and outside. They have the idea that the Arya Samaj should become like them: reviled because they are similar to Christians. For a virgin there is no sin in remarriage, and for her who has been with a man there is no fault in *niyoga*. To act against those principles will produce now or later great distress, because it will be in violation of the *Shāstras*: no doubt outcasting will follow.[59]

This is a very important and representative example of the exercise of authority by the Swami. Many Panjabi Aryas were in favour of widow-remarriage but did not accept *niyoga*. All Dayananda did was to reaffirm his own opinion, but he did not issue an injunction that the Aryas should follow it and stop their collaboration with the Brahmos. In fact, we know that the Panjabi Aryas actually increased their support for widow-remarriage: the Gurudaspur and Peshawar Samajes arranged such marriages,[60] and the *Arya Messenger*, which Dayananda regularly received, even ran a 'matrimonial notice' inviting widows and men prepared to marry widows to contact the Arya Samaj of Lahore or Sitapur.[61]

This same attitude of Dayananda's is also clearly evident in his correspondence with Mulraj, President of the Lahore Samaj and one of the Swami's closest advisers, whom he made vice-president of his Trust at the end of his life. Dayananda wanted to put a proposal to the Government to pass a regulation, 'by which children of widows be entitled to claim and obtain their rightful share of the property, both movable and immovable, of their parents, and by which anyone trying to malign a widow in any way be liable to punishment by the Government'. In a letter to Mulraj he stated quite clearly that the regulation should be applicable to both remarriage and *niyoga*. He asked Mulraj if he would agree to draft a legal document.[62] The Swami's next letter complained that Mulraj had not used the term *niyoga* in his draft but only the term remarriage, and it included a draft document of the Swami's own composition.[63] That seems to have been the end of the affair. Mulraj obviously did not agree with the Swami's theory of *niyoga* and was not prepared to comply with the Swami's wishes. Moreover, he must have realized the absurdity of including in such a legal document a term which had no legal standing. The important fact is that at no stage of the correspondence was anything like an order issued.

Another topic of correspondence between the two illustrates that relationship. In March 1881 Dayananda asked Mulraj if he would agree to translate the *Gokarunānidhi* into English. Three months later he complained that nothing had been done, and in November the Swami pleaded:

It would be such a good thing if you could do that translation, and do it quickly, but so far you have not had the time. But for the sake of the country's uplift time should be found. If you people do not do anything what can I do myself? If you cannot find the time, please send the pamphlet back to me. When I go to Bombay I may meet someone who knows English.

By December Mulraj had agreed to undertake it, but nothing materialized, and finally, after one year had elapsed, Dayananda wrote that he had found somebody else in Bombay, and told him to drop the matter now, 'as he had too heavy a burden to carry'.[64] At no stage in the correspondence was there ever a hint of command, and Mulraj's reluctance probably had something to do with the fact that many Panjabi Aryas were after all meat-eaters like Mulraj himself.

Some letters even show that certain Aryas did not hesitate to disapprove of some of the Swami's actions, and were prepared to give him advice. The Farrukhabad Samaj had started to publish a monthly, the *Bhāratsudashāpravartak*, which was warmly recommended by the Swami in his *Vedabhāshya* instalments.[65] A letter from Dayananda to its editor, Lala Kalicharan, who was the secretary of the local Samaj, indicates that the Aryas had strong reservations about publishing the Swami's tract against the Theosophists entitled *Theosophiston kī Golmāl-Polpāl*.[66] But worse was to come. When Jagannath Das published his *Ārya Prashnottarī*, a catechism of Arya doctrines, the Swami objected to a number of statements and wrote a lengthy answer. The Farrukhabad Samaj consistently refused to publish this, notwithstanding repeated requests from the Swami, who finally had to publish it elsewhere. Their objection was that the tract might well offend against the projected Press Act, but that seems to have been only a poor excuse.[67] There was another revealing aspect of this matter. From mid-1882 Jagannath Das and Munshi Indramani,[68] librarian and president respectively of the local Samaj had been giving considerable trouble. The Swami was aware of this, and suggested that they were unworthy of remaining in the Samaj. Yet it took the Farrukhabad Samaj a whole year, until May 1883, to expel the two gentlemen. This goes to show that the Swami's word certainly was not law, and that he might well advise and urge, but that the final decision and the practical steps had to be taken locally.

The Swami was not always a good judge of people, as the tribulations of his Press clearly show. The secretary of the Ajmer Samaj, Kamalanayan Sharma, wrote to him that he made too many wrong choices of people and that, therefore,

It is the wish of the committee members that I write to you that, when you intend to engage somebody, you should first consult the local samaj about that man . . . . If you had done so from the beginning and consulted the local samajes about Munshis Bakhtawar Singh and Indramani, we should not have been caught in such a net of deceit today.[69]

Lekhram, secretary of the Peshawar Samaj, felt that the Swami's intervention in the Jagannath Das affair was ill-considered, and told him so in his letter:

Such things have now been done that as it were hail has dropped onto a ripe crop. My plea to you now is that you please keep quiet, and that in future you do not break the heart of such able people. If you take heed of my plea, then it is not necessary to consider everything lost.[70]

Sunderlal, writing from the Vedic Press, also asked the Swami to temper his language: 'Do not write that a particular person is a lazy layabout, because on hearing those insults his love for you wanes, he becomes antagonistic and leaves us, and we cannot get another of the same quality.'[71] Both the secretaries of the Ajmer and the Lahore branches advised the Swami to leave the native states, where he could not achieve anything worthwhile, and to come back to the people through whom the real regeneration of the country could come about.[72]

In no circumstances did Dayananda act in the affairs of the Samaj as a dictator or an inspired *guru*, nor did the Aryas generally expect such an attitude of him. This does not mean that the Swami could not be authoritarian. He certainly could, but he did not act in that way towards the Samaj. His stubborn authoritarianism came to the fore in his management of his publications and of his Press. There he was the master and expected to be obeyed as a great number of letters show. In a letter to Pandit Bhimasena about his first will, he makes things quite clear:

It is written in my will that I will be the one to give to anyone the power to deal with money, and the committee will have the right to execute my wishes. I have invested myself with the full power to make any addition

or deletion to the will, or to make a second one, to expel any member or
to appoint another one. These rules have been made by me so that I am
able to do as I wish.[73]

This is a very different attitude from the one he adopted towards
the Arya Samaj. One last example will show conclusively that,
however much he was the inspirer and guide of the Aryas, he did
not wish to dictate to them, and the Aryas did not expect him to
do so. It was in 1877 that the Lahore Samaj wrote the new rules
of the Arya Samaj which were adopted by all subsequently founded
branches. But Bombay held on to its own original rules and
regulations. During his last visit to Bombay the Swami urged
the local Aryas to adopt the Lahore rules, and the manner in
which his plea is made is significant:

Brothers, the progress of the country is a task we have to accomplish
in unison. In some matters a difference of opinion has persisted among
us. Why should we not pull together in these too? Where we have differences
of opinion, a solution can be found as long as we sit down together and
discuss it in friendship. The bad condition of India has come about because
we have quarrelled when differences of opinion arose. Civilized people
first quench the fire of anger and debate the issues properly in friendship
and without prejudice, and that is the way the country may achieve progress. That is why the original rules were altered. And the Lahore rules
were formulated in such a way that nobody is able to put a false interpretation to them. That is why the Bombay rules too should be changed so that
there can be the same rules for the whole country. Certainly do alter the
regulations (*upaniyams*) for the administration of the Samaj. But as for
the rules, they should be uniform.[74]

These are not the words of a dictator, neither were they taken
as such. The local Aryas formed a committee to study the question,
and it was decided to adopt the Lahore rules and to adopt the
regulations also, but with some minor alterations. The Bombay
Aryas were most concerned that the Lahore regulations replaced
the hierarchic structure of the Bombay rules with too much local
autonomy.[75]

The life and activities of the branches in fact intensified and
diversified so much, especially in those last years while the Swami
toured Rajasthan, that it would have been very difficult to order
the Aryas about from a distance. The life of the branches shows
both their autonomy and their increased interrelationship.
From the biographies and the correspondence it is evident that
there was a constant traffic of Aryas between local samajes even
as far apart as Bombay and the Panjab. On the occasion of

Dayananda's visit to Hardwar quite a number of Aryas were present,[76] and one comes across constant references to addresses given in a particular branch by passing Aryas from other branches. Particularly in the Panjab and Western U.P., where the greatest number of branches were concentrated, this interaction was a growing phenomenon.

Moreover, among the Aryas there were now many able and prominent men, ready and eager to undertake responsible tasks. We have already noted Karsondas Sevaklal's collection and annotation of Jain works,[77] and Jivandas' tract in defence of the *Vedabhāshya*;[78] such tasks were to be increasingly undertaken. In fact, during this period the Aryas moved steadily into the arena of publication: no less than nine journals were started. From 1879 Shahjahanpur boasted of a monthy called *Āryadarpan*, whose editor and proprietor was Bakhtawar Singh, secretary of the local samaj, who also edited the *Ārya Bhūshan*.[79] The journal *Bhāratsudashāpravartak* of Farrukhabad was also edited by the local secretary, Kalicharan Ramcharan.[80] Meerut had a monthly in Urdū, the *Meerut Samāchār*, edited by Ananda Lal, the branch secretary, and another one in Hindī was published by the local Deva Nāgarī Prachārinī Sabhā, also under Arya management.[81] In Lahore three periodicals were being published by 1883. There were two English journals, *The Arya Magazine*, edited by R.C.Bary, and *The Regenerator of Aryavarta*, edited by Hans Raj and Guru Datt. Lajpat Rai was the initiator of an Urdū paper, the *Deshopakār*.[82] Ajmer had its own Arya periodical, the *Deshhitaishī*.[83] Although some of these journals were short-lived, they indicate the vitality of the Samaj, particularly in the Panjab and the U.P.

That was the area too where the Aryas started to produce pamphlets, a much-used contemporary means of propaganda. This was then, as it still is now, a most ephemeral type of literature, and most of it disappeared quickly, lost for ever. The few pamphlets we have knowledge of give some indication of the type of topics that were treated.[84] Jivandas wrote a tract supporting the cause of Hindī,[85] one defending the *Vedabhāshya*,[86] and another in which he pleaded for improvement in the conditions of women.[87] He also translated Dayananda's *Bhūmikā* into Urdū.[88] On the case for Hindī there was another pamphlet by Lala Dwarka Das.[89] Lala Mathura Das went to war against orthodoxy in his *Ārya Darshan*,[90] and Bawa Narain Singh wrote two pamphlets in which he attempted to present a clear statement of Aryan ideology.[91] We have already mentioned Jagannath Das's efforts where that subject was concerned. Pandit Umrao Singh wrote a pamphlet refuting the accusations made by the Theosophists in their journal.[92] This form of propaganda would increase as the years went by, and it was encouraged by the Swami, who was now acutely aware of the power of the printed word. He himself wrote a number of tracts, and he also composed two short pamphlets to be used by Aryas in controversy with Muslims and Christians.[93] He also urged that an American book against the Bible that he had come across be translated from English into the vernacular, which was eventually done.[94]

Another method of propaganda, no doubt inspired by the missionaries and the Brahmos, began to be used by the Samaj in these years: the employment of full-time preachers. There were two categories, the paid professionals and the *sannyāsīs*. During these last years Dayananda himself trained and sent out three *sannyāsīs* of his own order of the Dandīs: Swamis Atmananda, Ishwarananda, and Sahajananda, the latter two of whom were initiated into the order by himself. They combined study with touring and preaching, and were instrumental in founding new branches of the Samaj.[95] In Udaipur, Dayananda tried to train the blind *sādhu* Girananda for such work, but this attempt failed.[96] Ever since that time the Arya Samaj has always had a number of Arya *sannyāsīs*.

Apart from these the Samaj also sought to engage paid professional lay preachers. Swami Sahajananda wrote to the Swami about this need, because several branches in the Panjab were breaking up for want of instruction and encouragement.[97] The Jaipur Aryas felt the same need, and put forward a proposal by the branches in the area to engage Pandit Gaurishankar in that capacity.[98] Dayananda readily encouraged this step and worked out a plan by which the preacher would travel around in a methodical way amongst the different branches, so that the financial burden could be shared by all.[99] The idea was important in his eyes, and he prevailed upon the Raja of Shahpura to donate a sum of thirty rupees per month to support a preacher.[100] He saw the preachers' role as one of support for the local branches, and of stimulation of new growth, as he stated in a letter: 'If two such pandits in addition to people like Swami Sahajananda and Swami Atmananda travelled around constantly, it would bring joy to the old samajes, and it would also result in the creation of new branches'.[101] This was a way in which the Swami tried to see to the increasingly pressing needs of the growing Samaj without encroaching on his own precious time, which he felt was better spent in the work of reaching out to the wider world of Hinduism.

As the Samaj thus grew in membership and activities and as the number of able men with personality and initiative increased, it is no wonder that trouble arose in certain branches. Moreover, the branches, being autonomous, were at the mercy of their own members and their quarrels. There was no higher authority to arbitrate decisively, and differences had to be settled locally. Bombay had its early share when the local president Harischandra Chintamani was found to have mismanaged Samaj funds. The Bombay Aryas turned to Dayananda for intervention, but his answer was characteristic:

You write about your Samaj, saying that if I do not come the branch will disintegrate. Did you establish a Samaj because of faith in Harischandra Chintamani? If the condition of your Samaj depends on my coming and going, where am I, one person as I only am, going to run hither and thither? If there is an unworthy president in the Samaj, it is your business to dismiss him and appoint another one, and manage your branch in a proper way.[102]

Harischandra was expelled and replaced by Gopal Rao Hari Deshmukh.[103] In Ajmer trouble arose about the publication and finances of the Samaj journal, leading to a sorry wrangle and the resignation of the secretary. Here too, the Swami did not intervene directly, but let the branch work out its own solution.[104] The difficulties in Lucknow too were primarily clashes of personalities, who each in turn informed the Swami of their side of the story in long letters.[105] Even some Panjabi branches were collapsing,[106] and the trouble in Moradabad with Jagannath Das has already been referred to. Obviously the young Samaj ran into a lot of difficulties in the local branches, and they were mostly reported to the Swami and his advice was sought. Nevertheless, he did not intervene, and refused to come and clear matters up. He did give his opinion, but left action to the local members. His itinerary was his own, and to the distress of many Aryas he did not even consider cutting down his stay with the princes: in his own mind that work was more important than rushing around to help branches in solving their internal troubles.

Even if he was not an autocrat, there was one concern that Dayananda expressed so often that it must have been one of the most important things he felt about his Samaj: he repeatedly stressed that it was not a sect, and that nothing should be done to isolate it from the large community of Hinduism. 'I do not wish to be isolated like the Brahmos from the caste-life of society, for it is better to remain within that society and work at its uplift', he said when Pandit Ramadhar voiced the wish that the Arya Samaj should have a temple as big as the Moti Mahal, and he added, 'if you make the Swami of the temple into an Arya, then it becomes possible'.[107] On another occasion, while answering a Maulvi's questions, he made his idea very concrete:

The regulations and taboos of eating and drinking and marriage customs etc., have no connection with *dharma* or *adharma*, but they derive from the conduct of local custom and caste. But it is harmful to disregard them in one's behaviour with people of other religions. If a wise man acted that way, then the people of his caste would despise him and that community would remain deprived of the benefits which his wisdom could have bestowed on them.[108]

He used the same argument when declining to dine with Sayed Ahmed Khan in Aligarh.[109] He acknowledged that a Muslim could become an Arya, but he made it clear that this did not imply that immediate interdining could be expected.[110] The same reasons were offered when he refused to eat a Brahmo's food because it had been cooked by a low-caste female,[111] and when in Banaras he left a room where a Muslim was present to have a drink of water, because of the local taboo involved.[112]

In 1879 in Farrukhabad he related the parable he would repeat in his second *Satyārth Prakāsh*. A man in search of the true religion asked the advice of a pandit, who brought him to an assembly of a hundred sects and religions. He consulted them all, and everywhere he was told the same story: our religion is the true one, the other ninety-nine are false. In despair he returned to the pandit who told him

'Take heed only of those matters in which they all agree. Is there such a thing in which they all believe?' The man answered, 'Yes, there are some, e.g. they recognize one god, and worship him, they teach that truth should be spoken and not untruth, and that one should have mercy on the poor' Then the pandit said, 'Those are matters of religion, follow them. The rest are only misleading lies'.[113]

In other words, the advice of the pandit was: look for consensus not controversy. That became increasingly Dayananda's own watchword and the one he wanted the Samaj to adopt. Nowhere did he state this more clearly than in explaining the meaning of 'Arya' in a letter to Colonel Olcott:

The society of the Aryas, that is called the Arya Samaj, and all those who renounce the bad qualities of *dasyus* and adopt the good qualities of the Aryas, when they form a society, its name is Arya Samaj: therefore, there is no harm in calling all such good societies Arya Samaj: on the contrary, that name is their greatest ornament.[114]

In these final years Dayananda felt that within the Samaj there existed among a few people two pressures, very much part of the Hindu make-up. One was to involve him more and more in a role closer to the *guru* model, the other was to insulate the ranks of the Samaj against people who did not agree with all its ideas or with all the Swami's teachings. These pressures would split the Samaj into two sections after the Swami's death; but while he was alive he counteracted them wherever he could, because they were the pressures that tended to turn all Hindu reform into sectarianism.

The Swami's role as leader of the Arya Samaj in those final years now clearly emerges. In the first half of this period he concentrated on the U.P. and a good number of branches were established. In fact by 1881 the movement, with its concentration in the Panjab and Western U.P., had acquired a momentum of its own that carried it forward. There was some pressure from certain Aryas to involve the Swami more closely and constantly in the affairs of the branches, but he resisted it and adhered to his conviction that these should be democratically self-governing, without president, *guru*, or central seat and authority. As the Samaj grew stronger and as the Aryas increased their contacts with each other across town, district, provincial, and state borders, they grew more aware of their strength and cohesion, and of the way they differed from other Hindus; some Aryas would have liked to increase and foster that cohesion and that distinctiveness. But Dayananda saw in this the danger of sectarianism, and he counteracted this tendency by stressing the universal character of the Samaj, and insisting that the Aryas should take care to remain full and respected members of their caste.

As the life of the branches developed, and in turn fostered the growth of many new branches, and as the Aryas widened their interests and activities, Dayananda's direct involvement,

instead of increasing, decreased. He knew the needs of the adoles-
cent Samaj were pressing, and he tried to see to regular care for
these needs by the use of *sannyāsīs* and preachers. But he himself could not and would not see to them personally, because
his main energy was directed elsewhere. His six months' stay
in Bombay in the first half of 1882 clearly illustrates that
redirection. The Swami did not indulge in one single public debate,
and he gave very few lectures. His lectures did not deal with idol
worship or with the *Vedas*, but were mostly about cow-protection,
a cause for which he was launching an appeal at that time. Most
of his working time was absorbed by his writing: from 8 a.m.
to 4 p.m. he was at that task, and even a Ranade was not permitted
to interrupt that routine.[115] The young Samaj was in places
rent by dissension and even struggling for survival, and cried
out to the Swami for direction, and for the favour of a visit to
boost their spirits. But the Swami was not to be distracted, as
his gaze was now more than ever fixed on that wider community
of Hinduism that always beckoned him.

CHAPTER IX

The Final Years: The Wider World of Hinduism

When Dayananda left the Panjab in 1878, he was met with instant success: his stays in Roorkee, Delhi, and Meerut each resulted in the establishment of a samaj, and the Meerut branch was a major triumph: it had no less than eighty-three founding members, many of whom were prominent citizens.[1] It seemed that Western U.P. was just waiting for the Swami's appearance. One would have expected him to continue in that area, so ready for the harvest, but he did not. Instead, he went south into Rajputana, and on his return he moved straight up to Hardwar for the Kumbh Melā, thus delaying by about six months a tour of the U.P. that would result in the foundation of so many samajes. What was so important to the Swami that he thus postponed his visit to the U.P.? Two things called him south: an invitation from the Maharaja of Jaipur, Thakur Ranjit Singh, to come and assist at a great public sacrifice,[2] and the annual religious fair at Pushkar. These two occasions had one element in common: they represented the wider world of Hinduism, and that is why the Swami gave their call his preference. The native states had so far been little affected by the work of reform; they constituted the other half of India, where Dayananda's message had scarcely penetrated.

The attraction of the Pushkar annual fair, which Dayananda had visited in March 1866, and of the Hardwar Kumbh Melā, was that, however much the Swami despised the Hinduism they flaunted, they were still the only occasions when anything resembling a great council of Hinduism gathered. For that reason they kept attracting the Swami. He had visited Hardwar twice before at the time of the Kumbh Melā: in 1855,[3] when as a *yogi* in search of great teachers he avoided the *melā*, and again in 1867, when he went on his first great preaching expedition, but fled in despair.[4] Now, as the successful founder of the Arya Samaj and a public figure, he went up again to face the great throngs of *sannyāsīs*, pandits, and the faithful. On his arrival thousands of copies of a special announcement were distributed, in which he clearly set out the purpose of his visit. The dominant theme of this document was the need for unity and friendship among all Hindus for the sake of the well-being of the whole country, the need for collaboration among those Hindus who were permeated with a sense of truth and morality, concerned about the good of all, and ready to cooperate in harmony:

Where there are such people, there is no room for misery. These religious and wise people, whatever place, whatever community, whatever *sabhā* they belong to, adorn and strengthen their voices with love and wisdom. In the service of knowledge and the fight against ignorance, they fulfil themselves and they generate the feelings and the deeds of friendship. It is in the voice of such people that the glory and wisdom that bring prosperity, happiness, and the splendour of the universal kingdom, find their stable foundation. Those who are not determined to collaborate in providing that happiness remain for ever strangled by poverty and misery. Let us shed all hostility. . . . God has given us the way to happiness in the *Vedas*, . . . as the great Vedic age clearly demonstrates. Why have we Aryans changed so much?. . . . By going against the *Vedas*. The way to recapture that ancient glory is to act in accordance with the *Vedas*. That is what the Aryans who are members of the Arya Samaj are doing, that is what they want to foster. They wish to increase the number of Aryans who are concerned with the welfare of all, and who, without guile, are united in the desire of communicating the knowledge of truth to all. It is for that purpose that they have formed a group of preachers of the science of *dharma*, and schools for the study of the *Vedas* and of the true *Shāstras*.[5]

This statement is very significant, directed as it is to the great body of Hinduism on the occasion where it was best represented. It was an appeal to all Hindus to gather and unite, and it avoided that abrasive criticism of Hinduism the Swami so often voiced. Whereas earlier the stress had been mostly on controversy, now it was on consensus and collaboration. The prosperity and glory of the whole of Āryāvarta was held up as the one overriding goal. And the role of the Arya Samaj was put in bold relief: it was to be a gathering of all Hindus fired by that ideal, encompassing the whole Hindu commonwealth. The Samaj of itself had no particular aim; it was not meant to be just another sect or sabhā joining in petty controversies and jealousies, but rather an assembly of all Hindus committed to the ideal of the reconstruction of Āryāvarta. We have already seen how in his direction of the Samaj, the Swami constantly affirmed that idea and sought to prevent any actions that might cut the Aryas off from the great body of Hinduism.[6]

It is within this context that one should understand the eagerness with which Dayananda grasped the offer of collaboration from the Theosophists. Their involvement with the Arya Samaj started in February 1878 with a letter from Colonel Olcott to Dayananda and ended with the Swami's firm denunciation of the Theosophists in a public lecture in Bombay in March 1882. The lengthy and intricate details of this episode have often been retold,[7] and here it will suffice to enquire how it throws light on the mind and attitudes of the Swami.

Olcott's first letter could not but delight Dayananda:

A number of Americans and other students who earnestly seek after spiritual knowledge, place themselves at your feet, and pray you to enlighten them. They are of various professions and callings, of several different countries, but all united in the one object of gaining wisdom and becoming better. For this purpose, they, three years ago, organized themselves into a body called the Theosophical Society. Finding in Christianity nothing that satisfied their reason or intuition . . . they stood apart from the world, turned to the East for light, and openly proclaimed themselves the foes of Christianity. . . . For this reason, we come to your feet as children to a parent, and say, 'look at us, our teacher: tell us what we ought to do. . . . We place ourselves under your instruction'.[8]

The Swami was elated: at the time he was in the Panjab, where Christianity was felt as a real threat. The letter showed how some Westerners were turning away from Christianity, and looking to India for the true religion, thus confirming his thesis that Vedism was the original and true religion of the whole world. His answer expressed his delight; he promised to help all he could and to remain in contact by letter, and continued:

I am of the same opinion as you are concerning Christianity and other religions. Just as there is one God there should be one religion of all people. And that religion consists in worshipping one God, obeying his commandments, and working for the well-being of all. It is expounded in the eternal *Vedas*, practised by the wise, in conformity with reason, . . . and to be followed by all men. . . . We pray the Lord that by his grace and the effort of men one day these religions may disappear, and that in the midst of all people may be established the one true religion which throughout the tradition has been preserved by the Aryans.[9]

The Theosophists seem to have been in an indecent hurry, possibly because their Society was in bad straits,[10] and probably also because they were unduly encouraged by a misrepresentation of Arya ideology by their correspondent in Bombay, Harischandra Chintamani.[11] They did not wait for the Swami's answer, and resolved on 22 May 1878 to

. . . accept the proposal of the Arya Samaj to unite with itself, and that the title of this Society be changed to 'The Theosophical Society of the Arya Samaj of India'. Resolved, that the Theosophical Society, for itself and branches in America, Europe, and elsewhere, hereby recognize Swami Dayanand Saraswati, Pandit, Founder of the Arya Samaj, as its lawful Director and Chief.[12]

Olcott wrote another long letter to Dayananda in June asking for more information, but even before that he wrote in the *Indian Spectator* of 29 May, that 'Buddhism, or Wisdom-Religion'

is contained in the Vedas; hence the Aryans had it. It is this Wisdom Religion which the Theosophical Society accepts and propagates and the finding of which in the doctrines expounded by the Reverend Swami Dayanand Saraswati Pandit, has led us to affiliate our Society with the Arya Samaj and accept its chief as our supreme religious teacher, guide, and ruler.[13]

Dayananda's next letter, written on 26 July, was a lengthy one. He first accepted the amalgamation of the two bodies, and went on to answer Olcott's questions, stating with great clarity his monotheism and his belief in the *jīvas* as separate, eternal entities: thus he left no room for doubt about the essentials of his teaching. The letter also discounted the belief in ghosts, and declared the photo of a ghost which Olcott had sent to be a clever trick.[14] Moreover the Theosophists received in August from Shyamji Krishnavarma a translation of the rules of the Arya Samaj, setting out the conditions for membership. All this information was somewhat different from the misleading impression Harischandra had given in his letters, and it generated opposition within the ranks of the Theosophical Society. In September the Society resumed its former separate status and established 'The Theosophical Society of the Arya Samaj of Aryavart', a different body open to members of both organizations.[15] In fact, it seems that Dayananda himself had written a letter suggesting some similar arrangement, but that this letter had not been forwarded by Harischandra.[16] This new development was to grow into a major irritant in the relationship of the Aryas and the Theosophists.

Nevertheless, the Theosophist leaders were not to be discouraged: Col. Olcott and Madame Blavatsky arrived in Bombay in February 1879. They were warmly received by the Aryas in Bombay and Saharanpur, but on account of the Swami's current illness, they did not meet him until the first of May at Saharanpur, whence they proceeded to Meerut: all in all they spent five days together.[17] Their long talks through interpreters were very cordial and the Swami praised the two leaders highly in his subsequent letters.[18] They discussed the problems arising from the misrepresentations on the part of.Harischandra, who by this time had been removed as publisher of the *Vedabhāshya*. The Swami wrote:

When I spoke personally with the Colonel, he said that 'in our Theosophical Society up to now it was the rule to accept as members people of all religions. . . . Now that we have understood the rules of the Arya Samaj, it will be done according to your will. Henceforth it will not be thus, and whoever does not like the rules of the Arya Samaj will not remain in the Theosophical Society.'[19]

Although the text is not explicit, it seems that both understood that they were talking about the Vedic branch of the Theosophical Society only, and not about the whole body. Anyway, the Swami was still convinced of the honesty of the Theosophists, and harshly condemned Harischandra for suggesting that they were charlatans and tricksters.[20]

The Theosophists left for Bombay, but they kept in contact by correspondence. Dayananda encouraged them in their foundation of a journal, *The Theosophist*, suggesting the subtitle *Āryaprakāsh*,[21] and he wrote at length to Mme Blavatsky explaining his view of the fate of the soul after death.[22] The three met again in Banaras in December 1879. Olcott gave a public lecture in which he praised the *Vedas* as the oldest scriptures from which all wisdom spread over the world.[23] Relations were friendly, but the confusion about the relationship between the societies had not yet been cleared up. In May 1880 Dayananda published a notice in the *Āryadarpan* to be sent to all samajes: neither the Arya Samaj nor the Theosophical Society were branches of the other body, but the Vedic branch of the Theosophical Society, to which the two leaders belonged, was a branch of both organizations.[24] In a letter to Col. Olcott and Mme Blavatsky he asked them similarly to publicize this fact to their own members, 'as it should not be kept a secret'.[25] As a sign of his continuing goodwill, he included both as trustees in his first will.[26]

In Meerut, at the time of their third meeting, things came to a head. The Theosophist leaders had in the meantime visited Ceylon (Sri Lanka) in May 1880 and had been admitted into Buddhism.[27] In conversations they now admitted that they did not believe in a personal God. This shocked the Swami, and he insisted on discussing this with them, but they declined to stay and went on to Simla.[28] The Swami then advised the Meerut Aryas not to join any other Society if they were convinced that the Arya Samaj rules were right.[29] He now suspected that the Theosophists were deliberately keeping the relation between the two bodies vague in order to use his name and those of prominent Aryas to swell their own ranks. On hearing of this, Mme Blavatsky wrote an indignant letter to Babu Chhedilal of Meerut, accusing the Swami of setting himself up as a pope, and denying that the Theosophists tried to enrol Aryas. She complained that if they had received Dayananda as a member, why should her atheism prevent her from being an Arya. She boasted about their reception at Simla and their influence with people in high places, and also referred to 'feats' she had accomplished. She also mentioned that although American and British Theosophists considered all Aryas their brothers, the Europeans in India were not prepared to do so: only the Swami would they recognize as such. The letter ended, 'Please send a translation of this letter to the Swami for I want to know what his answer is to the question whether we will be friends or enemies. That is all I want to know.'[30]

Dayananda sent her a long answer on 23 October 1880, a courteous and detailed refutation of all her accusations. He stressed that the Aryas had never tried to enrol Theosophists, whereas the latter certainly had endeavoured to enrol Aryas, and he suggested that matters could be settled in face-to-face discussions.[31] Mme Blavatsky's reply of January 1881 was a retreat, in that it now laid the blame for 'misunderstanding' on the Arya interpreters. 'We have not changed our opinion of God, as the cause of all things visible . . . and of the *Vedas* as the fountain-head of all religions.' On the other hand, she affirmed that her society was not a religious body, but an organization for the study of old sciences and religions. She complained that whereas they had helped the Aryas all along, the latter were now turning against them.[32] Dayananda's answer was straightforward and dignified, affirming the constancy of the principles of the Arya Samaj in contrast with the Theosophists' change in belief. He denied any aspiration on his part for authority, 'I do not wish to found a new religion, I only preach the eternal Vedic faith. . . . I do not aspire to any position except that of preacher.' All his other statements and actions confirm the truth of that statement.

He finished by expressing the hope that they could discuss things later in Bombay.[33]

That was where interchange became confrontation. The two Theosophists were there from the very start of the year 1882, and Dayananda repeatedly urged them to have a discussion with him about the existence of God.[34] He finally sent letters in late March demanding a meeting, and stating that if he did not see them he would denounce them in a public lecture.[35] As they did not respond, the lecture was held on 28 March,[36] and followed by a public notice to all Aryas, entitled *Theosophiston kī Golmāl-Polpāl*, 'Humbuggery of the Theosophists'. This document set out in detail all the contradictions, changes, and lies in the writings and actions of the Theosophists from the very start, and concluded that 'no good but only harm can come to Āryāyarta and to the Arya Samaj from any connection with these people or their society'. He exposed them as tricksters and cheap jugglers who knew nothing of Yoga.[37]

Although initially some confusion was caused by Chintamani, the many documents leave no doubt that the Theosophists acted with duplicity, and tried to use the Swami and his Samaj for their own purposes. The subsequent history of their intrigues in India demonstrates quite clearly that such behaviour was in character.[38] The Swami was enthusiastic at first, but slowly grew suspicious of their beliefs and machinations. He patiently tried again and again to clear up the relationship between the two bodies, and to convince the Theosophist leaders of the wrongness of some of their beliefs. His letters show firmness and dignity, and a great amount of patience. But when he was finally convinced that his attempts were fruitless and that they obstinately refused to listen, he made the break publicly and with all the fire he could muster: the harsh tone of his final document was completely justified by the treatment he had received. Thus ended this attempt to widen the scope and influence of his Samaj: he certainly agreed to a very broad basis of cooperation, but some of his principles were too basic ever to become a bargaining point, and monotheism was categorically one of them.

It was this same conviction of the need to reach the wider community that made Dayananda spend more and more time on his writings. His Vedic commentary sometimes absorbed absolutely all his time, as in Kanpur,[39] and we have seen how in Bombay nine hours of his working day were reserved for it.[40] This is no wonder, because in these last years he wrote an average of a thousand pages of commentary per year over and above his other publications, including the very important new editions of his *Satyārth Prakāsh* and his *Sanskārvidhi.*

The decision of the Swami to acquire his own press was motivated by the urge to ensure the regular and continuing publication of the commentary: he did not want to be at the mercy of the convenience or whims of other printers. The Lazarus Press of Banaras was at first printing for him, but a man was needed to supervise and coordinate the publication. Harischandra Chintamani was appointed, but mismanaged affairs, and was replaced by Munshi Samarthadan.[41] The situation was still very unsatisfactory, and from early 1879 the Swami started asking people to subscribe funds to enable him to acquire his own press.[42] The Moradabad Samaj got the subscription going, followed by Meerut, Farrukhabad, and other branches; thus a sizeable amount of capital was gathered, and the Vedic Press was established on 12 February 1880. It was a great achievement, but to the Swami, who always considered himself a *sannyāsī*, becoming the owner of considerable property had a bitter taste: he said 'today I have fallen, I have become a householder'.[43]

The early years of the Press present a sorry history of mismanagement and misunderstanding, evidenced by the many letters that have been preserved. The first manager, Munshi Bakhtawar Singh, got the financial affairs of the Press into a mess, and was dismissed within a year to be replaced by Babu Sidaram, who was put under the authority of Ray Bahadur Pandit Sundarlal. The Press was shifted from Banaras to Allahabad in March 1881, and the managers followed each other quickly: Sidaram, Jwaladatt, Dayaram, Munshi Samarthadan. Finally, in May 1883, it was decided to have a managing committee of seven, of which Pandit Sundarlal was President, and Pandit Bhimasena secretary, to act as supervisory authority over the finances of the Press.[44] At a particular crisis point, the Swami wrote, '. . . if nothing is done, then even our books will be stolen from us, and we shall not be able to keep anything at all. We shall give up the *Vedabhāshya* and all our other work, and we shall happily roam around clad only in a loincloth.'[45]

The Swami's priorities were clear: he had acquired the Press

to ensure the regular publication of his *Bhāshya:* so that had
to come first. Repeatedly he wrote harshly asking Munshi
Samarthadan to put an end to all outside work, 'because this
press is not a business venture, but only for the propagation by
print of the true *Shāstras*'.[46] In this area the Swami claimed
and exercised a full authority, often harshly expressed in his letters
to his managers, who sometimes felt very hurt.[47] On 16 August
1880 he registered in Meerut his first *Svīkārpatra*, or will. Two
circumstances made him take this step. First, there was the long
illness that troubled him from April 1879 to May 1880,[48] which
made him realize that he could not necessarily count on a long
life. Secondly, the management of the Press had been erratic
and at times corrupt, and had constantly needed the strong hand
and decisive orders of the Swami. He had to make sure that in
the event of his death the Press could effectively continue its
printing and publication work. The will left the full control of
the Swami's property, 'clothes, books, money, Vedic Press, etc.' to
a body called the Paropkarinī Sabhā. These assets were to be
used only for the three objectives clearly stated:

1. The dissemination of the *Vedas*, *Vedāngas*, and other true *Shāstras*,
   namely by promoting the commentary, the reading, and the teaching
   of them.
2. The preaching and teaching of the Vedic *dharma* by instituting a body
   of preachers to be sent across India and outside so that truth may be
   accepted and falsehood rejected.
3. Helping and providing in the protection, feeding, and education of
   the orphans and destitutes of India.[49]

The fundamental task of the Paropkarinī Sabhā was to continue the Swami's work of propagation of the Vedic religion. It
is interesting that Dayananda added the third aim. Perhaps he
already felt that it was among the outcasts and the orphans that
both Christianity and Islam were having their greatest success.
This cause was to be taken up in earnest by the Arya Samaj at
the end of the century.

However, there was no direct connection between the Arya
Samaj and the Paropkarinī Sabhā, which had no authority over
the branches. Nevertheless, most trustees were prominent Aryas, as
the Swami stressed in a letter to Bhimasena.[50] Half the number,
nine, were leading Aryas from Western U.P., four of them from
Farrukhabad; three trustees were from Lahore, two from Bombay, and one from Danapur, with Ranade from Poona and the

two Theosophist leaders making up the total. Lala Mulraj was appointed President. It is clear that at that time the Swami considered the leading Aryas, especially those from the north, to be the people to carry on his work after his death, although he did include some persons whose connection with the Samaj was not so intimate: Ranade and the Theosophists.

On 27 February 1883, while in Udaipur, the Swami registered a new will that cancelled the first. This document is practically identical in wording with the first one.[51] The reason for the new will was that the Swami wanted to omit the names of four trustees: the two Theosophists, Munshi Indramani who had been expelled from the Samaj, and Dr Biharilal who had died. But the reconstruction of the list of trustees was much more drastic than the simple replacement of those names: the membership was enlarged from eighteen to twenty-three members, which means that nine new members were added to the remaining fourteen. The striking thing is that these new members all came from the ruling strata of the native states. The Maharana of Udaipur was the new President, and four members of his State Council were also included. Besides, there were the ruler of Shahpura, and the minor princely rulers of Delwara, Asind, and Masuda. These were all people whom the Swami came to know personally during his stay in Rajputana. This is a remarkable development: none of the nine additional members were Aryas. Moreover, they had three office-bearers, whereas the Aryas had only two. In the total membership the Aryas outnumbered the others 56.5 to 43.5 per cent. This was obviously a deliberate step taken by Dayananda to enlarge the base of the committee of trustees, and to make it more clearly representative of a wider group; thus he expressed his concern for the wider world of Hinduism, to which his publications and his reform were directed.

Dayananda's proclamation at Hardwar, his collaboration with the Theosophists, his overriding concern for his Press and the publications, and the content of his will clearly show that it was his intention that his work and his Samaj should reach out into the wider world of Hinduism. In the last three years of his life he actually managed to involve his Aryas in three successive agitations which brought them into close collaboration with a wide range of Hindus. The first opportunity came about by accident: it was the case of Munshi Indramani.[52] The Munshi was a well-known figure in Hindu circles: for twenty years he had been a vehement defender of Hinduism, writing numerous books and pamphlets against Islam. He first met the Swami at the gathering of reformers in Delhi in 1876, and a year later he was Dayananda's assistant in the Chandapur 'Melā disputation. In July 1879 he became the foundation president of the Moradabad branch of the Arya Samaj.

One year later, in July 1880, the Munshi was brought to court by Muslims for some of his inflammatory writings against Islam. The Magistrate of Moradabad, after seeking advice from a Muslim functionary about the publications before the court, convicted Indramani, and imposed a fine of five hundred rupees and confiscation of the offending books. The Munshi lodged an appeal, which was heard on 18 September; the fine was reduced to one hundred rupees. He then sought to appeal to the High Court. This was disallowed, but the provincial authorities, anxious to end the disruptive affair as quickly as possible, returned the fine to the Munshi.

This case was extensively written up in the Hindī newspapers of the U.P. and the Panjab, and the sympathy of all Hindus was with Indramani. As soon as he was convicted, funds to cover the costs of the appeal were collected among the Hindus, and even Banaras Hindu papers helped in the effort. In August Dayananda wrote a letter from Agra to the branches of the Arya Samaj, urging them to collect funds. There was a very unpleasant aftermath to the case: Indramani was accused of keeping for himself a substantial part of the money collected for his defence, a sum the Arya Samaj claimed was intended to become a standing fund for defraying the costs of similar cases in the future. This led to bitter public accusations by the Swami and the Aryas, and finally brought about the expulsion of Indramani from the Arya Samaj.

The case of Indramani is extensively reported by biographers of the Swami, and the main thrust of their argument is to show the dishonesty of Indramani and the correctness of the Swami's indignation, and of the drastic measures of the Arya Samaj. Their assessment seems right but, in presenting the case in that way, the biographers overlooked the most important aspect of the whole affair: the fact that for the first time the Swami succeeded in getting the Aryas deeply involved in an agitation in which the

Arya Samaj projected the image of being the defender of Hinduism and earned the sympathy of the majority of Hindus.

It seems quite probable that it was that wave of Hindu sympathy for the Arya Samaj that prompted the leaders of orthodoxy to call an extraordinary meeting shortly afterwards in Calcutta. On 22 January 1881 a council was convened which called itself the Ārya-Sanmārg-Sandarshinī-Sabhā, 'the council indicating the true Aryan way', which made it its business to pronounce on the orthodoxy of Dayananda.[53] Within the ambit of Hinduism such a display of authority in defence of orthodoxy was extremely rare, and its very occurrence demonstrates that a good number of the orthodox worried about the Swami's impact. Their line of attack was revealing: they tried to brand Dayananda as unorthodox, as a person beyond the pale of authentic Hinduism. They felt that the Swami's influence was reaching beyond the small group of Aryas; small sects never bothered the orthodox very much. It was that wider influence, exemplified in the agitation in support of Indramani, which they sought to counteract.

The Council was quite a grand affair: it was held in the Town Hall, and those present were about three hundred pandits mainly from Calcutta, with a few from the U.P. and even from South India, plus another two hundred notables, among whom there were many small rajas and zamindars. Some of the leading participants were old enemies of the Swami. The instigator was Seth Narayandas of Mathura, agent for Seth Lakshmidas; they were Vallabhāchāryas who had an old score to settle with the Swami. In fact they had already tried to get Dayananda thrown out of the house he occupied in Agra, and to lure him to Mathura for a public debate.[54] Pandit Maheshchandra Nyayaratna, Principal of Sanskrit College, had formerly attacked the *Vedabhāshya*, and had been answered by the Swami in a special pamphlet.[55] Another prominent figure was Pandit Ramsuba who had written a booklet against the Swami.[56] The Council's final decisions were the following:

1. The *Brāhmanas* are as authoritative as the four *Vedas*, and the other *Shāstras* as authentic as Manu.
2. Idol worship, *shrāddh*, and pilgrimages are sanctioned by the *Shāstras*.
3. The term *agni* in the *Vedas* means not God, but fire.
4. *Homa*, or offerings of clarified butter into the fire, is not for the purification of the air, but for the attainment of *moksha*.

They declared that those holding a contrary opinion, as Dayananda was well known to do, were in contravention of orthodoxy.

It is not likely that the Council decision carried much weight outside Calcutta. The Swami was well aware of these events, but he wrote to Kriparam, 'we don't have the leisure to write about the Calcutta Sabhā, we have too much work with the *Vedabhāshya*. If you have the time, publish something yourself'.[57] So he left it to his Aryas to give a detailed answer. But this attempt by the pandits to isolate him from the body of Hinduism was the reason why, immediately after the Council, he decided to launch an anti-cow-slaughter agitation: here indeed was an issue on which a great number of Hindus would sympathize with him, and through which his influence on the great body of Hinduism would grow.

Dayananda's concern for cow-protection appeared early in his career. In 1866, on his first visit to Ajmer three years after leaving Virjananda, he talked about it to Colonel Brooks, Agent to the Governor-General in Rajputana. His argument was already clearly established: the killing of cows was bad because of its economic consequences, as a dead cow provided little food whereas a live one provided for many.[58] In 1873 in Farrukhabad he asked Mr Muir, the Lieutenant-General of the N.W. Provinces, if he would use his influence to promote the ban on cow-slaughter when he became a member of the India Council in London.[59] He referred to the question in two places in his first *Satyārth Prakāsh*.[60] One of the duties of a king is to prevent the destruction of useful animals, because the people depend on them, an argument he elaborated in the section in which he criticized the British Raj. There he stated in full his economic argument: one cow can in the long run provide food for a hundred thousand, whereas its carcass scarcely feeds a hundred. The cow should not be killed because it is the basic condition of the good health and nutrition of all the people. The Swami restated this theme occasionally in the course of a lecture, for instance in Poona,[61] but it certainly was not yet a major concern of his.

It was only in 1877 that cow-protection became a major issue and that Dayananda started to devote special lectures to it. In fact, it was precisely in the beginning of that year that a group of Hindus sent a plea asking the Government to stop the slaughter of cows. When the Government answered that it could do nothing in the matter, Harischandra Bharatendu wrote bitterly about the injustice of a Government that favoured a minority of Muslims and Christians against an overwhelming majority of Hindus.[62] In 1879 the Swami made the following statement in Farrukhabad: 'There is no unity among us, that is why cow-slaughter keeps going on. If we petitioned the government all together, could it not come to an end?'[63] However, he did not take any specific action at that time.

Why then did the Swami, in early 1881, take the decision to launch a systematic agitation against cow-slaughter? In the beginning of that year the question once more hit the headlines in the north. The Hindus of Mirzapur came to know that a Muslim had acquired a cow for ritual slaughter. They managed to get from the authorities an injunction that the Muslim in question was not allowed to slaughter the animal, though he was its legal owner. This decision, however, was soon over-ruled by a new magistrate. He held that the legal owner could dispose of his property at will, but gave the Hindus the right of appeal within six weeks. This case brought the communities into action. The Muslims founded a committee called Anjuman-i-Islami to raise funds for the court case. The Hindus too started a money-raising campaign that was widely publicized in the papers.[64]

Swami Dayananda was at that time in Agra, and could not have missed the upheaval. The Calcutta Hindu Council's decision was only a few weeks old, and here the opportunity arose to involve his Samaj in another agitation that would find an immediate response in Hindu circles. He decided to launch a national cow-protection movement. Straight away he wrote his pamphlet *Gokarunānidhi*, 'The ocean of kindness to the cow', a work published within a few weeks, sold out quickly, and republished within a year. The Swami asked Mulraj to provide an English translation, but as Mulraj kept postponing the work, the translation was done in Bombay, but it is not known if it was published.[65] The first half of the booklet sets out at length the case for a ban on the slaughter of cows and other useful animals. The economic argument is elaborated and supported by scriptural arguments, and opponents' points are answered in detail. The fundamental ethical principle is simple: actions that cause injury to others are sinful. The killing of animals, in particular of the cow, leads to harm in two different ways. It causes the ruin of society by undermining the production of the best possible food; it also does untold damage by destroying the ecology: 'by the destruction of the natural order of the universe'.[66] This line of argument shows the Swami's concern for a healthy and pollution-free life, although its economics may be rejected. Animal slaughter, he says, leads to a greater dependence on grains, the cultivation of which increases wastage that pollutes earth, air, and water. Animals, even non-domesticated ones, have an important role in the cycle of nature: they clean up more than an army of sweepers could, and they are at the same time a great source of natural fertilizer. The protection of animals implies the protection of forests, which promote better rainfall and a purer atmosphere. Dayananda stressed that his argument thus encompassed the protection of the whole animal world, but he stated that the latter could only gradually be implemented. The immediate agitation was for the protection of the cow, which was selected by the ancient Aryans for special care because among the animals it is supremely useful, conferring the greatest benefits on man. In this work the Swami also stated his final attitude towards the consumption of meat: every form of it is sinful. The plea of the opponent, that a ritual context makes it morally right, was now rejected, and it was affirmed that the *Vedas* do not prescribe any rite involving killing or meat-eating.

The second part of the pamphlet contains the laws and by-laws of a society called the Gokrishyādirakshinī Sabhā, 'for the protection of kine, agriculture, etc.', usually shortened to Gorakshinī Sabhā. 'All men who wish to devote their effort and help by body, mind, or riches, to this work for the benefit of all' were invited to become members, and any society with similar aims was urged to associate itself. The Swami was very concerned that membership be kept open to all, as the explicit instructions to the secretary clearly show: 'It should be borne in mind that a member may belong to any community or group whatsoever, and that any community or organization affiliated should have a representative in the executive committee.' The document gives details of membership, organization and management. Such a society was immediately started at Agra, and several more followed soon, but the exact details are not available.

Apart from the pamphlet and the Sabhā, Dayananda's campaign had a third line of attack: he planned to give impetus and strength to the movement by collecting at least a hundred thousand signatures to a Memorial which was to be presented to Queen Victoria, the British Parliament, and the Governor-General of India. The document published in Bombay on 14 March 1882 outlined the case against cow-slaughter and asked the Government 'to quickly put an end to the slaughter of cows, bullocks and buffaloes'.[67] Hundreds of copies of this appeal were sent with an accompanying letter from the Swami to the Samajes, to leading personalities and institutions, and to the rulers of the princely states. It is difficult to assess the overall success of this campaign as it has to be judged from the few remaining letters that refer to it. In some places, the result was very quick and encouraging. There is a report of 40,000 signatures from Mewar,[68] of 60,000 in Patiala,[69] and a letter from Bombay mentions over 15,000.[70] The Swami complained of the slackness of some Aryas, e.g. those of Meerut, and also mentioned that his mail was being tampered with.[71] He was trying to communicate a sense of urgency; he felt that the Memorial, to be fully effective, should be presented during Lord Ripon's governorship which was due to run out in 1884.[72] However, his untimely death put an end to his own efforts, but on the whole the agitation generated was strong enough to bother the Indian Government.[73]

Did Dayananda succeed in his aim of attracting that collaboration in this matter of the wider world of Hinduism, an aim so clearly stated in the by-laws of the Sabhā? There are indications that he was indeed starting to achieve that end. The movement got the personal support of several ruling princes, notwithstanding the fact that, as kshatriyas, many of them were themselves meat-eaters. In the U.P. and the Panjab the response was assured, and regular incidents kept the issue on the boil.[74] In Bombay, the impact was remarkable. During that last half-year stay, the Swami did not direct his energies towards idol worship and other controversies, but he gave a number of lectures about cow-protection. The effect was that some people dropped their previous hostility and supported him on this new platform. The Bhatiyas especially, closely linked to the Vallabhāchārya sect, helped him to muster signatures for his Memorial, and even arranged for the Swami to give lectures on the subject in their halls.[75] A final indication of the spreading influence in this respect is a letter from Calcutta, from the editor of the *Bhārat-Mitra*, praising the movement, promising full collaboration, and asking for a parcel of copies of the Memorial to be sent to prominent personalities and associations in Bengal.[76]

In the early eighties another agitation gripped the Hindus of the North: the Hindī-Urdū controversy. This was not a new phenomenon, but the intense flaring-up of a movement that had started some twenty years earlier. In 1837 the Indian Government had decided that Urdū, written in the Persian script, would be the official language of the U.P., and in the sixties there came to be a movement to have Urdū replaced by Hindī in the *devanāgarī* script. Important landmarks in this campaign were Babu Shivaprasad's 'Memorandum on Court Characters' of 1868, the inauguration of the journal *The Reflector* in the same year, and the 1873 Memorial presented to Sir William Muir.[77] In these and many other writings and speeches the main arguments for Hindī and against Urdū were already clearly elaborated. Hindī was a 'pure' language, whereas Urdū was a barbarian mixture; the Persian script was hopelessly difficult and confusing, whereas *devanāgarī* was scientifically accurate and easy to learn. More important were the social arguments: the majority of the people of the U.P. were Hindī-speakers, and not only were they disadvantaged where education facilities were concerned, but the use of Urdū in official and court proceedings put them at the mercy of officialdom, as they could not understand the language used. The question was not, however, merely a social and linguistic one: by the seventies the movement for Hindī had already adopted as one of its main arguments the intimate connection between language, religion, and nation, in other words Hindu nationalism.[78] Another important aspect of the crusade was the fact that at every stage a number of Bengalis were among its leaders: thus the movement for Hindī was in a way connected with the growing movement of Hindu nationalism in Bengal.[79]

In 1881 Urdū was replaced by Hindī as the official language of the province of Bihar. This was an event that gave a new impetus to the promotion of Hindī in the U.P., which grew into a campaign, strongly supported by the prominent Bengalis Bhudev Mukhopadhyay and Rajendralal Mitra. When the Indian Education Commission, under the chairmanship of W.W. Hunter, came to the U.P. in 1882, the agitation was in full swing, and signatures for memoranda were being canvassed with great enthusiasm.[80] Dayananda's interest in Hindī began with his visit to Calcutta. Once he had decided, on the advice of Keshub Chandra Sen, to conduct his preaching and writing in Hindī,[81] he made great advances in that language, and it became the main vehicle for his teaching. Wherever he went, from Banaras to Lahore and Bombay, Hindī was the language he used. This was not just a policy of convenience, as Hindī was largely understood across the north, but also one of principle. In Gujarat the Swami could as well have preached in his own mother tongue, Gujarātī, and thus would have reached the masses there even better. Hindī was to him another major means of surmounting the divisive multiplicity of India and of promoting unity across the barriers of states and castes. To the question as to when India would again reach its full greatness and prosperity, he answered, 'When there is unity of *dharma*, of language, and of objectives'.[82] The idea of Hindī as a national language had probably been proposed to the Swami by his Bengali contacts, Bhudev Mukhopadhyay and Rajendralal Mitra,[83] and the connection of language and religion in a nationalist context had been, as we have seen, part of the Hindī movement since the seventies.

In 1878 Harischandra Chintamani advised the Swami to have his *Bhāshya* translated into English, Urdū, and other Indian vernaculars, but he was told this should not be done because it would tend to discourage people from studying Sanskrit and Hindī.[84] Mme Blavatsky got the same answer when she urged a translation of the *Bhāshya* into English;[85] and in Hardwar, when the Swami was again asked that question, he affirmed that all Indians should learn Hindī, and that if they could not make such a small effort, very little else could be expected from them.[86] The Swami encouraged the Aryas to use Hindī, and the volumes of incoming letters show how hard they tried: some of the letters written by Panjabis, Marathas, and Gujaratis are a strange mixture of Hindī and their own vernacular.[87] The case for Hindī was at the same time the case for the *devanāgarī* script, which the Swami promoted whenever he could. In Udaipur he urged the Maharana to introduce that script into the courts, and he also included the study of Hindī and *devanāgarī* in the educational curriculum of the young princes.[88] It was due to his pressure that Jodhpur made

Hindī in the *devanāgarī* script the state language in 1883.[89]

In 1882 the Swami, who was at that time in Bombay, heard about the Hunter Commission and the efforts being made to put the case for Hindī before it. The information came from the Panjabi Aryas; the Lahore and Multan branches had already taken the initiative and submitted their memorials. Dayananda wrote immediately to the Farrukhabad Aryas urging them to collect signatures and submit their own memorial. He also asked them to contact the other branches and to prompt them to do the same. Again and again he himself wrote to different branches pressing them to take part in the campaign.[90] As a result, no less than twenty-nine memorials were submitted by the Arya Samaj, about a dozen each from the Panjab and the U.P., and a few from Bombay and Rajputana.[91]

When the Swami thus urged his Aryas to write memorials, he was not taking a novel initiative, but rather he was pressing them to participate to the fullest extent in a campaign that was well under way. In fact, less than a quarter of the pro-Hindī submissions to the Hunter Commission came from the Arya Samaj.[92] The Swami was directing his followers to become closely involved in an agitation that stood for the intimate connection of language, religion, and nationalism, and which had a strong appeal for most Hindus of the North. The case for Hindī presented by the Arya Samaj can be gathered from the two memorials that are available, those of Meerut and Kanpur.[93] The linguistic and social arguments they used are identical with those that were already propounded in the seventies and nothing distinguishes them from most pro-Hindī statements of the decade.

Thus, in those last years of his life, the Swami devoted much time and energy to activities that involved him and his Samaj with the wider world of Hinduism. His public notice at Hardwar had clearly stated the policy: consensus, not controversy, was to be the guiding motto. The Arya Samaj, which was already showing some leanings towards sectarianism, had to become the rallying point of all Hindus of goodwill, and had to be accepted by Hindus as such. The collaboration with the Theosophists was prompted by that intention, and so was the composition of the board of trustees of the Paropkarinī Sabhā. But the most significant move in that direction was the involvement of the

Aryas in those three successive agitations: for the Indramani case, for cow-protection, and for Hindī. Each of these causes brought many Hindus together across the barriers of caste, sect, and provincialism. By its enthusiastic participation the Arya Samaj could project the image of being the protagonist of broad Hindu nationalism. None of these campaigns was created by the Swami: he came to the assistance of movements that were well launched, and to which many Hindus were deeply committed. All three movements also had a common factor in being directed against the Muslims, and containing a significant anti-British bias. Thus the Swami steered his Samaj towards closer cooperation with orthodox and sectarian Hindus, and anticipated the movement of *sangathan*, consolidation and integration of the whole Hindu community, that was later to flourish in the 1920s and 1930s.[94]

A final important indication of the widening of the Swami's outlook is that in the last year of his life he turned for the first time his attention to South India. Āryāvarta had always meant to him the region north of the Vindhya range. But as his concern broadened out and acquired national and political dimensions, his eyes turned towards the South. Letters to the Swami, written from early 1883, indicate that Dayananda had informed the Aryas of his intention to go to Madras after another visit to Calcutta.[95] The Aryas all over the North were clamouring for his presence, but the Swami had other plans: first he would visit Calcutta again, where he hoped to finally convert the Bengalis' admiration into cooperation, and then he would tour South India. But these grandiose all-India dreams were shattered by the Swami's untimely death.

CHAPTER X

The Ultimate Effort: The Princes of Rajputana

Why did Dayananda, after his great success in North India and at the very time that the spread of his Samaj was gathering momentum, move down into Rajputana to spend those years that tragically were to be his last among the princes of the native states? He always considered his mission to embrace the whole of Āryāvarta, and it was only natural that his interest should turn to the princely states, that other half of the country generally bypassed by the reformers. But one should not forget that he himself was born the subject of a raja in Kathiawar and that for the first twenty-one years of his life he knew no other than princely rule.[1] Moreover, in the early stage of his public preaching his eyes had been turned towards the rajas by his *guru*, Swami Virjananda, who had himself been a teacher of princes and had enjoyed their patronage in establishing his school. Virjananda had also dreamt of a great Council of Hinduism, wherein these princes would take into their hands the protection and the propagation of the works of the *rishis*.[2] One of the first areas where Dayananda himself preached was the state of Jaipur, where he converted the ruler to Shaivism and thus accelerated a conversion movement.[3] The Swami knew from experience the power of the princes in their domains, and he too had sometimes contemplated the idea of a great Council of Hinduism in which they would play an important role.[4]

The drift of Dayananda's early preaching had brought him to British India, and it was in the urban centres there that he had finally found response and success. He always believed that those in political power could and should exert their influence for the sake of *dharma*, as all his dissertations on statecraft amply demonstrate. On several occasions he had tried to convince the administrators of the British Raj that they should take some steps for the sake of the protection of *dharma*, specially by protecting the cow, promoting the study of the sacred language, and legislating to protect widows.[5] But none of these attempts had been blessed with success.

This failure convinced the Swami even more that the native princes might well be persuaded to exert their considerable power in the service of *dharma*. He asserted that the full prosperity of India depended on the unity of *dharma*, language, and aims, and he continued, 'That is why I wish that the rajas of our country bring about in their own territory that threefold unity'.[6] In his agitation against cow-slaughter he worked on two fronts: influencing the British to legislate against it, and urging the princes to ban it.[7] He complained about the fact that in Jaipur so many churches were being built, and that the missionaries were conducting intensive propaganda: 'The pandits and the rajas have not made any effort to remove them.'[8] These statements, his pronouncements on statecraft in his *Satyārth Prakāsh*, and also his directives to the princes that will be analysed later, indicate clearly that Dayananda was of the opinion that the princes could well apply their considerable power and influence to help in the reconstruction of Āryāvarta in a way in which the British were not prepared to do in British India.

Dayananda had occasionally visited raja states, mostly at the invitation of the rulers themselves. But the decision to make a protracted effort in their domains was a novel one, and there is no doubt that this decision was precipitated by his successful visits to Masuda and Chittor in 1881. Masuda was not a raja state proper, but a large estate within the British-administered territory of Ajmer-Mewara, only about thirty miles from Ajmer itself; yet in most ways Masuda was very much like the surrounding states of Rajputana. Dayananda had met Rao Bahadur Singh of Masuda, landlord and judge, at Pushkar in November 1878, and on his invitation he had spent a week with him in December. The Rao had attended the few lectures the Swami delivered, and had sealed their spontaneous friendship with a Rs 200 donation towards the *Vedabhāshya*.[9]

During the Swami's 1881 visit to Ajmer, the Rao sent Pandit Vriddhichand there to invite him for a longer stay, and the Swami accepted immediately; he was the guest of the prince for nearly two months.[10] The Rao Bahadur showed intense interest in the Swami's work; he attended his twenty-two lectures, and tried to arrange some public debates. He invited Dr Schoolbred for that purpose, but the latter declined a debate. The prince also put pressure on the Jains, who in fact invited Sādhu Siddhakaran to represent them, but the written debate that followed between him and the Swami was only shortlived.[11] Dayananda's preaching, with the wholehearted support of the Rao, was very successful, as was openly demonstrated at a public ceremony of investiture with the holy thread. It was a grand affair with all the pomp that could be mustered. A great Vedic altar was prepared, and the oblations were offered first by the Rao and then by four brahmins. Thirty-two people were initiated by the Swami himself while Vedic *mantras* were being chanted. Among the recipients of the sacrament were brahmins, kshatriyas, and kayasths, but the most striking fact was that half of the initiates were Jains. Another similar ceremony was held a few days later in which a smaller group was initiated, more than half of whom were Jains. This quite extraordinary event was reported not only in Arya journals, but even in the *Bhārat-Mitra* of Calcutta.[12]

In Masuda, some Muslims, converted from Hinduism during the Mughal period, had retained the custom of obtaining their brides from their former Hindu caste. When Dayananda heard of this, he berated the Hindus for this evil custom, and they agreed to terminate it. His friendship with the Rao had become very close, and the latter tried to persuade him to settle down in Masuda, promising that he would subsidize the *Vedabhāshya*. At his insistence the Swami prolonged his stay, but eventually he declared that his duty as a *sannyāsī* was to roam the land and instruct elsewhere. At last the Rao let him take his leave, and donated another Rs 400 for the *Bhāshya*.[13] The Rao kept in correspondence with the Swami, supported his cow-protection movement, and tried to dissuade him from moving to Mount Abu at the time of his final illness.[14]

From Masuda the Swami went, on the invitation of Thakur Hari Singh, to Raipur. Although a great *yajna* and a series of public lectures had been foreshadowed, nothing much resulted. The Raja did come to the Swami's discourses at his residence but the other matters kept being postponed. When a telegram arrived announcing the death of the Thakur's wife in Jaipur, the Swami asked leave to move on, and went to Beawar in the Ajmer-Mewara territory where he gave a series of lectures.[15] From there he went back to Masuda, where this time he only gave instruction to the Rao.[16] Dayananda's next stop was Banera, where he had been invited by Raja Govindsingh, a maternal uncle of the Rao of Masuda. There the Swami had some discussions with the Raja and his Rajpandits on Vedic matters.[17]

But the great chance came when the Swami met Maharana Sajjan Singh of Udaipur, ruler of one of the great states of Rajputana, with a princely pedigree that outshone that of most rajas. The prince had taken up the reins of government only five years previously, at the age of seventeen.[18] The house of Mewar was Shaivite, but the young prince had difficulties with Hinduism as he saw it around him, and became inclined towards atheism. Two of his closest advisers were very concerned about this development. Both were very learned men, Pandit Mohanlal Vishnulal Pandya, the Secretary of the Udaipur State Council, and Kaviraj Shyamaldas, a member of that Council and a famous historian. They made efforts to interest the young king in Dayananda's works and ideas. They told him all they knew about the Swami, and got him a copy of the *Satyārth Prakāsh* to read. The Maharana's interest was aroused, and the two councillors corresponded with the Swami in the hope of bringing the two together. There was, however, a procedural obstacle: Sajjan Singh would not meet Dayananda outside his territory, and the Swami was reluctant to go to Udaipur without a formal invitation. However, by chance, an occasion for their meeting arose. A durbar was arranged at Chittor, where Lord Ripon was to come specially to invest the young prince with the title of G.C.S.I. When Dayananda heard about this, he decided to go there, and informed Kaviraj Shyamaldas about it.[19]

No place in India symbolizes more the splendour, valour, and virtues of Hindu princedom than Chittor. 'My heart beat high', wrote Tod, 'as I approached the ancient capital of the Sesodias, teeming with reminiscences of glory, which every stone of her giant-like battlements attested.'[20] The Swami too was reminded of those glorious events as Maharana Sajjan Singh showed him around the historic monuments. They proclaimed the fight to death of the Rajputs and the self-immolation of their women at the conquest of Chittor by Ala-ud-din, and the similar rite performed when Akbar sacked the city. The 'Tower of Glory' recalled the victory of Rana Kumbha over the Sultan of Malwa; and the bards still sang the praises of the giant figure of Pratap

Singh whose heroic fight against the Mughals lasted a quarter of a century.

When the durbar was over, the Maharana and the Swami had several meetings and soon great affection and admiration sprung up on both sides. The ruler invited the Swami to accompany him to Udaipur right away, but Dayananda excused himself: he had urgent work to do in Bombay. However, he promised that after his stay in Bombay he would contact the Maharana, and that, if the prince still so wished, he would then go to Udaipur.[21] Many other princes met with the Swami and asked him to visit them in the near future.[22]

These were the events that drew the Swami to Rajputana. He had made close contact with one of its most powerful rulers, a young king earnest and keen to learn more about *dharma* and his kingly duties, who could have substantial influence not only in his own state, but also on the other rajas of the area: Sajjan Singh was noted for his concern to bring the native states closer together.[23] At Chittor Dayananda had also met the Raja of Shahpura, from the same illustrious Sesodia clan of Rajputs as the Maharana, and with him too a close bond had quickly developed. The meeting with these two men was to the Swami an unexpected revelation. He said to Sajjan Singh:

It was my opinion that in contemporary India the great majority of kings were a rather lazy lot, but having met you, I have come to believe that you are a very worthy person. Pandit Mohanlal had written to me that you are a lion for work, and that your virtues match your name. That is how I found you to be.[24]

The great success of his work at Masuda and the meeting with these two unusual princes were the deciding factors that took the Swami to Rajputana after his stay at Bombay: a new large sphere of influence called him, with the promise of reaching, through the goodwill and power of the princes, that ever beckoning wider community of Hinduism.

During his six months in Udaipur, the Swami concentrated his energies on instructing the Maharana and some of his family and main advisers. His mornings and early afternoons were taken up by his writing and correspondence, and the evenings were devoted to serious instruction; as soon as the pupils were sufficiently familiar with the elements of Sanskrit, the teaching

moved on to consider selected texts from the *Manusmriti*, the
political and ethical treatises of the *Mahābhārata*, and the six
darshanas.[25] The Swami praised the application and regularity
of his principal pupil in his letters to the Aryas.[26] He did not
give any public lectures, and he took part in only one public debate,
the one with Maulvi Abdul Rahman described in a previous
chapter.[27] If in the early days of Dayananda's stay, his pupils
did not know their teacher too well, they soon discovered his convictions. Some influential courtiers tried to convince the Swami
that, if he dropped his criticism of idol worship, he would get
many more people on his side. The answer was the usual one:
truth must come first.[28] When Kaviraj came up with the suggestion
of erecting some 'memorial' to the Swami, he was rebuffed in
plain language.[29] Some businessmen tried to get the Swami
involved in their judicial wrangles, no doubt to make use of his
influence on the Maharana in their favour, but the Swami made
it clear that that was completely outside his province.[30] One
day Sajjan Singh proposed to Dayananda that if he agreed to
become the Mahant of the great Shiva temple, he would command
much influence over the religion of the state. The Swami reacted
with indignation because he thought that the king was tempting
him with prospects of wealth: 'You can never force me to break
the commandments of the *Vedas*. Therefore, control your tongue.
Hundreds of thousands have put their trust in me. It is my firm
intention to follow the path of truth always and in every possible
way.'[31]

As the months went by Dayananda's instruction clearly started
to influence the life of the Maharana. When the Swami gave him
a suggested order of the day fit for a king, he accepted it and tried
to implement the demanding schedule.[32] He also seems to have
accepted Dayananda's doctrine of strict monogamy, even for
kings, for it is reported that at that time he declined to go ahead
with negotiations to take a second wife.[33]

But Dayananda's personal influence on Sajjan Singh spilled
over into the area of court life and of the administration of the
state. After the celebration of a great *yajna* that lasted several
days, the king ordered that a daily *havan* was to be held at the
court.[34] At the time of the Dashaharā festival, which celebrates
the descent of the river Ganga from heaven, many buffaloes were
ritually slaughtered in Udaipur. The Swami held in the court

a mock trial in which he played the role of the lawyer for the defence of the condemned animals. The ruler accepted the Swami's arguments, but pointed out that these customs could not be stopped overnight on account of their great popularity. He nevertheless promised that he would see to it that the slaughter was gradually reduced.[35] The Swami also proposed that the work of the courts be done in the *devanāgarī* script, and he supplied for that purpose a list of translations of Arabic terms into Sanskrit. Such a proposal could not be implemented quickly, as it involved wide-ranging administrative changes.[36] Another proposal was that a special school should be founded for the education of the sons of noble families where they would learn not only the military arts but also the *Shāstras*. Sajjan Singh accepted the proposal and took immediate action: plans for the building were drawn up forthwith; but the later illness of the ruler stopped further advance in the project.[37] The Maharana also accepted and ordered the implementation in the Government schools of the curriculum prepared by Dayananda, which included his own Sanskrit textbook.[38]

The Swami wrote for the king a long document containing advice on matters of statecraft:[39] the first section dealt with the judiciary, and the second listed fifty-one special instructions. The document, though arranged in a somewhat haphazard manner, shows that the Swami's ideas on statecraft had matured since he wrote his first *Satyārth Prakāsh*, where he remained too closely entangled in the material of Manu. In this document only the three rules pertaining to war and the spoils of war can be described as completely irrelevant to the actual situation. The section on the conduct of the judiciary advised the setting apart of special days for criminal and civil cases, and put great stress on the impartiality of all procedures, and on the great care that should be taken in the examination of witnesses and scrutiny of the evidence.

The affairs of state should be managed under the king by the three Councils, as described in the second *Satyārth Prakāsh*. In these there should be representatives of officials and non-officials; no one man should be given too much power; and the people should be consulted in all matters affecting them. The officials should be able men, and should be kept under careful surveillance: in fact a special day should be set apart for the ruler to act as an easily accessible ombudsman to whom any complaints about officials could be referred.[40] There is advice on the spending of the budget, but as regards taxation, only one point is emphasized: taxes should not fall heavily on the peasants, who are the main source of the prosperity of the state. A great deal of attention is given to the duties of the state in the area of social welfare. The state should provide education for all children and generous pensions to its retired servants, and it should take responsibility for widows and orphans. It should insist on monogamy, and implement the minimum age of marriage, sixteen for girls and twenty-five for boys.[41] As general guidelines, these suggestions are all very advanced for the age, and of high quality, but obviously their implementation would have to take a long time.

In his guidelines Dayananda intruded in an area where he had repeatedly shown his incompetence: that of sexual relationships, especially of newly-weds, under the heading 'secret rules'. In this particular matter he remained completely dependent on rules he found in the *Shāstras*; he could not come to grips with reality and his usually strong logical mind remained imprisoned by old formulas. For instance, he specified the particular nights of a woman's menstrual cycle when intercourse would lead to the conception of a male or of a female child; he also prescribed a special diet that would ensure impregnation if it did not occur promptly enough.[42]

There is no doubt that after six months in Udaipur the Swami rightly felt that a great deal had been accomplished. Not only had the Maharana accepted him in earnest as a close adviser and teacher, he had also started to implement in his state some of the Swami's most cherished dreams. Dayananda's letters show how enthusiastic he was about these results:

I have found the Maharana to be what all kings should be: lovers of truth above all, knowers of men and their qualities, and men aware of their own qualities and shortcomings. I have met many rulers but the mutual joy that pervades my relationship with the ruler of Udaipur, and that will remain strong in the future, such a pleasure I have but little hope of finding with any other ruler.[43]

He put the official seal on these high hopes by making the Maharana the President of the Paropkarinī Sabhā in his new will, and by including among its trustees no less than six members of his State Council, two of whom were on the Executive Committee.[44] Sajjan Singh showed his appreciation of Dayananda by expressing his thanks and his admiration in a farewell address. He also handed to the Swami various donations: Rs 1200 for the *Vedabhāshya* and Rs 600 for the Firozpur Arya Samaj orphanage. He presented the Swami with Rs 2000 as a personal gift, which the latter refused asking that it should instead be put into the Paropkarinī Sabhā Vedic Fund. The Maharana even proposed that, if the Swami would agree to write a commentary on the six *darshanas*, he would himself contribute Rs 20,000 towards its publication. The Swami declined this offer because he had first to complete his *Vedabhāshya*.[45]

From Udaipur the Swami took the road to Shahpura, which, although small in territory, was a very important chiefdom of Mewar.[46] Rajadhiraj Naharsingh had collected 40,000 signatures for the cow-protection memorial,[47] and had met the Swami at Chittor on the occasion of the durbar. He had ascended the throne fourteen years earlier and was a young man of only twenty-eight.[48] The Swami stayed just under three months with him.[49] In the first week they had long conversations and an excellent relationship was established. Then a regular order of the day was arranged, similar to the one adopted at Udaipur. The first half of the Swami's day was taken up with his regular work, and every evening he spent some hours instructing the prince, the topics being Manu, Patanjali Yoga, and the Vaisheshika system. The Swami was engaged in practically no public activity: no lectures or debates are mentioned. The intensive course indicates the keenness of the raja to learn, and the visit was a great success. In his farewell address, the ruler expressed his sorrow at Dayananda's departure but he agreed that he could not keep him any longer as the Swami had so much work to do elsewhere. As a token of his goodwill he donated Rs 250 for the *Bhāshya*, and promised to provide Rs 30 per month to pay for a preacher of the Vedic faith.[50] He would arrange for the regular performance of the *agnihotra*, and establish a Vedic school for the sons of kshatriyas. He remained in regular correspondence with the Swami throughout the following months.[51]

The success of his stays at Udaipur and Shahpura gave the Swami great confidence that he was indeed beginning to make a serious impact on the native states. In a letter written from

Shahpura to Jodhpur, where he had been repeatedly invited by its Maharaja, he exclaimed,

I accept with great joy the invitation to come to Jodhpur. And I thank Maharaja Jaswant Singh, Maharaja Pratap Singh, and you, Rao Raja Tej Singh, for the desire you have shown that I should come to Jodhpur. From this I have come to the firm conclusion that the time has arrived for the advancement of Āryāvarta, now that the ruler of Jodhpur and others have become enamoured with the true Vedic *dharma* and with ancient statecraft. . . I pray the Almighty that he may make you all of a determined mind, and that through you he may bring about the uplift of the whole of Āryāvarta, so that he may make you share in the glory of that great achievement.[52]

Little did the Swami anticipate what awaited him in Jodhpur: a bitter disappointment as far as the ruler was concerned, and a tragic illness that would carry him to his death.

However, Dayananda's enthusiasm was not surprising: after his achievements in one of the greatest states of Rajputana, Udaipur, he was now invited to Jodhpur, which also ranked among the most important of the area. It was the largest state territorially, the largest in revenue, and ranked only second to Jaipur in population. The princely house had an ancestry and a history that rivalled the glory of the house of Udaipur. The ruler, Maharaja Jaswant Singh, was forty-six and had ascended the throne eleven years previously. He was to occupy it till his death in 1895, and he had a good record as a ruler. His younger brother, Maharaja Pratap Singh, was his right-hand man, and acted as Prime Minister of the state from 1876 to 1902, when he was appointed ruler of Idar in Gujarat. Pratap Singh was looked upon as one of the most enlightened princes of India. His half-brother, Rao Raja Tej Singh, the illegitimate son of his father, was his protégé and close associate, and held a jagir from Jaswant Singh.[53] In Jodhpur there was another personality with enormous influence not only on the Maharaja but also on the nobles of the region: the Muslim minister Miyan Faizulla Khan.[54]

A series of letters written by the Swami during his stay give the surest and clearest picture of the development of his relations with the ruling family.[55] The Maharaja was indisposed at the time of the arrival of Dayananda, who was received with all honour by Pratap Singh and Tej Singh. The ruler himself paid his first visit to the Swami after about one month. It was a very friendly meeting: Jaswant Singh asked Dayananda to consider him his pupil, and the Swami spoke with him for three hours, mainly on the subject of statecraft. The ruler urged the Swami to instruct the people of Jodhpur as much as he could.[56] During this first month both Pratap Singh and Tej Singh had been visiting the Swami regularly and an excellent rapport had sprung up between them.[57] After this month, the Swami felt confident enough to put some advice in writing for Pratap Singh. The first part of the letter expressed his concern over the fact that the leaders of such a great state, with such immense responsibilities, were wasting their time and spoiling their health. They should arrange their lives more strictly so that they might be strong and live long to work for the advancement of the people and to share in the glory of the regeneration of Āryāvarta. The second part of the letter set out the conditions under which the Swami would be prepared to participate in debates with the local pandits mooted by the court: the princes should be present at these occasions and precise rules of procedure should be drawn up beforehand.[58]

By the end of July Dayananda had been in Jodhpur for two months. He wrote to a friend that he did not know when he would leave, but that he thought he would stay on for a while, as there had been some improvement but much remained to be done.[59] He had seen little of Jaswant Singh and decided to write him a letter: 'Though this is the first letter I send you, yet, if it is needed and I am not able to meet you personally, we will remain in touch by correspondence.' He praised the ruler's ability and his great qualities, and went on,

But it is such a great pity that, though you are such an intelligent man, you still keep engaging, I do not know why, in the following activities: drinking, consorting with prostitutes, kite-flying, gambling. If you do not give those pastimes up and devote at least six hours a day to state affairs, and if you do not show greater affection for your wives, princesses of great beauty, it is a great pity indeed. As a ruler is, so will the people be. All these bad habits are extremely injurious to your life expectation, your strength and health, your fame, to the achievement of the aims of *dharma*, *artha*, *kāma*, and *moksha*, and to the parental care for your subjects. . . . On the love of husband and wife depends the welfare of the whole family; its absence destroys the whole line. . . . Therefore, do not waste your precious time in drinking, womanizing etc., but spend it in the good work of looking after your subjects according to the sacred law of justice, and thus become worthy of universal fame and gratitude.[60]

It was an outspoken letter, but not a harsh one, giving plain advice without in any way belittling the ruler, and it seems that Jaswant Singh took it in that spirit. The Swami still hoped that things might improve, as his letter written a week later indicates: The king is somewhat inclined to listen to my instruction, I believe that some improvement may be expected. . . . The Maharaja's nature is excellent, but his attitudes have been influenced by the bad company he keeps. He has not yet fully given up his evil habits. May the Lord be merciful so that this ruler may become deeply involved in his duties of state, look with justice after his subjects like his own children, and thus become crowned with fame.[61]

But Jaswant Singh was not to become a regular visitor of the Swami, who therefore wrote him more letters. The second letter is not available, but the third, written on 8 September has been preserved.[62] By this time over three months had passed, and very little had been achieved as far as the Maharaja was concerned. Dayananda wrote, 'I will stay here for another three weeks or so . . . I have come to the conclusion that you have spent your money in vain on my hospitality here, because you have not profited in any way from my visit. As for me, you have satisfactorily taken care of all my needs.' The first part of the letter gave general advice: keep up your work in the affairs of state, and increase it if possible because it is your foremost duty; take great care of the health of the crown prince; never remove Pratap Singh from his state duties, as no one else is so concerned about the good of yourself, and of your state; and spend Rs 10,000 per year on *homa* sacrifice, which will improve the rainfall and reduce diseases in your domain. This section ended with an expression of the hope that the Maharaja would devote his great qualities to the administration of the state, and thus promote the welfare of the people, which would bring him fame throughout the continent.

This part of the letter was followed by seven more points headed 'personal'. Two of these concerned the education of the crown prince: no Muslim or Christian should be appointed as his tutor, as they would turn him away from the Vedic *dharma*; he should be taught Sanskrit and Hindī first, and only afterwards English. The other points had to do with the 'vices' of the Maharaja. This time the Swami's words were both outspoken and harsh. He condemned Jaswant Singh's adulterous association with the courtesan Nanni, and his involvement with a frivolous circle of courtiers as unworthy of a king, degrading, and injurious to the carrying out of his kingly duties. This was the type of behaviour that made Indians bow in shame before the Europeans. The king's own conduct had been influenced by his father, and if he continued in this way of life, then he should expect that his successors would go the same way.

Just as you have already given up the company of Ganeshpuri [the Shākta *Guru* of Nanni] and his cronies, who only teach evil things, why don't you likewise keep away from prostitutes and flatterers? Your person is not destined for such base activities, for pleasure, and luxurious leisure, but for building the prosperity of millions of people by dint of hard work with justice and humanity. Study the duties of rulers in chapters seven to nine of Manu, and learn what is forbidden to them. I feel certain that you will be pleased to listen to these words that are harsh, but are conducive to your welfare and that of the state.[63]

This was probably the severest reprimand Maharaja Jaswant Singh had ever had addressed to him, yet he seems to have taken it in the spirit in which it was written.

By the end of that month of September a quarter of a year had gone by, and the only contact between the Swami and the Maharaja had been some six short meetings[64] and three letters. Dayananda decided to leave soon, as a letter of 20 September indicates.[65] Was his connection with Jaswant Singh really such a failure, and what went wrong in Jodhpur? Dayananda came to Jodhpur with high hopes, raised by his success with the rulers of Udaipur and Shahpura. He anticipated a similar reception, and expected too much too soon. The circumstances in Jodhpur were quite different. The major difference was the age of the Maharaja. Whereas the rulers of Udaipur and Shahpura were young men in their early twenties, Jaswant Singh was a mature man of forty-six, twice their age. He had been brought up and had lived for nearly half a century in a court where courtesans and the gay court life were a tradition. By his mid-forties his habits of life had been strongly established. Moreover, in Pratap Singh he had a very able and dedicated prince who took charge of many of the affairs of state and left him plenty of leisure time.

Jaswant Singh was not a bad ruler, and he was obviously sympathetic to the Swami and his reforming ideas, and encouraged him to work among his people. On the other hand, he had no desire to become Dayananda's personal pupil or to drastically change his own way of life on the Swami's advice, though he received the latter humbly and without resentment. He did not counteract or even begrudge the profound influence the Swami exerted on Pratap Singh. Several events illustrate this influence. In August 1883 a branch of the Arya Samaj was established in Jodhpur under the patronage of Pratap Singh. In the same month Hindī was proclaimed the language of the state which was the first in India to take that step.[66] When the sick Swami left Udaipur on the 16 October, Jaswant Singh came personally to bid him farewell. He offered Rs 2500 to the Swami, and with Pratap Singh and Tej Singh he accompanied the Swami's *pālkī* on foot for some distance.[67] Those facts show that all did not go wrong in Jodhpur. The Swami expected too much, and he found it impossible in his personal relations with the Maharaja to overlook and condone his moral flaws, because in his mind the high personal morality of the ruler was inextricably connected with the prosperity and advancement of the state.

The Swami's public preaching in Jodhpur, encouraged by Jaswant Singh, took its usual form. Shortly after his arrival he issued a public notice announcing that he would give a series of lectures, which would last from four to six in the afternoon and be followed by a two-hour question session.[68] The earlier part of the day was taken up in writing, correspondence, and the reading of proofs.[69] Initially the accent of his teaching was on cow-protection, and on the duties of the kshatriyas. In a state like Jodhpur the latter probably aroused some antagonism among the nobles on account of the outspoken manner of the Swami. He also clashed in discussion with the Muslim minister Faizulla Khan, when he criticized Islam.[70]

As time went by the Swami's preaching took on the old aggressive tone: he gave lectures against the Vaishnavites; he had debates with Neo-Vedāntins, Shāktas, and Jains, and it seems that gradually a definite atmosphere of hostility developed.[71] Perhaps the Swami's own frustrating disappointment in the Maharaja somewhat sharpened his tongue. On the opponents' side, their awareness that their Maharaja kept aloof from the Swami may have encouraged them in their opposition. The Swami was certainly right that in the native states a person's relationship with the ruler greatly influenced the reaction and attitudes of the people towards him. In any case, the general atmosphere was such that the Swami felt that he could not do much more good in Jodhpur, and should move on.

In letters of 24 September, he announced his decision to leave on the first of October,[72] and on the twenty-seventh he formally asked Tej Singh to make the necessary arrangements for his departure. This involved many preparations, and two days later he reiterated his request.[73] But that departure was not to take place so soon. On 30 September he wrote that there had been a lot of rain, and that his departure would be delayed by a week.[74] It was in these last days that he was struck down by the illness from which he was not to recover.

The illness[75] started with what seemed a mild indisposition on 27 September, but within two days it had progressed fiercely and caused vomiting spells, acute colic in the stomach, and racking pains all over the body. Dr Suraj Mal was called in, but his treatment did not allay the condition. So Dr Alimardan Khan, Assistant Surgeon at the local hospital, took over, and he treated the Swami for the next two weeks. The medications he prescribed, in massive doses it is reported, did not help; on the contrary, the Swami's condition kept deteriorating. Within a week of Dr Khan's medication there was acute diarrhoea, so severe that it made the Swami faint repeatedly. Moreover, heavy coughing and racking hiccups now tortured him, and ulcers appeared on his body, on his head, and even inside his mouth.

In the meantime the Aryas had become aware of the Swami's illness through an announcement in the *Rajputana Gazette* of 12 October. Lala Jethmal of Ajmer was sent to Jodhpur and the main branches of the Samaj were informed of the situation. On 15 October Dr Khan advised that the Swami be moved to Mount Abu, and the Residency Surgeon Dr Rodan agreed with this advice: both thought that a cooler climate would help in the recovery. So the Swami's final journey began on 16 October. He was carried by *pālkī* for about seventy miles to Rohat, where he stayed a day and a night, and thence to Pali. From there he was transported by rail for about 120 miles to Aburoad. On the way, during a stop at Kharchi, the Swami was given some medicine prepared by the famous Hakim Pir of Ajmer. The Swami's condition had not improved at all: severe diarrhoea, continuous hiccups, and high fever sent him into spells of fainting. From Aburoad Station he was carried by *pālkī* up to mount Abu, arriving on 21 October.

There he was treated by Dr Lakshmandas, who was the first

to get some encouraging results : the Swami started to improve. But this doctor had been ordered to move to Ajmer to a new post, and he had already endangered his position by delaying his departure in order to take care of the Swami. In fact, Lakshmandas was quite willing to run that risk in order to look after his patient, for whom he had immediately felt affection and admiration. But when the Swami became aware of the situation, he ordered the doctor to leave at once for Ajmer. This unselfish act was a fateful decision: in the absence of Lakshmandas the Swami's condition deteriorated again. On 23 October, the prominent Aryas, Munshi Samarthadan, Babu Shivdayal Singh, Pandit Lakhmidas, and Karsondas Sevaklal had arrived at Mount Abu. The decision was made that the Swami, who had again become extremely feverish, should be taken by rail to Ajmer.

After a gruelling two hundred miles in the train they all arrived in Ajmer on 26 October, and Dr Lakshmandas immediately resumed his treatment. But things had gone from bad to worse, as the Swami had now contracted double pneumonia and was in a state of high fever. The Civil Surgeon Dr Newman was called in and confirmed the diagnosis. However, against the explicit orders of the doctors, the Swami, suffering intensely from high fever, was moved out of his room into the coolness of the verandah. His condition now became critical.

In the evening of 30 October the Swami knew that his end was near, and he asked all the Aryas to come to his room to bid a final farewell. He recited some Vedic *mantras*, and his last words were, 'Oh merciful and all-powerful Lord, this is your will, this is your will, let it be fulfilled. You have performed a good *līlā*'. Among the Aryas present was Pandit Gurudatt. The moving scene of the Swami's calm and resigned death forever wiped from his mind the lingering doubts the Pandit had entertained about the existence of God.

Two *sannyāsīs* came to claim the Swami's body in order to bury it according to the usual rites for *sannyāsīs*. But the Aryas told them that Dayananda had made it clear in his will that he wanted his body to be cremated according to the rites prescribed for all Hindus in his *Sanskārvidhi*. This rite was performed the following day, in the presence of Aryas from all over India, who were stunned by the immense loss they had suffered. The next day Pandit

Mohanlal Vishnulal Pandya took possession of the Swami's belongings in the name of the Paropkarinī Sabhā.

The account of the Swami's tragic last weeks leaves two strong impressions. The first is that of the remarkable willpower, resilience,and heroic patience of the Swami. The second impression is one of regrettable medical mismanagement. The Swami certainly had too many doctors, and probably also some ill-advised medicines, at least in the massive doses. His departure from Jodhpur was badly timed, and the fearful journey aggravated his condition; he might have had a better chance if he had left earlier or stayed on a little longer. For a man in his condition a journey of some four hundred miles was nearly fatal in itself. As the Swami weakened, too many people became involved in the decision-making. By the time he was brought to Ajmer, where he would have received the proper treatment, his condition had deteriorated to such an extent that the additional complication of double pneumonia could not be overcome even by a man of the Swami's constitution and willpower. It is impossible, however, to point the finger at any particular person for incompetence or malice, because the reports depend too much on hearsay from a later date.

It has been claimed that poison had been administered to the Swami in Jodhpur, on the instigation of the Maharaja's favourite, Nanni; she is said to have felt her position threatened by the Swami's presence. This tradition is very strong among the Aryas who claim that clear proof of poisoning exists, and who greatly resent any suggestion that their Swami did not die a martyr's death just as did his great follower Swami Shraddhananda. One cannot but respect their attachment to that tradition. The historian, however, may raise the following points. The story of the poisoning was not accepted by two of the earliest biographers, Gopal Rao Hari Deshmukh and Pandit Gopal Rao Hari.[76] The use of poison is on the one hand not implausible in the court atmosphere of native states, but on the other hand in such a context the sudden illness and ensuing death of an important public figure tended automatically to arouse the suspicion of foul play. From a strictly historical point of view it seems quite impossible to reach a complete positive or negative certainty about this matter that would satisfy the canons of historical proof. All one can do is to accept the possibility of the truth of the tradition. And in the final instance, it has no relevance to the greatness of the Swami himself whether he died by illness and medical mismanagement only, or whether the initial cause of the illness was poison.

Death cut short the life of Swami Dayananda at a very crucial stage in his development, when his efforts were turning in a new direction. Although he was a man of resolute, even stubborn convictions, he was always ready to learn from his mistakes, to adapt to new circumstances, and to change his course of action in conformity with new found aims. The fanatical lone searcher for *moksha* of the early years transformed himself into the fiery, abrasive, peripatetic preacher of the rural Doab. After his visit to Calcutta he became the reformer of the urban centres, and the propagandist of the pen. This led him to establish his own reform organization, the Arya Samaj, which soon achieved great success in the Panjab and in Western U.P. In the tradition of so many Hindu reformers, that achievement could have become the highpoint of his career, and his activity from then onward could have been concentrated on the consolidation and the growth of his Samaj. But his eyes were fixed on a much greater goal: the reconstruction of the whole of Āryāvarta. So he changed direction once more. It was the wider world of Hinduism that needed to be urged on to the road of reform. He threw himself into agitations that would affect all Hindus, and went into the princely states with the aim of influencing Hinduism as a whole by reforming the princes. Throughout all these transformations his stature grew steadily to become that of a figure of all-Hindu importance.

CHAPTER XI

The Final Years
The Last Legacy in Print

During his last five years the Swami wrote at a frantic pace. Apart from several written debates and a few pamphlets, he wrote three substantial works on Sanskrit grammar. He also completed thoroughly revised editions of his major works, the *Sanskārvidhi* and the *Satyārth Prakāsh*. On top of all this came the composition of his Vedic commentary, which accelerated to a rate of about a thousand pages a year.

In March 1880 Dayananda published in Banaras a booklet entitled *Vyavahārabhānu*, 'the sun of good behaviour'. It was a pocket handbook of general ethics for children and simple folk written in a question-and-answer form, and it included a wealth of illustrative stories. Its subject is basic morality: it treats the relationships of teacher and pupil, and husband and wife, parents and children, king and subjects, and it also includes topics like business ethics, the criteria of truth, and praise of *brahmacharya*. A high yet uncomplicated moral standard is combined with a sometimes charming simplicity.[1]

The teaching of Sanskrit was considered by Dayananda to be one of the main requirements for the regeneration of Āryāvarta. He set himself the task of providing textbooks that would make the teachers' work easier. At the highest level of instruction this task required a thorough knowledge of Pāṇini's *Ashtādhyāyī*; in 1878 the Swami started to write a commentary on that difficult work. He tried to find one thousand subscribers to guarantee the costs of its publication, but he never got anywhere near that number. Indeed, only very few Aryas would have been sufficiently advanced in Sanskrit to profit by such a work. As a result, the manuscript remained unpublished during the Swami's lifetime, and it was found among his papers on his death.[2]

But the Swami was not to be discouraged in his purpose, and proceeded to prepare two works that could be useful at a lower level. In March 1880 he published in Banaras the *Sanskrit Vākya*

Prabodh, a handbook for beginners. In his introduction he explained the pedagogic reason for his venture: exercises in speaking Sanskrit could be of great help to those learning the language. He therefore provided in this book a series of conversations in Sanskrit with Hindī translations facing them, systematically graduated from the very simple to the complex. The particular subjects of the lessons start with everyday items like food, shelter, the body, fauna, etc., and progress to geography, politics, and religion. They do not constitute only a linguistic exercise: the conversations are pervaded with the Swami's basic reform ideas. The first edition was lamentably produced and full of misprints, and it was severely attacked by Banaras pandits in a pamphlet called *Abodhanivārana*. Dayananda acknowledged the presence of many errors, which he attributed to three factors: his own illness, bad proof-reading by Bhimasena, and the lack of a good compositor at the Press. He also wrote a short note in answer to the Banaras pandits in the *Āryadarpan* of May 1880.[3]

However, this handbook, useful for beginners, was not enough; for the systematic teaching of Sanskrit there was a need for a manual that could be used by individuals and in schools. This need was pointed out to the Swami by some Panjabi Aryas as early as 1877. Dayananda was too busy to undertake the work himself, so he had most of it done by his collaborators under his direction. Bhimasena, Jwaladatta, and Dineshram were the main authors, and some advanced sections were prepared by the Swami himself. The work was called *Vedāngaprakāsh* and consisted of fourteen parts, the first one published in early 1880, and the last one in August 1883.[4]

The volumes vary greatly in size, from fifteen pages to over six hundred, and total some two thousand pages. The work is a very systematic one and the order in which it appears shows the clear conception behind it. The early parts deal successively with pronunciation, *sandhi*, the nouns, *samāsa*, the derivation of nouns, the indeclinable particles, and the verbs. Then follow more complex aspects of grammar: Vedic accentuation, grammatical maxims, roots and their meanings, series of words obeying similar rules, affixes, and finally the *Nighantu* glossary. With its systematic and progressive treatment of different aspects of grammar, the work no doubt constituted a very valuable teaching aid, probably outstripping anything available in Hindī at the time. It strictly adhered to the Pāninian norm; in fact three of the advanced books were a reproduction of texts of Pānini without commentary. However, the work as a whole contained 'many frightful impurities', because the Swami did not have the time to attend personally to each final press copy. Yudhisthir Mimamshak was so distressed about these deficiencies that he wrote, 'I do not understand how the Swami gave his permission for their publication'.[5] But the Swami recommended the work and even managed to have it introduced into the schools of Udaipur.[6] He was no doubt aware of the serious faults, but he was never a purist: the work represented a considerable advance in Sanskrit textbooks, and could enhance the teaching of the sacred language. Moreover, there was a pressing need for it, so he thought it better to publish it as it stood than to further delay its availability.

In this period the Swami also published a small booklet entitled *Gotama-Ahalyā kī Kathā*, which unfortunately has not been recovered so far, but which was on sale in early 1880. It contained his interpretation of the ancient Vedic myths of Gotama and Ahalyā and of Indra and Vritra.[7] It therefore clarified an important aspect of Dayananda's method of Vedic interpretation: the way he gave meaning to mythological stories. But his commentary on the *Veda* also throws some light on this problem, as will be seen below.

Among the effects left by the Swami to the Paropkarinī Sabha there were a large number of manuscripts.[8] Many were drafts of future instalments of the *Vedabhāshya*, but there were also a large number of papers not intended for publication: they were the Swami's own tools of research; as such they throw some light on his methods. Nearly all were collections of passages from texts he had studied. Of these twenty-six documents, seven were anthologies of the four *Vedas*, five of different *Brāhmanas*, and another five of grammatical works, including one on the relation of Sanskrit to Prākrit which was particularly important for the interpretation of Jain texts. There were selections from Manu, and from the ethical portions of the *Mahābhārata*. And, finally, there were anthologies of texts from the Bible, the Koran, Jain literature, and Rāmsnehī literature. These many manuscripts show the Swami's earnest application to his research and writing. He did not rely on his memory or on vague references.

He took pains to study the original sources carefully and to take notes to which he could refer while composing his commentaries and criticisms.

One of these manuscripts is of particular interest: it is a translation of the Koran into Hindī. At that time there was no Hindī translation of the Koran in existence, and the Swami did not know Urdū or Persian. He therefore had this translation done for him by an unknown scholar, but we know that he had it checked by Munshi Manoharlal of Patna, who was versed in these languages. The Munshi had helped him in the writing of the chapter on Islam for the first *Satyārth Prakāsh*, which was not included in the first edition, and the translation was no doubt used by the Swami in the preparation of the second edition of the work. In fact, he seriously considered publishing the translation, but this did not materialize.[9]

Dayananda completely re-wrote his *Sanskārvidhi* for republication, and in his introduction he gave his reasons: the first edition had been sold out, and it needed to be restructured because it was unsatisfactory in plan, especially the way in which the Hindī explanations were too widely separated from the long Sanskrit texts. He finished this work a couple of months before his death, but it was not published until 1884.[10] His constant efforts towards self-criticism and improvement are clearly evident in this new edition. The work now starts with an introductory chapter. This contains all the essential rites common to all sacraments. It also gives a definition of the officiant of the rite: he should be a householder who is wise, religious, and selfless, and who is of good character and knows the *Vedas*.[11] Thus Dayananda removed the professional ritualist from the scene, and put the rites back into the hands of all worthy Aryas. This chapter also describes in detail the construction of the altar and the instruments and ingredients of the rites, and it stresses that a quiet and meditative dignity should pervade all ceremonies. Each subsequent chapter on a particular sacrament starts with an explanation of the meaning of the rite, and of the proper time to perform it. Then follows a description of the rite itself. Clear rubrics are given throughout, indicating what actions were to be performed, which texts to be recited. It is an admirably organized handbook which is totally self-explanatory and makes it possible for any intelligent Arya to perform the ceremonies. The rites abound with a wealth of

the most beautiful Vedic texts, showing how much the Swami
had become a real master of the *Vedas*.

The nine sacraments that pertain to the pre-natal and childhood
periods have a great and simple beauty, and at all stages the rites
involve both parents 'so that the love between father, mother,
and child may ever grow'.[12] In the rites and the accompanying
instructions a constant preoccupation with the physical well-
being of mother and child is expressed, and also great concern
for their happiness, peace, and contentment. In the chapters on
the wedding ceremony and on the stage of the householder, there
is an abundance of beautiful prayers, many taken from the
Atharvaveda, invoking blessings on the family; the constant
themes are love and kindness, faithfulness, happiness and joy,
prosperity and long life. They draw a touching picture of ideal
family happiness, the dominant refrain of these pages. The chapter
on family life is very long, eighty pages as compared with
the fifteen of the first edition. It includes a detailed description
of the daily home ritual, and of the special domestic rites to be
performed at the time of the full moon, in the harvest season,
and on the occasion of building a new house. There is also a
lengthy exposition, based on Manu, of the domestic and civic
duties of the four classes. The chapter on the hermit and the
sannyāsī continues further along the lines the Swami's thought
had taken even in the first edition: it minimizes the concrete
prescriptions and stresses the spirit of these stages of life. In
particular the *sannyāsī's* foremost duty as a preacher is put into
constant perspective. It is also noteworthy that the many references
to *niyoga* contained in the first edition have been eliminated.
The Swami had not changed his mind on this matter, but he thought
that this topic was not one that had direct relevance to the sacraments; he was to deal with it extensively in his second *Satyārth
Prakāsh*.

The re-writing of this last work was to Dayananda of the same
order of importance as was the writing of his *Vedabhāshya*; it contained the full systematic treatment of the whole range of his ideas.
Seven years had passed since the first edition was published, and
many of his ideas had changed considerably in the meantime. The
work was done in 1882, and the proof-reading was finished not
long before the Swami's death.[13] Although much of the material
was the same, the second edition constituted a very thorough

revision. By now the Swami had become a master of Hindī, and the language he used was an excellent sanskritic Hindī, clear and fluent. The work was now neatly paragraphed and much easier on the eye than the first edition. Several chapters had been drastically reorganized.' Whereas the first edition often tended to amble along from question to question as a conversation or a debate does, picking up the problems as the spoken word throws them up, the new edition sought to treat a subject systematically. The chapter on the *Vedas* moves from the method and means of revelation to the proof, and the necessity of it. The section on God treats successively the unity of God, the proof of his existence, his attributes, and his relation to the soul; that on the relations of God and the cosmos starts with the proof from scripture, goes on to discuss the object of creation and the three causes of the world, and ends up with the process of creation.

There is also a striking change in the use of quotations. Dayananda now carefully avoided earlier mistakes such as quoting a text as illustration without necessarily agreeing with the full implication of the quotation. He now conscientiously screened his texts and made it clear how far he accepted their content or authority. The new edition also drew on a wider wealth of sources: over two hundred different works are referred to.[14] The Swami's deeper knowledge of the *Vedas* shows itself in the multitude of Vedic quotations, greatly exceeding those used in the first edition. Manu remained one of the main sources, and the principal *Upanishads* were still used, but with more discrimination: the author carefully warded off any possibility of advaitic interpretation. The Swami's knowledge of the six systems of philosophy had deepened: about one hundred and fifty references to them are scattered throughout the work.

In the following analysis of the contents of this work the arrangement of topics is the same as that used in the analysis of the first *Satyārth Prakāsh* in Chapter V, in order to facilitate comparison; but only those points will be raised which are new, or in which there is a noticeable change. In the doctrine of Vedic revelation there is no change, except that two problems that had frequently arisen in the interval and upon which a clear decision had been reached, are treated specifically. These are the essential differences between the four *Vedas* and the *Brāhmanas*, and the non-existence of lost branches of the *Vedas*.[15] The first chapter, where the names of God are listed, remains substantially the same, but some names mentioned previously are now left out: the names of the five senses, and seven adjectives describing attributes of God. Some names are added, six of these probably because in the intervening years the Swami decided that in some Vedic texts they had to refer to the divinity: Yama, Purusha, Shesha, Mahādeva, Svayambhū, and Kavi. The two other new terms, *āchārya* and *guru*, may well have been added by the Swami in order to stress that these titles, so abused by sectarians, should not be claimed by mere mortals, and he himself avoided them because they properly belonged only to the Lord. Dayananda's theology of the nature of God-in-himself, never of great interest to him, did not develop at all in these years. In his first edition Dayananda had given proof of the existence of God and had refuted atheism. In the new edition the proof is very much the same, but there is a much greater subtlety and clarity in the refutation of atheism. Whereas the first edition presented an awkward and unreadable commentary upon verses of the *Nyāyasūtras*,[16] the new edition dispenses with the *sūtras* and gives a simple and lucid answer.[17] Similarly the new and very lengthy criticism of the Chārvāka doctrine is far superior to the previous one.

Dayananda's theory of God's relation to the cosmos had changed enormously since 1876: his new theory of *traitavāda* had taken full shape as early as 1877 at the time of the Chandapur Melā,[18] and was followed at the end of the same year by the revision of the doctrine of *moksha* in his *Āryoddheshya Ratnamālā*.[19] The full integrated theory is elaborated in the second *Satyārth Prakāsh*. On account of its central importance it is analysed at length in the following paragraphs.

Traitavāda is the theory that there exist three eternal substances without beginning or end: God, the *prakriti*, and the *jīvas*. They are always co-existent and their nature, qualities, and activity are equally eternal. This is the level of absolute being, where the concept of causality does not apply: they are simple uncaused causes, the only truly absolute and eternal entities. Causality only applies on the lower level of becoming: that of cosmic evolution and involution, and of the drama of bondage and liberation of the souls. Causality can never be 'total creation', because no entity that did not exist before can be brought into being. All causality, therefore, is but a transformation of existing entities.

The cosmic cycle of evolutions and dissolutions, to which the Swami had formerly attributed an absolute beginning and an absolute end, is now de~lared to be eternal.

Evolution is preceded by dissolution, dissolution by evolution; evolution is followed by dissolution and dissolution by evolution: from beginningless time that cycle has been revolving. There is no beginning or end to it. Whereas the Lord, the *jīvas*, and *prakriti* are eternal by nature, the evolution, preservation, and dissolution of the cosmos are eternal by rhythm (*pravāh se*).[20]

The evolution of the world from the dormant, undifferentiated *prakriti* proceeds by association of the subtle *gunas* (the constituents of *prakriti*), and out of this progressive association the whole manifest universe evolves. Whereas in the explanation of this cosmic process Dayananda had previously used only the Nyāya atomic theory, now he combined the latter with the evolution theory of classical Sāmkhya, which describes the twenty-three evolutes from the subtlest *buddhi* to the gross elements.[21] It is on this cosmic level of activity that the three causes play their part. God is the chief efficient cause, who is the prime mover behind the cosmic emanations and involutions, steering them along their proper path. *Prakriti*, on the other hand, is the purely passive material cause, capable of producing an endless variety of forms by the combination of its basic simple constituents, the *gunas*. In the hands of the divine potter *prakriti* is but malleable clay without will, direction, or activity of its own. Man is a secondary efficient cause: he can effect changes upon the world as it comes from the Potter's hands, but these changes are always very restricted in time and space.[22]

Dayananda had obviously been strongly influenced by Sāmkhya ideas since he wrote his first *Satyārth Prakāsh*. It is interesting to note that some tenets which he himself had earlier held, like 'God is the material cause of the universe', 'the universe had a beginning and will have an end', were now rejected as false doctrines of the Neo-Vedāntins.[23] Thus he himself obliquely acknowledged what a strong hold some 'Vedāntic' ideas had had over his thought until recently. In his first edition he had criticized 'Vedānta' only incidentally, limiting himself to two of its tenets, namely the identity of *brahman* and *ātman* and the illusory nature of the world. The second edition, on the other hand, contains no less than five lengthy refutations, all running

to between four and six pages.[24] There we find a re-interpretation
of excerpts of the *Vedānta-Sūtras* showing that they did not contain
the false doctrines of the Neo-Vedāntins. Moreover, there is a
detailed analysis of the latter's use of the concepts of *upādhi,*
adhyāropa, māyā, and *chidābhāsa,* a criticism of their doctrine
of causality, and a refutation of their interpretation of dreams
and illusions. About Shankara, whom the Swami greatly admired
as one of the greatest reformers of Hinduism, he said: 'If the
doctrine of the identity of the soul and *brahman* and of the illusory
nature of the world was really Shankarāchārya's own belief,
then it was not a good one; but if he assumed it only to refute
the Jains, then it did have some virtue.'[25]

There was another way in which the Swami showed both his
deeper study of philosophy and his different attitude to the
Vedānta system. In both editions he replied twice to the objector
who states that the six systems of philosophy are mutually contradictory in their doctrine of creation and that, therefore, none
of them can be accepted as the authority Dayananda acknowledged them to be. In the first edition Vedānta was said to be
the school that gave the most complete, penetrating, and the
final answer on the question of creation, in contrast to the partial
and incomplete answers given by the other schools. Whereas,
in the matter of involution, the other schools referred to
mahāpralaya, a partial dissolution that stopped short at a subtle
form of matter, Vedānta spoke of *atyant pralaya,* the total dissolution where even subtle matter is dissolved in the ultimate
brahman.[26] The second edition deprives Vedānta of that place
of prominence, and all systems are put on the same level: 'There
are six causes of the creation of the world. Each of these is explained by one author of the *darshanas.* Therefore, there is no
contradiction between the *darshanas.*'[27] In other words, causality,
when referring to the world as a whole, is a very complex matter,
and the different systems specialize in different aspects. Whereas
Vedānta says that 'nothing can originate without the action of
an efficient cause', Sāmkhya says that all origination presupposes
a material cause.[28] Thus the second edition demoted Vedānta
from its position as the ultimate source of philosophical truth
to being just one of the six.[29]

Dayananda's concept of 'original' creation in the first edition,
according to which previously non-existent man came into being,

had thrown up some logical problems. To these the Swami had given the following answers: since there was no previous *karma*, God's justice required that all beings be created perfectly equal; therefore, all men were born in the bloom of youth, innocent of good and evil, and there was no distinction between men and animals. That first creation happened in the Himalayas.[30] Since the new edition discarded the concept of original creation, these particular problems did not now present themselves. Dayananda still referred to the beginning of our world, but he now meant the beginning of our particular cosmic cycle, which happened 1,960 million years ago, leaving about 2,360 million years of the cycle to run.[31] This calculation is according to Manu.[32] Humans were created in great numbers, and also animals of all kinds. There was no injustice in that discrimination, because it resulted from *karma* incurred in the previous cycle. Men originated first in Tibet, all in youth and without differences. But soon a differentiation occurred: the wise and the best were called the Aryans, the others the *Dasyus*; and the Aryans divided themselves up into the four classes. When there came to be increasing hostility between Aryans and non-Aryans, the former migrated to the best country in the world: the land between the Himalayas and the Vindhyas, bordered by the Indus in the west and the Brahmaputra in the east. That land was therefore called Āryāvarta, and the Aryans were the first to settle it. Dayananda rejected the theory that the Aryans came from the Middle East into a country already settled by savages, a theory propounded by Western Orientalists.[33] Thus Dayananda's theory had developed considerably, especially with its clear statement on the early colonization of Āryāvarta; this was to be the foundation for his conception of the Vedic Golden Age.

Dayananda's basic theory of the nature of the *jīva* as propounded in the first edition remained very much the same in the second. It is a limited spirit, conscious, free, and active, and it is joined with a subtle and gross body in its peregrination through successive lives. However, very drastic changes were brought about by the new theory of *traitavāda*: there is no absolute beginning or end to the existence of the *jīva*. This new framework forced Dayananda to completely rethink the eschatology, and in this transformation he showed more clearly than anywhere else some of the most fundamental traits of his thought.

KING ALFRED'S COLLEGE
LIBRARY

According to the first edition, the *jīva* is initially created, and on reaching *moksha* 'its *karma* is shed with its very root'. In that state, the *jīva* remains separate from the Lord, and enjoys beatitude through its subtle body. In *atyant pralaya*, the final dissolution occurs of all subtle matter, and therefore also of the subtle body; the state of *moksha* and the entity of the *jīva* come to a final end.[34] The new edition eliminates all absolute beginning and end, and, therefore, neither the *jīva* nor the cosmos is to disappear. At this point one would expect Dayananda to come back to the traditional Hindu concept of endless *moksha*, but he did not; as early as 1877 he had proposed the doctrine that *moksha* itself comes to a conclusion at the end of a *mahākalpa*, but that the *jīva* returns to the cycle of rebirth.[35] When the objector said, 'All the world believes and all the books proclaim that one never comes back to rebirth', Dayananda did not deny this statement, but simply wrote, 'That cannot be so', and proceeded to give the reasons for that impossibility.[36] He must have considered these reasons to be extremely cogent, to affirm his new doctrine against the weight of the whole tradition. These reasons are repeated and reinforced throughout the work, and their total coherent structure is presented here.

The argument can be summarized as follows: perpetual salvation would mean boundless bliss. Man is finite in his instruments of action, therefore he cannot produce an infinite effect. Man is finite in his powers, therefore he cannot enjoy an infinite bliss. Man is finite in his works, therefore he cannot earn an infinite reward.[37] They are all variants of the one simple argument of the irrevocable opposition between finite and infinite. They appear to have a simple logical cogency, but their strength depends entirely on the theological presuppositions that hide behind the argument.

The finite works of man are indeed incapable of meriting infinite *moksha*, but only if one accepts that *moksha* must be exclusively earned by works. The finite powers of the soul are incapable of sustaining infinite bliss, but only if any other divine agency in the *jīva* is excluded, for instance 'grace' in any form. Finite means of the *jīva* cannot produce an infinite effect only if one accepts the tenet that *moksha* is effected exclusively by the *jīva's* actions. Dayananda's arguments are based on the presupposition that *moksha* in all its aspects, as effect, as state, and as reward, must be directly commensurate with human activity alone, excluding all other intervening powers. If one accepts that presupposition, then the finitude of the *jīva* necessarily implies the finitude of *moksha*. However, in this presupposition Dayananda takes a stand apart from most of the Hindu tradition, which consistently affirms that the process of liberation and the state of *moksha* entail more than just the finite powers of the *jīva*. Theologians accept some form of divine agency, some form of grace, *prasāda*, and others hold that at the very centre of the *jīva* there exists a deeper entity, a divine, absolute being, which they call *ātman*, or *purusha*, or *brahman*. For them *moksha* is a function of that entity, and the role of the *jīva* is often no more than that of unveiling that hidden, absolute reality.

The Hindu theologians who ascribe to man a more than human power, often identify that power as *jnāna* or *vidyā*, knowledge or wisdom. This power is said to override ordinary karmic processes: it gives dispensation from *dharma* duties, it transcends the level of distinction of good and evil, it removes the veil of *māyā*: *jnāna* reveals the *ātman*, and full *jnāna* is *moksha*. The first edition of the *Satyārth Prakāsh* retained many traces of that conception: those who have full knowledge, the perfect *sannyāsīs*, are freed from all outward ritual duties, are not bound by works, and can dispose freely of accumulated *karma*; knowledge is the instrument of *moksha*, destroying all *karma* with its very root; knowledge makes the knower *sarvajna*, omniscient.[38]

The second edition omits all these special powers of the *sannyāsī*: he remains bound by works.[39] It clearly states that the *jīva's* knowledge, even in *moksha*, can never become unlimited,[40] and goes as far as declaring that 'the relation between the *jīva* and *karma* is an eternal one'.[41] The essence of Dayananda's argumentation is as follows: *moksha* is achieved by the application of certain means, these being right actions. Whatever change is affected by the application of means can be undone by the application of means of the same order. *Moksha*, a change of condition effected by human action, can be undone by human action. Man's activity itself is an eternal quality, but its effects, even its major effects, bondage and liberation, are necessarily of limited duration: *moksha*, therefore, must be limited in time.[42]

As that eternal quality of man, activity, is intrinsically bound up with the law of *karma* and with matter, these links must persist in *moksha* and inevitably cause an eventual return of the *jīva* to the realm of transmigration. *Moksha* is not a transcendent state, as all Hindu systems declare it to be, but, because it is effected by transient means, it is itself necessarily transient, just like the state of bondage. The *jīva* enjoys the bliss of emancipation through its own innate powers;[43] that means all its powers, excluding only the gross physical body which is only an evolute of subtle matter. Even the *turīya* body, the most subtle body through which the soul is absorbed in the contemplation of God, and which is developed by yogic practices, is but a human body evolved by human action.[44] No divine, transcendent power is communicated to the soul in its enjoyment of beatitude, and therefore its bliss cannot but be finite. In fact, wrote Dayananda, the long duration of *moksha* fades the palate like an overdose of sweets, and must come to an end.[45] Even stronger than that: the taint of sin can soil the *jīva* even in *moksha*, and draw it back into the realm of rebirth.[46]

The description of the state of *moksha* reinforces that same pattern of thought. Dayananda described it as follows:

The emancipated soul roams about at will in the boundless all-pervading God. He sees the whole cosmos through pure knowledge and meets other emancipated souls. Aware of all the laws of nature in their ordered processes, he roams about in all worlds visible and invisible. He understands all objects as he comes face to face with them, and the more his knowledge increases, the more his bliss grows. Being altogether pure in the state of *moksha*, the soul becomes a full knower and acquires insight into all the things he comes across.[47]

This is essentially a cosmic experience, and the deliberate choice of words shows that the emancipated soul himself is essentially cosmic: his knowledge, though pure compared to that he acquired on earth, remains limited by time and space. Although he moves 'freely', because now he only has a subtle body, yet he obviously still has to *move* through space, and his experiences remain successive. He does not have that divine knowledge which transcends and envelops all time and space. When the objector mentions among others the Paurāniks who believe that *moksha* means union with God, Dayananda answers, 'That is self-evident, because the *jīvas* are present within the all-pervading Lord'.[48] Even on earth the *jīva* can become aware of the presence of God in meditation and yogic contemplation, and it is that same 'union' that continues and intensifies in the state of *moksha*.[49] In other words, the contemplation of God in emancipation is not different in kind from the one man can experience here on earth; it is nothing but the natural consequence of God's presence and of the knowledge capacity of the soul, and it does not entail communication to the soul of any superhuman power.

Dayananda's persistent stressing that *moksha* in all its aspects is effected by and commensurate with the activity of man necessitates the question: what then is God's function in the process of emancipation? God is essentially active, and his activity is repeatedly referred to as causing the evolution, maintenance, and involution of the cosmos.[50] Two more activities of God are mentioned by Dayananda, and these are connected with the process of emancipation: God is the dispenser of the *Vedas* and the administrator of justice. The revelation of the *Vedas* is no doubt necessary for the emancipation of man, because by himself he could not rise to that infallible knowledge; therefore, revelation is an act of kindness on God's part.[51] But neither that revelation nor even man's knowledge of it are by themselves the cause of *moksha*; only man's acts performed in the light of that knowledge can produce it. No doubt it is the law of *karma* that rewards man's acts with *moksha*, and God is the dispenser of that law. But in the process itself God acts only as the administrator of the law of moral retribution. This law is God's eternal creation, and it runs its course automatically, just like the laws that govern the physical universe.

It is not surprising that, in this context, Dayananda repeatedly stressed God's justice: 'If God were to give the soul unlimited happiness as the fruit of its limited actions, his justice would be destroyed.'[52] The same argument is used to condemn the Christian conception of eternal reward, and the 'last day of judgment' is similarly indicted because the balancing out of sins and good against one another is an injustice:[53] each act, good or bad, should separately find its individual inexorable bitter or sweet fruit.[54] Forgiveness of sins is not only unjust, it is wicked, because it promotes sin, and it would make God immoral.[55] Yet Dayananda holds that God is merciful as well as just. Mercy, he wrote, is the intense desire to bestow happiness on all, and God's mercy expressed itself in the very creation of everything for the good of all. Justice, on the other hand, is the equitable infliction of punishment and reward. But the object of both is the same: to rescue all from sin and the suffering that results from it. In other words, God's mercy expresses itself in the continuous act of creation and in the revelation of the *Vedas*, whereas his justice is exercised in the administration of the law of *karma*. As the ultimate objective of justice and of mercy is the same, they are but different words for the same quality in God.[56] Dayananda did not see the law of *karma* as a purely automatic one, acting like a chemical combination, but as needing the superior intelligence of God to guide it,[57] in the same way as he is needed to guide the emanation of the cosmos along its proper path. Although justice and mercy were attributed to God by Dayananda, he emptied these concepts of that interpersonal quality that most theistic faiths ascribe to them. According to the Swami, mercy can in no way interfere with that final determinant of punishment, reward, and *moksha*, which is the deed of man.

These principles of *moksha* were extensively used by Dayananda in his refutation of the eschatology of other religions, most of which suffer from one or more of three fundamental flaws. The idea that *moksha* entails a divinization of man is denounced in the sections on the Neo-Vedāntins and the Jains.[58] The Tīrthānkaras, the great saints of Jainism, cannot become divine 'because what is not free by nature must necessarily become subject to bondage again'.[59] A second flaw that mars many concepts of salvation is that they conceive of a limited physical heaven, full of sensuous pleasures: Hindus, Jains, Muslims, and Christians all make that mistake. Dayananda's conception is one that tries to walk the tightrope between these two pitfalls: on the one hand a *moksha* where man is divinized, on the other, one that is but a glorified earth. In his *moksha* man does not lose himself in the absolute, nor does he remain enmeshed in the crudely physical: with his subtle body he roams freely in the immense cosmic expanse that is pervaded by God.

The third way in which most eschatologies go wrong, according to Dayananda, is in that they all map out short-cuts to salvation, or prescribe miracle pills to induce it. Pilgrimages are useless, because 'no place can sanctify, only acts can do so'.[60] Idol worship cannot help because it is a sinful act,[61] and *tilaka* and *japa* are deeds too insignificant to arouse any expectation of fruit.[62] The mere belief in a master, a book, or a doctrine, cannot save: 'what an idiotic creed it is to believe that *moksha* can be gained without having to do anything at all!'[63] The dogma of the Neo-Vedāntins that *moksha* is achieved simply by the very conviction of one's identity with *brahman* is declared to be equally absurd.[64] Only one single means of salvation is accepted as valid by the Swami: moral action guided by reason. Since that action is always finite, *moksha*, its result, must also be finite. But since the activity of man is an eternal attribute of the *jīva*, the movement of souls from bondage to salvation and back to bondage, must be eternal too; it is, said Dayananda, eternal by rhythm (*pravāh se*) like the succession of cosmic evolutions and involutions.[65]

Chapter eleven of the new *Satyārth Prakāsh*, devoted to the critique of Hinduism, is by far the largest in the book: it is half as long as the sum of the ten chapters that precede it, and twice as long as any other chapter. In general it repeats the topics treated in the first edition, but there are some significant developments. The panegyric on the Vedic Golden Age has acquired a new dimension: not only was Āryāvarta the origin of all wisdom and science, but its king-emperors were the universal sovereigns of the whole earth from the earliest days till the great war of the sons of Bharat five thousand years ago.[66] This claim of absolute political supremacy stretching over an immense period, when all other kings were vassals of the Aryan empire, is but one aspect of a new type of nationalism that manifests itself in Dayananda's last work.

The Swami's treatment of the history of Hinduism after the devastation wrought by the great war was much improved. The description of the emergence of the sects and of the new literature of *Purānas* and *Tantras* is more historical and systematic. Shaivism and Tantra, neglected in the first edition, receive extensive coverage and the mediaeval and more recent sects previously glossed over, are now given a thorough treatment: the Kabīrpanth, Sikhism, Dādūism, the Rāmsnehī and the Swāmīnārāyana sects are criticized in detail. In fact, the Swami had taken part in discussions and confrontations with representatives of those sects in the years between the writing of the two editions. There is also a considerable enlargement of the sections on idolatry and astrology: their absurdity and their pernicious influence on society are denounced at length.[67]

The Swami increased threefold his discussion of the Brahmo and Prarthana Samajes,[68] with whose members he had had considerable dealings after the establishment of his Samaj, especially in Maharashtra and the Panjab. He wrote that they deserved praise for fighting idolatry and denouncing superstitious books, and also for the additional reason that they had kept a number of people from conversion to Christianity. The denunciation of their doctrinal errors remained substantially the same, although more elaborate and detailed. The most interesting aspect of this section, however, is a new slant that pervades it right through: again and again the reformers are accused on the ground that their love for their own country is but small, and repeatedly it is shown how they always imitate foreigners and agree with foreign religions. That lack of loyalty to their own nation had made them ineffective in working for its uplift, and had caused other Indians to look upon them not as of their own kind, but as foreigners. Dayananda closed this section with an impassioned appeal to the members of those Samajes that has strong nationalistic overtones.

If you wish to work for progress, then join the Arya Samaj and agree to act according to its ideals and aims, otherwise your efforts will be in vain. Because it is most proper both for you and for me that we collaborate in love with all the resources of our body, mind and possessions for the uplift of that country, from whose substance our bodies were fashioned, and upon which they still feed and will keep depending.[69]

Dayananda finished his chapter on Hinduism with the lengthy parable of the assembly of a thousand faiths that he had related at Farrukhabad in 1879.[70] A king who wants to find the true religion asks the preachers of the different faiths represented in the assembly in succession what their religion consists of.

He asked a thousand teachers and found that they all contradicted one another. He decided that none of them was worthy of being his *guru*, because there were 999 witnesses to the falsehood of each of them. They were like deceitful shopkeepers, prostitutes, and procurers, praising their own wares and belittling those of others.[71]

A real sage then told the king to ask all these teachers on what points they did agree. The basic issues of agreement were that religion consists of truth, knowledge, and a moral life. When asked why they peddled all those other wares, the preachers answered that it enabled them to live in ease and luxury, and they declared that anyway it was impossible to have only one faith because people were too different. This last objection was countered thus by the sage: that education of the young and a concerted effort by all learned people could ensure that the unification of religion was not delayed too much. The chapter ends with a bitter denunciation of devious and corrupt *sādhus*, who are the main reason why false faiths are visibly increasing and people are becoming Christians and Muslims.[72]

Now we turn to Dayananda's positive preaching of the Aryan way of life. Some new ideas on schooling are put forward: that segregated schools should be completely egalitarian in the treatment of all children, who should have no contact, not even by letter, with their families,[73] and that these schools should be placed away from populated areas. Whereas the first edition excluded the shūdras from the study of the *Vedas* proper,[74] the new edition passionately defends their right to that study:

Does the Lord not wish the well-being of the shūdras? Is he so biassed as to forbid the study of the *Vedas* to them and to prescribe it for the twice-born? If it had not been his intention that the shūdras and others should be educated, why would he have put speech and hearing in their bodies? Just as the Lord has created the four elements, the sun, and the moon for all mankind, in the same way has he made the *Vedsa* shine for all.[75]

In fact even the *ati-shūdras*, very lowest of castes, are included in a previous line. The section on the education of girls has also been expanded. They should study the *Vedas* and the *Shāstras*, they should learn about the special skills their husbands need in their occupations, and they should be informed about medicine, dietary science, and book-keeping so that they can run the household perfectly.[76] With such an education they would be able to undertake with competence their full share in both public and domestic life as the great women of ancient India used to do.

The Swami's conception of married life had not changed in any important way. He had clarified his idea of *niyoga* in the intervening years in the *Sanskārvidhi*,[77] and he had even tried to draft some appropriate legislation.[78] Although he had never found, even among the Aryas, support for this aspect of his programme, he restated the theory of it in great detail.[79] He took great care to give scriptural proof for his stand and emphasized some new points. The partners of a *niyoga* contract were not to live together, but to keep their separate households: they should come together only for intercourse; and they were not to have

any obligation to provide mutual financial support. Here again
Dayananda's undue stress on the sexual aspect somehow vitiates
the solution to the problem of the widows, which he clearly realized
not to be just a sexual one. That same bias shows itself in the
fact that he now allowed a *niyoga* contract even for the husband
who found the obligatory year's sexual abstention during his
wife's pregnancy intolerable.[80] Every child begotten by a *niyoga*
union was to belong, by mutual agreement, to one particular
partner, and, to acquire full legal rights within that partner's
family.

In an interesting new paragraph the Swami explained the
rationale of the institution of marriage. It safeguards the basic
structures of society: it ensures that inter-personal service remains
stable and that the young and old are properly cared for, and it
also upholds and protects private property. If marriage were
abolished, there would be a fatal increase in adultery and sen-
suality, and the sense of moral values would be eroded, leading
to the weakening and destruction of the race.[81] The Swami seems
to have been obsessed with the idea that sexuality is the root of
all moral degradation. Nevertheless, throughout the chapter, the
lofty ideal of married life which he preached in his *Sanskārvidhi*
is held high.

Dayananda had thoroughly rewritten the chapter on the hermit
and the *sannyāsī*. The mass of Manu material, from which he
could not extricate himself in the first edition, has been drastically
cut down to one-third. All references to the special powers, privileges, and dispensations of the *sannyāsī* have been omitted,
and also those numerous verses from Manu that prescribe petty
details relating to food, cover, and shelter. *Sannyāsa* was open
only to the brahmins, which in Dayananda's terms meant not
the caste, but the group of people who excel in wisdom, piety,
and charity.[82] The main thrust of the chapter is that *sannyāsīs*
should be dedicated to the good of the people, and promote it
by example and by their preaching.

The chapter on the state had also been drastically overhauled.
There is more logic in the development, and whereas some fifty
verses of Manu have been dropped, some hundred new ones have
been added. The Swami remained very much the pupil of Manu
in statecraft. A few new ideas have been developed. There should
be three Councils of State, on Education, Religion, and Admi-

nistration. The king, who is president of the Rāja Sabhā is chosen by the people and can be removed by them: all the powers of the state, king, Sabhā, and people, are mutually subordinate, and no one has dictatorial powers. Village, district, and provincial administrations receive more attention, and it is stressed that all forms of corruption should be eliminated, one of the best methods being for the state to pay its civil servants well and assume responsibility for their families and widows. There is also a longer section on the conduct of diplomacy and war, again completely taken from Manu. Whereas the first edition mentioned the performance of the great public sacrifices as being a duty of the king, the second edition is completely silent on that matter.[83]

Some ideas, already mooted earlier by the Swami, were emphasized to the point that they now became key notions in his concept of the state. Those involved in government affairs must be held responsible and accountable: all, from the king to the village administrator, are appointed to their posts, and all can be removed for incompetence or corruption. The members of the Councils of State are ultimately subject to the people, as is the king himself, who should always implement the majority decisions. In a way they are all but functionaries of the people. The only person with divine rights is the supreme King, God himself; the prime representative of his command is not the ruler, but *danda*, the law, which transcends the king.

Dayananda's ideal state is certainly not a theocracy; in fact he excludes one class of people from becoming members of the Councils of State; the *sannyāsīs* of the fourth order![84] In order to prove the divinity of the king the Hindu tradition had sometimes used certain verses of Manu which declare that the king was created from particles of eight Vedic gods. The Swami interpreted this text in a different way. He said that it is only an allegory that shows the basic qualities a king should possess.[85] Dayananda's state was in a way a social welfare state, with wide-ranging obligations: it should provide universal education and protect the *dharma*; it should be responsible for social welfare, providing support for widows and orphans, and pensions for state servants; and it should root out the evil practices of child-marriage and polygamy. By stipulating that only the most able people should be involved in the administration, Dayananda proposed an aristocratic regime. However, he held that these 'aristos' had to be held in check by two higher principles: the law and the commonweal. But he did not specify clear procedures for appointing 'the best' or for checking them once they were in power. A page of praise of the benefits of the British Raj that featured in the first edition[86] has been deleted. Elsewhere a paragraph explains the Swami's different approach in this matter. After describing the universal rule of the Vedic age, he lamented:

But now, due to the onset of misfortune and to the laziness, pride, and mutual hostility of the Aryans, far from them being the rulers of other countries, there is even in Āryāvarta no more that undivided, free, independent, and peaceful rule of the Aryans. What little power they have, even that is trodden underfoot by foreigners: only a few kings are still self-governing. When such bad times come, then the people have to suffer great misfortune. However much good may be achieved by foreign rule, indigenous rule is by far the best of all. Foreign rule cannot be fully conducive to happiness, even when it is conducted with mercy and justice and with parental solicitude for the people and is devoid of all racial and religious bigotry. But it is very difficult to eradicate the mutual hostility that arises from the great variety of languages, education systems, and customs. Without the removal of those differences, it is difficult to achieve the full realization of the aim of a perfect commonweal.[87]

Here again Dayananda's new political nationalism showed itself; for the full realization of the reconstruction of the glory of the Vedic Age would necessarily imply political independence. The contrast between alien rule (*videshī rāj*) and indigenous rule (*svadeshī rāj*) mentioned in the long quotation, was repeatedly and forcefully emphasized by the Swami in this work. The following few instances give some impression of the thrust of the idea: 'when foreigners trade or rule in our country, then poverty and misery are inevitable';[88] 'ever since meat-eating and spirit-drinking aliens have come to our country, the suffering of Indians has steadily increased';[89] when defeated by their enemies, 'the Indians become subjected to foreigners, and they suffer manifold distress like the pony of the inn-keeper and the donkey of the potter'.[90]

In 1875 Dayananda knew very little about Jainism, but his knowledge had grown vastly by 1883 due to the pressure of his controversy with Thakurdas. Sevaklal Karsondas had helped the Swami at that time: he had supplied books on Jainism, and had gathered information such as the list of books of the Jain scriptures, which Dayananda reproduced in his introduction to the *Satyārth Prakāsh*.[91] Karsondas acquired for the Swami twenty volumes of the most ancient works, supplemented by over fifty volumes of authoritative commentaries and of contemporary works.[92] Some of these volumes were used by the Swami to write his new chapter, which runs to over a hundred pages and abounds in quotations. Few of the latter come from the Jain scriptures themselves; most are taken from contemporary works, which, though often commentaries on other commentaries, certainly represented Jain doctrines as preached in those days.

The treatment of Jainism is systematic and wide-ranging, covering topics like Jain atheism, the doctrine of matter and spirit, *syādvāda*, or the doctrine of relative pluralism, *karma*, and *moksha*. The innumerable 'absurdities' of Jain mythology, astronomy, and geography are ridiculed in the same way as those of Hinduism had been in the previous chapter. The most bitter words are directed at Jain exclusivism: the way their books propounded denunciation and vilification not only of all other faiths, but also of whatever a non-Jain might do or think. For advocates of non-violence that was unforgivable: 'Very few people would personify hatred to the extent the Jains do.'[93] Dayananda's technique of criticism was the one he used against Hinduism. Reason, logic, common sense, and morality are the touchstones of truth, and they are applied to the texts taken in their most literal sense. No effort is made to grasp the deeper meaning of myth or symbol, or to probe the religious and historical rationale of a custom or rite. In this same chapter, Chārvāka and Buddhism are also subjected to a criticism that is completely based on the *Sarvadarshanasamgraha*. Buddhism is treated very superficially; being a negligible sect on the contemporary Indian scene, it did not interest the Swami at all.

The chapter on Christianity can unfortunately not be compared with the one the Swami wrote for his first edition, as this was never published. The chapter treats Christianity as a 'religion of the book' and concentrates exclusively on the Bible. Dayananda mentioned in his introduction that he used a Sanskrit and a Hindī translation of the Bible, but he did not specify which ones they were.[94] At the time Carey's full translation into Hindī and Sanskrit were available: they had been completely published by 1819. Dr Wenger's revised re-publication of Carey's translation of the Old

Testament into Sanskrit was published in 1876. Two more Hindī translations were on the market: one by Bowley of the C.M.S., and one by Parsons, Holcomb, and Owen, published in 1868.[95] It is impossible to work out which ones Dayananda used, but we know that the basic text comes from translations by missionaries. His method of interpretation is most simplistic: he takes the words in their immediate literal sense and makes no effort whatsoever to apply the following rules which he himself, in his introduction to the *Satyārth Prakāsh*, recommended for the interpretation of his own words: the interpreter should be aware of the intention of the author, of the total context, of the word-meaning the author intends, and he should also give preference to an interpretation that gives rationality to the text.[96]

The thesis presented in this chapter is a very simple one: the claim of Christianity stands or falls with the Bible; the Bible is not the word of God; therefore, the Bible is not revelation and Christianity is not the true religion. To prove that the Bible is not God's word several arguments are used. The Bible is not universal, but particularistic and embedded in history.[97] It contains a great number of statements that offend reason. By presenting a God who is limited by space and time, temperamental, deceitful, jealous, cruel, and a tawdry magician to boot, it contradicts the essential divine qualities. It also abounds in logical impossibilities, contradictions, and absurd miracles, and it displays a crude ignorance of scientific truth. Moreover, it contains many stories and precepts that are immoral, praising cruelty and deceit and encouraging sin. These are the basic arguments that are exemplified, page after page, in the many texts chosen from both Old and New Testaments.

Although the reader is assured in the preface that 'this expose is intended only to propagate truth and suppress untruth, and not to injure anyone's feelings or impute untrue faults',[98] there is quite a lot of sarcastic bitterness in it. Repeatedly, up to a dozen times, it is asserted that the idolatry, mythology, and cultural degradation of Christianity outstrips that of the *Purānas* and the *Tantras*.[99] It is a hard judgment, but understandable: after all, the Swami was paying the missionaries back in the same coin some of them had used so extravagantly in their attacks on Hinduism.[100] Another theme runs right through the chapter, that of 'barbarism': over twenty-five times the term 'barbarous' (*jangalī*) is applied to the Christians, their God, their scripture, and their prophets. This again is explicable when put in the context of the late nineteenth century, when a feeling of not only cultural, but racial superiority prevailed among many British people in India.[101]

But there is more: a number of statements denounce the Christians (and to Dayananda and his readers this meant primarily the British in India) with what can only be called savage, resentful bitterness. Referring to *Exodus* 20, 17, 'Thou shalt not bear false witness against thy neighbour. . . .', the Swami exclaims, 'That must be why Christians descend on the property of foreigners like the thirsty upon water and the starving upon food!'[102] After commenting on the injustice of the Last Judgment, he sarcastically adds, 'I suppose that explains why the Christians are so biassed in favour of their own that when a black man is killed by a white man, they acquit the murderer in court'.[103] Since their God enjoys animal sacrifices, 'why should Christians not fill their belly with the slaughter of beef?'[104] and if they believe that sacrifice deletes sin, 'why should their rulers, judges, and generals be afraid of acting immorally?'[105] Christians are essentially a people who delight in war, because 'they have taken war as their *guru-mantra*',[106] and even their heaven is a place of carnage, and therefore, 'fit for Christians only'.[107]

Thus this chapter too exhibits the new aggressive nationalistic leanings of the Swami. There seems no doubt about it that this attitude originated in the Panjab, where he was continuously confronted with aggressive Christian propaganda, and where he came into closer contact with the missionaries' pamphlet literature. His contact with the Theosophists, who were vehemently anti-Christian, would have helped to foster these sentiments. Nowhere else in his earlier writings does one find even an echo of that militant nationalism.

The chapter on Islam follows very closely the argument presented against Christianity, applying it to the Koran. As there was no current Hindī translation of the Koran, Dayananda had one especially made.[108] There are some differences in emphasis. The text stresses very heavily, nearly page by page, that the doctrines of Islam in all its aspects offend natural justice by their enormous bias in favour of the Muslims. Another theme that recurs very often is that Islam sanctifies war and plunder and the slaughter of non-believers. Dayananda did not spare Islam the harsh condemnation he had meted out to Hinduism and Christianity. But, nevertheless, it is significant that we do not find in this chapter those bitter, sarcastic remarks that feature in his attack on the Christians; his attitude here is in general more moderate. This fits in with his behaviour during his visit to the Panjab: the missionaries were his prime target, whereas the Muslims were only incidentally attacked.

This is the work that was to become the principal textbook of the Aryas. As the final major work of the Swami it presented a great advance on his earlier writings in many ways: language and style had improved; there was greater clarity and simplicity, and a more systematic arrangement; and the fruits of his deep study of the *Vedas*, of the philosophical systems, and of many other works, were apparent in a wealth of quotations. But, more importantly, as his final legacy to the Arya Samaj, this work presented a set of attitudes and ideas which, though they were not completely novel, had acquired a bold new perspective within the totality of his thought, and were destined to greatly influence the Samaj after his death.

The fully worked out doctrine of *traitavāda* with its strong anti-Advaita bias, is the most important theoretical advance. Within this doctrine the concept of *moksha* is the central one: it emphasizes that man's moral activity must be the very soul of the Aryan ethos. The second important legacy is the clearer and stronger elaboration of the myth of the Vedic Golden Age, with its religious, scientific, and political supremacy over all other races and nations, an age that is to be brought to life again in the reconstruction of Āryāvarta. Thirdly, in this book Dayananda's criticism of Hinduism is heavily counterbalanced by his criticism of Jainism, Christianity, and Islam, and this new emphasis greatly influenced the growing Samaj. Finally, whereas the nationalism of the earlier Dayananda was not so much nationalism as it was Aryan 'Vedism', the new *Satyārth Prakāsh* repeatedly reflects a new nationalism with aggressive, anti-British, and political overtones.

In those last years Dayananda's greatest effort was devoted to the composition of his Vedic commentary. Only part of this work was published during his lifetime: fifty-one fascicules each of the *Rigvedabhāshya* and of the *Yajurvedabhāshya*. It took the Paropkarinī Sabhā another six years to complete the publication of the latter, and no less than sixteen years to finish that of the former.[109] The total output comprises over seven thousand large pages of print, treating the whole of the *Yajurveda*, and the *Rigveda* from the beginning up to *Rigveda* 7.4.60. All this was written over a span of six years, which means an average rate of twelve hundred pages per year. Even when one takes into consideration the fact that two pandits were continuously working on the Hindī translation, the task was still a remarkable one.

How did Dayananda himself conceive the value of this work? First of all, his decision to write a Vedic commentary was not a precipitous one. He made the resolution seven years after leaving his *guru* Virjananda, at the time of his visit to Calcutta. A year earlier he had still refused to consider the idea, but now he diagnosed the scant interest shown in the *Vedas* by the Calcutta intelligentsia as the root cause of their divisiveness. He decided there and then that he would himself write a commentary on the *Vedas* which would clearly vindicate their supreme importance.[110] After his visit to Calcutta it took the Swami another three years to actually embark on his work.

Dayananda never claimed his own commentary to be definitive or infallible, and he never imposed its acceptance or its study on the Aryas. However, he did state that his work was different from and better than the other current interpretations, because they were influenced mainly by later commentators, whereas his own work was based on the earliest commentaries. He also asserted that his new study would stimulate research in the *Vedas*, for which there was a crying need.[111] One may disagree with both these claims, but it could not be held that they were in themselves either irrational or extravagant.

Dayananda's interpretation is of a very special type. On the one hand it proceeds in the usual fashion by way of grammatical and semantic analysis to the establishment of the meaning of a text. First the composite words of a passage are clearly separated into their single components according to the rules of *sandhi*. Then follows the *padārtha*, the systematic explanation of all these components, indicating their meaning and their function in the sentence, which establishes the meaning of the text. This is followed by the reconstruction of the whole sentence in a straight grammatical form; and finally comes the *bhāvārtha*, a sentence which explains the purport of the text, indicating if it is an injunction, a statement of principle, or some kind of comparison. All this is in Sanskrit, and it is followed by Hindī translations of the *padārtha* and the *bhāvārtha*. It is all very traditional so far, but it is quite clear that the interpretation thus arrived at is not simply the result of that analysis. Other powerful factors were directing every step taken by the Swami, namely his own theological presuppositions about the *Vedas*. There were four such basic assumptions, the influence of which is detectable in almost every page of the commentary.

Since, according to the Swami, the *Vedas* literally contained the eternal wisdom of God, all their statements had to be of a universal nature. Therefore, they could not possibly refer to historical or geographical data. Other commentators, especially the historically minded Western orientalists, interpreted a number of Vedic texts as containing historical references. For Dayananda historical considerations were *a priori* excluded, because in his mind the *Vedas* antedated all history. He went to great lengths of semantic contortion to explain away all terms that could be taken as names of historical persons or that mention geographical features.[112] What other interpreters consider to be statements of fact, Dayananda explained as statements of principle or as injunctions. Hence his commentary abounds in pronouncements on politics, because all texts referring to kings or battles were interpreted as giving directives on the arts of statecraft, diplomacy, or war.

A second assumption of Dayananda's was that the *Vedas* proclaimed a pure monotheism. Therefore, the names of the many *devas* were re-interpreted in the light of that presupposition. For instance, when the name Agni occurred in a context of divine action, it was said to signify the one Lord; outside such a context the same term was understood to mean simply 'fire'. The Swami treated in a similar way the 'hundred names of God' which he listed in the first chapter of his *Satyārth Prakāsh*. To contemporary Hindu orthodoxy that procedure of Dayananda's was probably the most objectionable aspect of his work, and the Calcutta Hindu Council made a special point of declaring it unorthodox.[113]

The third necessary consequence of the divine nature of the

Vedas, in Dayananda's view, was that they could not possibly contain anything that offended reason or morality. According to the Swami all myths and miracles were irrational, and also sometimes implied immoral acts: no such nonsense could be part of the *Vedas*. Those myths that most commentators accept as an integral part of Vedic lore were therefore thoroughly demythologized by Dayananda. An interesting example of this procedure is to be found in his interpretation of the myth of the fight between Indra and Vritra, so often referred to in the hymns. According to the Swami this episode has two levels of meaning: on the one hand it explains scientific truths about the interaction of sun and clouds, and on the other hand it proposes rules for the conduct of battle. In other words, the myth has nothing to do with the divinity as such or with his relation to the cosmos.[114]

A final assumption that directs some of the Swami's interpretations is his unique doctrine that the *Vedas* were also the repository of scientific truth. As the Swami's own scientific knowledge was rudimentary, this aspect was only rarely elaborated. Some texts were shown to propound the theory of the relatively new process of telegraphy,[115] and others were said to explain the principles of mechanical locomotion by means of steam and electricity over land, water, and by air.[116]

These four basic assumptions were the overriding factors that directed Dayananda's interpretation. He used his wide and subtle knowledge of grammar and semantics in their service. Since the revival of Vedic studies had been launched by Western orientalists in the nineteenth century, most Vedic scholars had looked on the *Vedas* as historical documents, expressing aspects of Aryan civilization at a particular stage of its development. They attempted to unravel the meaning of these obscure documents by the application of a wide spectrum of research approaches. Besides linguistic tools like grammar, semantics, prosody, and etymology, they also used other methods involving protohistoric data, comparative philology, internal dating, comparisons with historical data of post-Vedic literature, etc. In Dayananda's view only the linguistic tools were appropriate, because he held that the documents were not of a historical nature. Vedic scholars attacked the Swami on the ground that such a presupposition vitiated his interpretation *ab ovo*. The Swami's retort would have been that, on the contrary, their interpretation was valueless because they wrongly assumed that the *Vedas* were historical documents. In a way the Swami's approach in his commentary is very similar to that of the commentaries of great interpreters of Hinduism like Shankara and Rāmānuja. They too manipulated the sacred texts with the subtle tools of linguistics, and forced them to yield the meaning that fitted in with their theological presuppositions. Perhaps the most striking examples of that technique are the commentaries on the *Brahmasūtras* and the *Bhagavadgītā* of Shankara and Rāmānuja respectively. But there is an important difference between these ancient theologians and Dayananda They did acknowledge that Hinduism found its authoritative sources in ancient texts, but they were not committed, as Dayananda was, to the dogma that the four *Vedas* by themselves contained the total and infallible revelation of the wisdom of God.

That dogma was new in the history of Hinduism, which had never been strictly a religion of the book. Dayananda's conviction that it was, did not stem from the Hindu tradition. He evolved that dogma over many years, and the decisive influence in its emergence cannot have been any other than that of the Christian missionaries, and, to a much lesser degree, of Muslim theologians. One should remember that most of the missionaries with whom Dayananda came into contact belonged to the Protestant churches: their religion was primarily a religion of the book, and the Bible occupied the centre of their theology. Their propaganda concentrated on two fronts: they showed on the one hand the absurdity and immorality of the Hindu scriptures, and, on the other, they tried to prove the absolute and definitive truth of biblical revelation. That was exactly the approach Dayananda applied in reverse: he wanted to prove that Christianity fell with the Bible, and that the truth of Vedic religion was demonstrated by the absolute veracity of the *Vedas*. In other words, Dayananda accepted the Protestant premise that God has revealed himself in a book, and that the very content of that book proves its authenticity. The Swami, however, went even further than the Christians in his claim that the *Vedas* contained the totality of truth, both theological and scientific. Thus Dayananda accomplished in his Vedic theory what he did in other fields: he took an ancient Hindu tradition and gave it a new direction all of his own.

What, in the final instance, is the lasting value of Dayananda's Vedic commentary? As a stage in the ongoing decipherment of

Vedic literature it must be considered of little importance. It does not have a place in modern Vedic science, and, outside the ambiance of the Arya Samaj, no Vedic scholar takes any account of it.[117] Nevertheless, it remains an astounding monument to the convictions and efforts of Swami Dayananda, and it may well be the last of the great Vedic commentaries in the traditional Hindu mould. The *Bhāshya* has another claim to greatness: the fact that it constitutes the very first effort, and a very massive effort at that, to bring the *Vedas* out of the sanctuary of brahmin dominance into the open and to make them accessible to all Hindus. This may well be the strongest argument in favour of him being called the Luther of India. After Dayananda no brahmin would get away with claiming exclusive rights to the sacred heritage. The Swami's great commentary will retain its place in history for a third reason: even if few people, and few Aryas, read and study it, many are proud to know that it symbolizes the Vedic Golden Age, the superiority of Hinduism, the greatness of ancient India, ideas that have become, thanks to Dayananda, an integral part of a nationalist spirit, the strong echo of which one can hear in India even today.

CHAPTER XII

A Dynamic View of Swami Dayananda

A. THE THEOLOGIAN: GOD AND THE *Vedas*

When Dayananda left his home his concept of God was probably still vague, but it contained two important characteristics: his Shaivite background had imprinted on his mind the profound idea of a personal God enshrined in the numinous figure of Shiva, and an abhorrence of Vaishnavite mythology.[1] His first study of Advaita as a *sannyāsī* then convinced him of the identity of *brahman* and *ātman*. However, this inquiry was not very deep; his limited knowledge of Sanskrit restricted him to rudimentary texts, and his temperamental preference for practice over theory cut this study short. He soon turned to the cultivation of Yoga, which dominated his next ten years of wandering. His passion was not for speculation but for the mastery of techniques that would bring spiritual fulfilment. This blissful goal seems to have eluded the pilgrim, but on that long road his assiduous practice of Yoga made him into a man of astounding physical and mental power.

Dayananda's period in Mathura as a pupil of Virjananda brought back to the fore his earlier monotheism with its strong Shaivite tinge, no doubt partly as a reaction to the stifling Vaishnavite atmosphere of that city of Krishna. In subsequent years of study this monotheism was gradually purged of all its Purānic and Shaivite elements, and combined with some Advaitic notions. Although *sat-chit-ānanda* was now declared to be the proper name of God, it did not signify an impersonal entity, but was another name for *parameshwar*, the Lord. Thus arose an uneasy compromise between theism and monism, for the Swami still held the doctrines of the fundamental identity of *brahman* and *ātman* and of the ultimate unreality of the world. These two doctrines were repudiated by him during his years in the Doab, and he arrived at the basic tenets of his monotheism: God is a transcendent person, distinct from the world and the souls, original creator of all, and through his power immanent in all creation. The lofty monotheism of Debendranath's *Brahmo Dharma* helped the Swami to clarify the details of his theism in his first *Satyārth Prakāsh*. He adopted the Maharshi's formula that made it possible to describe God as both *sa-guna* and *nir-guna*: the *gunas* in the first term refer to perfect qualities and those in the second to finite ones. Thus some more lingering traces of monism were eliminated. The greatest theological difficulty Dayananda then faced was that of conceiving between God and the non-divine a relationship that did not in any way impair God's perfection. This problem was complicated by the fact that the Swami then held that cosmos and *jīvas* were originally created out of God's infinite potentiality, a doctrine probably also influenced by Debendranath. The derivation of the created world from God's potentiality did confuse the distinction between God and his creation. The Swami adopted the old principle of *bhedābheda* to deal with this delicate point: God and his potentiality are in a *bhedābheda* relation. In one way God's potentiality is not distinct from him, and therefore God is the real material cause of the universe; but, at the same time, the two are also distinct, and therefore one cannot say that the Lord himself was transformed into the universe.

Discussions with Christian missionaries made Dayananda feel that this solution was not a satisfactory one. It was in his subsequent study of Sāmkhya and of Nyāya-Vaisheshika that he discovered the elements that helped him formulate his final doctrine of *traitavāda*: the cosmos as *prakriti*, and also the *jīvas* are co-eternal with God. Thus the intricate problem of their origination completely evaporated; nevertheless, according to the Swami, they remain utterly dependent on God in their evolution.

This gradual development of Dayananda's concept of God clearly shows that basically he always adhered to the monotheism he inherited in his youth. Although monism influenced his thought for a while, its impact was not very deep, and the Swami progressively freed himself of all monistic ideas. Three external sources of influence were at work in this process: the Swami's discussions with missionaries, the impact of Debendranath's *Brahmo Dharma*, and concepts of Sāmkhya and Nyāya-Vaisheshika. Sāmkhya contributed the idea of the co-eternity of the three ultimate substances, and Nyāya-Vaisheshika helped shape the idea of God's activity in the processes of creation.

On the Swami's side, the primary force directing his thinking was his concern to develop an idea of God that would rule out even the slightest imperfection, and yet would safeguard God's personality. That is why he retained the simple *sat-chit-ānanda* formula, why he eliminated the concept of *sāmarthya*, and why he persistently denied any historical divine intervention in the affairs of the cosmos and the souls. However, this negative process of dissociating God from all possible imperfections led to a final conception that constitutes an uneasy compromise between theism and deism. God pervades and sustains the cosmos, and dispenses the fruits of *karma*, but in both these functions he somehow remains at a distance, uninvolved, as the eternal divine architect of the physical laws of the universe and of the moral law of retribution. There is no doubt that in the Swami's personal devotion and in his devotional works God is much nearer and dearer, but Dayananda did not succeed in integrating that personal closeness of a loving and concerned Lord into his theological structure, which remained a syncretic amalgam of basic tenets without profound integration.

This lack of integration shows up in one particular aspect of Dayananda's theology. Although he was obsessed by the idea of a completely infinite and independent divinity, he ended up with a God who in a certain way needs the world as much as the world needs him. God's relationship with the world is the only sphere in which he can fulfil his 'natural' powers and attributes of omnipotence, mercy, and justice. Creation, preservation, and salvation, said the Swami, are the 'natural' functions of God, just as seeing is the natural function of the eyes.[2]

Dayananda was hampered in his theological thinking by his complete inability to grasp the value and meaning of myth and symbol in the elucidation of the sacred. To him only pure rationality was acceptable in the realm of theology. This radical rationalism prevented him from appreciating the depths of the theological speculations of Hindu thinkers like Rāmānuja or Madhva: in the Swami's eyes their attempts at plumbing the mysteries of God's love violated God's pure infinity. That same rationalism steered his mind also in the direction of a vague deism. Dayananda was no great theologian of the divine. After all, his primary interest was never really directed towards the mysteries of God, but rather towards the strivings of man; the first period of his life he devoted to his personal search for *moksha*, and the second he dedicated to the regeneration of Hindu man and Hindu society.

The development of Dayananda's conception of the *Vedas*, so intimately attached to his name, was a very long and slow process. Firm foundations for it were laid in his youth. As a Kathiawari Shaivite he inherited a tradition which prided itself on its adherence to the most ancient aspects of Hinduism, the Vedic rites and the *Dharmashāstras*; as a youth he learned the *Yajurveda* by heart. But for the first twenty years of his adult life the *Vedas* had no place among his concerns.

It was Virjananda who turned Dayananda's mind again towards the ancient roots of Hinduism: he taught him that the authentic sources of pure Hinduism were contained in the most ancient works of the *rishis* alone. But the *guru* himself does not seem to have been clear as to exactly which these works were. Dayananda set himself the task of finding that out. In the seven years after leaving his *guru* he studied all the Hindu works he could find, and progressively decided to eliminate all *Tantras* and *Purānas*, the *Mahābhārata*, the *Upanishads*, the *Manusmriti*, etc. Finally, around 1870, he crossed the *Brāhmanas* out too, and declared that the original revelation of God was contained only in the four *Samhitās*, the *Rig*, the *Yajur*, the *Sāma*, and the *Atharva*.

Thus Dayananda went much further than simply answering his *guru's* question as to which the books of the *rishis* were. He made a radical distinction between the four *Samhitās* as revelation of God transmitted through the *rishis*, and other works composed by the *rishis* themselves, which he regarded as authoritative only in a secondary way. But at that time he had as yet no definite ideas as to what exactly the *Vedas* contained and in what manner they revealed God's message.

It was in Calcutta that these problems forced themselves on the Swami's attention. Questions about 'revelation' had been considered by the Bengali reformers since the time of Rammohan Roy. They had thought about them in a wide context, as they were challenged by the claims of Christianity and Islam, 'religions of the book'. Their general conclusion had been to reject all claims to exclusive revelation, and to accept that different religions presented in their sacred writ complementary aspects of a universal rational religion. From that premise followed their practical eclecticism in borrowing from different scriptures, an eclecticism carried to its greatest lengths by Keshub. In the seventies that universalistic and eclectic approach was being increasingly challenged by a newly emerging movement supporting Hindu pride and nationalism spearheaded by the Adi Brahmos, according to which Hinduism was not just one among equals in the brotherhood of world religions, but was superior to all the others.

It was his reflections about the ideas that confronted him in Calcutta that led the Swami to formulate his own particular concept of Vedic revelation by combining two separate doctrines. He adopted the view that true religion must come directly from God in the definite form of a book, and combined this with the dogma of the superiority of Hinduism. Authentic religion was revealed by God in the *Vedas*, which constituted the only real divine revelation. All the other books of Hinduism, and also the scriptures of other religions such as Islam and Christianity, were mere secondary works of human origin without any inherent authority. The Swami also insisted that the content of revelation was completely rational, and as such comprised of necessity all that was rationally true in all other religions which were the imperfect efforts of men.

Such a concept of revelation is not to be found in the Hindu tradition. Though it always recognized that the most ancient scriptures had a special authority, it tended to class together all the early works from the *Rigveda* to the *Brahmasūtras* and the *Bhagavadgītā*. Moreover, the Hindu tradition did not generally look upon that great collection as necessarily comprising the final word, but often accepted an ongoing process of revelation in new eras in many later works such as the hymns of the early *bhakti* teachers of South India, the *Purānas*, the *Tantras*, and works of medieval *bhakti* saints. Dayananda's restrictive concept of true religion as the religion of the one book was no doubt inspired by the concept prevalent among Protestant missionaries. He accepted their premise of a divine revelation given once and for all time, and applied it to the four *Vedas*. But he went even further than any Christian fundamentalist would have dared to go by claiming that the *Vedas* contained the totality of all know-

ledge, spiritual, moral, social, political, and even scientific.
That is the conception Dayananda enshrined in his *Vedabhāshya*,
which he considered his major contribution to knowledge and
legacy to posterity. The *Bhāshya* has not played that vital role
in the regeneration of Hinduism which Dayananda hoped it
would, and has become to many of his followers an inert monument
to which one occasionally pays tribute. However, the work still
remains important to many as a symbol and a reminder of the
material, cultural, and spiritual greatness of the Vedic Golden
Age, and of the absolute superiority of Hinduism, both lasting
ingredients of the spirit of Hindu nationalism.

B. The Moralist: Man and *Dharma*

Dayananda's first explicit theory of man was an advaitic one:
the *ātman* is in the final instance identical with *brahman*, and the
supreme goal of life is the realization of that identity. The
sannyāsī who completely dedicates his life to the pursuit of that
ideal is elevated above the restrictions of the *varna-dharma*. The
Swami lived according to this ideal from the age of twenty-one
to the age of thirty-six, when he went to study under Virjananda.
During his stay in Mathura his attention was diverted from his
own super-self and directed towards the humanity around him,
as at the same time his theistic approach reasserted itself.[3]
This new view of life gradually led the Swami to deny the monistic
identity of God and man, and to affirm that man's deepest essence,
the *jīva*, though dependent on the Lord for its existence, was
essentially distinct from God and always remained so. During
the long years in the Doab, Dayananda's constant concern with
morality made him reflect much on the essence of man and his
relation to God. His subsequent reading of the *Brahmo Dharma*
and his discussions with Bengali moral thinkers like A.K.Datta
helped him to clarify his ideas.
A year after his visit to Calcutta the Swami formulated his
first comprehensive view of man in his *Satyārth Prakāsh*. The
jīva, created by God 'at the beginning', at the time of *ādisrishti*,
remains a separate entity. Consciousness is his deepest essence,
and he is linked to the gross body by the subtle body. The *jīva*
is active, a free agent, and totally responsible for all his deeds.
He peregrinates through successive lives until he reaches fulfilment

in the state of *moksha*. There he remains until 'the end of time', *atyant pralaya*, when he is reabsorbed with the whole cosmos into God's potentiality. This eschatology ascribes to the *jīva* some striking characteristics. The *jīva* is finite, having both a beginning and an end in time; he is essentially active and cosmic even in *moksha*, where he enjoys the bliss of emancipation through his subtle body which is a cosmic entity; he cannot act or exist without this connection, and when the cosmos is finally dissolved, both the *jīva* and his subtle body are included in that dissolution.

Thus Dayananda had now arrived at a concept of man radically different from the advaitic one: the deepest essence of man was to be active and cosmic. Yet there still remained what could be called an inconsistency, or a vestige of monism, in this conception: in *moksha* both *karma* and *avidyā* were totally destroyed. From this it logically followed that *moksha*, though it was restricted in time, was irreversible as a state, because the very seeds of *samsāra*, namely *karma* and *avidyā*, had been eliminated. Two considerations had moved the Swami to that conclusion. He applied the ancient Hindu principle that whatever has a beginning must also have an end. Secondly, his concern to safeguard the distinction between God and man, the infinite and the finite, made him adhere to the doctrine of the cosmic nature of man, even if this meant accepting man's eventual disappearance.

The second *Satyārth Prakāsh* propounds the Swami's final conception of man. His study of Sāmkhya and his discussions with missionaries had made him doubt the logical soundness of an initial creation out of God's potentiality. This led him to the doctrine of *traitavāda*: God, the cosmos, and the *jīvas* are eternal substances. But if one concedes to the *jīva* co-eternity with the Lord, how can one safeguard the basic distinction between the two? By linking man *eternally* to the cosmos and its tyranny of time and space this can be done, and Dayananda now realized that if man remained active and cosmic even in the state of *moksha*, then he also had to retain his freedom, and with his freedom the possibility of relapse. He therefore stated that man always remained bound to *karma* and that his knowledge always remained imperfect; these conditions would eventually bring man back from the state of *moksha* into the cycle of rebirth.

Two basic ideas were so dear to the Swami that he was prepared to go against the whole Hindu tradition in his new eschatology.

The first idea was the distinction between God and man, which had to be preserved at all cost. The second, and even more compelling concept was that man's salvation had to be achieved completely by his own works and by nothing else; moral action guided by reason was the one and only power effective in the process of salvation. Dayananda ruthlessly eliminated all other roads to *moksha*, all the short cuts, the easy rides, the instantaneous transformations that Hinduism had devised over the centuries. *Moksha* was to be earned by action alone, its achievement was regulated by the law of *karma*, an inexorably just law that man never escaped, not even in *moksha*. Although this law was administered by the Lord, he never interfered with it just as he never interfered with the physical laws of nature, for both these laws were perfect from the beginning.

The long and gradual emergence of Dayananda's final concept of man had an overall direction. Progressively it disentangled man from that basic identity with God which Advaita ascribes to him. In this process of disentanglement more and more stress was laid on the essential attributes of man: he is active, always free, and bound to cosmic existence. Freedom, activity, and involvement in the world constituted for Dayananda the basic nobility of man, the source of his greatness, for which he owes God gratitude, but for which he is wholly and solely responsible. Even the *sannyāsīs'* pride should lie in that, and not in an escape from the world.

Within the Hindu tradition this is a remarkable conception, indeed a unique one. No other Hindu theologian has elevated man's moral action to such a rank in the scale of human endeavour, far above the powers of ritualism, the raptures of mysticism, or the wondrous effectiveness of devotional love which are given a place of prominence in the Hindu theologies of *karma*, *jnāna*, and *bhakti*. This conception of man is no doubt Dayananda's greatest theoretical achievement and his main contribution to Hindu speculation. At the same time it is the most perfect expression of the Swami's own approach to life.

As Dayananda's vision of man evolved, his conception of *dharma* developed correspondingly. *Dharma* here is taken to refer to the complex of duties man has to perform to achieve his fulfilment. It was only after leaving Virjananda that the Swami

allocated not by the accident of birth, but by the state according to each man's abilities and behaviour. By ascribing to the classes a purely secular status, he took away from the *Shāstras* that religious authority in caste matters that orthodoxy attached to them, which meant that all their statements had to be judged from the ethical point of view.

Two other doctrines of the Swami's reinforced this strong accent on moral action. He condemned the way of *nivritti*, renunciation of action, and stated that not even the *sannyāsī* was exempt from the fundamental commandment of positive moral action. The other doctrine was that sins cannot be forgiven; the law of karmic retribution allows for no exception as it is the basis of morality, and every single act must bear its own fruit. In this search for the roots of morality Dayananda was determined as an individual to challenge the taboos of Hindu social life; he repeatedly acted against them, and also exposed some of his followers to excommunication.

We can detect two major sources of influence on the Swami in his search for basic moral principles. First there was the example of the Sādhs: their simple moral code with its stress on basic attitudes and its freedom from ritual and superstitious regulations was a model for Dayananda. So too was the ethical teaching of Debendranath's *Brahmo Dharma*, with its emphasis on the three fundamental qualities of all morality: rationality, activity, and truthfulness.

By the time the Swami wrote his first *Satyārth Prakāsh* his own concept of *dharma* had fully matured. Man's ritual duties were domestic, sacramental, and public Vedic rites; and his social life was to be regulated by the authentic Vedic *varna-dharma*. The responsibility for the regulation of this lay with the state, but the whole programme basically depended on everyone living a morally good life. The very essence of this righteous life was the practice of virtue, for wisdom and truthfulness are the roots of justice, tolerance, and peace. Dayananda's moral man is consumed with a thirst for knowledge, he is self-controlled and ever-active, and guides his social relations by truth, justice, and tolerance. Although the state must be the guardian of *dharma*, the state's effectiveness depends on the righteousness of all its members, from the ruler to the commoner. It is this conception that made it impossible for the Swami to overlook the moral flaws of the ruler of Jodhpur.

Dayananda's deep sense of morality shows itself in his balanced treatment of the major aspects of human relationships. To him marriage should be a permanent union where partners share everything; a full education is the right of every man; the state must bear wide social responsibilities; foreign travel is excellent, because 'evil springs from the heart, not from the location'; food and interdining taboos are valueless, because 'there is no direct connection between eating and drinking and *dharma*'; non-violence is not an absolute law, but must be judged in accordance with the greatest benefit to all. The only weak points in the Swami's treatment of moral issues were two: his doctrine of *niyoga* betrayed the inability of the *sannyāsī* to fully comprehend the sexual aspects of life; and in his remarks on the state of *sannyāsa* he had not yet fully drawn the radical conclusions of his premises.

The second *Satyārth Prakāsh* changed little in this concept of *dharma*, but there was a development in two areas. The Swami took away all the residual privileges of the *sannyāsī* and put him on an equal footing with every other human being; the only thing that should distinguish him was a more radical dedication to work for the good of all mankind. The second edition also exhibits a deeper concern for the lower ranks of society: the shūdras had hitherto been excluded from the study of the *Vedas*; now the Swami declared that as human beings they had as much right to that study as anybody else. There was one other new development in the later years of the Swami's life. During his search for true morality in those years in the Doab, Dayananda had not shrunk from offending orthodox taboos and exposing his followers to the punitive sanctions such offences entailed. Now, although he did not reject the principle that these taboos had no religious or authoritative value, he became careful not to break them, and he urged his Aryas to be similarly cautious. This constituted no dereliction of principle, but rather a practical policy. If he and his Aryas were to be a leaven within the body of Hinduism, then they had to avoid any actions that might force that body to expel them. Expulsion from the body would mean that, like the Brahmos, they would become ineffective outsiders.

Thus Dayananda's concept of *dharma* developed parallel with his concept of man. As he elevated man gradually to a position of complete freedom and responsibility within his 'natural elements', society and cosmos, so he elevated *dharma*. From its early beginnings as lip-service to traditional taboos and regulations, it gradually grew into a plan for pure, responsible moral action. This action of necessity had to involve all men, even the *sannyāsīs*, in society and the world. Man's ultimate goal, his ascent to the highest state of *moksha*, was to be conditional on such involvement. This high moral code was perhaps Dayananda's greatest legacy to his followers. The best of the Aryas have been people inspired by that ideal of a man dedicated to action, socially· committed and humanistic, who tries to guide his life by simple and clear moral principles.

C. THE REFORMER: THE RECONSTRUCTION OF ĀRYĀVARTA

The picture that is sometimes presented of Dayananda receiving his mission to reform the whole of India from his *guru* Virjananda, is nothing but a fantasy. Every idea that became part of the ethos of the Dayananda of the final years took long to mature and develop, and so did his ideal of the reconstruction of Āryāvarta. For the first thirty-five years of his life Dayananda was not concerned with the physical, moral, or religious state of his fellow-men, but only with his personal search for *moksha*. No doubt the influence of his *guru* and of the city of Mathura redirected his concern to the world around him. But when he left his *guru* and started to preach, the content of his instruction was still very tentative, and his teaching work took second place to study. He had no general plan, but he instructed wherever his studies brought him, simply responding to the needs of the moment; in fact very much in the manner of the wandering *sannyāsī*.

His visit to Hardwar in 1867 and his campaign at the Kumbh Mela was his first planned and concerted effort to make an impact on the Hindu world. But this attempt was a miscalculation and ended in failure and disappointment. Then, after desolately wandering along the banks of the Ganga, the Swami slowly drifted into a new type of reform work. This was a very localized effort along a stretch of the Ganga only one hundred miles long, in an essentially rural setting. Dayananda was still thinking in local and immediate terms, and his movements were not clearly planned. His preaching was directed to individuals, his moderate success was with individuals, and in a caste-dominated society such attempts at individual reform were always precarious. But as the Swami moved about, he engaged more and more often in public disputations with pandits. As in most cases he easily vanquished them, his fame spread, more important pandits challenged him, and some antagonists were brought in from the cities to try to defeat the iconoclast who was making too strong an impression. This process of challenge and response finally brought the Swami to Banaras, the citadel of orthodoxy.

The Banaras *shāstrārth* was most important, in that it put the Swami on a more than local stage; the challenge of the Banaras pandits had in itself made him into a figure of all-Hindu importance. Moreover, here in Banaras Dayananda met reformers from Bombay and Calcutta. It was here that he spoke for the first time of his dream of the regeneration of Āryāvarta through a return to the Vedic religion. However, at that stage this was only a vague ideal, not a concrete programme. In fact, although his performance in the disputation had strengthened the Swami's self-confidence, the collapse of his influence in Banaras after the pandits declared him defeated and unorthodox made him realize that his work so far had had little effect. That is why he again spent more time in study and reflection. At the Allahabad Kumbh Melā he met Debendranath Tagore who invited him to Calcutta.

The Calcutta visit was a cardinal turning point in the Swami's career. The Bengalis steered Dayananda's mind out of the narrow ambit it had been moving in. They opened up new perspectives, and helped the Swami to think in broader social and national terms: to see education as the most important factor in the uplift of the people; to consider the wide social responsibilites of the state; to be aware of the different aspects of the plight of Hindu womanhood; and to think of Hinduism in a comparative framework. Dayananda saw at close quarters a superbly-organized effort at social and religious reform, and his eyes were opened to a new range of approaches. In Calcutta he discovered the great power of lectures and publications, the strength of organization, and the receptivity of the urban middle classes to the call for reform.

The transformation was remarkable; the roving *sannyāsī* of the rural Doab overnight became the fiery lecturer of the North Indian cities, a public figure of imposing stature. He also started his work as a publicist of the pen by bringing out in his first

Satyārth Prakāsh a full statement of his reform programme. His impact and appeal were great, yet all his attempts at organization still failed; his schools proved ineffective, and the Banaras Sabhā, which he established, died a quick death.

It was Bombay that offered the Swami the chance effectively to add a new dimension to his reform efforts in the form of a solid organizational base. A small but compact group of people, primarily from the Gujarati merchant castes, had been looking towards the *Vedas* for the reformation of their religion. They found in Dayananda an inspiration and a leader, and he found in them the first members of his own Samaj. Nevertheless, the Swami was cautious, as he was too conscious of the dangers of sectarianism he had witnessed among the Brahmos. He would have preferred a broader base for his Arya Samaj, and tried unsuccessfully to persuade existing Prarthana Samaj branches to join. So he had to be satisfied with a small group of people who were neither socially nor intellectually influential. He also made it clear to the Bombay Aryas that their organization was their own responsibility, and that they had no exclusive rights over him.

If Bombay gave the Arya Samaj a start, the Panjab proved a much greater success. One of the reasons for this success was that the Hindu élite of the Panjab had broader-based needs than those of the Bombay Aryas. Whereas the latter's needs were primarily religious, that of the former were also social, cultural, and even political. Moreover, the Panjab castes who were drawn towards the Swami included the intellectual and social leaders in their areas. Compared to the Bombay Aryas they were a much more influential group. Whereas the Bombay Aryas constituted only a small selection of people from the Gujarati trading castes, the Panjab Arya Samaj captured a significant number of the leading elements in the influential Khatri community.

As the success achieved in the Panjab spread into Western U.P; and many branches of the Samaj sprang up in this area, Dayananda saw his dream of creating a movement with a broader base become reality. The Panjabis had convinced him that it was necessary to lessen the doctrinal content of the Samaj rules and this resulted in the enrolment of a more varied type of people, including even Sikhs. Whereas previously the target of the Swami's caustic criticism had been mostly sectarian Hinduism, in the Panjab it found a further butt — Christianity. The Swami's anti-Christian attitude was another element that increased his appeal among a wider section of Hindus. As the Samaj spread over North-West India and as his Vedic commentary went to thousands of subscribers from Calcutta to Lahore and Bombay, it was obvious that the Swami was making a serious impact on North Indian Hinduism.

But as the Samaj grew, orthodox opposition intensified, precisely because it noticed the widening impact of the Samaj, and hoped to isolate the Samaj by branding its Swami unorthodox. Within the Samaj there was among some Aryas a tendency towards consolidation, closing the ranks, accentuation of their distinctiveness, and a desire to involve the Swami more closely with the Samaj. To Dayananda these looked like steps in the direction of narrow sectarianism. It was not his dream to be the founder and *guru* of a reformed sect, but to work for the regeneration of the whole of Āryāvarta. His own efforts and those of his Samaj were not only for the sake of the Aryas, but for the sake of the larger body of Hinduism. The larger community was still in the grip of orthodoxy, and the Samaj could reform it only if its members took care to remain within its fold.

So the Swami once more redirected his inexhaustible energies, this time with the aim of involving himself and his Samaj as much as possible with Hindus generally. The union with the Theosophists, the agitation to support Indramani, the movements for cow-protection and for Hindī, and finally the Swami's campaign in the princely states of Rajasthan were all directed towards the same end: on the one hand they took the Swami away from Samaj affairs, and on the other hand they pushed the Aryas out of their isolation into collaboration with the orthodox and sectarians. Dayananda replaced the cry for controversy by the cry for consensus. He carefully avoided breaking taboos so as not to antagonize the orthodox, and advised his Aryas to act likewise. He was also becoming more interested in the low castes and the untouchables, for Hindus generally started to realize that it was amongst that section of Hindu society that Christians and Muslims were becoming increasingly successful. In the last year of his life the Swami also cast his eyes for the first time across the Vindhya range to South India, which had hitherto been completely outside his concern.

As the Swami thus redirected his energies towards the larger community of Hinduism, his thought gained a new dimension. Whereas so far his preoccupations had been primarily religious and social, with an almost complete negelect of the political side of the situation, now a new concern with political matters came more and more often to the fore. His writings and speeches now frequently contained references to political nationalism, to political independence, and to the evils of the British Raj. This new spirit was often fully expressed in the second *Satyārth Prakāsh*, in its bitter anti-Christian and anti-British pronouncements. It was also very much part of the three agitations in which the Swami involved the Arya Samaj: the agitations for Indramani, cow-protection, and Hindī. In each of these movements resentment against the British was combined with a strong anti-Muslim bias.

Thus towards the end of his life the Swami's eyes became more firmly focussed beyond the Arya Samaj upon the total religious, social, and also political regeneration of India as a whole. That final vision evolved over many years. After localized attempts, false starts, and ten years of reflection, it was only in 1870 that he first spoke of the general ideal of a reconstruction of the Vedic Golden Age. But it took twelve more years to work out in detail what exactly that ideal consisted of in terms of the individual, the family, society, and the state. During these years the Swami kept looking for new and more effective means by which that ideal could be gradually realized.

Dayananda's ideal was a peculiar combination of radicalism and gradualism. If one looks at his proposals of reform in the spheres of ritual, education, social organization, and political structure, and at the drastic abolition of existing customs and structures they imply, one can scarcely think of a more radical programme. However, strictly speaking, these proposals did not constitute a programme, but an ideal. They presented the ideal conditions which once existed in the Vedic Golden Age and would one day again prevail in India. The realization of that ideal could only be very gradual, as the Swami well knew; that is why he demanded even from the Aryas very little practical and immediate reform action. How then did he envisage his function and that of the Samaj in this process of reform? The Swami was a strong believer in the power of truth, of ideas. He was convinced that once people accepted the truth of the ideal, they would conform their life to it. Whereas during his period in the Doab he sought to reform the lives of individuals, after his visit to Calcutta he was more concerned with the wider propagation of his ideas. His Samaj, his publications, his Vedic commentary, his involvement with all-Hindu agitations, and his work among the princes were different phases of that ever-widening effort to disseminate the ideal. Dayananda was convinced that once there was a widespread belief in the ideal, the actual implementation of reform would naturally follow.

D. THE MAN

Dayananda's personality was not one easily captured in a simple formula, for it had many different complementary facets. Of these the most immediately obvious is that from his youth to his full maturity he was a self-directed, self-sufficient, rugged individualist. Neither parents nor teachers could map his road for him; neither religious nor political authority could coerce him. He always had to discover his own way and to decide for himself what direction he would take. Not even his own Samaj was able to imprison him in the role of leader or *guru*. This bold individualism was the fountainhead of the astounding originality of many facets of his thought and endeavour. It was also the source of a self-assurance that sometimes grew into an arrogance that alienated people and made him many bitter enemies, and of an inner rigidity that made him a poor judge of people.

The strong individualism was connected with an exceedingly active temperament. Dayananda was eminently a man of action. To become a *sannyāsī* never meant to him an escape into a sanctuary of contemplative isolation. Although he spent the first fifteen years of his adult life in the search of the personal goal of *moksha*, this search was never the patient awaiting of a dawn, but an active, frantic pursuit that sometimes drove him to the utter limits of physical and psychic endurance. In his long practice of the techniques of Yoga he trained himself to become a man of enormous bodily and mental resources, who was able to sustain a pace of work that astonished even the most vigorous. Activity was to him the first commandment. This side of his temperament was expressed to the fullest in his moral teaching that the very essence of man, his greatest nobility, is to be free,

ever active, and deeply involved. This explains the extreme severity
of his judgement on all forms of living he considered parasitic,
such as those of the lazy *sannyāsīs* who live off the charity of the
poor, of priests who sell wares worth nothing, or of kings who
enjoy the luxuries of court life. In the Swami's letters one often
finds harsh words for Aryas and helpers when he suspected them
of taking things too easily.

Dayananda's approach to life and its problems was characterized
by two tendencies which at first may seem contradictory: a high
regard for principle and a common-sense pragmatism. Once the
Swami had clearly perceived a moral or theological principle,
nothing was allowed to stand in its way. Throughout his life
very influential people and well-meaning friends on occasion
tried to make him compromise on such a principle; they always
met with a fearless and blunt refusal. Neither threats of loss of
influence, of ostracism, of the demise of friendship, even of danger
to his life, nor promises of wealth or of success in his reform work,
could dislodge the Swami from his stand. His adherence to principle was of an inflexible and narrowly rationalistic type; he
tended to judge things in terms of black and white, and had little
appreciation of all the grey areas, the shades of meaning, the
ambiguities and uncertainties that are inherent in· so many
spheres of human thought and of ethics. This passion of Dayananda's for high principle and its concomitant rationalism
often made him dogmatic, and prevented him from genuinely
appreciating the point of view of others. His narrow literalism
blinded him to the deeper truths that may be hidden in myth,
symbol, and allegory.

Yet, this strict adherence to principle went hand-in-hand with
a sound, common-sense pragmatism. This allowed him to look
at a situation, judge its elements in the light of a clear scale of
values, and make an appropriate decision. As a youth he decided
to take *sannyāsa* because this would free him for study, which
he considered his most important task; the same motive made
him surrender his *danda*. When he felt he needed to study Sanskrit
he did not hesitate to sit as a mature man among the youngsters
at the feet of Virjananda, because he was the best teacher available.
The naked *sannyāsī* of the Doab started without any scruples
to acquire books, clothes, servants, and eventually his own press,
because all this was necessary for his work. When his schools

did not achieve their aims he simply abolished them. When the Panjabis argued that the Bombay rules of the Samaj contained too much doctrinal matter, he agreed to minimize it so as to ensure wider appeal. Although he considered all food and pollution taboos utterly valueless, he obeyed them because, if by breaking them he became branded as an outcaste, he would lose his influence on the body of Hinduism. The Swami's pragmatism was best expressed in his judgement of widow-remarriage. He was convinced that *niyoga* was the only proper procedure for the twice-born, but he admitted that if *niyoga* were not to be accepted, then widow-remarriage was infinitely better than the contemporary oppression of widows. However, his pragmatism was not unprincipled or cynical; it was cool, deliberate choice according to his own scale of values. In the eyes of those who did not agree with that scale, the Swami's pragmatism appeared ruthless opportunism.

Dayananda, with all his inner resources and his self-control, was yet basically an extrovert, a doer, whose mind was fixed on the present and on the future. This made him into a dominating presence, an eloquent orator, a man of magnetic charisma. He never dwelt upon his past. When he became convinced, after due deliberation, that some idea or approach he had long cherished was not right, he simply discarded it. He did not laboriously and painfully dwell upon this change, he did not even bother to repudiate his former belief. If someone drew his attention to a discrepancy, he simply declared that after due consideration he had changed his mind and that what he previously held was due to ignorance on his part. He told his Aryas that he expected the same attitude from them. He never wallowed in the ashes of the past; they had to be thrown away and forgotten. His opponents have accused Dayananda of inconsistency, fickleness, and even duplicity, by pointing out the discrepancies between the two editions of his *Satyārth Prakāsh*. The Aryas have defended their Swami by explaining away the differences or by trying to prove that mischievous interpolators had been at work. Dayananda's answer would have been simpler: 'what I wrote eight years ago is irrelevant now, because I have changed my mind; tell me what is wrong with the position I hold today'.

How was it that the ideas of such an individualist, a man of such high principles, changed so often and so thoroughly? Every important idea held by the Swami of the eighties had taken many years to evolve and had undergone many transformations. The reason is that Dayananda was open to new ideas and perspectives, always keen to widen his learning and his horizons. The present study has identified many of the sources of profound influence on the Swami, such as Virjananda and the ambience of Mathura, the community of Sādhs, the Bengali intelligentsia, the aspirations of the Khatris and the atmosphere of the Panjab, Christian ideas, the *Brahmo Dharma*, the Sāmkhya system, and the growing Arya Samaj. But the receptivity of the Swami to outside influence was never passive. Every new idea had to be tested in his own fire of reason and of action, and only what withstood that heat was kept, and hammered into a new shape. One may trace the stages in the gradual growth of Dayananda's conceptions of God, of man, of the *Vedas*, of the Vedic Golden Age, of the function of the Arya Samaj, of the duties of the state and the nature of nationalism, and detect the successive influences that helped shape them, but the finished product was always unique, a new creation. The Swami's mind was open to new ideas, but anything that entered it was transformed in an original manner. Those of his followers who have raised him to the exalted stature of a *guru* have minimized and even denied that dominant aspect of his personality, his dynamism, his genius for transformation, his receptivity to new ideas and vistas.

There is another aspect of the Swami's view of life that is too often overlooked because it is overshadowed by other facets, that is his humanism. We refer here to the central meaning of that term, a concern for humanity-in-this-world, and not to the refined and aesthetic connotations it evokes. Dayananda was not a man of refinement, he was basic, direct, and even blunt; he was no aesthete, and in fact there is no indication that he had time or need for the appreciation of art and beauty in any form. He was a humanist because his deep concern for man was not limited to man's ultimate religious fulfilment. For Dayananda that fulfilment comprised also a full and rich life here on earth. This is evident in his many descriptions of an ideal family life: prosperity, peace, contentment, close relations between family members are emphasized again and again. His description of the ideal society and state always included references to a prosperous economy, abolition of poverty, just distribution of wealth and education, and satisfying occupations for all men according to their abilities. Dayananda did not see any positive value in starvation, poverty, suffering, or asceticism in themselves. This humanism of the *sannyāsī* is evident even in his concept of *moksha*: to him it is a state that comprises, besides the contemplation of God, also deep interpersonal relations between the *jīvas* and their continuing interaction with cosmic life.

Such was Swami Dayananda: an individualist consumed by a passion for action, principled yet pragmatic; a man with great inner depth yet totally involved in the present and always working for a better future; a mind receptive to the rapidly changing world around him but never passively submitting to its pressures; a man consumed by the dream of a better life for all, a happiness not only religious, but also social and economic. In the light of those basic characteristics one comes to understand better the Swami's limitations and excesses, his severity, his dogmatism, his blind spots. In the final instance they are but the contrasting shadows that accentuate the basic greatness of a man who made himself into one of the giant figures of nineteenth-century India.

Notes and References

CHAPTER I
A Brahmin Youth from Kathiawar

1. Dayananda delivered fifteen lectures in Hindī in Poona, which were extensively reported in the vernacular papers, and then separately published in Marāthī and Gujarātī translations. Later a re-translation into Hindī was also published. Cf. *Poona Pravachana arthāt Upadesh-Manjari*, ed. Yudhisthir Mimamshak, Delhi, 1969, Introduction. This is the best edition now available. Lecture fifteen is autobiographical.

2. This autobiography was written in Hindī by the Swami on the invitation of Colonel Olcott of the Theosophical Society. Three instalments in an English translation were published in *The Theosophist*, vol.I, pp.9-13 (Oct.1879), pp.66-8 (Dec.1879), and vol.II, pp.24-6 (Nov.1880). Recently the Paropkarinī Sabhā at Ajmer discovered a manuscript of the original Hindī version. This was published with the English translation of *The Theosophist* in *Paropkārī*, 17, no. 5 (March 1975). This autobiography is incomplete: Dayananda's complete break with the Theosophists put an end to further instalments.

3. Cf. the introductory paragraphs to the Poona lecture and the autobiography in *The Theosophist*.

4. The first extensive treatment of this theory was proposed in Pandit Jīyālāl's *Dayānanda-Chhal-Kapat-Darpan* (Ahmedabad, 1894) and regularly repeated in works like *Swami Dayananda in the Light of Truth*, ed. Amar Singh, Lahore, 1925. In short, their story is that Dayananda was born in Rampur, Morvi, son of a poor agriculturist. His father had been declared outcast for living with a woman married to another man, belonging to the caste of Kapris, professional travelling singers and dancers who prostitute their wives. It is also suggested that Dayananda was probably the illegitimate son of that Kapri woman.

5. *AUTO*, p.1.

6. *PP*,. p.148.

7. GHII, p.301; the two versions of the will are reproduced in *PV*, pp.217-20, and pp.386-9.

8. His arguments are extensively stated in GHII, pp.362-81, and have been examined in GR, pp.27-46.

9. The *Pārthiva pūjā* is the daily ceremony of moulding a *linga* shape out of black earth, which is then consecrated, worshipped, and then de-consecrated. For details, cf. Mrs Sinclair Stevenson, *The Rites of the Twice-born*, O.U.P., 1920, pp.234-5.

10. The five great daily sacrifices of the orthodox Hindu, the worship of *brahman*, of the ancestors, of the gods, of all living creatures, and of men, had to be performed at the *sandhyās* or times of worship at sunrise, noon, and sunset. The word *Sandhyā* refers to that worship.

11. *Shivarātri*, 'the night of Shiva', is one of the most important fast days devoted to the god Shiva. For the myth, cf. B.A.Gupte, *Hindu Holidays and Ceremonials*, Calcutta, 1919, pp.214-23, and Stevenson, pp.276-7.

12. The *Purānas* are great collections of legendary and mythological stories and religious instruction dealing with the great gods of Hinduism. They were composed from the 4th cent. A.D., and eighteen are accepted as the important ones.

13. This sacrament is called the *upanayana*, the second birth which makes the boys of the three high classes, brahmins, kshatriyas, and vaishyas into 'twiceborn'. From that time on they had the right and duty to wear the sacred thread, to study the *Vedas*, and to perform the daily sacrifices.

14. The *Yajurveda*, or book of sacrificial formulae, is the third of the books of the *Veda* proper, preceded by the *Rigveda*, book of hymns, and the *Sāmaveda*, or collection of *Rigveda* verses arranged for liturgical purposes, and followed by the *Atharvaveda*, book of spells and incantations.

15. The *Nighantu*, a very ancient list of words used in the *Rigveda*.

16. The *Nirukta*, Yāska's etymological commentary on the previous work, dated the 5th cent. B.C.

17. The Pūrvamīmāmsā, 'earlier system of inquiry', was one of the six orthodox *darshanas* or systems of salvation. It originated as a system of explanation of the *Vedas*. Later it developed its own system of salvation, stressing the study of the *Vedas* and the observance of social and ritual rules. From the eighth century it began to merge with the Vedānta school of philosophy, which was called the Uttaramīmāmsā, or the later Mīmāmsā.

18. *Moksha* or *mukti*, the liberation of the spirit from the round of transmigration.

19. Āyurveda medicine is the ancient Indian science of medicine, 'the science of longevity'.

20. Cf. *Selections from the Records of the Bombay Government*, no. 37, New Series, 'Report upon the general condition, in the year 1842, of the Province of Kattywar . . .' by G. Le Grand Jacob, pp.28-9.

21. Cf. S.N.Hay, 'Jain Influences on Gandhi's early Thought', in S.N.Ray, *Gandhi, India and the World*, Melbourne, 1970, pp.29-38; A.L.Basham, 'Traditional influences on the thought of Mahatma Gandhi', in R.Kumar, *Essays on Gandhian Politics*, O.U.P., 1971, pp.17-42; H.Spodek, 'On the origins of Gandhi's Political Methodology: the Heritage of Kathiawad and Gujarat', *The Journal of Asian Studies*, 30 (1971), pp.361-72; C.D.S.Devanesen, *The Making of the Mahatma*, Orient Longman, New Delhi, 1969.

22. S.N.Hay, *Asian Ideas of East and West, Tagore and His Critics in Japan, China, and India*, Harvard U.P., 1970, p.309.

23. *Gazetteer of the Bombay Presidency*, vol.9, part 1: *Gujarat Population*, Bombay, 1891, pp.136, 541.

24. B.A.Saletore, *Main currents in the Ancient History of Gujarat*, Baroda, 1960, pp.45-7; also K.M.Munshi, *Somanatha, The Shrine Eternal*, Bombay, 1965.

25. K.M.Munshi, *Gujarat and its Literature*, Bombay, 1935, p.xxl.

26. *Gazetteer, Guj.Pop.*, p.541; *Gazetteer of the Bombay Presidency*, vol.8, *Kathiawar*, Bombay, 1884, pp.355-692.

27. GHI, p.47.

28. *Gazetteer,Guj.Pop.*, pp.31, 530, 541. For the works mentioned, cf. P.V.Kane, *History of Dharmashāstra*, vol.I, Poona, 1930, *passim*.
29. L.Renou & J.Filliozat, *L'Inde Classique*, vol.I, Paris, 1947, p.623.
30. *Gazetteer, Guj.Pop.*, p.533.
31. J.N.Farquhar, *Modern Religious Movements in India*, reprint, Delhi, 1967, p.308.
32. *Gazetteer, Guj. Pop.*, p.3.
33. Ibid., pp.4-9.
34. Ibid., p.31.
35. Ibid., p.7.
36. Ibid., p.13.
37. Ibid., p.546.
38. Ibid., 'Religious Sects', pp.530-50.
39. Ibid., p.532.
40. Ibid., p.537.
41. Ibid., p.541.
42. M.K.Gandhi, *An Autobiography, or The Story of My Experiments with Truth*, tr. from Gujarātī by Mahadev Desai, Ahmedabad, 1927, p.16.
43. *Gazetteer, Guj.Pop.*, p.70; *Gazetteer, Kathiawar*, vol.VIII,B, p.34.
44. *Selections*, p.291.
45. *Gazetteer, Kathiawar*, p.148.
46. E.Reclus, *The Universal Geography*, ed. A.H.Keane, vol.III, *India and Indochina*, London, n.d., p.167.
47. H.von Glasenapp, *Der Jainismus*, Hildersheim, 1964, pp.74-5.
48. Farquhar, pp.327-9.
49. S.N.Hay, 'Jain influences . . .', pp.31-2.
50. Cf. von Glasenapp, p.48.
51. Mrs Sinclair Stevenson. *The Heart of Jainism*, O.U.P., 1915, p.17.
52. *Gazetteer, Kathiawar*, p.147.
53. Munshi, *Gujarāt*, p.73
54. von Glasenapp. p.325
55. *Gazetteer, Guj.Pop.*, pp.111-13; A.K.Forbes. *Rās Mālā*, London. 1878, p.598.
56. von Glasenapp. p.325; V.A.Sangave, *Jaina Community, a Social Survey*, Bombay. 1959. p.267.
57. von Glasenapp. p.443
58. Ibid.. p.74.
59. For references, cf. S.N.Hay, *Asian Ideas*, pp.398-9, note 59.
60. von Glasenapp, p.444.
61. *Gazetteer, Guj. Pop.*, p.106.
62. Farquhar, pp.104, 327.
63. von Glasenapp, pp.69-72; *Rās Mālā*, pp.610-11; V.A.Sangave, pp.56-7.
64. *Gazetteer, Guj. Pop.*, pp.xxvi, 50; Stevenson, *The Rites*, pp.158, 175.
65. Ibid., p.102.
66. *Rās Mālā*, p.644; V.A.Sangave, pp.269, 361.
67. *Gazetteer, Guj. Pop.*, 49.
68. Cf. von Glasenapp. Stevenson, and *Gazetteer, Guj.Pop.*
69. *PV*, pp.219, 388.
70. *Gazetteer, Guj. Pop.*, p.115.

71. von Glasenapp, p.335; *Selections*, p.29.
72. For the use of meat in *Shrāddh*, cf. P.V.Kane, *History of Dharmashāstra*, vol.II, part II, Poona, 1941, pp.776-83; and D.R.Shastri, *Original Development of the Rituals of Ancestor Worship in India*, Calcutta, 1963, pp.161-3.
73. R.C.Majumdar (ed.), *The History and Culture of the Indian People*, vol.V, *The Struggle for Empire*, Bombay, 2nd. ed., 1966, p.78.
74. J.Jordens, 'Gandhi's Religion and the Hindu Heritage', in S.N.Ray, *Gandhi, India and the World*, Melbourne, 1970, p.48.
75. *Gazetteer, Guj. Pop.*, p.530.
76. S.N.Hay, *Asian Ideas*, p.287.
77. J.Jordens, 'Gandhi's Religion', pp.51-2; cf.R.Williams, *Jaina Yoga*, O.U.P., 1963.
78. Cf. Ch. II, p.20.
79. Cf. Ch. II, p.27.
80. Cf. references in note 21 of this chapter.
81. *Gazetteer, Kathiawar*, p.116.
82. Ibid.; Devanesan, pp.41-3; G.B.Malleson, *An Historical Sketch of the Native States of India in Subsidary Alliance with the British Government*, London, 1875, p.369.

CHAPTER II

The Search for *Moksha* Leads to Grammar

1. *AUTO*, p.6.
2. GHI, p.63.
3. *AUTO*, p.7.
4. *PP*, p.151.
5. Ibid.
6. *AUTO*, p.7.
7. Ibid.
8. GHI, p.72.
9. *AUTO*, p.7.
10. J.N.Bhattacharya, *Hindu Castes and Sects*, Calcutta, 1896, p.160.
11. Jadunath Sarkar, Sir, *A History of Dasnami Naga Sanyasis*, Allahabad, n.d., p.55.
12. H.H.Wilson, *Religious Sects of the Hindus*, 2nd ed., Calcutta, 1958, p.115.
13. G.S.Ghurye, *Indian Sadhus*, Bombay, 1953, p.94.
14. J.Sarkar, pp.66-75.
15. 'The three debts', every orthodox Hindu has to pay before his death.
16. *AUTO*, p.8.
17. J.Oman, *The Mystics, Ascetics, and Saints of India*, London, 1903, p.160.
18. Swami Agehananda Bharati, *The Ochre Robe*, London, 1961, p.154.
19. *AUTO*, p.8.
20. Ghurye, p.107.
21. Agehananda Bharati, 'Pilgrimage Sites and Indian Civilization', in J.W.Elder, ed., *Chapters in Indian Civilization*, Dubuque, 1970, vol.I, p.96.
22. Ghurye, p.124.

23. *AUTO*, p.8.
24. O.H.K.Spate, *India and Pakistan*, London, 2nd ed., 1963, p.401.
25. Cf. S.M.Bhardwaj, *Hindu Places of Pilgrimage in India*, Los Angeles, London, 1973.
26. H.G.Walton, *British Garhwal, a Gazetteer*, being volume XXXVI of the *District Gazetteers of the United Provinces of Agra and Oudh*, Allahabad, 1910, pp.55-6.
27. H.G.Walton, p.176.
28. *AUTO*, p.9.
29. *AUTO*, p.8.
30. H.G.Walton, *Dehra Dun, a Gazetteer*, being vol.I of the *District Gazetteers of the United Provinces of Agra and Oudh*, Allahabad, 1911, p.263.
31. *AUTO*, p.8.
32. Ibid., p.9.
33. Ibid., p.12.
34. Ibid.
35. Ibid., p.9.
36. H.G.Walton, *Garhwal*, p.167.
37. Ibid., p.202.
38. The Autobiography, p.9, literally says: 'after visiting Gaurikund and Bhima Gupha, I arrived at Kedar where I spent a few days'. This 'Kedar' has always been interpreted as referring to the Kedarghat in Srinagar (e.g. GHI, p.78) because of a misleading English version in the *Theosophist*. There are strong reasons, particularly now that we have the original Hindī version, to understand that Kedar here rather referred to Kedarnath. Dayananda was within eight miles of that most famous of Shaivite shrines, why would he have neglected visiting it? If he indeed was proceeding back to Srinagar, why did he go north from Guptakashi instead of south? He says he observed at Kedar the Jangama ascetics, but Kedarnath is the great centre of these ascetics. And finally, he says that from Kedar he went to roam the mountains and that, having wandered for twenty days, he ended up at Tunganath. Geographically this makes perfect sense if the starting point was Kedarnath.
39. *AUTO*, p.9.
40. Cf. R.G, Bhandarkar, *Vaisnavism, Saivism, and Minor Religious Systems*, Banaras, 1965, pp.131-40; L.Renou, *Inde Classique*, vol.I, Paris, 1947, 1300-1.
41. *AUTO*, p.9.
42. Ibid.
43. Ibid.
44. H.G.Walton, *Garhwal*, p.177.
45. *AUTO*, p.9.
46. Ibid., p.10.
47. Agehananda Bharati, 'Pilgrimage Sites', p.104.
48. *AUTO*, p.10.
49. H.G.Walton, *Garhwal*, p.182.
50. *AUTO*, p.10.
51. *PP*, p.107.
52. Ibid., p.153.
53. *AUTO*, p.11.

54. Ibid.
55. Ibid.
56. The *Theosophist* version mentions 'Sibsanda' and 'Yog-Bij', whereas the Hindī version mentions 'Shiva Sandhyā' and 'Kesharāni Sangīt'.
57. *AUTO*, p.12.
58. Ibid.
59. Ibid.
60. *Gazetteer of the Bombay Presidency*, vol.IX, part I, pp. XXXIII.
61. Cf. Agehananda Bharati, *The Tantric Tradition*, London, 1965, pp.235, 289, 301.
62. *AUTO*, p.12.
63. Ibid., p.13.
64. There has been recurrent speculation about the Swami having played an important and leading role in the Mutiny of 1856-57. Cf. App.I.
65. Quoted from Tod, frontispiece of F.S.Growse, *Mathura, a District Memoir*, 2nd ed., Allahabad, 1880.
66. Growse, p.168.
67. D.L.Drake-Brockman, *Muttra: a Gazetteer*, being vol.VII of the *District Gazetteers of the United Provinces of Agra and Oudh*, Allahabad, 1911, p.94.
68. Growse, p.48.
69. Ibid., p.72.
70. *History of the Sect of the Mahārājas or Vallabhāchāryas in Western India*, London, 1865, p.45.
71. *Mathura Gazetteer*, p.300.
72. Ibid., p.88.
73. *PP*, p.153.
74. Devendranath Mukhopadhyay, *Virjānandacharit*, trans. into Hindī by Ghasiram, Agra, 1918, p.192.
75. *GR*, pp.112-13.
76. Shri Ram Sharma 'The earliest autobiography of Swami Dayananda', *Punjab University Research Bulletin (Arts)*, vol.III (1972), p.219, n. 26.
77. *GHI*, p.97.
78. Bholanauth Chunder, *The Travels of a Hindoo*, vol.II, London, 1869, p.28.
79. *SPII*, p.488.
80. Growse, p.9.
81. B. Chunder, p.29.
82. *Mathura Gazetteer*, pp.99, 306.
83. S, p.44.
84. Bhimasena Shastri, *Virjānanda-Prakāsh*, 2nd.ed., Delhi, 1969, p.12.
85. Whether the *sūtra AJĀDYUKTI* of the *Siddhānta Kaumudī* was a genitive or a locative *Tatpurush* compound.
86. *Virjānandacharit*, p.79.
87. Ibid., pp.108-11.
88. Ibid., p.147.
89. This document is reproduced in Ibid., pp.201-15.
90. Ibid., p.119.
91. Ibid., p.162.
92. J.Robson, *Hinduism and its Relations to Christianity*, London, 1893.

93. *Bhāgavata-Khandanam*, ed. Yudhishthir Mimamshak, Sonipat, 1971.
94. GHI, p.107.
95. Ibid.
96. *PV*, p.21.
97. GHI, p.107.
98. L, pp.51,55. ·
99. Robson, p.219, and 218.
100. L, p.49.
101. GHI, p.115.
102. ·L, p.58.
103. GHI, p.115.
104. L, p.58.
105. Ibid., p.62.
106. Ibid., p.63.
107. Robson, p.217 n.
108. *Kena Upanishad*, 1, 4-5, translation R.E.Hume, *The Thirteen Principal Upanishads*, 2nd. ed., O.U.P., 1958, p.336.
109. *PP*, p.154.
110. L, p.68.
111. GHI, p.123.
112. This misnomer obviously refers to Dayananda's belief in 'the identity of the divine and the human spirits', a typically Upanishadic and Vedāntic doctrine. Cf. Robson, p.217, n. 4.
113. Robson, p.218.
114. Ibid., p.219.
115. The only book explicitly declared by Virjananda to be non-authentic in his *Sārvabhauma Sabhā* document.
116. GHI, p.118.
117. *Bhāgavata-Khandanam*, p.18.
118. At least that is what the text says: *ityāha Vishnupurāna*. But the commentator and editor Yudhisthir Mimamshak comments: *anupalabhdamūlamidam*.
119. In his appendix to the work, the editor of the *Bhāgavata-Khandanam* has shown that a number of the criticisms in this work have been reproduced practically word for word later on in the first and second editions of the *Satyārth Prakāsh*.
120. *Bhāgavata-Khandanam*, p.1.
121. GHI. p.111.
122. *Bhāgavata-Khandanam*, p.20.
123. Robson, p.219.
124. L, pp.58, 59, 68.
125. Ibid., p.65.
126. GHI, p.130.
127. Robson, p.219.
128. L, p.50; YM, p.9.
129. L, pp.53, 58; GHI, p.120.
130. L, p.131.
131. L, p.50; GHI, p.111.
132. L, p.70.

CHAPTER III

The New Reformer in the Rural Doab

1. For the details cf. L, pp.72-4.
2. Ibid., pp.74-5.
3. GHI, p.137.
4. L, p.76.
5. GHI, p.139.
6. Ibid., p.138.
7. Bhīmasena Shāstrī, *Virjānanda-Prakāsh*, Delhi, 2nd.ed., 1969, p.12.
8. L, p.112.
9. O.H.K. Spate, *India and Pakistan*, London, 2nd.ed., 1963, p.500, quoting *U.P. Gazetteer*, vol.I, Calcutta, 1908, p.8.
10. Ibid., p.505.
11. Ibid., pp.505-8.
12. H.R. Nevill, *Bulandshar: A Gazetteer*, being vol.V of the *District Gazetteers of the United Provinces of Agra and Oudh*, Allahabad, 1903, p.74.
13. E.R. Neave, *Etah: A Gazetteer*, being vol.XII of the *District Gazetteers of the United Provinces of Agra and Oudh*, Allahabad, 1911, p.78.
14. Ibid., p.223.
15. L, p.110.
16. E.R. Neave, *Farrukhabad: A Gazetteer*, being vol.IX of the *District Gazetteers of the United Provinces of Agra and Oudh*, Allahabad, 1911, p.215.
17. Cf. the appendices of the relevant District Gazetteers.
18. GHI, pp.141, 142, 158, 145, 163, 235.
19. *Bulandshar Gazetteer*, pp.172, 180.
20. Ibid., p.250.
21. Ibid., p.284.
22. *Etah Gazetteer*, 223-4.
23. Ibid., p.217.
24. *Farrukhabad Gazetteer*, p.215.
25. Ibid., p.195.
26. GHI, p.105.
27. L, p.90.
28. GR, p.129.
29. L, p.126.
30. GHI, pp.88, 125.
31. L, pp.96, 108, 120, 124. Cf. also T.J. Scott, *Missionary Life in the Villages of India*, New York, 1876, p.162.
32. L, p.95.
33. Ibid., p.113.
34. Ibid., pp.93, 97.
35. GHI, p.146.
36. S, p.58.
37. L, p.96.
38. Ibid., p.121.
39. Ibid., p.166.

started to think about this question, and at first he adhered closely to traditional guidelines. As regards ritual duties, he taught a very traditional Vedic *Sandhyā*, and advocated the reading of some *Purānas* and the wearing of the Shaivite rosary. His main preoccupation in these years was still study, and the kind of *dharma* he preached was only a tentative choice from among the many available systems of conduct. He gradually came to discourage idol worship and all sectarian devotions. In the field of personal and social morality he still adhered to the *varnāshrama dharma* as stipulated by Manu, although he was conscious of its inadequacies.

It was during the years in the Doab, when the Swami was fully engaged in the work of reform, that his ideas on *dharma* started to mature. On the ritual side he now made a complete break with all non-Vedic practices and scriptures, advocating the performance of Vedic rites only. As his study of the *Vedas* deepened he completely opted for the pure Vedic ritual, and the propagation of that ritual to the exclusion of all other rites was to remain one of the major efforts throughout his life.

But even more important were his reflections on moral action. In his daily contact with people and his efforts to guide them he had to reflect on the ethics of concrete human behaviour. The individualism that was asserting itself in his Vedic interpretation also came to the fore in this sphere; he freed himself from the tyranny of the *Shāstras* and their commentaries, and judged the morality of actions on the basis of general principles he evolved himself. Manu had been his guide so far, but now he cut loose from that norm and accepted Manu's authority only when it was in agreement with reason. Thus we find the Swami now asserting basic moral principles, such as that food can only be polluted by impure ingredients or by the immorality of its acquisition; that good works are morally superior to the mere observance of ritual rules; that charity should be directed to the needy and not to useless temple-building; that *moksha* does not come from Ganga water, but from works. His important Kanpur declaration laid great stress on the basic moral attitudes that should guide man's life.

These reflections on ethics made Dayananda reject Manu's *varnāshrama dharma*. Denying any validity to the caste divisions of Hindu society, he replaced them by his system of the four classes,

40. GHI, p.192.
41. L, pp.86, 87, 90; GHI, p.144.
42. Cf. Ch. V, p.313, n. 90.
43. GHI, p.192, and p.168, note.
44. L, p.77.
45. Ibid., p.127.
46. Ibid., pp.77, 85, 86, 96, 112, 114, 125.
47. Ibid., p.112.
48. Ibid., pp.77, 85, 148.
49. Ibid., pp.82, 85.
50. Ibid., p.86.
51. Ibid., pp.88, 90, 93, 104, 114.
52. Ibid., p.114; GHI, p.157.
53. J. Robson, *Hinduism and its Relations to Christianity*, new ed., Edinburgh and London, 1893, p.219.
54. L, pp.86, 90.
55. Ibid., p.98.
56. Ibid., p.210.
57. Ibid., p.632.
58. Article reproduced in full in Lajpat Rai, *A History of the Arya Samaj*, rev.ed. by Shri Ram Sharma, Bombay, 1967, pp.28-38.
59. L, p.632.
60. GHI, p.240.
61. Lajpat Rai, p.32, n. 4.
62. *DSS*, pp.27, 31, 32, 36.
63. Lajpat Rai, pp.37-8.
64. L, p.126.
65. Ibid., p.213.
66. Ibid.
67. GHI, p.229.
68. Cf. R. Lovett, *The History of the London Missionary Society, 1795-1895*, 2 vols., London, 1899, *passim*.
69. GHI, p.229.
70. Lajpat Rai, pp.33-4. ..
71. *DSS*, p.231.
72. Robson, pp.218-19.
73. *DSS*, p.23.
74. Lajpat Rai, p.29.
75. Ibid.
76. L, p.632.
77. Lajpat Rai, p.34.
78. *DSS*, p.35.
79. Ibid., p.226.
80. L, pp.631-2.
81. Lajpat Rai, p.33.
82. *DSS*, p.232.
83. L, p.633.
84. L, pp.90, 107, 148, 159; GHI, pp.144, 165.

85. L, pp.148, 159, 210; GHI, p.143.
86. GHI, p.199.
87. L, p.159; GHI, p.230.
88. L, p.159.
89. Ibid.
90. GR, p.128.
91. Lajpat Rai, pp.34-5.
92. L, p.129.
93. Ibid., p.97.
94. Ibid., p.634.
95. GHI, p.236.
96. L, p.619.
97. Ibid., p.132.
98. Robson, p.219.
99. GHI, pp.135-6.
100. Lajpat Rai, pp.35-6.
101. GHI, p.143.
102. L, p.87.
103. GHI, p.169.
104. Ibid., p.252.
105. Ibid., p.245.
106. Ibid., pp.137, 165, 169, 181, 190, 239, 242.
107. Ibid., p.256.
108. Ibid., p.224.
109. Ibid., p.159.
110. L, p.634.
111. Ibid., p.124.
112. GR, p.128.
113. Lajpat Rai, p.30.
114. L, p.807.
115. Ibid., p.809.
116. Ibid., pp.807, 808.
117. Ibid., pp.812, 813.
118. Ibid., pp.807, 813.
119. YM, app. no. 6.
120. Bholanauth Chunder, *The Travels of a Hindoo*, vol.I, London, 1869, pp.249, 251, 271, 275.
121. Lajpat Rai, p.30.
122. L, p.164: the *Hindu Patriot* of 17 Jan. 1870.
123. For detailed description and reports of the debate, Cf. L, pp.142-200, 613-18; DSS, pp.9-44, 211-38.
124. Cf. Ch. II, p.36.
125. Lajpat Rai, p.32.
126. GHI, p.242.
127. L, p.213.
128. Ibid., pp.91, 92, 105, 108, 137-8.
129. L, pp.89, 92, 104, 125, 128; GHI, pp.238, 240.
130. Cf. above, p.66.

131. Cf. above, p.68.
132. L, p.135.
133. Cf. Ch. VI, p.128; GHI, p.322.
134. *PVP.*, p.51; Satyavrat Samashrami's report is published in *DSS*, pp.214-38.
135. GHI, p.221.
136. Lajpat Rai, p.35.
137. L, pp.82, 148, 158; GHI, p.143.
138. GHI, p.230.
139. L, p.165.
140. GHI, p.231.
141. L, p.137.
142. Ibid., p.124.
143. GHI, p.229.
144. Scott, pp.162-7.
145. Lajpat Rai, p.38.
146. W. Crooke, *The Tribes and Castes of the North-Western Provinces and Oudh*, vol.IV, Calcutta, 1896, p.252.
147. W.L. Allison (*The Sādhs*, O.U.P., 1935) estimated their total number at a maximum of 6,000. Farrukhabad had about 2,000, Mirzapur 1,000, and the rest were scattered over villages.
148. Crooke, p.246.
149. Allison, p.69.
150. Crooke, p.248; Allison, p.54.
151. Crooke, p.248.
152. Cf. Allison, Ch. VI. Cf. Bhavāni Dās 'Account of the Religion of the Sād Sect'. Original MS in the Royal Asiatic Society Library, London.
153. Allison (p.102) quoting Chaplain Fisher's article, 'Authentic Account of the Saadhs', *C.M.S. Register of 1819*, p.24.
154. Allison, Ch. VII; Crooke, pp.248-9.
155. Crooke, pp.246-7.
156. L, p.129; GHI, pp.169, 170, 173, 174.
157. L, p.129.
158. GHI, p.180.
159. Allison, p.102.
160. Ibid., p.103.

CHAPTER IV

Calcutta: A Cauldron of New Ideas

1. GHI, pp.248-50, 255.
2. Ibid., pp.244-6, 249, 255.
3. Ibid., p.249.
4. *PVP*, pp.51-5.
5. GHI, pp.257, 259.
6. *PVP*, pp.51-5.
7. Cf. N.S.Bose, *The Indian Awakening and Bengal*, Calcutta, 1969, pp.220-5.

8. B.B.Majumdar, *History of Indian Social and Political Ideas from Rammohan to Dayananda*, Calcutta, 1967, p.116.

9. *PVP*, p.53; GHI, p.259.

10. Rajnarayan Basu, *Hindudharmer Shreshtatā*, Calcutta, 1872.

11. Meetings recorded in *PVP*, pp.51-5. For A.C.Sarkar, cf. B.B.Majumdar, pp.118-20; for R.K.Gupta, cf. N.Sinha, ed., *Freedom Movement in Bengal 1818-1904, Who's Who*, Calcutta, 1968, pp.384-6; for Bhudev Mukhopadhyay, cf. N.S.Bose, pp.151, 221.

12. Lajpat Rai, *A History of the Arya Samaj*, revised by Sri Ram Sharma, Bombay, 1967, p.38.

13. GHI, p.259.

14. We have used the English translation by Hem Chandra Sarkar, *Brahmo Dharma of Maharshi Debendranath Tagore*, Calcutta, 1928.

15. Ibid., p.10.

16. Ibid., pp.57, 66.

17. Ibid., pp.94-5.

18. Ibid., pp.167, 194.

19. Ibid., pp.199, 200, 203.

20. Ibid., p.227.

21. Ibid., pp.188-90.

22. N.S.Bose, p.277.

23. Cf. B.B.Majumdar, pp.67-72; A. Poddar, *Renaissance in Bengal, Quests and Confrontations, 1800-1860*, Simla, 1970, pp.159-64.

24. *Bhāratbarshīya Upāsak Sampradāy*, Calcutta, 1870; based on H.H.Wilson's *Hindu Sects*.

25. Roper Lethbridge, ed., *A History of the Renaissance in Bengal, Ramtanu Lahiri: Brahman and Reformer*, from the Bengālī of Pandit Shivanath Shastri, new reprint, Calcutta, 1972, p.152.

26. C.H.Heimsath, *Indian Nationalism and Hindu Social Reform*, Princeton, 1964, p.95.

27. *PVP*, p.52.

28. GHI, pp.261, 263.

29. Ibid., p.261.

30. Ibid., p.262.

31. Ibid., p.283.

32. Ibid., p.262.

33. L, p.230.

34. Ibid., p.244.

35. Ibid., p.173.

36. GHI, p.306.

37. Cf. N. Sinha, p.385; S.P.Sen, ed., *Dictionary of National Biography*, vol.III, Calcutta, 1974, p.161; A.Poddar, p.40; S.P.Sen, vol.III, p.156; N.S.Bose, pp.315-17.

38. For references, cf. Ch. IX, note 79.

39. Meeting recorded in *PVP*, p.53.

40. N.S.Bose, p.136.

41. Meeting recorded in *PVP*, p.53.

42. Cf. P.S.Basu, *Life and Works of Brahmananda Keshav*, Calcutta, 1940, pp.295-300.
43. Four meetings are recorded in *PVP*, pp.51-5.
44. B.Ghose, *Iswar Chandra Vidyasagar*, Delhi, 1965, p.123.
45. Ibid., *passim*.
46. *PVP*, p.52.
47. S.K.Sen, *History of Bengali Literature*, New Delhi, 1960, p.196.
48. Lethbridge, p.85; S.P.Sen, vol.II, Calcutta, 1973, pp.387-8.
49. N.S.Bose, p.186.
50. The articles are reproduced in C.Y.Chintamani, *Indian Social Reform*, Madras, 1901, pp.255 ff, 272 ff.
51. *PVP*, p.52.
52. S.P.Sen, vol.III, pp.160-2.
53. GHI, p.264.
54. Ibid.; S.K.Sen, p.239.
55. *PVP*, p.53.
56. Ibid.
57. Cf. N.S.Bose, pp.17, 315, 317; S.P.Sen, vol.III, pp.129-32.
58. *PVP*, p.53; Cf. N.Sinha, pp.384-6.
59. GHI, p.221.
60. *PVP*, p.52.
61. GHI, p.260.
62. Ibid., p.261.
63. Lālā Lājpat Rāi, *Maharshi Swāmī Dayānanda Saraswatī aur unkā kām*, re-edited in *Sārvadeshik*, Aug. 1967, p.181.
64. Cf. S.P.Sen, vol.III, pp.155-6.
65. Ibid., pp.129-32.
66. Cf. Lethbridge, *passim*; N.S.Bose, p.77.
67. N. Sinha, p.384.
68. S.P.Sen, vol.II, Calcutta, 1973, pp.23-5.
69. Cf. B. B.Majumdar, pp.66-72.
70. Ibid., p.120; B.C.Pal, *Memories of my life and Times*, 2nd rev. ed., Calcutta, 1973, p.222.
71. N. Sinha, pp.384-6.
72. S.P.Sen, vol.III, p.288; Lethbridge, p.131.
73. S.P.Sen, vol.I, pp.131-3.
74. *PVP*, p.54; from 1 to 21 Feb.
75. Excerpts are reproduced in S.P.Kulyar, *Swami Dayanand Saraswati, His Life and Teachings*, rev. ed., Patna, 1938, pp.96-102; also in S, p.88.
76. Excerpts in Kulyar, pp.99-102; also GHI, pp.265-8.
77. Kulyar, p.101; GHI, p.267.
78. Kulyar, p.101.
79. *PVP*, p.51.
80. He wrote *Jalpakalpataru*, a commentary on the famous medical treatise, the *Charaka Samhitā*; Cf. R.C.Majumdar (ed.), *The History and Culture of the Indian People*, vol.IX, *British Paramountcy and Indian Renaissance*, part II, Bombay, 1965, p.165.
81. L, p.230.

82. GHI, p.269.
83. Ibid., p.270.
84. It was published by Babu Harischandra at the Light Press of Banaras, and it was a Hindī translation of a previous Bengālī version, which has remained unrecovered. Cf.YM, pp.179-81.
85. GHI, p.261.
86. During this period there is only a single mention by Lekhram that the Swami recommended the remarriage of widows: L (p.642) mentions that testimony, which is repeated in GHI (p.192). This, however, is an account given by only one man, and recorded by Lekhram many years after the events. Since Dayananda revisited Kanpur several times after his visit to Calcutta, this particular testimony becomes very suspect, as the informant could easily have confused the different visits of the Swami. This statement is an isolated one and it is not confirmed by independent reports of newspapers or missionaries or by any other reports. Ghasiram's statement that the Swami preached widow-remarriage at Arrah in August '72 is even more suspect for two reasons: Ghasiram gives no source for this information, and the Swami revisited Arrah shortly after his stay in Calcutta, in June '73.
87. *SPI*, p.395.
88. GHI, p.306.
89. Ibid., p.283.
90. Ibid., p.291.
91. Satyananda, *Shrīmaddayānandaprakāsh*, Delhi, 1964, p.260.
92. GHI, pp.278, 286.
93. Ibid., pp.283-5, 298.
94. Ibid., p.294.
95. Ibid., pp.280, 290, 293, 311.
96. Ibid., pp.284, 290.
97. Ibid., p.302.
98. Ibid., pp.307-8.
99. Ibid., p.308.
100. L, p.257.
101. GHI, p.309.
102. YM, pp.21-3; *PV*, pp.20-2.
103. *PV*, pp.23-4.

CHAPTER V

The First *Satyārth Prakāsh*

1. This analysis and comparison has so far not been attempted. One of the reasons is probably the great difficulty of finding access to the very few copies of the book available, mostly kept at Arya Samaj institutions. Cf. our article 'Dayananda Sarasvati and Vedanta: A comparison of the First and Second Editions of his *Satyārth Prakāsh*', *The Indian Economic and Social History Review* (1972), pp.367-9.
2. The pamphlet war against the Arya Samaj was extensive. Just to mention

some recent important booklets: Amar Singh, *Views on Meat-Diet and Forgeries suppressing Swami Dayananda's Opinions*, Lahore, 1941; and its answer contained in H.B. Sarda, *Works of Maharshi Dayananda and Paropkarini Sabha*, Ajmer, 1942.

3. Cf. *SP* II, pp.31-8 of the introduction.
4. *PV*, p.94. Dayananda had a similar experience later with his *Sanskritavākyaprabodha*, which came from the press full of mistakes. He wrote, 'There are three reasons for this impurity. First, the haste in the composition and my bad health; second, the fact that the correction of the proofs was left to Bhimasena and that I did not see them; third, there was no able compositor at that time in the press, and there was a shortage of type.' *PV*, p.221. Dayananda was much more careful in the later years of his life.
5. *PV*, p.109.
6. *PV*, pp.329, 331. I have not found any evidence at all that would support Graham's statement (in a note on GR, pp.151-2), 'Whether for doctrinal or linguistic reasons Dayananda hastened shortly after publication to call in the whole First edition and had it burnt'. He himself gives no source at all for this extraordinary statement that is contradicted by scores of letters published in *PV*.
7. *SP* II, p.1.
8. *Vedāntidhvāntanivārana*, cf. Ch. VI, p.150, and *Vedavirruddhmatkhandana*; cf. Ch. VI, p.149.
9. Two other works were written by Dayananda in that year, the *Panchamahāyajnavidhi*, and the *Áryābhivinaya*. But the only editions now available are those revised by Dayananda years later. They cannot, therefore, be used in our argument.
10. Chapter eight contains twenty Vedic quotations, half of which are taken from the *Rigveda*.
11. *SP* I, pp.147-8. Dayananda quotes the *Chāndogya Upanishad* to show that in ancient times Manu was considered the only final authority because of his conformity with the *Vedas*.
12. *SP* I, p.78.
13. Most of these are used in the final chapter on Jainism, where different types of atheism are refuted by means of Nyāya verses.
14. *SP* I, pp.76-80.
15. Ibid., pp.25-6, and 361-71. Examples of infringement of morality are: denial of the law of *karma*, praise of immorality, contempt of *Vedas* and *rishis*.
16. Ibid, p.311.
17. Ibid., pp.315, 361.
18. Ibid, p.194.
19. Ibid., p.242-3.
20. Ibid., pp.244-6.
21. Ibid., pp.241-3.
22. Ibid., pp.249-51.
23. This does not refer to the shūdras of the time, because the society had not yet been properly structured.
24. Ibid., p.252.
25. The theory alluded to is that of the Chārvākas; cf. also note 27 of his chapter.

26. Ibid., pp.221-8.
27. The Jains were accused of atheism, and some Chārvāka verses of the *Sarvadarshanasamgraha* were attributed to them on page 402. This was resented by some Jains who went so far as to threaten to take Dayananda to court over misrepresentation. Cf. Ch. VIII, pp.190-3. Cf. also this chapter's section on Jainism, p.113.
28. Ibid., pp.403-7.
29. Ibid., pp.5, 6, 14, 17.
30. Ibid., pp.18, 240...
31. Ibid., p.21; cf. Ch.IV, p.80.
32. Ibid., pp.5, 6, 17, 19, 26.
33. Ibid., p.14, 17.
34. Ibid., p.227.
35. Ibid., pp.271-2.
36. Ibid., pp.256, 262, 245.
37. Ibid., p.257.
38. Ibid., p.295.
39. Ibid., p.83.
40. Ibid., p.257.
41. Cf. Ch. IV, p.80.
42. *SP* I, pp.259-63.
43. Ibid., pp.261, 264.
44. Ibid., p.230.
45. Ibid., p.292.
46. The inner organ includes the Sāmkhya entities *buddhi*, *manas*, *ahamkāra*, *chitta*, the five senses of knowledge, the five senses of action, and the ten *prānas*. Cf. ibid., pp.231-3, 294. Here there is also reference to the *kāran sharīr*, the causal body, which is the subtle potential of all bodies, the subtlest form of *prakriti*. From this causal body the *jīva* receives its higher faculties, knowledge, will, etc., and from the gross body it receives the sensations.
47. Ibid., p.292.
48. Ibid., p.233. Dayananda here favours the Nyāya doctrine of soul and knowledge.
49. Ibid., p.236.
50. Ibid., p.252.
51. Ibid., p.291.
52. Ibid., pp.279-82.
53. Ibid., p.263.
54. Ibid., p.284.
55. Ibid., pp.284-90. Dayananda here quotes twenty-six verses from Manu's twelfth chapter, describing the many types of births from animals to gods, according to the different admixture of the three *gunas*. The weird list goes from insects through horses and gamblers to nymphs and *rishis*. It was reproduced wholly in the second edition.
56. Ibid., p.237: '*parameshvar ne jīv race hain*'.
57. Ibid., pp.243, 253.
58. Ibid., p.280.
59. Ibid., p.373.

60. Ibid., p.394.
61. Ibid., pp.282-4.
62. Ibid., p.295.
63. Ibid., p.296.
64. Ibid., pp.294, 296.
65. Ibid., p.297.
66. Ibid., pp.225, 295.
67. Ibid., p.291.
68. Ibid., p.394.
69. Ibid., pp.308-9, 373.
70. It would be interesting to know where Dayananda got that idea from.
71. Ibid., pp.310-12. This may at first seem an extraordinary statement, but it is not really so. The idol-worshipping Jains themselves claimed their idol worship to be very ancient, going back to Mahāvīra and to the first emperor Bharata himself, who built a temple with 24 Jain statues (H. von Glasenapp, *Der Jainismus*, Hildersheim, 1964, p.386). Dayananda's strongest argument for deriving idol worship from the Jains were the claims of the Jains themselves. In fact, the Jains never objected to this statement which was repeated in several places in the second edition.
72. Ibid., pp.312-26.
73. Ibid., pp.361-71.
74. Ibid., pp.337-51.
75. Ibid., pp.216-19.
76. Ibid., pp.328-9.
77. Ibid., pp.331-2.
78. Ibid., p.329.
79. Ibid., p.333.
80. Ibid., pp.351-61.
81. Ibid., pp.29-30, 311.
82. Ibid., p.86.
83. Ibid., p.382.
84. Ibid., pp.214-15.
85. Ibid., pp.393-5; cf. Ch. IV, pp.77-9.
86. It should be remembered here that Dayananda wrote a chapter on Islam and one on Christianity which remained unpublished on account of the great pressure on the press. Cf. p.98.
87. Ibid., pp.398, 402. He mistakenly attributed some Chārvāka verses of the *Sarvadashanasamgraha* to the Jains, for which the Jains would attack him. Later on he tried very hard to inform himself better about the religion of the Jains, cf. Ch.VIII, pp.190-3.
88. Ibid., pp.398-9.
89. Ibid., pp.40-3.
90. Although the falsification by the pandits is accepted, it seems that the Swami did not completely exclude at this stage a certain form of commemoration of the deceased. Indeed, in answer to the question what the use may be of tarpan and shrāddh, it is said that the service of the dead makes people realize so much better the need of the service of the living; thinking of the dead makes people reflect on their own death and live a life of *dharma*; the recitation

of the names of the fathers, grandfathers, etc. will help people to remember their ancestry of six generations, and so avoid many quarrels that arise on the breaking-up of the patrimony. These reasons (pp.47-8) seem genuine enough and do not read like a wholesale interpolation. And they do imply that the Swami did approve of some commemoration of the dead.

91. Ibid., pp.45-7.
92. Ibid., pp.123-4.
93. Ibid., p.158. To prove his position Dayananda refers to Manu's fourth chapter.
94. Ibid., p.187.
95. Ibid., p.47.
96. Ibid., p.28.
97. Ibid., pp.38, 49.
98. Ibid., pp.49-50.
99. Ibid., p.58.
100. Ibid., pp.86-7.
101. Ibid., pp.59-60.
102. Ibid., pp.94-5, 193.
103. Ibid., p.140.
104. Ibid., p.99.
105. Ibid., pp.104-6. Dayananda reproduces from Manu a list of women to be avoided as marriage partners however rich they may be. It is a strange list including some sensible criteria, but also some very irrational ones like the exclusion of girls with too much hair on their body, redheads, and girls with ugly or inauspicious names! Ibid., pp.100-1.
106. Ibid., p.110.
107. Ibid., pp.139-40. .
108. Ibid., pp.108, 111-15, 153.
109. Ibid., pp.123-7.
110. Ibid., p.153.
111. Ibid., p.141.
112. Ibid.
113. For this cf. P.V. Kane, *History of Dharmashāstra*, vol.II, pt.I, Poona, 1941, pp.599-607.
114. *SP* I, pp.143-6, 186.
115. Ibid., pp.145-6. It is puzzling that whenever, in this context of *niyoga*, Dayananda refers to the woman, he uses the expression 'let her contract *niyoga*', whereas whenever he speaks about the man he uses the expression 'let him contract a second marriage', *dūsrā vivāh karle*. Why is the word marriage used here when Dayananda has stated quite clearly the principle that there cannot be a second marriage for either man or woman!
116. Dayananda tied up many loose ends of his *niyoga* theory in his second edition, but there was no retraction of any point, only clarification.
117. Ibid., p.141.
118. Ibid., pp.32, 91.
119. Ibid., pp.140, 150-1.
120. Ibid., p.156.
121. Ibid., p.162-3.

122. Ibid., pp.160, 172.
123. Ibid., p.161.
124. Ibid., pp.159, 163, 174.
125. Ibid., pp.165-6.
126. Ibid., pp.158, 172.
127. Ibid., pp.166-7.
128. Ibid., pp.299-301.
129. Ibid., pp.301, 306.
130. Ibid., pp.301-3.
131. Ibid., p.303.
132. Ibid. Dayananda takes great pains to show that *go-medha*, the sacrifice of kine, refers most of the time to bulls, whose economic value is less than that of cows. And when the texts unmistakably refer to a female animal, then a barren cow is meant, he says, showing again how the economic argument was foremost in his mind.
133. Ibid., pp.304-7, 213.
134. Ibid., pp.175, 177, 184, 185, 196.
135. Ibid., pp.191-3.
136. Ibid., pp.294-5.
137. Ibid., pp.197, 199.
138. Ibid., pp.202-5, 214-15.
139. There are rules about ambassadors, exposition of the *mandala*-theory and all the means of diplomacy, a section about weapons and the ethics of war. Ibid., pp.189-96.
140. Ibid., pp.219-20.
141. Ibid., p.384.
142. Ibid., pp.384-9.
143. Ibid., p.389.
144. Ibid., pp.271, 293.
145. Ibid., pp.130-8, 169, 270, 298.

CHAPTER VI

Bombay: the Foundation of the Arya Samaj

1. The Swami's detailed itinerary was as follows: Bombay, 20 Oct. – 1 Dec. '74; Surat, Broach, Ahmedabad, Rajkot, Ahmedabad, Bombay, 29 Jan. – June '75; Poona, June – Sept.; Satara, Bombay, Oct. – Dec.; Baroda, Ahmedabad, Bombay, March – April '76.
2. GHI, p.322.
3. Cf. B.N. Motiwala, *Karsondas Mulji, a biographical study*, Bombay, 1935; *Report of the Maharaj Libel Case and of the Bhattia Conspiracy Case connected with it*, Bombay Gazette Press, 1862; *History of the Sect of Mahárájas, or Vallabháchāryas in Western India*, London, 1865 (published anonymously by Karsondas Mulji); D.F. Pocock, *Mind, Body and Wealth*, Oxford, 1973.
4. *Report*, p.180. Cf also pp.77, 93, 123-4, 128, 201, 211, 213.
5. Motiwala, pp.318-19.

6. Cf. C. Dobbin, *Urban Leadership in Western India*, O.U.P., 1972, p.254; also GHI, p.322.

7. L, p.259.

8. Cf. J.N. Farquhar, *Modern Religious Movements in India*, reprint 1967, Delhi, pp.77-80.

9. Dobbin, p.251.

10. Ibid., p.247-9; also C.H. Heimsath, *Indian Nationalism and Hindu Social Reform*, Princeton, 1964, pp.147-8.

11. GHI, p.268.

12. L, p.262.

13. Ibid., p.266.

14. GHI, p.352.

15. Ibid., pp.354-7. The details are as follows. The Rajkot Samaj invited Pandit Gattulal to give a demonstration of his ability to compose Sanskrit stanzas extempore. He did so, but he made a verse about the dethronement of the Gaekwad. This was published and the political agent threatened the office-holders of the Samaj, mostly government servants, with dismissal. They were much alarmed, and the Samaj disintegrated.

16. Ibid., pp.358-61.

17. Cf. Krishnarao Bholanath, *The Life of Bholanath Sarabhai*, Bombay, 1867, pp.7-8; *PV*, pp.24, 28; L, p.286. It has been repeatedly suggested by opponents of the Arya Samaj that the Swami admitted to Bholanath that he did not himself believe in the infallibility of the *Vedas*, but held on to them for the sake of tactics: they were the rallying point of all Hindus. This contention, however, completely lacks any convincing proof. Cf., *inter alia*, *Swami Dayananda in the Light of Truth*, pub. by Amar Singh, Lahore, 1925, pp.183 ff.

18. L, p.269.

19. GHI, pp.366-7.

20. Ibid., p.367-70.

21. L, p.279. In a letter of 10 Oct. 1875 to Gopalrao Hari Deshmukh, Dayananda says that he had heard that a Poona Arya Samaj had been founded with Ranade as president and 60-70 members. I have not found that report confirmed elsewhere. *PV*, p.30.

22. Dobbin, pp.153, 162-7.

23. Cf. E. McDonald Gumperz, 'English education and social change in late nineteenth century Bombay 1858-1898', unpublished Ph.D thesis, Univ. of California, Berkeley, 1965.

24. Dobbin, p.195.

25. Ibid., p.247.

26. J. Houston, *Representative Men of Bombay*, Bombay, 1897, p.83.

27. Dobbin, p.129.

28. Indulal Yajnik, *Shyamji Krishnavarma, Life and Times of an Indian Revolutionary*, Bombay, 1950, p.9; Dobbin, p.255; GHII, p.288.

29. Yajnik, p.12.

30. *PV*, p.29.

31. L.V. Kaikani, ed., *The Speeches and Writings of Sir Narayan G. Chandavarkar*, Bombay, 1911, p.543.

32. *PV*, pp.218, 387.

33. D. Keer, *Mahatma Jotirao Phooley, Father of our Social Revolution*, Bombay, 1964, pp.137-8.

34. Cf. Keer, pp.22, 135; Heimsath, pp.23-4.

35. *PV, passim; Lokahitavādī*, 2 (1884), pp.1-37.

36. Dāmodar Sundardās, *Mumbai Āryasamājano Itihās* (Gujarātī), Bombay, 1933, pp.31-6.

37. The details are as follows: 37 Brahmins, 22 Bhatias, 17 Vanias, 6 Bhanshalis, 3 Lohanas, 2 Khatris, 1 Soni; the remainder were three Bengalis, probably Kayasths, one Prabhu and one Udasi. The last does not seem to be a proper caste name, but rather a name of sectarian adherence indicating followers of the Sikh religion. Cf. H.H. Wilson, *Religious Sects of the Hindus*, reprint, Calcutta, 1958, pp.149-51.

38. That is how we interpret the two categories that frequently recur: *sādhāran jñān*, ordinary knowledge, and *khānagī abhyās*, domestic training.

39. Fourteen had matriculated, one was a B.A., one a B.A.,LL.B., one an M.D., and the four who were actually studying at High School have been included among those of matriculation standard.

40. One member puts down 'Doctor Marāthivarg', which may refer to an indigenous medical degree.

41. 28 per cent matriculation and above, 'as against 24 per cent.

42. 37 per cent of the brahmins had little schooling; over 50 per cent of the Maratha brahmins had matriculation or above, as against only 14 per cent of the Gujaratis.

43. Of the 14 Maratha brahmins 5 were in the professions, 5 were students, 3 were in clerical service, and only one in business.

44. I am indebted for this observation to C. Dobbin.

45. Cf. Yajnik, op.cit.

46. 66 per cent as against 50 per cent.

47. 33 per cent as against 40 per cent.

48. Dāmodar Sundardās, p.40.

49. Motivala, pp.43, 194.

50. Dobbin, pp.255-6.

51. Dāmodar Sundardās, pp.2-4.

52. GHI, pp.367, 372.

53. C.Y. Chintamani, *Indian Social Reform*, Madras, 1901, pp.300-1. The other member who would become an outstanding figure was the Chitpavan brahmin Dr Moreshwar Gopal Deshmukh, president of the Bombay Arya Samaj from 1897. However, at this time he was only a medical student.

54. There were among them four teachers, three clerks, six in lower clerical services, one doctor, one editor, one translator, one printer, and one *shāstrī*.

55. It has been suggested by Dobbin (op.cit., p.256)'that the Maratha membership and leadership increased after 1876 with the enrolment of Harischandra Chintamani. However, the committee lists of 1884, 1888, 1892 and 1896 suggest this trend was short-lived. All these committees had three Maratha brahmins on them, only one of whom was an office-bearer. Moreover, these three were always the same recurring names of the three original supporters: Gopalrao Hari Deshmukh, Anna Martand Joshi, and Moreshwar Gopal Deshmukh. Cf. Dāmodar Sundardās, *passim*. The total membership list of 93 for 1894 to be found (ibid., p.35) contains scarcely half a dozen names that may belong

to Maratha brahmins, whereas the 1875 list contained fourteen.
56. Dāmodar Sundardās, *passim*.
57. Cf. App. II for these rules.
58. Rules 1 & 17.
59. Rule 14.
60. Cf. rules 8, 9, 22, 23, 26, 27.
61. Rules, 3, 4, 5, 21.
62. Rules 8 & 24.
63. Rules, 6, 16, 19, 20, 21, 28.
64. Rules, 9, 23, 24, 28, 11, 15, 12, 27.
65. GHI, p.348.
66. Dāmodar Sundardās, pp.8-9.
67. GHII, pp.383-4.
68. *PP*, Introduction.
69. Ibid., pp.126-8. In these lectures Dayananda also tidied up his muddled treatment of *niyoga* in the *Satyārth Prakāsh*. See p.152 for this aspect.
70. Dayananda has obviously tried to clarify his ideas on early Buddhism and Jainism, and their relationship, for long a problem to nineteenth century scholars. He now clearly distinguished them, but was still unsure about their historical relationship to each other. Cf., ibid., pp.134-7.
71. GHI, p.322.
72. They are fully reported in L, pp.260-2. Little is known about Swami Purnanand. We know he translated some pamphlets of Dayananda into Hindī (YM, p.65), and the volumes of letters mention him occasionally as a close collaborator of Dayananda.
73. GHI, p.327.
74. Ibid., pp.335-7.
75. Ibid., pp.364-5.
76. Ibid., p.272.
77. Reproduced in GHI, pp.272-9; and in Bawa Chajju Singh, *Life and Teachings of Swami Dayanand Saraswati*, reprint, Delhi, 1971, pt.l, pp.107-15.
78. L, p.288.
79. GHI, pp.324-5.
80. Ibid., pp.362, 370, 399. Monier-Williams reported this meeting in his *Brahmanism and Hinduism*, 4th ed., London, 1891, pp.529-31.
81. YM, pp.62-5. The pamphlet was published by the Nirnaysagar Press, Bombay, in 1875, and included a Sanskrit text by Dayananda and a Gujarātī translation by Shyamji Krishnavarma. It treats the nature of the *guru*, of idol–and temple–worship, of God and incarnation, of *māyā* and *moksha*; the conception of Krishna; a refutation of the philosophy of *Shuddhādvaita*. Later on it was translated into Hindī by Pandit Bhimasena. The pamphlet was republished by Govindram Hasanand, Delhi, n.d.
82. For these works, cf. S.N. Dasgupta, *A History of Indian Philosophy*, vol.IV, Cambridge U.P., 1961, Ch. XXXI; Karl H. Potter, *Bibliography of Indian Philosophies*, Delhi, 1970, *passim*.
83. GHI, p.330.
84. Ibid., pp.272-3.

85. YM, pp. 60-2. Dayananda wrote this pamphlet, published by the Oriental Press, Bombay, in a couple of days in rather poor Hindī. For the second edition, published during the Swami's lifetime, Munshi Samarthadan polished up the language. This pamphlet too was republished by Govindram Hasanand, Delhi, n.d.

86. Cf. Manilal C. Parekh, *Sri Swami Narayana, a gospel of Bhagwat-Dharma or God in Redemptive Action,* Rajkot, 1936; H.T. Dave, *Shree Swaminarayan,* Bombay, 1967; Pocock, pp.127-44; B.G. Desai, *Ethics of the Shiksapatri,* Baroda, 1970.

87. YM, pp.65-8. The booklet was written in Sanskrit, accompanied by a Gujarātī translation done by Shyamji Krishnavarma, and published in 1876 by the Oriental Press, Bombay. Later on it was translated into Hindī and the pamphlet was republished by Govindram Hasanand, Delhi, n.d.

88. *Sanskārvidhi,* 1st ed., p.2.

89. Ibid., title page. The book was proofread by Pandit Lakshman Shastri, subsidized by Keshavlal Nirbhayram, and published in 1877 by the Asiatic Press, Bombay.

90. Cf. R.B. Pandey, *Hindu Sanskāras, Socio-Religious study of the Hindu Sacraments,* Delhi, 1969.

91. These were the following: *Garbhādāna* (Conception), *Pumsavana* (Quickening of Male Child), *Sīmantonnayana* (Hair Parting), *Jātakarma* (Birth Ceremonies), *Nāmakarana* (Name-Giving), *Nishkramana* (First Outing), *Annaprāshana* (First Feeding), *Chūḍākarma* (Tonsure), *Karnavedha* (Piercing the Ears), *Upanayana* (Initiation), *Vedārambha* (Beginning of Vedic Study), *Samāvartana* (The End of Studentship).

92. *Sanskārvidhi,* 1st ed., pp.105, 108, 150-2.

93. Ibid., pp.132-9.

94. YM, p.9.

95. Ibid., pp.49, 52.

96. Ibid., pp.69-79. Originally the Swami planned a much larger work, with selected verses from at least the other two *Vedas,* and perhaps also from the *Brāhmanas* and the *Upanishads.* However, pressure of work prevented him from executing that plan. The work was proofread by Pandit Lakshman Sharma, subsidized by Vaijanath Atmajal, and published by the Aryamandal Press. It has been republished very often.

97. *PV* (pp.24-5) reproduces a letter of Dayananda to Gopalrao Hari Deshmukh that mentions the sending of Prarthana Samaj prayer books. *PVP* (p.60) reproduces a list of books in Dayananda's possession at the time of his death. This list includes several publications of the Samajes.

98. GHI, p.331; YM, pp.91-2.

99. The following was his itinerary: Farrukhabad, Banaras, 27 May–14 Aug. '76; Jaunpur, Ayodya, Lucknow, Shahjahanpur, Moradabad, Karnavas, Chalesar, Delhi, 17 Dec. '76–16 Jan. '77; Meerut, Saharanpur, Shahjahanpur, Ayodhya Chandapur, 22 March '77.

100. GHII, pp.1-4.

101. Ibid., pp.4-14.

102. Cf. Ch. II, pp.37-8.

102. Cf. Ch. II, pp.

104. L, p.299.
105. Published in *DSS*, pp.71-104.
106. Cf. Ziya-ul Hasan Faruqui, *The Deoband School and the demand for Pakistan*, Bombay, 1963, ch. II.
107. Cf. P.A. Parapullil, *Swami Dayananda Saraswati's Understanding and Assessment of Christianity*, Rome, 1970, pp.50-1.
108. *DSS*, pp.83,85,86,89-91,94,103.
109. YM, pp.99-100.
110. GHII, pp.7, 11.
111. *DSS*, pp.89-90.
112. *Rigvedādibhāshyabhūmikā*, ed. Y. Mimamshak, Amritsar, 1967, pp.45, 130, 131, 136, 137, 145. This is the best edition available at this time.

CHAPTER VII
Success in the Panjab

1. The exact figures are 50.12% Muslims, 36.65% Hindus, and 12.80% Sikhs. *Census of India 1891, The Punjab and its Feudatories*, pt.I, *The Report of the Census*, ed. E.D.Maclagan, Calcutta, 1892, p.88.
2. N.G.Barrier, 'The Punjab Government and Communal Politics 1870-1908', *The Journal of Asian Studies*, 27 (1968), p.528.
3. K.W.Jones, 'The Arya Samaj in the Punjab: a study of social reform and religious revivalism, 1877-1902', unpublished Ph.D thesis, Univ. of California, Berkeley, 1966, p.9. For this chapter we have benefited greatly from this excellent work.
4. Prakash Tandon, *Punjabi Century, 1857-1947*, Univ. of California Press, 1968, p 76. Cf. also P.H.M.van den Dungen, 'Changes in Status and Occupation in Nineteenth Century Punjab', in D.A.Low, *Soundings in Modern South Asian History*, A.N.U.P., 1968, p.61.
5. Jones, p.10.
6. Ibid., p.11.
7. Quotation from the *Ethnology of India*, in H.A.Rose, *A Glossary of the Tribes and Castes of the Punjab and North-West Frontier Province*, Lahore, 1911, p.506.
8. Ibid., p.507.
9. Jones, p.295.
10. K.W.Jones, 'The Bengali Elite in Post-Annexation Punjab: an example of Inter-Regional influence in 19th Century India', *The Indian Economic and Social History Review*, 3 (1966), pp.376-95.
11. Cf. H.R.Mehta, *History of the Growth and Development of western Education in the Punjab (1846-1884)*, Punjab Government Records Monograph No. 5, n.p., Punjab Government Printing, 1929.
12. van den Dungen, p.80.
13. K.W.Jones, 'Communalism in the Punjab, the Arya Samaj Contribution', *The Journal of Asian Studies*, 28 (1968), p.41.
14. Tandon, p.28.

15. van den Dungen, p.86.
16. Jones, thesis, pp.14-18.
17. Jones, 'The Bengali Elite . . .', p.377.
18. N.G.Barrier, 'The Punjab Government . . .', p.526.
19. H.M.Clark, *Robert Clark of the Punjab, Pioneer and Missionary Statesman*, London, 1907, pp.301-2.
20. E.Stock, *The History of the Church Missionary Society*, vol.III, London, 1899, p.148.
21. Jones, thesis, pp.33-6.
22. *Idem*, 'The Bengali Elite . . .', p.379.
23. *Idem*, thesis, pp.30-1.
24. Ibid, pp.31-2.
25. *Idem*, 'The Bengali Elite . . .', p.388.
26. GH II, pp.72, 81.
27. Ibid., p.18.
28. In Jullundur and in Multan 35 lectures in 36 days; in Ludhiana seven in a week; and in Firozpur eight in so many days. Cf. GHII, pp.36, 67, 72, 101.
29. Bhagat Lakshman Singh, *Autobiography*, ed. Ganda Singh, Calcutta, 1965, p.24.
30. List available in L, p.407.
31. GH II, p.63.
32. Ibid., pp.40-9.
33. Ibid., pp.64, 75, 95, 87, 90, 104.
34. Ibid., p.86.
35. Ibid., p.76.
36. Ibid., p.101.
37. Ibid., p.41.
38. L, p.362.
39. Ibid., p.389.
40. GHII, p.62.
41. Full account in L, pp.751-8. Also reproduced in *DSS*, pp. 105-17. The latter includes the Urdū introduction to the original pamphlet.
42. *DSS*, p.117.
43. L, pp.401-3.
44. Jones, thesis, p.19.
45. Stock, vol.II, p.65, vol.III, pp.150, 132; J. Richter, *History of Missions in India*, transl. Sydney H.Moore, Edinburgh, 1908, p.290; GH II, pp.42-3.
46. Jones, thesis, p.15.
47. GH II, p.66.
48. Ibid., p.40.
49. Ibid., p.72.
50. Stock, vol.III, p.144; GHII, p.105.
51. Cf. P.V.Kane, *History of Dharmashāstra*, vol.IV, Poona, 1973, pp.268-9.
52. Cf. C.H.Heimsath, *Indian Nationalism and Hindu Social Reform*, Princeton, 1964, *passim*.
53. An interesting case was that of the brahmin boy, Shripat Sheshadri Parilakar, in Bombay in the early 1850s. Cf. T.V.Parvate, *Mahadev Govind Ranade: A Biography*, Bombay, 1963, pp.35-6; and Dhananjay Keer, *Mahatma Jotirao Phooley, Father of our Social Revolution*, Bombay, 1964, pp.59-60.

322   *Dayananda Sarasvati*

54. Cf. Kane, vol.II, pt. I, Poona, 1941, pp.385-7 and 285-9. It is interesting to note that it was not until the 1920s that the *Devalasmriti*, and until the 1930s that the *vrātyastoma*, arguments were rediscovered by both the orthodox and Aryas for proving the lawfulness of *shuddhi*. Cf. GR, pp.511, 560; and G. Thursby, 'Aspects of Hindu-Muslim Relations in British India: a study of Arya Samaj activities, Government of India policies, and communal conflict in the period 1923-1928', unpublished Ph.D. dissertation, Duke University, 1972, pp.40-1.
55. GH II, p.37.
56. L, p.371.
57. C.F. Andrews, *In North India*, London, 1908, p.139: referred to in GR, p.201. Later on Kharak Singh turned back to Christianity.
58. GH II, pp.106-7.
59. Cf. Ch. IX, pp.209-10
60. *SPI*, pp.347-8.
61. GH II, p.205.
62. K.W.Jones, '*Ham Hindū nahīn*: Arya-Sikh relations, 1877-1905', *The Journal of Asian Studies*, 32 (1973), pp.457-75.
63. GH II, p.39.
64. Ibid., pp.41,49. Pandit Agnihotri became a bitter enemy of the Arya Samaj, as did the organization he founded in 1887, the Deva Samaj, of which he became the Supreme Divine Guru. Cf. J.N.Farquhar, *Modern Religious Movements in India*, Delhi, reprint, 1967, pp.173-7.
65. L, pp.358-9.
66. GHII, pp.75, 79, 95, 98.
67. Jones, 'The Bengali Elite . . . ', p.381.
68. GHII, p.53; L, p.351.
69. L, p.383.
70. GHII, pp.81, 89. Later on he became an Arya, and even president of the Gujarat Arya Samaj.
71. Jones, thesis, p.31.
72. L, p.355; GHII, p.57.
73. The full list is given in L, p.352; this list is reproduced with some additional information in Bawa Chajju Singh, *Life and Teachings of Swami Dayanand Saraswati*, 2nd ed., New Delhi, 1971, vol.I, p.156; some additional information was also gained from the list of subscribers in the first edition of the *Vedabhāshya*. Our computations take into account the total information from those three sources.
74. Cf. Mehta, p.50; J.P.Naik, *Selections from Educational Records of the Government of India*, vol.II, Delhi, 1963, pp.238. 256, 476.
75. I accept and apply here the criterion proposed by Jones in his thesis (p.84) that the Hindu honorific 'Lala' indicates a largely Khatri group. However, the total information to which this is applied is greater than that available to Jones. Cf. note 73.
76. Altogether thirty-four names are available in L, pp.362, 376, 384, 388, 390, 398, 404, 409.
77. In fact, the list mentions no less than twenty-five different Government Departments, or offices, from the Accountant General's Office to the Traffic Mana-

ger's, from the Forestry Department to the Female Penitentiary.
78. For a list of the rules see. App. III.
79. In Hindī: *Veda satvidyāon kī pustak hai.*
80. Cf. App. III.
81. A lecture by Mulraj, 'Arya Samaj and Swami Dayananda Saraswati', in Lala Jivan Das, ed., *Papers for the Thoughtful*, No.3, being Essays on Swami Dayananda Saraswati and the Arya Samaj, Lahore, 1902, pp.3, 6. For even more detailed information and the full text of several lectures of Mulraj, all supporting the case argued here, c.f. the newly published *Beginnings of Punjabi Nationalism, Autobiography of R.B.Mul Raj,* Hoshiarpur, 1975.
82. Cf. App. III.
83. Ibid., p.5.
84. Ibid., p.8.
85. Dāmodar Sundardās, *Mumbhài Āryasamājano Itihās* (Guj.), Bombay, 1933, pp.25-9.
86. Cf. App. III.
87. YM, pp.91-2.
88. GHII, pp.43-7; the Hindī version of the documents is available in L, pp.827-35, and an English version in Jivan Das, pp.45-53.
89. Jivan Das, p.53.
90. The scholars referred to are the following: Benfey, Bollenson, Bopp, Burnouf, Colebrook, Coleman, Garrett, Griffith, Langlois, Max Müller, Roth, Schlegel, Stevenson, Tawney, Weber, Wilson.
91. Jivan Das, p.49.
92. YM, p.112, republished by Govindram Hasanand, Delhi, 1952.
93. Ibid., pp.29, 31.
94. YM, pp.109-10; republished by Govindram Hasanand, Delhi, 1970.
95. Ibid., p.6.
96. L , p.353; GHII, p.99.
97. Cf. Ch. V., p.109.
98. Cf. Ch. VI, p.157.
99. Cf. A.L.Basham, *History and Doctrines of the Ājīvikas*, London, 1951; especially p.259.
100. PV, pp.87-8.
101. Ibid., p.53.
102. Ibid., pp.48, 52, 75-8, 80.
103. Ibid., pp.84, 89, 90.
104. Figures compiled from the list of subscriptions published in the first edition of the *Vedabhāshya*.
105. GHII, pp.59, 101; L, pp.386, 390.
106. Cf. Lālā Lājpat Rāi, *Maharshi Dayānand Saraswatī aur unkā kām,* reprinted in *Sārvadeshik,* 20 Aug. 1967, pp.109-10.
107. Jones, thesis, p.31.
108. N.G.Barrier, 'The Arya Samaj and Congress Politics in the Punjab, 1894-1908', *The Journal of Asian Studies,* 26 (1967), p.366.
109. Jones, thesis, pp.295-6.

CHAPTER VIII

The Final Years: The Founder and the Samaj

1. For a detailed chronology, see. *PVP*, pp.41-51; S, pp.341-3.
2. GH II, p.120.
3. *PV*, p.135; Bawa Chajju Singh, *Life and Teachings of Swami Dayananda*, New Delhi, 1971, vol.II, p.17.
4. GH II, p.168.
5. *PV*, p.139.
6. GH II, p.176.
7. Ibid.; *PV*, p.158.
8. GH II, pp.200, 210, 220, 221, 234, 237; *PV*, p.168.
9. GH II, p.183.
10. Ibid., p.152.
11. L, p.561.
12. GH II, p.266.
13. Ibid., pp.114-17; full account with documents, L, pp.758-86, and 787-95.
14. GH II, pp.121-8.
15. Ibid., pp.165-6.
16. Ibid., p.170.
17. Ibid., pp.193-8.
18. Ibid., p.253; L, p.556.
19. GH II, p.268.
20. Full report in L, pp.737-45; *DSS*, pp.118-25; and also *The Theosophist*, 2 (1880), pp.98-100.
21. Cf. Ch. III, p.72.
22. Cf. Ch. VI, p.156.
23. Full report in L, pp.479-502, and *DSS*, pp.129-71.
24. GH II, pp.190, 199.
25. Ibid., pp.201-7; L, pp.522-7.
26. GH II, p.236; YM, pp.129-33; *PV*, pp.186-7. The available edition, of the *Bhramocchedan* is by Pandit Jagatkumar Shastri, Delhi, 1952. The Raja's account was also published: Rājā Shivaprasād Sitāre Hind, *Nivedan*, Banaras, 1882, and *Dūsrā vā Pichlā Nivedan*, Banaras, n.d.
27. *PVP*, p.68.
28. Full account in L, pp.730-6, and *DSS*, pp.172-86.
29. Cf. Ch. X, p.229.
30. Full report in L, pp.795-804, and *DSS*, pp.191-205.
31. Full report in L, pp.702-29. Thakurdas himself also published the documents: Thākurdās Mūlrāj, *Dayānanda-Saraswatī-mukh-chapetikā*, Bombay, 1882.
32. L, p.712; Thākurdās, p.20.
33. *Sarvadarshanasamgraha*, Ch. I.
34. M I, pp.253-64.
35. Ibid., p.264.
36. *PVP*, App. no. 7.
37. L, pp.714-16.

38. Cf. W. Schubring, *The Doctrine of the Jains*, tr. by W. Beurlen, Banaras, 1962, pp.1-6.
39. C.J.Bleeker and G. Widengren, *Historia Religionum*, vol.II, *Religions of the Present*, 'Jainism' by Carlo Della Casa, Leiden, 1971, p.370.
40. L, p.717.
41. *PVP*, App. no. 7.
42. MI, p.265.
43. To determine the caste we have to depend on the names. We have described our critera in Chapter VII,note 75.In this analysis we assume that names prefixed with Pandit refer to brahmins, and those prefixed with Babu or Munshi refer to kayasths. Most names are preceded by some prefix, which allows for a reasonably probable assumption of the caste, especially when combined with the name itself.
44. L, pp.448-9. We use the same criteria as above.
45. Branches were established at Roorkee, Meerut, Delhi, Dehra Dun, Moradabad, *Badaun, Shahjahanpur, Farrukhabad* (2), Kanpur, *Mirzapur, Danapur,* Banaras, Lucknow, Mainpuri, Agra (2). Cf.GH.II., *passim*. The towns in italics are those where the branches were established before the Swami's arrival.
46. GH II, pp.120, 176.
47. Ibid., p.210.
48. Ibid., p.176.
49. Ibid., pp.149, 172.
50. M I, p.371.
51. GH II, p.250.
52. Indra Vidyāvāchaspati, *Āryasamāj kā Itihās*, vol.I, Delhi, 1957, p.158.
53. A complete list of branches has not yet come to hand. These estimates are calculated from the names of sixty branches collated from the biographies, the letters, and contemporary journals.
54. Cf. Chs. VI, VII.
55. GH II, p.120.
56. Ibid., p.155.
57. Ibid., p.260.
58. PV, pp.462, 466; MI, pp.177-9, 194-5.
59. PV, p.327.
60. *The Arya Magazine*, ed. R.C.Bary, Lahore, vol.I (1882-3), p.85.
61. Ibid., p.86.
62. PV, pp.211-12.
63. Ibid., pp.216, 224-7.
64. Ibid., pp.280, 291, 304, 326.
65. Ibid., p.333.
66. Ibid., p.328.
67. Ibid., pp.335, 336, 344, 352, 353, 355, 356, 376.
68. For details about Munshi Indramani, cf. Ch. IX, pp.217-18.
69. M I, p.167.
70. Ibid., p.311.
71. Ibid., p.61.
72. Ibid., pp.159, 192.
73. PV, p.204.

74. Dāmodar Sundardās, *Mumbai Āryasamājano Itihās (Guj.)* Bombay, 1933, p.26; the Swami's speech is reproduced in Hindī.
75. Ibid., pp.25 ff.; GH II, p.292.
76. GH II, p.152.
77. Cf. above, p.193.
78. Cf. Ch. VII, p.178.
79. *PV*, p.161; Chajju Singh II, p.33.
80. *PV*, p.333.
81. *The Arya Magazine* I (1882-3), pp.136, 180.
82. K. W. Jones, 'The Arya Samaj in the Panjab', unpublished Ph.D. thesis, Univ. of Calif., Berkeley, 1966, p.83.
83. M I, pp.180-1, 192, 196-9.
84. Most of this information was collected by K.W.Jones, 'Sources of Arya Samaj History', *The Indian Archives*, 18 (1969), pp.20-36.
85. *Hamarī Deshī Zubān*, Lahore, 1882.
86. Cf. Ch. VII, p.178.
87. *Sada-e-Haqq*, Lahore, 1882.
88. Y.M., pp.100-1.
89. *Hindi versus Urdu*, Lahore, 1882.
90. Lahore, 1879.
91. *Vedon ton Budhan dā Dharm Sambandh*, Amritsar, 1878; & *Dharm Vichar*, Lahore, 1882.
92. *Reply to the Extra Supplement to the Theosophist for July 1882*, n.p., 1882.
93. *PV*, pp.438, 446.
94. *PV.*, p.435, note 4. The book was entitled *Self-Contradictions of the Bible*, probably by W.H.Burr, and its Hindī translation was published by Nandkishor Singh. Cf. also YM, pp.41-2.
95. GH II, pp.306, 319; MI, pp.1-39, 307.
96. GH II, p.305.
97. MI, p.37.
98. Ibid., pp.103-4.
99. *PV*, p.472.
100. GH II, p.323.
101. *PV*, p.472.
102. Ibid., p.132.
103. Ibid., p.150.
104. M I, pp.180-9, 192, 196-9.
105. Ibid., pp.340-64.
106. Ibid., p.37.
107. GH II, p.237.
108. Ibid., p.310.
109. Ibid., p.120.
110. Ibid., p.153.
111. Ibid., p.171
112. Ibid., p.228.
113. L, pp.516-18.
114. Ibid., p.900.
115. GH II, pp.288-9.

CHAPTER IX

The Final Years: The Wider World of Hinduism

1. Full list in L, pp.444-9.
2. GH II, p.132.
3. Cf. Ch. II, p.24.
4. Cf. Ch. III, p.46.
5. Full text in *PV*, pp.127-30.
6. Cf. Ch. VIII, p.204.
7. Most documents have been gathered in L, pp.854-905; GH II, pp.382-416; S, pp.519-951. All the Swami's letters and announcements can be found in *PV*, *passim*. For a continuous story, cf. Shyam Sundarlal, *Treatise on the Arya Samaj and the Theosophical Society as once Amalgamated Bodies*, Mainpuri, 1925; S.R. Sharma, 'Swami Dayanand and the Theosophical Society', *Purba, Punjab University Research Bulletin (Arts)*, 4 (1973), pp.117-35. The Theosophists' version can be found in *The Theosophist*, July 1882, 'Extra Supplement'.
8. Cf. S, pp.522-3.
9. Sanskrit text: *PV*, pp.90-1; Hindī text: L, pp.896-7. The letter was dated 21 April, and the Sanskrit version was accompanied by an English translation.
10. Cf. Sharma, pp.118, 124
11. *PV*, p.207.
12. S, p.525.
13. Ibid., pp.529-30.
14. Full text in Sanskrit, *PV*, pp. 95-102; Hindī in L, pp.897-904; extracts in English, S, pp.530-4.
15. Cf. Joan Leopold, 'The Aryan Theory of Race', *The Indian Economic and Social History Review*, 7 (1970), p.291.
16. *PV*, p.207.
17. GH II, pp.172-3.
18. *PV*, pp.139, 140.
19. Ibid., p.143.
20. Ibid., p.144.
21. Ibid., p.152.
22. Ibid., pp.153-5.
23. GH II, pp.223-4; L, p.187
24. *PV*, p.207.
25. Ibid., p.209.
26. Aug. 1880 at Meerut, cf. *PV*, p.218.
27. Sharma, p.121.
28. GH II, pp.245-7.
29. Ibid., p.246.
30. S, pp.539-41.
31. S, pp.541-6 in English; Hindī: *PV*, pp.254-8.
32. S, pp.549-51.
33. S, pp.552-4 in English; Hindī: *PV*, pp.282-3.
34. GH II, p.408.

35. *PV*, pp.316-17.
36. GH II, p.409.
37. Full text in Hindī: *PV*, pp.319-23; English: S, pp.556-60. Colonel Olcott wrote an answer to this document in the July 1882 issue of *The Theosophist* as an 'Extra Supplement'. This was answered in detail by Pandit Umrao Singh in a pamphlet, 'Reply to the Extra Supplement to the Theosophist for July 1882', Oct. 1882, Roorkee.
38. Cf. J.N. Farquhar, *Modern Religious Movements in India*, Delhi, 1967 (reprint), pp.232-67.
39. GH II, p.209.
40. Ibid., p.289.
41. For the early history of the Vedic Press, cf. YM, Appendices, pp.92-4.
42. *PV*, p.140.
43. GH II, p.226.
44. Cf. YM, *loc.cit.*; *PV*, pp.469-70.
45. *PV*, p.280.
46. Ibid. p.413; also pp.415, 416, 426-7, 432.
47. MI, pp.416, 418.
48. Cf. Ch. VIII, p.185.
49. Full text of will, *PV*, pp.217-20.
50. Ibid., p.204.
51. Full text, *PV*, pp.386-9.
52. For details, cf. GH II, App. III, pp.417-42; *PV*, *passim*, but especially pp.479-83, 401-4, for Dayananda's published announcements of the affair; Von Jürgen Lütt, *Hindu-Nationalismus in Uttar Pradeś 1867-1900*, Stuttgart, 1970, pp.120-1.
53. Full report in L, pp.671-701.
54. L, p.672; GH II, p.259.
55. Cf. Ch. VII, p.178.
56. GH II, p.259.
57. *PV*, p.285.
58. GH II, p.128.
59. Ibid, p.290.
60. *SPI*, pp.212, 389.
61. *PP*, p.75.
62. Lütt, p.134.
63. GH II, p.200.
64. Lütt, p.139.
65. YM, pp.136-8. The pamphlet is available in the edition of Govindram Hasanand, Delhi, 1969.
66. Expression used by the Swami in his article, 'The killing of cows and other useful Beasts', *The Theosophist* 2 (1880), p.52.
67. *PV*, p.313.
68. M II, p.17; *PV*, p.341.
69. MI, p.140.
70. Ibid., p.269.
71. *PV*, p.352.
72. Ibid, p.451.

Notes and References 329

73. Cf. G. Thursby, 'Aspects of Hindu-Muslim Relations in British India', unpublished Ph.D. thesis, Duke University, 1972, p.170.
74. Lütt, pp.139-41.
75. GH II, pp.288-9.
76. MI, pp.66-8.
77. Cf. P.R. Brass, *Language, Religion and Politics in North India*, Cambridge U.P., pp.129-31; Lütt, pp.40-6; J.Das Gupta, *Language Conflict and National Development*, Univ. of Calif. Press, 1970, p.84.
78. Lütt, pp.44, 47.
79. Lütt, pp.41, 42, 44, 47; Das Gupta, pp.83-4; B.B. Majumdar, *History of Indian Social and Political Ideas*, Calcutta, 1967, p.109.
80. Das Gupta, p.103; Lütt, p.50.
81. Cf. Ch. IV, pp.82-3.
82. GH II, p.307.
83. Cf. Ch. IV, p.83.
84. *PV*, p.81.
85. Ibid., p.155.
86. GH II, p.163.
87. Cf. MI, MII, *passim*.
88. GH II, p.302; *PV*, p.464.
89. *PVP*, p.71.
90. *PV*, pp.318, 353, 355, 357.
91. L.N. Gupta, *Hindī Bhāshā aur Sāhitya ko Āryasamāj kī den*, Lucknow Univ., 1971, p.254.
92. Lütt, p.50, mentions that a total of 118 lists of signatures were submitted.
93. They are reproduced in *PVP*, pp.22-30.
94. Cf. Bhāī Paramānand, *Hindu Sangathan*, Lahore, 1936.
95. MI, pp.117, 159, 192.

CHAPTER X

The Ultimate Effort: The Princes of Rajputana

1. Cf. Ch. I.
2. Cf. Ch. II pp.36-7
3. Cf. Ch. II, p.42.
4. Cf. Ch. VI, pp.132, 153
5. Cf. Ch. II, p.44, Ch. IV, p.95-6; Ch. VII, p.177; Ch. VIII, p.197; Ch. IX, pp.222, 225.
6. GH II, p.307.
7. *PV*, p.324.
8. Ibid., p.332.
9. GH II, p.143; L, p.582.
10. GH II, pp.269-76.
11. Cf. Ch. VIII, p.189.
12. GH II, p.275; L, pp.736-7.
13. GH II, pp.275-6.

14. Letters in M II, pp.73-85.
15. GH II, pp.277-9.
16. Ibid., p.279.
17. Ibid., pp.280-1.
18. Cf. *Rajputana Gazetteers*, vol.II A, 'The Mewar Residency', text compiled by K.D.Erskine, Ajmer, 1908, p.28; S, pp.286-7.
19. GH II, pp.282-4; about the two councillors, cf. *PVP*, pp.69-70. Vishnulal was author of a dozen works, and Shyamaldas wrote in Hindī a famous history of Udaipur in four volumes called *Vīra-Vinod*.
20. J. Tod, *Annals and Antiquities of Rajasthan*, ed. W. Crooke, vol.III, London, 1920, p.755.
21. GH II, p.284.
22. L, p.594.
23. S, pp.287-8.
24. GH II, p.284.
25. Ibid., pp.299.
26. *PV*, pp.375, 379, 390.
27. Cf. Ch. VIII. pp.189-90
28. L, p.597.
29. GH II, p.301.
30. Ibid., p.304.
31. L, p.600.
32. *PV*, p.449; GH II, p.303.
33. GH II, p.303.
34. L, p.600.
35. Ibid., p.599.
36. GH II, p.302.
37. Ibid.
38. Ibid.; also *PV*, p.390.
39. *PV*., pp.449-52; also M II, pp.135-43.
40. *PV*, p.450.
41. Ibid.
42. *PV*, pp.451-2.
43. *PV*, p.390, also pp.375, 379, 392.
44. *PV*, p.387.
45. GH II, p.316; *PV*, p.392.
46. Cf. J. Tod, vol.I, p.198.
47. M II, pp.17-18.
48. *PVP*, p.69.
49. From 6 March to 23 May 1883.
50. GH II, pp.318-23.
51. *PV*, p.436-7; M II, pp.24, 34, 36.
52. *PV*, p.410.
53. *Rajputana Gazetteers*, vol.III A, 'The Western Rajputana States Residency and the Bikaner Agency,', text compiled by K.D.Erskine, Allahabad, 1909, pp.74-6; *PVP*, pp.70, 71.
54. GH II, p.328.
55. All reproduced in *PV*, *passim*; also M II, pp.89-104.

56. GH II, pp.325-6.
57. *PV*, p.436.
58. Ibid., p.430.
59. Ibid., p.438.
60. Ibid., pp.443-5.
61. Ibid., p.447.
62. Ibid., pp.463-5.
63. Ibid., p.465.
64. GH II, pp.329-30.
65. *PV*, p.468.
66. *PVP*, p.71.
67. GH II, p.343.
68. *PV*, p.426.
69. GH II, p.330.
70. Ibid., p.328.
71. Ibid., pp.328, 329, 332.
72. *PV*, pp.472, 473.
73. Ibid., pp.476, 481.
74. Ibid., pp.482.
75. Cf. GHII, pp.336-54; L, pp.913-25.
76. Cf. *Lokahitavādī*, Jan.-Feb.1884, pp.3-4; Gopalrao Hari, *Dayānanda Digvijayārk*, re-edited by B. Bharatiya, Delhi, 1974.

CHAPTER XI

The Final Years: The Last Legacy in Print

1. YM, pp.127-8. The booklet has been republished recently by the Ramlal Kapur Trust, Amritsar, 1970.
2. YM, pp.114-20. Part of the manuscript has been edited by Pandit Raghuvir, and published at Ajmer, vol.I in 1927, and vol.II in 1949.
3. Ibid., pp.124-7. Also republished by the Ramlal Kapur Trust, Amritsar, 1969.
4. Ibid., pp.141-54. All parts have been republished by the Vedic Yantralay, Ajmer, from 1945, and are continuously being reprinted.
5. Ibid., p.146.
6. *PV*, p.390.
7. YM, pp.128-9; *PV*, p.358.
8. Cf. YM, pp.190-2; also *PVP*, pp.56-64
9. YM, pp.192-4.
10. Ibid., pp.85-6.
11. *Sanskārvidhi*, pp.30, 76. Our references are to the excellent edition prepared by Y.Mimamshak, and published at Sonipat, 1971.
12. Ibid., p.82.
13. *Satyārthprakāsh*, ed. Y.Mimamshak, Sonipat, 1972. Introduction, pp.31-8, refers to all the letters that prove that statement. We use this edition throughout, as it is by far the best so far published, endeavouring to produce a version

text-critically accurate. We refer to this edition by the letters *SP II*, and references to the first edition of the work are referred to by the letters *SP I*.
14. These works are listed in App. VI of *SP II*, pp.967-74.
15. *SP II*, pp.300-2.
16. *SP I*, pp.403-7.
17. *SP II*, pp.316-22.
18. Cf. Ch. VI, p.157.
19. Cf. Ch. VII, p.179.
20. *SP II*, pp.329-30. *Pravāh* means literally 'flow', 'current', and hence 'waves', 'continuous movement'. Since the continuous 'flow' of evolution and dissolution entails alternation, the most appropriate translation here is 'rhythm'.
21. Ibid., p.327.
22. Ibid., pp.309-10.
23. Ibid., pp.310-13.
24. *SP II, passim* in Chs. VII, VIII, IX, & X.
25. Ibid., p.430.
26. *SP I*, pp.80-3, 271-2.
27. *SP II*, p.107.
28. Ibid., p.325.
29. For a more detailed treatment of this topic, cf. J. Jordens, 'Dayananda Saraswati and Vedanta: a comparison of the first and second editions of his *Satyarth Prakash*', *The Indian Economic and Social History Review*, 9 (1972), pp.367-79.
30. *SP I*, pp.282-4, & 373.
31. *SP II*, p.332; cf. also *Bhūmikā*, p.26.
32. Manu I, 69-73.
33. *SP II*, pp.329-34.
34. Cf. Ch. V, pp.109-10.
35. Cf. Ch. VII, p.179.
36. *SP II*, pp.356-7.
37. Ibid., pp.350-5.
38. *SP I*, pp.123, 158, 166, 167, 228, 285, 296.
39. *SP II*, p.191.
40. Ibid., pp.332, 358, 658.
41. Ibid., p.659.
42. Ibid., pp.659-62, 638-40, 332, 350-8, 579-80.
43. Ibid., p.351.
44. Ibid., p.360.
45. Ibid., p.873.
46. Ibid., pp.659-60.
47. Ibid., p.372.
48. Ibid., p.365.
49. Ibid., pp.271, 282, 365.
50. Ibid., p.272.
51. Ibid., p.302.
52. Ibid., p.357.
53. Ibid., pp.780, 828, 881.
54. Ibid., p.880.

55. Ibid., pp.579, 876, 897.
56. Ibid., p.260.
57. Ibid., p.885.
58. Ibid., pp.345-9, 430-40.
59. Ibid., p.646.
60. Ibid., p.486.
61. Ibid., p.470.
62. Ibid., pp.537, 548.
63. Ibid., p.679.
64. Ibid., p.584.
65. Ibid., pp.581, 646.
66. Ibid., pp.407-12.
67. Ibid., pp.489-91, 510-14.
68. Ibid., pp.572-83.
69. Ibid., p.582.
70. L, pp.516-18.
71. *SP II*, pp.585-6.
72. Ibid., pp.592-9.
73. Ibid., p.58.
74. *SP I*, p.50.
75. *SP II*, p.110.
76. Ibid., p.111-12.
77. Cf. Ch. VI, p.152.
78. Cf. Ch. VIII, p.197.
79. *SP II*, pp.163-72.
80. Ibid., p.175.
81. Ibid.
82. Ibid., p.191.
83. Ibid., Ch. VI.
84. Ibid., p.207.
85. Ibid., pp.203-4; Manu VII, 4-7.
86. *SP I*, p.384.
87. *SP II*, pp.334-5.
88. Ibid., p.391.
89. Ibid., p.397.
90. Ibid., p.470.
91. Ibid., pp.7-8.
92. MI, pp.256-64.
93. *SP II*, p.681.
94. Ibid., p.719.
95. Cf. J. Richter, *Indische Missionsgeschichte*, Gütersloh, 1906, pp.280-2.
96. *SP II*, p.9.
97. Ibid., pp.779, 783, 799.
98. Ibid., p.719.
99. Ibid., pp.761, 768, 770, 772, 797, 799, 800, 802, 807, 811.
100. One example of this type of literature is J.M.Mitchell, *Letters to Indian Youth*, Bombay, 1857. This was the third edition.
101. Cf. T.R.Metcalf, *The Aftermath of Revolt*, Princeton U.P., 1964, Ch. VIII.

102. *SP II*, p.755.
103. Ibid., p.780.
104. Ibid., p.756.
105. Ibid., p.759.
106. Ibid., p.775.
107. Ibid., p.804.
108. Cf. this chapter, p.248.
109. YM, pp.103-5.
110. Cf. Ch. IV, p.91.
111. Cf. Ch. VII, pp.177
112. For examples of Dayananda's interpretation of names of historical persons, cf. his commentary on *Rigveda* 6.16, and 6.20; for geographical names cf. *Rigveda* 4.22, and 5.52.
113. Cf. the pamphlet by Pandit M.Nyayaratna, *Pandit Dayananda Sarasvati's Veda Bhāshya*, Calcutta, 1876; the comments of Western orientalists in L, pp.827-35; and the account of the Calcutta Hindu Council, Ch. IX, pp.218-19.
114. Cf. Dayananda's interpretation of the Vritra myth, *Rigveda* 1.32. Cf. also his comments on the Gotama-Ahalyā and other myths in his announcement published in *PV*, pp.33-9.
115. Cf. Dayananda's commentary on *Rigveda* 1.119.10.
116. Ibid., 1.34 & 1.85.
117. Cf. *inter alia*, Renou's comment in L.Renou, *The Destiny of the Veda in India*, tr. by Dev Raj Chandra, Delhi, 1965, p.4.

CHAPTER XII

A Dynamic View of Swami Dayananda

1. Cross-references are not given in this concluding chapter because they would run into the hundreds and unnecessarily overload the text. The index is a sure guide to the reference required.
2. Cf. *SPII*, p.313; *DSS*, pp.88-9.
3. Constantin Regamey has proposed the very interesting hypothesis that Dayananda may have derived his activistic philosophy from Virjananda, who may have taught him the activistic theories of the Nairukta grammarians. There is no evidence whatsoever that Virjananda knew or taught that system. An even more compelling argument against this attractive theory is that, as we have shown, Dayananda's activistic theory of man took many years to evolve after he left his *guru*. Cf. C. Regamey, 'The Origin of the Activistic Trends in the Doctrine of Svāmī Dayānand Sarasvatī', in R.N. Dandekar, ed., *Proceedings of the Twenty-sixth Congress of Orientalists*, vol.III, pt. I, Poona, 1969, pp.452-4.

Appendices

Appendix I. *Swami Dayananda and the Sepoy Mutiny*

The Swami's autobiographical fragments tell us very little about the period 1857-60: he travelled towards the sources of the Narmada in the fearful territory of the Vindhya range, and finally ended up in Mathura. It was during this period that the Sepoy Mutiny occurred. Some devotees of the Swami, intent on exalting his patriotism, found in these years a vacuum that cried out to be filled in. The earliest suggestion that Dayananda played an important role in the Mutiny appears to have been contained in Swami Vedananda's *Virjānanda-Charit*, a work I have been unable to find.

Although that suggestion was repeated from time to time, it seems that it is only in recent years that major attempts have been made to claim such a revolutionary role for the Swami. Satyapriya Shastri's work *Bhāratīya Swātantrya Sangrām men Ārya Samāj kā Yogdān*, published in Jullundur probably in 1970, was the first attempt in book-form I have come across. This writer fails to produce even one solid historical argument for his assertions. The next publication in book-form was Pindidas Jnani's *1857 ke Swātantrya Sangrām men Swārājya Pravartak Maharshi Dayānanda Saraswatī kā kriyātmak Yogdān*, Amritsar and Delhi, 1971. This work recounts in great detail how Dayananda met the leaders of the Mutiny at the Hardwar Kumbh Melā in 1855, and planned the uprising with them. Occurrences and conversations are boldly described without any supporting evidence. The whole episode reads like a fairy-tale, but is presented as historical fact.

In 1972 a new publication caused quite a stir in Arya Samaj circles: *Yogī kā Ātma-Charitra (39 varsh kī ajnāt jīvanī)*, edited by Pandit Dinbandhu Shastri and Swami Saccidananda Yogi, and published in Rohtak by the Pātanjal Yog Sādhanā Sangh. This voluminous work of some five hundred pages set out to prove once and for all the historicity of the story of Dayananda's involvement in the Mutiny by putting it in the mouth of the Swami himself, in 'the long-lost autobiography of Swami Dayananda Saraswati'. The editors' explanation is as follows. During his stay in Calcutta in 1872-3, the Swami related the real story of his life to a group of twelve Bengalis, who each wrote down a fragment of the tale. These scribes had to promise not to divulge these facts during the Swami's lifetime. However, these manuscripts were not revealed after the Swami's death on account of the antagonism that had arisen in the meantime between the Brahmos and the Aryas. After a long search Dinbandhu recovered the fragments from twelve Bengali families, and in his book he gave the Hindī translation of this long-lost autobiography.

Dinbandhu went much further than his predecessors. Not only did he present in detail the Swami's involvement in the Mutiny; he also described a fabulous journey made by the Swami through the Himalayas, part of Tibet, and to the southernmost point of India, Kanyakumari; and he detailed at length the stupendous‑ yogic accomplishments of the Swami. This 'autobiography' is surrounded by some two-hundred-and-fifty pages of introductions and appendices, which desperately try in a jumbled way to prove the authenticity of the document.

The document was quickly denounced as a fake by serious Arya Samaj historians such as B. Bharatiya and Shri Ram Sharma, who wrote articles revealing numerous historical and other impossibilities (Cf., e.g. *Paropkārī*, June '72, July '72, Oct. '73, Nov. '73). It is unnecessary to go into all the details here. I have myself applied the following three simple tests, the results of which discredit different and vital parts of Dinbandhu's work.

The 'autobiography' contains the record of a visit made by Dayananda to the ancient monastery of Hemis in Ladakh; there he found a Tibetan manuscript giving a version of the life of Jesus in Pālī. This is reproduced in the 'autobiography' in a Hindī translation. In my article '*Yogī kā Ātmacharitra*: another nail in the coffin of a fake autobiography' (*Paropkārī*, 16 March 1974, pp.15-17), I have conclusively demonstrated that this account of 'the life of Jesus' is dependent in detail on the work of Nicholas Notovitch (*The Unknown Life of Christ*, translated from the French by Violet Crispe London, 1895). It follows that the autobiography cannot have been dictated by Dayananda in 1873, over twenty years before the publication of Notovitch's work.

Another aspect of Dinbandhu's work considerably intrigued me: the list of Bengalis who had written down the autobiographical fragments, and the list of Bengalis from whom Dinbandhu recovered the manuscripts. I did not have the time nor the inclination to check this information in detail. However, during a visit to Calcutta I showed this list to D.K. Vishwas of the Sadharan Brahmo Samaj. He recognized the name of one person who was supposed to have been custodian of one of the fragments, and who had died. D.K. Vishwas told me that this man was his most intimate friend and associate, and that he had taken care of all his papers after his death; never had he hinted that he was in possession of such a document. I was able to establish that much on a short rushed visit to Calcutta. One wonders if any of the other names mentioned would stand up to close scrutiny.

A third test was carried out by one of my students, R. Thwaytes, in his B.A. Hons. thesis, 'Dayananda Saraswati and the Sepoy Mutiny of 1857' (A.N.U., Canberra, 1973). He carefully studied the possibility of the presence at Hardwar of the Mutiny leaders who visited the Swami there according to the 'autobiography'. He clearly established, among other things, that Azimulla Khan, who was recorded as having visited the Swami at Hardwar in early 1855, was in fact in July 1855 still in the Crimea, on his way back to India from England, and could not have been back in India until the end of that year. These three instances alone disprove the authenticity of the 'autobiography'. Many additional arguments have been presented by the scholars previously mentioned, showing that in many instances the documents contradict what we know from elsewhere about the Swami. The many pages about the Swami's yogic accomplishments read like the translation of an obscure and dry commentary on the *Yoga-Sūtras* and completely lack the impression of being personal experiences. The description of the Swami's Himalayan journey shows all the signs of having been copied from an old travel book. The work is a wholesale fabrication; even if Dinbandhu did discover some Bengali fragments, then these were products of somebody's fertile imagination. Although some Aryas still believe in its authenticity, it is gratifying to know that most have accepted the arguments against it brought forward by their own scholars. The book is a vain and pitiful attempt to replace the eminently real figure of the Swami by a hollow myth.

Appendix II. *The Bombay rules of the Arya Samaj*
(My translation of the Hindī rules as recorded in L, pp.270-2.)

1. The Arya Samaj is necessary for the good of all people.
2. In this Samaj the *Vedas* shall be considered as the primary and self-evident authority. For the purpose of testimony and of understanding the *Vedas* and Aryan history, the following works shall have secondary authority: the four *Brāhmanas* including the *Shatapatha*, the six *Vedāngas*, the four *Upavedas*, the six *darshanas*, and the 1127 *Shākhās* (expositions of the *Vedas*), because they are recognized ancient works of the *rishis* and are in accordance with the *Vedas*.
3. In this Samaj there shall be in the centre of each province a Principal Samaj, of which the others shall be branches.
4. The branch Samajes shall be managed according to the model of the Principal Samaj.
5. In the Principal Samaj books in Sanskrit and Hindi that are in conformity with the *Vedas* shall be kept for the propagation of truth; and a weekly periodical called *Āryaprakāsh* shall be published. The books and the periodical shall be disseminated amongst all branches.
6. In every Samaj there shall be a president and a secretary. Others, men and women, shall be members of the committee.
7. The president shall properly look after the affairs of the Samaj, and

the secretary shall take care of the members' register and of the correspondence.

8. Those people shall be enrolled as members of this Samaj who are truthful, upright, of good conduct, and concerned with the welfare of mankind.

9. The householder shall devote the leisure time his household duties leave to the uplift of this Samaj, with even more determination than that he applies to his household duties; he who is free from household duties shall be ever at work for the progress of the Samaj.

10. Every eighth day the president, the secretary, and the members shall gather in the Samaj hall, and they shall give this function precedence over all other work.

11. At that gathering they shall all be composed in their minds. They shall first converse with one another with mutual affection and without prejudice. Then there shall be songs from the *Sāmaveda*, etc., with instrumental accompaniment; these songs shall be about God, true *dharma*, true morality, and the teaching of truth. Then there shall be a discourse upon the meaning of the *mantras*, and a lecture. Then there shall again be songs, explanation of *mantras*, lecture, songs, and so on in succession.

12. Each member shall contribute to the Samaj fund one-hundredth part of what he earns for an honest living, for the running and progress of the Samaj, the schools, and the periodical. The more someone gives, the greater shall be his merit. That money shall be spent exclusively for the purposes specified.

13. Whoever does his utmost for the promotion of these causes shall be encouraged by the proper recognition of his efforts.

14. In this Samaj there shall be praise, invocation, and adoration of the one and only God according to the *Vedas*; that Lord is bodiless, almighty, just, unborn, unending, immutable, unbeginning, incomparable, merciful, father and mother of the whole world, supporter of the world and Lord of all, possessor-in-full of the qualities of being, intelligence, and bliss, all-pervading and dwelling in the heart of all beings, immortal, fearless, all-pure and all-wise, always totally free, infinite, giver of happiness, and bestower of the boons of *dharma*, *artha*, *kāma*, and *moksha*. The members shall praise him by lauding his qualities; they shall pray to him by asking for help in their good works; they shall contemplate him by becoming absorbed in his bliss; they shall give him their love. None other but the one Lord shall be venerated in that way.

15. In this Samaj all sacraments including the funeral rites shall be performed according to the *Vedas*.

16. In the Aryan school there shall be instruction in the *Vedas* and the other ancient works of the *rishis*; thus all men and women shall acquire

the knowledge of truth in the proper Vedic way.

17. In this Samaj efforts shall be made for the reformation of this country, both spiritual and material. Reform along those two lines shall lead to the purification and uplift of the whole world.

18. This Samaj shall recognize only what is right and just, that is the true Vedic *dharma* which is free from bias and established by the authoritative sources of knowledge. This Samaj shall not admit anything that does not agree with it, as far as it is possible.

19. From this Samaj excellent and learned men shall from time to time be sent out to preach the truth everywhere.

20. Aryan schools shall be founded everywhere, as much as is possible; there will be separate schools for the training in wisdom of women and men. In the schools for women the teaching and the services shall be managed by women only; in the schools for men, by men only. Not otherwise.

21. The running of these schools shall be organized according to the directives of the Principal Samaj.

22. For the sake of mutual affection, the president and all other members shall shed all pride, stubbornness, hatred, anger, etc.; they shall practise friendliness and helpfulness without any animosity; thus they shall love each other as much as they love themselves.

23. At times of deliberation decisions shall be made with justice and with careful consideration of the well-being of all. The decisions shall be made known to all members, who shall hold on to them as the right ones, and in no other way. Only such a procedure can be called rejection of all prejudice.

24. The person who behaves according to these rules, who is religious and virtuous, shall be made a member of the superior order of the Samaj; the others shall be ordinary members. He who is wicked in an excessive and public manner shall be expelled from the Samaj; but this shall not be done in prejudice, but only after due deliberation on the part of the best members, not otherwise.

25. The president and other committee members shall do their utmost to promote the Arya Samaj, the schools, the periodical, and the Arya Samaj fund.

26. Whenever a member of the Arya Samaj is available for a job, that job shall not be given by a member to an outsider. The two concerned shall afterwards act in the proper relationship of master and servant.

27. Whenever there shall be an occasion for making a donation, such as a wedding, the birth of a son, good fortune, a death in the family, or any other reason, then that gift should be directed to the Arya Samaj. There is no greater source of merit. Let this be known and never forgotten.

28. Any addition to, deletion or alteration of, these rules, shall be done in the proper way: all the best members shall be notified beforehand, and the change shall be done according to the outcome of their deliberations.

Appendix III. *The Lahore rules of the Arya Samaj*
(My translation of the Hindī rules as recorded in L, p.350.)

1. God is the primary source of all knowledge, and of all things that can be known through it.
2. God is by essence being, truth, and bliss; he is bodiless, almighty, just, merciful, infinite, unchangeable, beginningless, incomparable, the support and Lord of all, all-pervading and present in all that lives, imperishable, immortal, fearless, holy, and the maker of the universe. He alone is worthy of worship.
3. The *Veda* is the book of true knowledge. It is the highest duty of all Aryans to study and propagate the *Veda*.
4. All should always be ready to accept truth and abandon untruth.
5. All actions should be performed according to *dharma*, that means after due consideration of right and wrong.
6. The principal aim of this Samaj is to promote this world's well-being, material, spiritual, and social.
7. One should treat all with affection, according to *dharma*, and with due consideration of their merits.
8. Ignorance should be destroyed and knowledge increased.
9. Nobody should remain satisfied with his own progress, but everybody should consider his own uplift to depend on the uplift of all.
10. All should be subordinate to social laws that govern the well-being of all; and all should remain self-governed in regulating their personal affairs.

BY-LAWS

[Reproduced by permission of the Director of the India Office Library and Records]

N.B. The earliest version of the Lahore by-laws that have come to hand are included in Ganeshi Lal, *The Arya Samaj or 'The New Light of Asia'*, Lahore, 1889. There is very little possibility that the original rules formulated in Lahore had been changed by that time, because the Arya Pratinidhi Sabhā of the Panjab was formed only at the end of 1886. There is no evidence anywhere that any change in the rules was effected before the 1890s. I reproduce here literally the English version as available in Ganeshi Lal's work.

(1) The Arya Samaj recognises the four Texts of the Vedas, viz. Rig, Yajur, Sama, and Atharva, as containing all that is necessary to constitute them as an extraordinary authority in all matters relating to mundane and spiritual progress of man. The Brahmanas, the six Darshanas (six schools of philosophy), 1127 Shakhas (lectures on the Vedas), Ashtadhyai and Mahabhashya (Vedic grammars) and ten Upanishads, viz. Isha, Kena, Katha, Prashna, Mundaka, Māndūkya, Aitteriya, Taitereya, Chhandogya and Brahdaranyaka, are accepted as the exponent of the meaning of the Vedas, as well as the history and the scheme of studies of the Aryas. So far as these concur with the views of the Vedas they shall be considered as an ordinary authority.

(2) Any person who is not less than 18 years of age, bears good character, and professes his belief in the fundamental principles of the Arya Samaj, shall be eligible for membership in the Samaj as an Arya. If a member shows great zeal and interest in the affairs of the Samaj during his first year of probation and contributes one per cent or more of his income, monthly or yearly, he shall be an Arya member, be entitled to give his votes in the meetings of the Executive Committee. Whoever does not strictly follow the principles of the Arya Samaj, shall forfeit his membership.

(3) He who pays 10 Rs. or more monthly as one per cent of his income or contributes 250 Rs. as a lump sum, or who is proficient in learning or possesses influence, shall be considered an active Arya member.

(4) Weekly meetings of the Arya Samaj will be held once a week, in which Vedic prayers will be offered and lectures on the physical, social and spiritual subjects delivered together with interpretation of Vedic hymns. Before and after the lectures, the songs treating of the Deity, shall be sung according to the Sama Veda system and when possible with musical accompaniments. Any particular thing that may be worth telling the members, shall also be intimated to them on the occasion.

(5) Annual meeting of the Arya Samaj will be held once a year to celebrate the Anniversary and to elect members of the Executive Committee and office-bearers. Annual report of the working of the Samaj during the past year shall be read in the meeting. The date fixed for the celebration of the Anniversary shall be notified a month before.

(6) Extraordinary meeting will assemble at the request of the President, the Secretary, Executive Committee and one-twentieth number of Arya members, to carry out, whenever found necessary, any special work. Due notice shall be given of the day and hour appointed for this meeting.

(7) The management of the spiritual and pecuniary affairs of the Arya Samaj shall be the duties of the Executive Committee. It will consist of representative Arya members of respectability and office-bearers. The members represented by their parties shall be the representative members. Any party can change its representative member when it wishes to do so.

(8) The duties of the representative member shall be:
  1. To obtain the opinions of his party.

2. To intimate such resolutions of the Executive Committee to his party as are worth communicating to it.

3. To collect subscriptions of his party and to make them over to the treasurer of the Samaj.

(9) The election of Arya members òf respectability shall be made in the annual or special meeting of the Samaj. The number of such members shall not exceed one third of the members of the Executive Committee.

(10) The election of the Arya members of respectability and the office-bearers of the Arya Samaj shall be made once a year in the annual meeting of the Samaj when an old respectable Arya member and office-bearer can be re-elected.

(11) In the place of a respectable Arya member or office-bearer which may fall vacant before the expiration of a year, the Executive Committee has power to elect a competent man.

(12) The Executive Committee can appoint trom its members a sub-committee to consider and dispose of special work.

(13) A member of the Executive Committee can with the consent of the President intimate, a week before, to the Secretary that he wishes to bring up a certain question. If five members of the Executive Committee agree to bring up a certain question, it shall necessarily be placed before the Committee.

(14) The Executive Committee shall meet with the consent of the President once a fortnight. But when five members of the Executive Committee apply to the Secretary it can also assemble at any other time.

(15) The office-bearers will be — (1) President, (2) Vice-President, (3) Secretary, (4) Treasurer, and (5) Librarian.

If a necessity arises, the Executive Committee can appoint assistants to the Secretary, Treasurer and Librarian, and distribute duties among them.

DUTIES OF THE PRESIDENT

(16) The President shall be the chairman of all the meetings of the Samaj, and direct the proper and regular management of the affairs and progress of the Arya Samaj. If there is a difficult and urgent matter he should immediately attend to it and be held responsible for it. He shall also be a member of all the sub-committees appointed by the Executive Committee.

(17) The Vice President will act for the President when he is absent. If there is more than one Vice President, the senior Vice President with the consent of the Executive Committee will officiate for the President. The principal duty of the Vice President shall be to assist the President in all the affairs of the Samaj.

DUTIES OF THE SECRETARY

(18) The Secretary acting under the orders of the Executive Committee, shall conduct correspondence and keep all letters received and issued in a proper order and a record of the proceedings.

He shall read in the monthly meetings names of the persons admitted into the Samaj and of those who resigned their membership, in the previous month. He shall keep control over the Establishment of the Samaj and see that the Principles, Rules and Bye-laws of the Samaj are strictly observed.

He shall under the orders of the sub-committee appointed for the purpose undertake the management of the School, if attached to a Samaj in which instruction in the philosophy of the Vedas and works of the ancient sages will be imparted. He should see that every member of the Samaj is included in some party which is represented in the Exec. Committee. He shall receive the members with all honours and respect due to them, be punctual in his attendance and stay till the meetings of the Samaj are over.

DUTIES OF THE TREASURER

(19) He must give receipt for all money realised on account of the Samaj and keep a proper account of it.

He should disburse no money without the sanction of the Exec. Committee and no more even to the President and the Secretary than what has been authorised to be paid to each of them for expenditure. That official of the Samaj by whom money is spent, shall only be held responsible for it.

The Treasurer shall keep a proper account of the income and expenditure and submit it for check and audit in the monthly meetings.

DUTIES OF THE LIBRARIAN

(20) He shall be in charge of the books forming the Samaj Library as well as those available for sale. He shall keep a catalogue of the former and an account of the latter. He shall collect money due for the books sold and pay for those received. He shall also lend books of the Samaj to its members for perusal and take them back when done with.

(21) Written opinions of the Arya members shall be taken in the cases noted below:-

(a) The Executive Committee considers for the benefit of the Samaj that any particular resolution of an ordinary meeting shall not be carried out but the opinions of the Arya members should be obtained.

(b) One twentieth number or more of the Arya members write to the secretary on the subject.

(c) Any suggestion about heavy expenditure, management, rule or resolution has to be made.

(d) The Exec. Committee wishes to get the opinions of all the Arya members.

(22) The Executive Committee can elect a competent member to act for an office-bearer when he is absent in a meeting or for some time.

(23) If no office-bearer is elected in the annual meeting of the Samaj, the incumbent then in office will continue to do his work till another person is appointed in his place.

(24) A record of the Proceedings of all the meetings of the Samaj shall be kept and all the Arya members shall be allowed to read it.

(25) When there are one third of the members present, the work of all the meetings can be proceeded with.

(26) The matters brought up in all the meetings shall be decided by a majority of votes.

(27) One tenth of the income of the Samaj shall be deposited as a reserve fund.

(28) All the Arya members of the Samaj should know Sanskrit or Arya Bhasha.

(29) All the members shall offer a donation at the celebration of a marriage, the birth of a child and when they are in any way highly benefited.

(30) It is the paramount duty of all the members of the Samaj to sympathise with one another when in sorrow and distress; but on an auspicious and happy occasion, they should join only when invited. The ideas of superiority and inferiority should be avoided.

(31) If a member loses his parents, his wife is left a widow or his children are deprived of their parents and when there is no means of their livelihood, the Arya Samaj having ascertained about the matter shall arrange as far as lies in its power for their support.

(32) If any difference arises among the members of the Samaj, it shall be settled amongst them and decided by a Sub-Committee of the Arya Samaj.

(33) The members must invariably treat one another with great love and respect for the good of the Samaj laying aside all party spirit, malice, anger and all disorganising vices.

(34) Every member of the Samaj shall be expected (even if necessary at the expense of his fortune and life) to use his utmost endeavours to defend the rights, elevate the position and extend the influence of the Arya Samaj and everything connected with it.

Bibliography

A. COMPLETE WORKS OF DAYANANDA SARASVATI

I. *Books and pamphlets* (in chronological order)

1. *Sandhyā*, published by the Jwalaprakash Press, Agra, 1863. No copy of this work has so far been recovered.
2. *Bhāgavata-Khandanam*, published in Agra in 1864. A copy of this work was discovered recently, and published with notes by Y. Mimamshak, Sonipat, 1971.
3. *Advaitamat-Khandanam*, published by the Light Press, Banaras, 1870. No copy of this work has so far been recovered.
4. *Satyārth Prakāsh*, first edition, published by the Star Press, Banaras, 1875. Only very few copies of this work remain available.
5. *Panchamahāyajnavidhi*, first edition, Bombay, 1875. This edition has not been recovered. A second revised edition was published by the Lazarus Press, Banaras, 1878. Many reprints of this edition are available.
6. *Vedaviruddhmatkhandana*, published by the Nirnaysagar Press, Bombay, 1875. Available in the edition published by Govindram Hasanand, Delhi, n.d.
7. *Vedāntidhwāntanivārana*, published by the Oriental Press, Bombay, 1875. Available in the edition published by Govindram Hasanand, Delhi, n.d.
8. *Shikshāpatridhwāntanivārana*, with a Gujarātī translation by Shyamji Krishnavarma, published by the Oriental Press, Bombay, 1876. Available in the edition published by Govindram Hasanand, Delhi, n.d.
9. *Āryābhivinaya*, published by the Aryamandal Press, Bombay, 1876. Many editions are available.
10. *Sanskārvidhi*, first edition, published by the Asiatic Press, Bombay, 1877. Only very few copies of this edition are available.
11. *Rigvedādibhāshyabhūmikā*, published first in sixteen fascicules, from 1877 onwards, by the Lazarus Press; the last two were published by the Nirnaysagar Press, Bombay, 1878. The best edition available is that edited by Y. Mimamshak, Amritsar, 1967.
12. *Bhrāntinivārana*, published in 1887, probably at the Ārya-Bhūshan-Yántrālay, Shahjahanpur. Available in the edition published by Govindram Hasanand, Delhi, 1952.
13. *Āryoddheshya Ratnamālā*, published by the Chashmanur Press, Amritsar, 1878. Available in the edition published by Govindram Hasanand, Delhi, 1970.
14. *Vedabhāshya*, published in monthly fascicules. The first fourteen issues were published by the Lazarus Press, Banaras, from 1877; the rest were published by the Vedic Yantralay, in 1880 in Banaras, in 1881-91 in Allahabad, and from 1891 in Ajmer. Fifty-one fascicules each of the *Rigvedabhāshya* and of the *Yajurvedabhāshya* were published during the Swami's lifetime. The publication of the remaining manuscript continued after the Swami's death. It took another six years

to publish. the rest of the *Yajurvedabhāshya*, which covers the whole book. The *Rigvedabhāshyā*, which only goes up to RV.7.4.60, took sixteen years to complete. Both commentaries are available in the edition published by the Vedic Press, Ajmer, the former in four volumes, the latter in nine.

15. *Autobiography*, written in Hindī by the Swami, and published in an English translation in *The Theosophist* in three instalments: vol.I (Oct. 1879), pp.9-13; vol.I (Dec. 1879), pp.66-8; vol.II (Nov. 1880), pp.24-6. The Hindī version was recently recovered by the Paropkarinī Sabhā, Ajmer, and was published with the English version from *The Theosophist* in *Paropkārī* 17, no.5 (March 1975).

16. *Ashtādhyāyī-Bhāshya*, not completed, and not published in the Swami's lifetime. It has been partly published by Pandit Raghuvir, Ajmer, vol.I in 1927, vol.II in 1949.

17. *Gotama-Ahalyā kī Kathā*, was published by 1879, place unknown. This short work has so far not been recovered.

18. *Sanskrit Vākya Prabodh*, published by the Vedic Yantralay, Banaras, 1880. Available in the edition published by the Ramlal Kapur Trust, Amritsar, 1969.

19. *Vyavahārabhānu*, published by the Vedic Yantralay, Banaras, 1880. Available in the edition published by the Ramlal Kapur Trust, Amritsar, 1970.

20. *Bhramocchedan*, published by the Vedic Yantralay, Banaras, 1880. Available in the edition published by Govindram Hasanand, Delhi, 1953.

21. *Anubhramocchedan*, published by the Vedic Yantralay, Banaras, 1880. Available in the edition published by Govindram Hasanand, Delhi, 1953.

22. *Vedāngaprakāsh*, published in fourteen parts by the Vedic Yantralay, Banaras and Allahabad, from 1880 to 1883. All parts are available from the Vedic Press, Ajmer.

23. *Gokarunānidhi*, published by the Vedic Yantralay, Allahabad, 1881. Available in the edition published by Govindram Hasanand, Delhi, 1969.

24. *Satyārth Prakāsh*, second revised edition, published by the Vedic Yantralay, Allahabad, 1884. Numerous editions are available. The best by far is that edited by Y. Mimamshak, Sonipat, 1972.

25. *Sanskārvidhi*, second revised edition, published by the Vedic Yantralay, Allahabad, 1884. The best edition available is the one edited by Y. Mimamshak, Sonipat, 1971.

II. *Reports of disputations and lectures*
(in chronological order)

26. *Shāstrārth-Kāshī*, first published by the Light Press, Banaras, 1869. Another version was published by Pandit Satyavrat Samashrami in

The Hindu Commentator of Dec. 1869. Both versions are available in *DSS*.

27. *Shāstrārth-Huglī*, first published in a Bengālī version at Calcutta in 1873, which has so far not been recovered. Later a Hindī version was published by Harischandra Bharatendu at the Light Press, Banaras, in 1873, under the title *Pratimā-Pūjan-Vichār*. Available in *DSS*.

28. *Pūnā-Pravachana,* first published in a Marāthī version, and in a Gujarātī translation, in 1875. Later translated into Hindī and published in Ajmer, 1893. None of these are available in full. The text has been reconstructed by Y. Mimamshak, and is available in *PP*.

29. *Shāstrārth-Jālandhar*, published at the Panjabi Press, Lahore, 1877. Available in *DSS*.

30. *Shāstrārth-Melā-Chāndāpur*, first published in Urdū in 1878, but this edition has not yet been found. Later both a Hindī and an Urdū version were published by the Vedic Yantralay, Banaras, 1880, under the title *Satyadharm Vichār*. Available in *DSS*.

31. *Shāstrārth-Barelī*, first published under the title *Satyāsatya-Vivek* in an Urdū version by the Aryabhushan Press, Shajahanpur, 1879. Available in *DSS*.

32. *Shāstrāth-Ajmer*, first published in Hindī and Urdū in the *Āryadarpan* of Ajmer, June 1880. Available in *DSS*.

33. *Shāstrārth-Masūdā*, first published in the *Deshahitaishī* of Ajmer, 1880. Available in *DSS*.

34. *Shāstrārth-Udaypur*, held in December 1882, not published during the Swami's lifetime. The manuscript notes of this discussion were recovered by Lekhram and published in his biography of Dayananda. Available in *DSS*.

III. *Letters and notices*

35. *Rishi Dayānanda kā Patravyavahār*. A collection of letters received by the Swami, and also of some written by him. Edited by Munshīrām Jijnāsu, Gurukul Kangri, vol.I in 1910, vol.II in 1935.

36. *Rishi Dayānanda Saraswatī ke Patra aur Vijnāpan*. Collection of letters and notices written by Dayananda. First edition by Pandit Bhagavaddatta, Lahore, 1945; second revised and enlarged edition by Y. Mimamshak, Amritsar, 1955.

37. *Rishi Dayānanda Saraswatī ke Patra aur Vijnāpanon ke Parishisht*, ed. Y. Mimamshak, Amritsar, 1958.

B. SELECT WRITINGS ON DAYANANDA AND THE ARYA SAMAJ

I. *English*

Arya Pratinidhi Sabha Punjab, *The Arya Samaj from the Outsiders' Point of View*, Lahore, 1902.

348   *Dayananda Sarasvati*

Arya Samaj Calicut, *Swami Dayananda Saraswati, A Critical Review of his Career, together with a Short Life Sketch. Being a Collection of articles written by several distinguished men,* Calicut, 1924.

Barrier, N.G., 'The Punjab Government and Communal Politics 1870-1908', *The Journal of Asian Studies,* 27 (1967-8), pp.523-39.

—— 'The Arya Samaj and Congress Politics in the Punjab, 1894-1908', *The Journal of Asian Studies,* 26 (1967), pp.363-79.

Chand, Gokal, *The Luther of India,* reprint, Lahore, 1913.

Das, Lala Jivan, ed., *Papers for the Thoughtful. Being Essays on Swami Dayanand Saraswati and the Arya Samaj,* Lahore, 1902.

Datta, Pandit Ram Bhaj, *Agnihotra Demolished, being a thorough Refutation of his Dayanand Unveiled and its Rejoinder,* Lahore, 1892.

Durrani, F.K. Khan, *Swami Dayanand, A Critical Study of His Life and Teachings,* Lahore, 1929.

Forman, H., *The Arya Samaj, Its Teachings and an Estimate of it,* Allahabad, 1887.

Gajra, T.D., *The Life of Swami Dayanand Saraswati,* Lahore, 1915.

Ghose, Aurobindo, *Bankim-Tilak-Dayananda,* Pondicherry, 1955.

Graham, J. Reid, 'The Arya Samaj as a Reformation in Hinduism with special reference to caste', unpublished Ph.D. thesis, Yale Univ., 1942.

Griswold, H.D., *The Arya Samaj, A Paper read before the Victoria Institute,* Calcutta, 1903.

Jijyasu, Munshi Ram, and Rama Deva, *The Arya Samaj and its Detractors, A Vindication,* Gurukul Kangri, 1910.

Jones, K.W., 'The Arya Samaj in the Punjab: a study of social reform and religious revivalism, 1877-1902', unpublished Ph.D. thesis, Univ. of California, Berkeley, 1966.

—— 'The Bengali Elite in Post-Annexation Punjab: An Example of Inter-Regional influence in 19th century India', *The Indian Economic and Social History Review,* 3 (1966), pp.376-95.

—— 'Communalism in the Punjab, the Arya Samaj Contribution', *The Journal of Asian Studies,* 28 (1968-9), pp.38-45.

—— '*Ham Hindū nahīn:* Arya-Sikh Relations, 1877-1905', *The Journal of Asian Studies,* 32 (1973), pp.457-75.

—— 'Sources of Arya Samaj History', *The Indian Archives,* 18 (1969), pp.20-36.

Jordens, J.T.F., 'Dayananda Saraswati and Vedanta: a comparison of the first and second editions of his Satyarth Prakash', *The Indian Economic and Social History Review,* 9 (1972), pp.367-79.

—— '*Yogī kā Ātmacharitra:* another nail in the coffin of a fake auto-biography', *Paropkārī,* 16 (March, 1974), pp.15-17.

Kishore, L. Nand, ed., *A General Survey of the Life and Teachings of Swami Dayananda,* Lahore, 1925.

Kulyar, S.P., *Swami Dayanand Saraswati,His Life and Teachings, and other papers reprinted from the Vedic Magazine,* rev. ed., Patna, 1938.

Leopold, Joan, 'The Aryan Theory of Race', *The Indian Economic and Social History Review,* 7 (1970), pp.271-97.

Lillingston, F., *The Brahmo Samaj and Arya Samaj in their bearing on Christianity: a study in Indian Theism*, London, 1901.

Mal, Bahadur, *Dayanand, A Study in Hinduism*, Hoshiarpur, 1962.

— *Swami Dayanand and His Teachings*, Sholapur, 1956.

Müller, F. Max, *Biographical Essàys*, London, 1884.

— *Chips from a German Workshop*, 2 vols., London, 1867.

Mulraj, *A Lecture on the Arya Samaj*, Lahore, 1894.

— *Beginnings of Punjabi Nationalism, Autobiography of R.B. Mul Raj*, ed. Ajit Nath, Hoshiarpur, 1975.

Murdoch, J., *Papers on Indian Reform*, part III, *Vedic Hinduism*, Madras, 1888.

— *Papers on Indian Reform*, part IV, *Brahma Samaj and other Modern Eclectic Systems of Religion in India*, Madras, 1893.

— *.Vedic Hinduism and the Arya Samaj*, London, 1902.

Nigama, Z. Singh, *The Vedic Religion and its Expounder Swami Dayananda Saraswati*, Allahabad, 1914.

Nyayaratna, Maheśa Chandra, *A few remarks on Pandit Dayananda Saraswati's Veda Bhashya*, 2nd ed., Calcutta, 1890. (First ed. 1876).

Olcott, Col. Henry S., *An address by Col. Olcott to the Arya Samaj of Meerut*, Roorkee, 1879.

Pandey, Dhanpati, *The Arya Samaj and Indian Nationalism*, New Delhi, 1972.

Parameswaran, C., *Dayananda and the Indian Problem*, Lahore, 1944.

Parapullil, P.A., *Swami Dayananda Saraswati's Understanding and Assessment of Christianity*, Rome, 1970.

Pareek, Radhey S., *Contribution of Arya Samaj in the making of Modern India 1857-1947*, Univ. of Jaipur, 1965.

Paropkarini Sabha, A Member of, *Swami Dayanand Saraswati and Satyarth Prakash*, Ajmer, 1944.

Prakash, Satya, *A Critical Study of Philosophy of Dayananda*, Ajmer, 1938.

Prakash, Vishwa, *Life and Teachings of Swami Dayanand*, Allahabad, 1935.

Prasad, Durga, *Maharshi Dayanand Saraswati*, Lahore, 1892.

Punjabi Brahmo, A, *The Arya Samaj and a Refutation of its Tenets*, Lahore, 1883.

Purohit, B.R., *Hindu Revivalism and Indian Nationalism*, Sagar, 1965.

Rai, Lala Lajpat, *The Arya Samaj, An account of its Aims, Doctrine and Activities with a Biographical Sketch of the Founder*, London, 1915.

— *Autobiographical Writings*, ed. V.C. Joshi, Delhi, 1965.

— *A History of the Arya Samaj*, rev. ed. by Shri Ram Sharma, Bombay, 1967.

— *Life and Work of Pandit Guru Datta Vidyarthi, M.A.*, Lahore, 1891.

Ramanand to Ramtirth, Life of the Saints of Northern India including the Sikh Gurus, anon., Madras, n.d.

Rama Deva, cf. Jijyasu, Munshi Ram.

Regamey, Constantin, 'The origin of the activistic trends in the doctrine of Swāmī Dayānand Saraswatī', R.N. Dandekar, ed., *Proceedings of the Twenty-Sixth International Congress of Orientalists*, vol.III, part I, Poona, 1969, pp.452-4.

Robson, J., *Hinduism and its Relations to Christianity*, new ed., London, 1893.

Sadik, Gulam Mohamed B.H.H., *A Refutation of the Satyarth Prakasha of Pandit Dayanand Saraswati, the founder of the Arya Samaj*, Surat, 1910.

Sarda, Har Bilas, *Dayanand Commemoration Volume*, Ajmer, 1933.

— *Life of Dayanand Saraswati, World Teacher*, 2nd ed., Ajmer, 1968.

— *Sankara and Dayanand*, Ajmer, 1944.

— *Works of Maharshi Dayanand and Paropkarini Sabha*, Ajmer, 1942.

Scott, T.J., *Missionary Life in the Villages of India*, New York, 1876.

Sharma, B.M., *Swami Dayanand, His Life and Teachings*, Lucknow, 1933.

Sharma, Shri Ram, 'The earliest autobiography of Swami Dayananda', *Purba, Punjab University Research Bulletin (Arts)*, 3 (1972), pp.211-50.

— 'Swami Dayanand and the Theosophical Society', *Purba*, 4 (1973), pp.117-35.

Shastri, Vaidyanath, *The Arya Samaj, Its Cult and Creed*, 2nd ed., New Delhi, 1967.

Shraddhananda, Swami, *Autobiography*, translation into English by M.R. Jambunathan, Bombay, 1961.

Singh, Amar, ed., *Swami Dayanand in the Light of Truth. A True and Critical Biography of the Founder of the Arya Samaj*, Lahore, 1925.

— *Views on Meat-Diet and Forgeries suppressing Swami Dayanand's Opinions*, Lahore, 1941.

Singh, Bawa Arjan, *Dayanand Saraswati, Founder of the Arya Samaj*, Lahore, 1901.

Singh, Bawa Chajju, *A Few Specialities of the Arya Samaj*, Lahore, 1925.

— *Life and Teachings of Swami Dayanand Saraswati*, Lahore, 1903. (Reprint, Delhi, 1971).

Singh, B.K., *Swami Dayanand*, National Biography Series, New Delhi, 1970.

Singh, Pandit Umrao, *Reply to Extra Supplement to the 'Theosophist' for July 1882*, Lahore, 1882.

Sundarlal, Shyam, *Treatise on the Arya Samaj and the Theosophical Society as once Amalgamated Bodies*, Mainpuri, 1925.

Thursby, G., 'Aspects of Hindu-Muslim Relations in British India: a study of Arya Samaj activities, Government of India policies, and communal conflict in the period 1923-1928', unpublished Ph.D. thesis, Duke Univ., 1972.

Thwaytes, R., 'Dayananda Sàraswati and the Sepoy Revolt of 1857', unpublished B.A. Hons. thesis, A.N.U., Canberra, 1973.

Upadhyaya, Ganga Prasad, *Landmarks of Swami Dayanand's Teachings*, Allahabad, 1947.

— *The Origin, Scope and Mission of the Arya Samaj*, Allahabad, 1940.

— *Philosophy of Dayananda*, Allahabad, 1955.

— *Swami Dayanand's Contribution to Hindu Solidarity*, Allahabad, 1939.

Vidyarthi, Pandit Gurudatta, *A Reply to Mr Williams' Criticism on Niyoga*, Lahore, 1890.

— *Wisdom of the Rishis, or works of Pandit Gurudatta Vidyarthi*, 3rd ed., New Delhi, n.d.

Williams, T., *Exposure of Dayananda Saraswati and his followers both as to their deliberate falsification of the Rigveda and their immorality,* Delhi, 1889.

II. French

Morin, Louise, *Swāmi Dayānanda Saraswatī, Satyārtha Prakāsh, Le Livre de l'Arya Samaj,* Brussels, 1940.

III. German

Lütt, Von Jürgen, *Hindu-Nationalismus in Uttar Prades 1867-1900,* Stuttgart, 1970.

IV. Gujarātī

Sundardās, Dāmodar, *Mumbai Āryasamājano Itihās,* Bombay, 1933.

V. Hindī

Bhāratendu, Harischandra, *Bhāratendu Granthāvalī,* vol.III, ed. Vrajaratna Dās, Banaras, 1953.

Bhāratīya, Bhawānīlāl, *Maharshi Dayānanda aur Rājārammohanrāy,* Agra, 1955.

— *Maharshi Dayānanda aur Swāmī Vivekānanda, ek Tulanātmak Adhyayan,* Abohar, 1972.

— *Paropkarinī Sabhā kā Itihās,* Ajmer, 1975.

Rishi Dayānanda aur Ārya Samāj kī Sanskrit Sāhitya ko Den, Amritsar, 1968.

Dās, Jagannāth, *Dayānandajīvancharitra aur Samālochanā,* Bombay, 1898.

— *Satyārthaprakāshasamīkshā,* Etawah, 1926.

Ghāsīrām, *Maharshi Dayānanda Saraswatī kā Jīvan-Charit,* 2 vols., Ajmer, 1957. Based on the material collected by Devendranāth Mukhopādhyāy. (First published in 1933.)

Gopal Rao, Hari, *Dayānanda-Digvijayārk,* parts I and II published in 1881, part III in 1887, at Farrukhabad. Republished by B. Bhāratīya, Delhi, 1974.

Gupta, Atrideva, *Sanskār Vidhi Vimarsh,* Banaras, 1951.

Gupta, L.N., *Hindī Bhāshā aur Sāhitya ko Āryasamāj kī den,* Lucknow Univ., 1971.

Gupta, Nāthūlāl, *Ārya-Samāj men krāntī karnevālī naī-khoj, arthāt Traitavād Samshodan,* Shivapuri, 1894.

Gupta, Veda Prakāsh, *Dayānanda-Darshan,* Meerut, n.d.

Jaimini, Mehtā, *Jagadguru Dayānanda kā Samsār par Jādū,* Moradabad, 1924.

Jīyālāl, Pandit Jainī, *Dayānanda-Chhal-Kapat-Darpan,* Ahmedabad, 1894.

Jnānī, Pindīdās, *1857 ke Swātantrya Sangrām men Swarājya-Pravartak Maharshi Dayānanda Saraswatī kā kriyātmak Yogdān,* Amritsar, 1971.

Kushavāhā, Shivapūjansingh, *Maharshi Dayānandjīkrit Vedabhāshyānu-shīlan*, Baroda, 1950.

Lekhrām, *Maharshi Dayānanda Saraswatī kā Jīvan Charitra*, transl. from the original Urdū by Kavirāj Raghunandansingh 'Nirmal', ed. by Pandit Harischandra Vidyālankār, Delhi, 1972. The first and only edition of the Urdū version was published in Lahore, 1897.

Mīmāmshak, Yudhisthir, *Maharshi Dayānanda Saraswatī kā Bhrātrivamsh aur Swasrivamsh*, Delhi, 1959.

— *Rishi Dayānanda ke Granthon kā Itihās*, Ajmer, 1949.

Mukhopādhyāy, Devendranāth, cf. Ghāsīrām.

— *Virjānandacharit*, transl. from the Bengālī by Ghāsīrām, Agra, 1918.

Mūlshankar, Vijayshankar, *Tankārāshatābdī tathā Dayānanda Janmasthān Nirnay*, Bombay, 1930.

Nambardār, L.B.P., *Dayānanda-mat-vidrāvan arthāt Satyārth Prakāsh par Shankāpravāh*, Etawah, 1908.

Premī, V.S., *Uttarākhand ke van-parvaton men Rishi Dayānanda*, Delhi, 1956,

Rāi, Lālā Lājpat, *Maharshi Dayānanda Saraswatī aur unkā Kām*, Lahore, 1912. (Reprinted in *Sārvadeshik*, Aug. 1967).

Sahāy, Yaduvamsh, *Maharshi Dayānanda*, Allahabad, 1971.

Sarda, Rām Bilās, *Ārya Dharmendra Jīvan*, Ajmer, 1904.

Satyānanda, Swāmī, *Shrimaddayānanda Prakāsh*, New Delhi, 1964.

Sharma, Bhīmasena, *Sanskār-Chandrikā, arthāt Maharshi Dayānanda pranīt Sanskārvidhi kī vistrit vyākhyā*, Baroda, 1924.

Shāstrī, Ajitkumār, *Satyārth-Darpan*, Firozpur, n.d.

Shāstrī, Bhīmasena, *Virjānanda-Prakāsh*, 2nd ed., Delhi, 1969.

Shāstrī, R.N., *Satyārth Prakāsh ke Samshodanon kī Samīkshā, arthāt Rishi-Gāmbhīrya kā Samarthan*, Delhi, 1966.

Shāstrī, Satyapriya, *Bhāratīya Swātantrya Sangrām men Ārya Samāj kā Yogdān*, Jullunder, n.d.

Shāstrī, Vaidyanāth, *Dayānanda-Siddhānta-Prakāsh*, Delhi, 1962.

— *Tattvārthādarsh*, New Delhi, 1967.

Shivaprasād, Rājā, *Nivedan*, Banaras, 1882.

— *Dūsrā va Pichlā Nivedan*, n.p., n.d.

Shivdayālu, ed., *Ārya Samāj kī Pragatiyon evam Ārya Pratinidhi Sabhā Uttar Pradesh kā 75 wārshīya Itihās*, Lucknow, 1963.

Shraddhānanda, Swāmī, *Ādim Satyārth Prakāsh aur Ārya Samāj ke Sid-dhānt*, Delhi, 1917.

— *Swāmī Shraddhānanda kī Dāyarī se*, ed. Chatursen Gupta, Delhi, 1961.

Siddhāntālankār, ʸ.N., *Maharshi Dayānanda: Jīvan aur Darshan*, Delhi, 1967.

Swāmī, Pandit Tulsīrām, *Bhāskaraprakāsh, arthāt P. Jwālāprasād krit Dayānanda Timirbhāskar kā uttar*, Meerut, 1921.

Thākurdās, Mūlrāj, *Dayānanda-Saraswatī-Mukh-Chapetikā*, Bombay, 1882.

Vasu, Jagadīshchandra, *Maharshi Dayānanda tathā Strī va Shūdra Jāti*, Meerut, 1965.

Vedānanda, Swāmī, *Satyārth Prakāsh kā Prabhāw*, Ghaziabad, 1959.

Vidyālankār, Bhīmasena, *Ārya Pratinidhi Sabhā Panjāb kā Sachitra Itihās,* Lahore, 1935.
Vidyāvāchaspati, Indra, *Maharshi Dayānanda,* Delhi, 1950.
— *Āryasamāj kā Itihās,* vol.I, Delhi, 1957.
Viramāni, K.C., *Dayānanda-Siddhārta-Bhāskara,* Rawalpindi, 1933.
Yāmtol, Maharsingh, *Satyārth-Prakāsh-Prashnottarī,* Lahore, 1965.

VI. *Marāthī*

Deshmukh, Gopāl Rāo Hari, 'Pandit Swāmī Shrīmaddayānandasaraswatī', *Lokahitavādī,* 2 (1884), pp.1-40.
Rānade, Rāmābāī, *Āmachyā Āyushyāntīl Āthavanī,* Bombay, 1910.

C. SELECT LIST OF GENERAL WORKS

I. *English: official sources*

District Gazetteers of the United Provinces of Agra and Oudh,
— vol.I, *Dehra Dun: a Gazetteer,* by H.G. Walton, Allahabad, 1911.
— vol.V, *Bulandshar: a Gazetteer,* by H.R. Nevill, Allahabad, 1903.
— vol.VII, *Muttra: a Gazetteer,* by D.L. Drake-Brockman, Allahabad, 1911.
— vol.IX, *Farrukhabad: a Gazetteer,* by E.R. Neave, Allahabad, 1911.
— vol.XII, *Etah: a Gazetteer,* by E.R. Neave, Allahabad, 1911.
— vol.XV, *Badaun: a Gazetteer,* by H.R. Nevill, Allahabad, 1907.
— vol.XXXVI, *British Garhwal: a Gazetteer,* by H.G. Walton, Allahabad, 1910.
Gazetteer of the Bombay Presidency, vol.9, part 1: *Gujarat Population,* Bombay, 1884.
— vol.8, *Kathiawar,* Bombay, 1884.
Growse, F.S., *Mathura, a District Memoir,* 2nd ed., Allahabad, 1880.
Kathiawor Directory, The, rev. ed., 2 vols., compiled by Dhanjishah Harmasji Kadaka, Rajkot, 1886.
Mehta, H.R., *History of the Growth and Development of Western Education in the Punjab (1846-1884),* Punjab Government Records Monograph no. 5, n.p., 1929.
Naik, J.P., *Selections from Educational Records of the Government of India,* vol.II, Delhi, 1963.
Rajputana Gazetteers, vol.II A, *The Mewar Residency,* text compiled by K.D. Erskine, Ajmer, 1908.
— vol.III A, *The Western Rajputana States Residency and the Bikaner Agency,* text compiled by K.D. Erskine, Allahabad, 1909.
Selections from the Records of the Bombay Government, no. 37, New Series, Bombay, 1856.

II. *English: non-official sources*

Allison, W.L., *The Sādhs,* O.U.P.. 1935.

Andrews, C.F., *In North India*, London, 1908.
Basham, A.L., ed., *A Cultural History of India*, O.U.P., 1975.
— *History and Doctrine of the Ājīvikas*, London, 1951.
Basu, P.S., *Life and Works of Brahmananda Keshav*, 2nd ed., Calcutta, 1940.
Bayly, C.A., 'Patrons and Politics in Northern India', *Modern Asian Studies*, 7 (1973), pp.349-88.
Bhandarkar, R.G., *Vaisnavism, Saivism, and Minor Religious Systems*, reprint, Banaras, 1965. (First ed. 1913)
Bharati, Agehananda, *The Ochre Robe*, London, 1961.
— 'Pilgrimage Sites and Indian Civilization', J.W. Elder, ed., *Chapters in Indian Civilization*, vol.I, Dubuque, 1970, pp.83-126.
— *The Tantric Tradition*, London, 1965.
Bhardwaj, S.M., *Hindu Places of Pilgrimage in India*, Univ. of Calif. Press, Berkeley, 1973.
Bhattacharya, J.N., *Hindu Castes and Sects*, Calcutta, 1896.
Bose, N.S., *The Indian Awakening and Bengal*, Calcutta, 1969.
Brass, P.R., *Language, Religion and Politics in North India*, Cambridge U.P., 1974.
Chatterton, Eyre, *A History of the Church of England in India since the Early Days of the East India Company*, London, 1924.
Chintamani, Y., ed., *Indian Social Reform*, Madras, 1901.
Chunder, Bholanauth, *The Travels of a Hindoo to various parts of Bengal and Upper India*, 2 vols., London, 1869.
Clark, H.M., *Robert Clark of the Punjab, Pioneer and Missionary Statesman*, London, 1907.
Crooke, W., *The Tribes and Castes of the North-Western Provinces and Oudh*, 4 vols., Calcutta, 1896.
Das Gupta, J., *Language Conflict and National Development*, Univ. of Calif. Press, 1970.
Dasgupta, S.N., *A History of Indian Philosophy*, 5 vols., Cambridge U.P., 1922-55.
Dave, H.T., *Life and Philosophy of Shree Swaminarayan (1781-1830)*, Bochasan, 1967.
Desai, B.G., *Ethics of the Shikshapatri*, Baroda, 1970.
Devanesen, C.D.S., *The Making of the Mahatma*, New Delhi, 1969.
Dobbin, C., *Urban Leadership in Western India: politics and communities in Bombay City, 1840-1885*, O.U.P., 1972.
Enthoven, R.E., *The Tribes and Castes of Bombay*, 3 vols., Bombay, 1920-2.
Farquhar, J.N., *Modern Religious Movements in India*, reprint, Delhi, 1967. (First ed., 1914.)
Forbes, A.K., *Rās Mālā, or Hindoo Annals of the Province of Goozerat in Western India*, new ed., London, 1878.
Gandhi, M.K., *An Autobiography, or The Story of My Experiments with Truth*, tr. from Gujarātī by Mahadev Desai, Ahmedabad, 1927.
Ghose, B., *Iswar Chandra Vidyasagar*, Delhi, 1965.
Ghurye, G.S., *Indian Sadhus*, Bombay, 1953.
Gumperz, Ellen McDonald, 'English education and social change in late

nineteenth century Bombay, 1858-1898', unpublished Ph.D. thesis, Univ. of Calif., Berkeley, 1965.

Gupta, Atulchandra, ed., *Studies in the Bengal Renaissance*, Jadavpur, 1958.

Gupte, B.A., *Hindu Holidays and Ceremonies*, 2nd rev. ed., Calcutta, 1919.

Hay, S.N., *Asian Ideas of East and West, Tagore and his Critics in Japan, China, and India*, Harvard U.P., 1970.

Heimsath, C.H., *Indian Nationalism and Hindu Social Reform*, Princeton U.P., 1964.

Houston, J., *Representative Men of the Bombay Presidency: a collection of biographical sketches, with portraits*, Bombay, 1897.

Jordens, J.T.F., 'Gandhi's Religion and the Hindu Heritage', in S.N. Ray, ed., *Gandhi, India and the World*, Melbourne, 1970, pp.39-56.

— 'Hindu Religious and Social Reform in British India', in A.L. Basham, ed., *A Cultural History of India*, O.U.P., 1975, pp.365-82.

Kane, P.V., *History of Dharmashāstra*, 5 vols., Poona, 1930-62.

Keer, D., *Mahatma Jotirao Phooley, Father of Our Social Revolution*, Bombay, 1964.

Kumar, Ravindra, ed., *Essays on Gandhian Politics: the Rowlatt Satyagraha of 1919*, O.U.P., 1971.

— *Western India in the nineteenth century*, A.N.U.P., Canberra, 1968.

Le Grand Jacob, Maj.-Gen. Sir George, *Western India Before and During the Mutinies: Pictures drawn from Life*, London, 1871.

Lethbridge, Roper, ed., *A History of the Renaissance in Bengal, Ramtanu Lahiri: Brahman and Reformer*, from the Bengālī of Pandit Shivanath Shastri, reprint, Calcutta, 1972. (First ed. 1907.)

Lovett, R., *The History of the London Missionary Society, 1795-1895*, 2 vols., London, 1899.

Low, D.A., ed., *Soundings in Modern South Asian History*, A.N.U.P., Canberra, 1968.

Majumdar, B.B., *History of Indian Social and Political Ideas from Rammohan to Dayananda*, Calcutta, 1967.

Majumdar, R.C., ed., *History and Culture of the Indian People*, 11 vols., London, Bombay, 1952-65.

Malleson, G.B., *An Historical Sketch of the Native States of India in Subsidiary Alliance with the British Government*, London, 1875.

Metcalf, Thomas R., *The Aftermath of Revolt: India 1857-1870*, Princeton U.P., 1964.

Monier-Williams, Sir Monier, *Brahmanism and Hinduism; or, Religious thought and life in India, as based on the Veda and other sacred books of the Hindus*, 4th ed. enlarged and improved, London, 1891.

Motiwala, B.N., *Karsondas Mulji, a biographical study*, Bombay, 1935.

Mozoomdar, P.C., *The Life and Teachings of Keshub Chunder Sen*, 3rd ed., Calcutta, 1931.

Mulji, Karsondas, (publ. anon.), *History of the Sect of Mahārājas, or Vallabhāchāryas in Western India*, London, 1865.

Munshi, K.M., *Gujarāt and its Literature, from early times to 1852*, Bombay, 1935.

356   *Dayananda Sarasvati*

―― Somnatha, *The Shrine Eternal*, 3rd rev. ed., Bombay, 1965.

Oman, J., *The Mystics, Ascetics, and Saints of India*, London, 1903.

Pal, B.C., *Memoirs of my Life and Times*, 2nd rev. ed., two vols. in one, Calcutta, 1973.

Pandey, R.B., *Hindu Samskāras: Socio-Religious Study of the Hindu Sacraments*, 2nd rev. ed., Delhi, 1969.

Parekh, Manilal C., *Sri Swami Narayana, a gospel of Bhagwat-Dharma or God in Redemptive Action*, Rajkot, 1936.

―― *Sri Vallabhacharya, Life, Teachings and Movement*, Rajkot, 1943.

Parvate, T.V., *Mahadev Govind Ranade: A Biography*, Bombay, 1963.

Pocock, D.F., *Mind, Body and Wealth, A Study of Belief and Practice in an Indian Village*, Oxford, 1973.

Poddar, A., *Renaissance in Bengal, Quests and Confrontations, 1800-1860*, Simla, 1970.

Potter, Karl H., ed., *The Encyclopedia of Indian Philosophies*, vol.I, *Bibliography of Indian Philosophies*, Delhi, 1970.

Ranchodji, Amarji, *Tarikh-i-Sorath, A History of the Provinces of Sorath and Halar in Kathiawad*, transl. from the Persian, Bombay, 1882.

Ray, S.N., ed., *Gandhi, India and the World*, Melbourne, 1970.

Reclus, E., *The Universal Geography*, ed. A.H. Keane, vol.III, *India and Indochina*, London, n.d.

Report of the Maharaj Libel Case and of the Bhattia Conspiracy Case Connected with it, Bombay Gazette Press, 1862.

Rose, H.A., *A Glossary of the Tribes and Castes of the Punjab and North-West Frontier Province*, 3 vols., Lahore, 1911-19.

Saletore, B.A., *Main currents in the Ancient History of Gujarat*, M.S. Univ. of Baroda, 1960.

Sangave, V.A., *Jaina Community, a Social Survey*, Bombay, 1959.

Sarkar, Sir Jadunath, *A History of Dasnami Naga Sanyasis*, Allahabad, n.d.

Sen, P.K., *Biography of a new Faith*, 2 vols., Calcutta, 1950, 1954.

Sen, S.K., *History of Bengali Literature*, New Delhi, 1960.

Sen, S.P., ed., *Dictionary of National Biography*, 3 vols.+, Calcutta, 1972+

Shastri, D.R., *Origin and Development of the Rituals of Ancestor Worship in India*, Calcutta, 1963.

Singh, Bhagat Lakshman, *Autobiography*, ed. by Ganda Singh, Calcutta, 1965.

Sinha, N., ed., *Freedom Movement in Bengal, 1818-1904; Who's who*, Calcutta, 1968.

Spate, O.H.K., *India and Pakistan: a general and regional geography*, 3rd ed., London, 1967.

Spodek, H., 'On the origins of Gandhi's Political Methodology: the Heritage of Kathiawad and Gujarat', *The Journal of Asian Studies*, 30 (1970-1), pp.361-72.

Stevenson, Mrs Sinclair, *The Heart of Jainism*, O.U.P., London, 1915.

―― *The Rites of the Twice-born*, O.U.P., London, 1920.

Stock, E., *The History of the Church Missionary Society; its environment, its men and its works*, 3 vols., London, 1899.

Tagore, Debendranath, *Brahmo Dharma of Maharshi Debendranath Tagore*, transl. into English by Hem Chandra Sarkar, Calcutta, 1928.

Tandon, Prakash, *Punjabi Century, 1857-1947*, Univ. of Calif., 1968.

Thoothi, N.A., *The Vaishnavas of Gujarat, Being a study in methods of investigation of social phenomena*, Calcutta, 1935.

Tod, James, *Annals and Antiquities of Rajasthan or the Central and Western Rajput States of India*, ed. W. Crooke, 3 vols., Delhi, 1971. (First ed., 1920.)

Wilson, H.H., *Religious Sects of the Hindus*, 2nd ed., Calcutta, 1958. (First ed., 1861.)

Yajnik, Indulal, *Shyamji Krishnavarma, Life and Times of an Indian Revolutionary*, Bombay, 1950.

III. French

Renou, L., and Filliozat, J., *L'Inde Classique, Manuel des études Indiennes*, 2 vols., Paris, 1947 and 1952.

IV. German

Richter, J., *Indische Missionsgeschichte*, Gütersloh, 1906.

von Glasenapp, H., *Der Jainismus: eine Indische Erlösungsreligion*, Hildersheim, 1964.

V. Gujarātī

Bholanath, Krishnarao, *The Life of Bholanath Sarabhai*, Bombay, 1867.

Shāshtrī, D.S.K., *Shaivadharmano Sanskshipt Itihās*, Bombay, 1936.

— *Vaishnavadharmano Sankshipt Itihās*, 2nd. rev. ed., Bombay, 1939.

Index

KING ALFRED'S COLLEGE
LIBRARY

KING ALFRED'S COLLEGE
LIBRARY